How EU Member States Represent the Common Purpose of Migration Management

Nijhoff Studies in European Union Law

Series Editors

VOLUME 26

The titles published in this series are listed at *brill.com/seul*

How EU Member States Represent the Common Purpose of Migration Management

By

Sebastian Meyer

BRILL | NIJHOFF

LEIDEN | BOSTON

Library of Congress Cataloging-in-Publication Data

Names: Meyer, Sebastian, author.
Title: How EU member states represent the common purpose of migration management / by Sebastian Meyer.
Other titles: How European Union member states represent the common purpose of migration management
Description: Leiden ; Boston : Brill, 2025. | Series: Nijhoff studies in European Union law, 2210-9765 ; 26 | Includes bibliographical references and index. | Summary: "Since the 'refugee crisis' in 2015, EU Member States have claimed to represent or act on behalf of the Union when regulating migration. Some measures were outside or at the margins of the EU legal order"– Provided by publisher.
Identifiers: LCCN 2024036280 (print) | LCCN 2024036281 (ebook) | ISBN 9789004695726 (hardback) | ISBN 9789004695733 (ebook)
Subjects: LCSH: Emigration and immigration law–European Union countries. | European Union countries–Emigration and immigration–Government policy. | Immigrants–Government policy–European Union countries.
Classification: LCC KJE6044 .M49 2025 (print) | LCC KJE6044 (ebook) | DDC 342.2408/2–dc23/eng/20240807
LC record available at https://lccn.loc.gov/2024036280
LC ebook record available at https://lccn.loc.gov/2024036281

Typeface for the Latin, Greek, and Cyrillic scripts: "Brill". See and download: brill.com/brill-typeface.

ISSN 2210-9765
ISBN 978-90-04-69572-6 (hardback)
ISBN 978-90-04-69573-3 (e-book)
DOI 10.1163/9789004695733

This book is printed on acid-free paper and produced in a sustainable manner.

Contents

Acknowledgements

This book is based on my dissertation, submitted at the University of Basel in 2021. I owe the utmost gratitude to my supervisor Prof. Dr. Christa Tobler for her continuous intellectual and personal support and for the challenging opportunities, in particular as far as academic teaching is concerned. I would also like to thank Prof. Dr. Peter Uebersax and Prof. Dr. Jorrit Rijpma for serving on the doctoral committee. The pleasure of doing research at the Institute for European Global Studies inspired me to examine the law of EU migration management from an external point of view. I am therefore indebted to my former colleagues for the stimulating working environment and the warm atmosphere. Turning the dissertation into a monograph would have been impossible without the support from Prof. Dr. Linda Senden, Prof. Dr. Sybe de Vries and Prof. Dr. Michiel Luchtman, who supervised me when I was a postdoc at the Utrecht Centre for Regulation and Enforcement in Europe (Renforce). Likewise, I would like to express my sincere gratitude to the publisher for making this book possible in the first place.

Introduction

1 The Rise of 'Team Europe' in Migration Management

In the summer of 2023, the Commissioner for Neighbourhood and Enlargement signed a Memorandum of Understanding (MoU) between the European Union (EU) and Tunisia,[1] announced as a 'strategic and global partnership'[2] but intended first and foremost to reduce irregular migration to Europe. A photograph on the website of the European Commission shows the Commissioner and his Tunisian counterpart holding a wrapper with the signed document into the cameras.[3] In the background, we see the President of the European Commission and the President of Tunisia, flanked by the Dutch and the Italian Prime Minister. Each of the political leaders is standing in front of the flag of the political association he or she represents. If the Dutch and the Italian Prime Minister each represent a European nation state, what explains their presence at the signing of a cooperation agreement between the EU and Tunisia? From a legal viewpoint, the answer is clear: the national heads of government do not belong there because the Commission is responsible for most matters of the Union's external representation,[4] which the MoU confirms.[5] What is worse, it has been reported that the Prime Ministers sidelined the Council as the decision-making forum authorising the Commission to sign an agreement on behalf of the Union.[6] Yet another complaint concerns the choice for a political rather than legal agreement, evading the procedure for the conclusion

1 European Commission, 'Memorandum of Understanding on a Strategic and Global Partnership between the European Union and Tunisia' (Press release 16 July 2023) <https://ec.europa.eu/commission/presscorner/detail/en/ip_23_3887> accessed 1 March 2024.

2 Ibid, see the title.

3 European Commission, 'The European Union and Tunisia: Political Agreement on a Comprehensive Partnership Package' (News article 16 July 2023) <https://neighbourhood-enlargement.ec.europa.eu/news/european-union-and-tunisia-political-agreement-comprehensive-partnership-package-2023-07-16_en> accessed 1 March 2024.

4 Art 17(1) TEU.

5 The MoU states that the European Union is 'represented by the European Commission', see (n 1).

6 See Paula García Andrade & Eleonora Frasca, 'The Memorandum of Understanding between the EU and Tunisia: Issues of Procedure and Substance on the Informalisation of Migration Cooperation' (2023) EU Immigration and Asylum Law and Policy <https://eumigrationlawblog.eu/the-memorandum-of-understanding-between-the-eu-and-tunisia-issues-of-procedure-and-substance-on-the-informalisation-of-migration-cooperation/> accessed 1 March 2024.

 | DOI:10.1163/9789004695733_002

of international agreements under EU law and thus democratic and judicial safeguards.[7]

In contrast, according to the European Commission, the presence of the national leaders signifies a 'Team Europe spirit'.[8] Placed into context, this means that EU migration management has for some time relied on national contributions in the form of, amongst others, financial resources, operational assistance or, as this case suggests, diplomatic means to conclude international treaties or political declarations with third countries where migrants originate from or transit through. From this angle, the presence of the Italian Prime Minister makes more sense since she entered into bilateral negotiations with the Tunisian President in preparation for the MoU,[9] based on the historical ties between the two countries. The role of the Dutch Prime Minister is, however, more obscure. On a benign interpretation, he was there not for domestic political gains but to showcase a united European response to a common challenge. Of course, a national head of government cannot do that on his own: the joint presence with the Italian Prime Minister was meant to suggest that Europe has managed to overcome the fractions between Northern and Southern states, which had so far characterised the common immigration policies. Indeed, in a letter to the members of the European Council, the Commission President writes the following: 'Your bilateral contributions also make a real difference as part of a Team Europe approach, alongside the powerful symbolism of the joint missions showing a united EU approach.'[10]

What has just been described is but one of the most recent manifestations of European migration management, which can no longer be reduced to the EU institutions adopting laws and other measures and the Member States implementing these, each acting in accordance with the principles, rules and procedures of the EU Treaties. Instead, since the so-called 'refugee crisis' in 2015/2016, Member States have claimed to represent or to act on behalf of the Union, especially in unforeseen or novel situations outside or at least

7 See Annick Pijnenburg, 'Team Europe's Deal: What's Wrong with the EU-Tunisia Migration Agreement?' (2023) Verfassungsblog <http://www.printfriendly.com/print/?source=site&url=https://verfassungsblog.de/team-europes-deal/> accessed 1 March 2024.

8 See (n 3).

9 See Federica Pascale, 'Italy Works to Secure Tunisia IMF Funding for Stable Cooperation' *Euractiv* (7 June 2023) <https://www.euractiv.com/section/politics/news/italy-works-to-secure-tunisia-imf-funding-for-stable-cooperation/> accessed 1 March 2024.

10 European Commission, Untitled letter from European Commission President Ursula von der Leyen to the members of the European Council (25 June 2023) 2 <https://www.statewatch.org/media/3945/eu-com-von-der-leyen-letter-euco-25-6-23.pdf> accessed 1 March 2024.

at the fringes of EU law. Other examples than the one mentioned include national border protection in Greece, which led the President of the European Commission to 'thank Greece for being our European *ασπίδα* [English: shield] in these times'.[11] Or think of the coordination of search and rescue operations on the Mediterranean and the ensuing relocation of rescued protection seekers to a small number of participating Member States, pending the adoption of common EU rules.[12] In a basic sense, claiming to act on behalf of the Union, or interpreting and recognising an action in that light, is thus part of the discourses on migration management.

2 The Aims and the Conceptual and Theoretical Framework of This Book

It is the aim of this book to discuss to what extent law – EU law in particular – can channel these discourses so as to both frame the exercise of national power on behalf of the Union and to constrain it according to the rule of law. The book intends to answer the following research questions:

> How do the Member States claim to represent the Union in the management of migration, and when is such a claim legal and legitimate? In particular, what is the role of EU law in constraining and constituting (or framing) the exercise of national power on behalf of the Union?

Crucial for this endeavour is the concept of representation, whose essential meaning comes down to 'the making present of something which is nevertheless not literally present'.[13] Like a visitor of a museum who is admiring a painting of a magnificent landscape cannot be certain that the painter depicted the landscape just as it is (instead of how the painter saw it), a citizen in a democratic state cannot be certain that what a politician is presenting as 'the will

---

11 European Commission, 'Remarks by President von der Leyen at the Joint Press Conference with Kyriakos Mitsotakis, Prime Minister of Greece, Andrej Plenković, Prime Minister of Croatia, President Sassoli and President Michel' (Statement 3 March 2020) <https://ec.europa.eu/commission/presscorner/detail/en/statement_20_380> accessed 1 March 2024.

12 'Joint Declaration of Intent on a Controlled Emergency Procedure – Voluntary Commitments by Member States for a Predictable Temporary Solidarity Mechanism' (23 September 2019) <http://www.statewatch.org/media/documents/news/2019/sep/eu-temporary-voluntary-relocation-mechanism-declaration.pdf> accessed 1 March 2024.

13 Hanna Fenichel Pitkin, *The Concept of Representation* (University of California Press 1967) 144.

of the people' in fact corresponds to what the 'the people' wants. At best, he has an idea as to whether the politician's claim aligns with his own interests. Assuming there is a mismatch in this regard, would that be problematic from a democratic point of view? No, because it is not the task of elected politicians to pursue the interests of his voters but to represent them.[14] Whereas the former is rather the unfiltered transmission of his voters' interests through the political process, comparable to a mirror image, representation requires abstraction, opening a space for political imagination.[15] The politician is then not indifferent to his voters' interests either, but he does relate them to other concerns as well.

That is not to suggest that preferences should just be aggregated. Instead, politicians and public authorities in general ought to represent the common good. Under the classical legal tradition, the common good includes but cannot be reduced to certain political aims, the most fundamental of which are peace, justice and abundance (welfare); rather, it transcends these in the sense that their realisation is geared at the flourishing of the polis, which is the highest goods of individuals.[16] This orientation is due to human nature: we need meaningful social relationships for a good life. Although it is impossible to develop such relationships on the scale of a political association like the nation state, the latter is instrumental for securing the conditions for a good life within our dense social communities of families and friends.[17] In addition, the representation of a shared past through, for instance, political speech, rituals and symbols has created an imagined national bond, which has become 'real' in the sense that people are willing to make sacrifices on that basis, such as risking one's life in times of war.[18] To be sure, the (credible) representation of the common good has material consequences insofar as it constitutes the basis upon which political action for the flourishing of the polis unfolds.

Representing the common good, what does that has to do with the role of EU Member States in migration management? At first sight, not that much. For migration management seems to be a technocratic exercise of detecting

14 See Edmund Burke, 'Speech to the Electors of Bristol' in Philip B Kurland & Ralph Lerner (eds), *The Founders' Constitution* (volume 1, web edition, University of Chicago Press) ch 13, document 7 <https://press-pubs.uchicago.edu/founders/documents/v1ch13s7.html> accessed 1 March 2024.

15 See Frank R Ankersmit, *Political Representation* (Stanford University Press 2002) 112–118.

16 See Adrian Vermeule, *Common Good Constitutionalism* (Polity Press 2022) 26ff.

17 On the important distinction between state and society, see Andreas Kinneging, *Hercules op de Tweesprong* (Prometheus 2023) 215–232.

18 See Benedict Anderson, *Imagined Communities: Reflections on the Origin and Spread of Nationalism* (revised edition, Verso 2016).

routes of migrants and refugees; then channelling, controlling or restricting those movements; and doing so in a manner that appears to be compliant with the law, even if in fact legal standards are evaded like in the case of the cooperation between the EU and Tunisia. Hence, decision-makers seem to be so obsessed with 'responding to' and 'managing' new challenges that the space for political imagination, which representation is all about, has been lost – like our museum visitor who stands so close in front of a painting that he cannot see it in full. And the common good? If migration management is indeed technocratic in nature, it will rather not be transcendent at the same time. And even if it was, should we not care about individual human rights as opposed to the common good, since migration management at the margins of the law is a brute exercise of power over vulnerable people? At most, one could state that the commitment to human rights and the other values listed in the EU Treaties corresponds to the common good of the Union, although the language of values and their translation into legal principles and rights is in fact much more prominent. Apart from the rights of nationals from third states (refugees and migrants), the rights of EU citizens are centre stage. The Schengen acquis, for example, is a project fostering a European sense of belonging because the abolition of internal border controls, together with the constitutional right of free movement, enables EU citizens to experience European integration.[19] The fundamental task of the nation state to protect its citizens is relegated to a derogation regime under the EU Treaties, which (on a generous interpretation) require a 'fair balance'.[20]

This book offers a new angle, based on a number of definitions and assumptions. First, for our purposes, migration management covers all policies to govern the regular and irregular migration to Europe, while the emphasis lies with international protection policies. That ties in with the predominant political interest to govern migration on all fronts, under a so-called 'comprehensive approach'.[21] While several elements of this multi-dimensional phenomenon are rather technical, it still triggers the fundamental political question what constitutes us as a polity, who belongs to us and who is excluded. In short: what

19 See Stefan Salomon & Jorrit Rijpma, 'A Europe Without Internal Frontiers: Challenging the Reintroduction of Border Controls in the Schengen Area in the Light of Union Citizenship' (2023) 24(2) German Law Journal 281.

20 See Jonas Bornemann, 'Competing Visions and Constitutional Limits of Schengen Reform: Securitization, Gradual Supranationalization and the Undoing of Schengen as an Identity-Creating Project' (2024) German Law Journal 1, 7.

21 See eg European Council, 'Conclusions' (Meeting of 14 and 15 December 2023) EUCO 20/23, para 29.

is the good life under conditions of large-scale international migration? Second, apart from national communities, the EU as a union of sovereign states should also ask itself this question. Although, as will be argued throughout this book, the EU does possess constitutional characteristics, its potential to represent a common good is more limited than that of its Member States,[22] considering its apolitical beginnings and the continuous importance of nation states for citizens' political, social and cultural identification. At the same time, it cannot be denied that several European nation states are also EU Member States, not just because the Treaties established that status but because their self-perception has changed since most of them have shaped and experienced European integration for decades.[23] Representing the common good must thus not proceed from either an EU or a national point of view: both must be reconciled.

What is, third, the role of law in this regard? To reconcile EU and national positions does not mean here to subject national ideas of the good to EU law, specifically to EU fundamental rights and the sophisticated judicial enforcement mechanisms. That implied a liberal constitutional imagination,[24] purporting to be neutral on the good life because all that it seems to be doing is to protect individual life choices through rights. Law, on this view, recognises and enforces rights, trumping or constraining the common good as the latter inhibits the individual from doing as he pleases. In an age of 'postnational' governance, the constraining effect often emanates from supranational courts, curtailing democratic political representation in nation states.[25] We see this in the field of migration management, where human rights have tightened a stiff net of rules and procedures over political communities. One might even ask whether there is a 'human rights overreach'.[26] At least, it is undesirable when rights function as external constraint on the common good. For the classical legal tradition, rights are rather an integral part thereof, and the right balance is as much a legal as a political question.[27] Law is thus 'ordered'[28] to the common good in the twofold sense that it is meant to preclude arbitrariness and to

22 See Neil Walker, 'The European Public Good and European Public Goods' in Jan Komárek (ed), *European Constitutional Imaginaries: Between Ideology and Utopia* (OUP 2023).

23 See Chris J. Bickerton, *European Integration: From Nation States to Member States* (OUP 2012).

24 Regarding the EU, see Jan Komárek, 'Why Read *The Transformation of Europe* Today? On the Limits of a Liberal Constitutional Imaginary' in Komárek (n 22).

25 See Martin Loughlin, *Against Constitutionalism* (Harvard University Press 2022).

26 See Anuscheh Farahat & Ingrid Leijten, 'Human Rights Overreach?' (2022) 40(2) Netherlands Quarterly of Human Rights 83.

27 See Vermeule (n 16) 164–169.

28 Ibid 30.

channel legitimate political power. To be legitimate, legal and political power must aim at the common good.

This third assumption is the predominant concern of the present study. However, assuming is not enough because it is rather uncommon to think of the Member States using (rather than abusing) EU law to represent the Union.[29] In respect of migration management, this book thus argues that EU law can fulfil the dual function of constraining and empowering the Member States to represent the Union or, what is the same, to pursue the Union's common good. So far, it has been explained what the concepts of representation and the common good mean in the context of EU migration management, which has been defined as covering all (internal and external) dimensions of regulating – through EU and national policies – migration to Europe, with an emphasis on refugee movements. It has also been mentioned that the 27 Member States of the EU should still be seen as sovereign nation states. Now, what is the theoretical approach that brings these concepts and ideas together?

This book builds on and further develops the idea of European spheres,[30] of which there are three: the inner sphere of the EU Treaties; the intermediate sphere of the 27;[31] and the outer sphere of international relations. Their governing mechanisms differ, as it is EU law that governs the inner sphere, whereas national interests and power politics determine actions in the outer sphere. The intermediate sphere is an 'in-between' in the sense that EU membership is not limited to compliance with EU law, nor is the pursuit of national interests per se selfish or 'nationalistic'. Rather, the intermediate sphere operates on the basis of Member States' legal *and* political obligation towards the Union, that is, towards the idea of joint action. EU law is crucial in this respect as it provides an institutional framework for acting together and the means to curtail unilateralism. That is thus the common, albeit 'thin' purpose[32] of the Union

29 A special case exists in EU external relations law when international fora limit or exclude the participation of the EU (as an international organisation), even though it is competent to act according to its own rules. In this case, it shall act 'through the medium of the Member States', see *Opinion 2/91* (*ILO*) EU:C:1993:106, para 37. See also Marise Cremona, 'Member States as Trustees of the Union Interest: Participating in International Agreements on Behalf of the European Union' in Anthony Arnull et al. (eds), *A Constitutional Order of States? Essays in EU Law in Honour of Alan Dashwood* (Hart 2011).

30 See Luuk van Middelaar, *The Passage to Europe – How a Continent Became a Union* (Yale University Press 2013), Prologue.

31 The '27' means collective action of the Member States in the intermediate sphere, outside or at the margins of the EU legal order. That said, unilateral action by a single Member State may also fall within the intermediate sphere.

32 When reference is made to the fundamental political goals of the EU, this book prefers the term 'common purpose' over 'common good'. The latter carries such a deep philosophical

because it does not indicate what joint action should aim at.[33] Of course, the EU Treaties do list values, principles and rights that should guide the exercise of public powers. However, as we shall see, these EU norms rather constrain in the name of the rule of law than animating national political action in the governance of migration. As a result, we should not neglect the outer sphere. It is there where a shared moral, historical and cultural consciousness and actual social-economic relationships help determine what ought to be done in the face of international migration. Taken together, and without complicating matters further at this stage, EU law and a (national) political imagination inform how the 27 or single Member States act in the intermediate sphere.

The main task of the following chapters is to show that EU (asylum and migration) law directs – in the sense of constraining and empowering – the Member States to represent the Union. As Figure 1 shows, EU law determines when Member States are permitted to move 'inside-out', that is, from the inner to the intermediate sphere. EU law is, as it were, a 'gatekeeper' in the twofold sense of a 'guardian' and a 'signpost'. Hence, it both monitors compliance with the Treaties and, at the same time, opens a path towards a deeper political meaning in the intermediate sphere. Union law itself carries political meaning as it promises to ensure that Member States act in common, relegating blatant unilateralism to the past. But, in the intermediate sphere, this 'thin' common purpose comes together and interacts with a deeper national consciousness, tapped from the outer sphere. In that sense, EU law both constrains and empowers.

It is called upon to fulfil that function when Member States claim to represent the Union. Claims to representation take the form of political speech, legislation, executive acts and judicial pronouncements. Representation is thus the mechanism according to which Member States navigate between the spheres. Of course, not all claims can be cast into the language of EU law; or doing so at least causes conceptual problems such as the delineation of law

meaning that it cannot be transposed writ large to the EU, whereas the former better reflects the functional orientation of the EU qua international organisation. However, the relationship between both notions is tight insofar as working together on certain fundamental political goals may foster a shared sense of being a political community. Hence, the 'common purpose' of the EU may over time develop into a richer 'common good'. The idea behind using both terms is thus not to establish a binary opposition between the EU and the Member States.

33 See also Gerhard Seel, 'What is the Common Good and Why Should We Pursue it? A Philosophical Foreword to a Current European Debate' in Sonja Puntscher Riekmann et al. (eds), *Is There a European Common Good?* (Nomos 2012) 38–42, who however argues to develop the EU into a federal state to better realise human rights, amongst others.

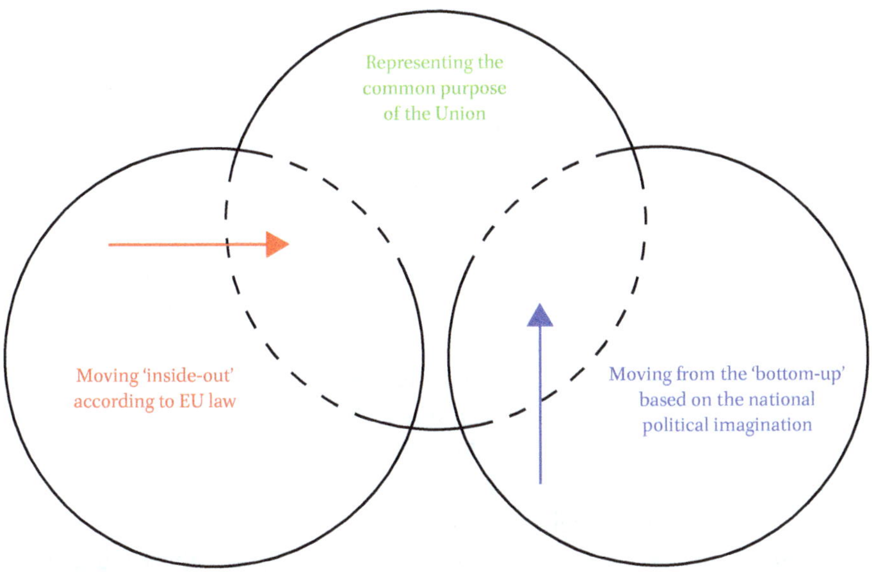

FIGURE 1 The three European spheres

and 'governance'.[34] The guarantee function of EU law therefore has limits, as we will see throughout the book. For that reason, it is crucial that Member States feel responsible for both the Union and for their national communities. In other words, law alone cannot stabilise the intermediate sphere. Maintaining the European political bond is thus as a much a legal as a political (and ethical) question.

This connects to the common good. For doing the good requires an ethics of virtue. According to the classical legal tradition, the four cardinal virtues are: (1) reason, understood as prudence and wisdom as opposed to the modern rational cost-benefit calculation; (2) justice in the sense of giving each his due; (3) courage; and (4) self-control in the sense of taming one's desires for the benefit of reason and action in pursuit of the common good.[35] Law in a positivist sense cannot be good, unless the people who make it do their best

---

34 See Mark Dawson, *The Governance of EU Fundamental Rights* (CUP 2017) 3, who defines governance as 'the exercise of public power in conditions under which normative authority and steering capacity are dispersed'.

35 See Andreas Kinneging, *De Onzichtbare Maat: Archeologie van Goed en Kwaad* (Prometheus 2020) 76–80, 291–313.

to be virtuous, at least. And that is learned and practiced in social interaction, passed on from generation to generation, and reflected upon also from a larger national angle when historical developments and events force us to rethink and to represent (present anew) what we ought to do. Apart from political leaders, parliamentarians and other public officials, this also concerns individual citizens and European societies.

Finally, the foregoing hints at the reasons from proceeding from the inner as opposed to the outer sphere. That is, other than one might think, an important difference. Of course, it would not be wrong to state that the outer sphere and the national interests it encapsulates often stimulate political action, and it is then for EU law to set and enforce legal limits. But that conforms to the mentioned liberal constitutional paradigm according to which law is but a constraint of power and not also its source. As explained, that is undesirable, and so too are movements 'outside-in'. By contrast, representing the Union from the 'inside-out' means that adhering to EU law is what nation states qua members of the Union ought to do. It is less a legal obligation than a political command, imposed not in the form of abstract values, principles and rules but emanating from within responsible Member States.

3 How the Book Proceeds

This book is divided into two parts, the first being theoretical and the second more practice-oriented. Chapter 1 further explores what it means to represent the Union through a Member State lens. It explains that a Member State embodies the constitutional imagination of both the Union and its national polis. EU law facilitates the representation of both, dividing competences between the EU and the Member States and providing for different categories of national discretion in the exercise of those competences. Chapter 2 delves deeper into the constitutional foundations of the Union, for matters of legal-institutional design will not be sufficient to help Member States reconcile their double bind qua members of the Union and qua sovereign nation states. Discussing several possibilities for ordering the constitutional relationships between the EU and its Member States, the chapter argues for placing the common good at the apex of the shared constitutional order. This has implications for the interpretation of EU legal principles such as mutual trust, and for the conceptual relationship between EU law and other forms of governance. Therewith, the book concludes its theoretical investigations, moving in the second part to the practice of EU migration management.

Chapter 3 identifies the common purpose of European integration in the field of immigration policies. It conducts a historical examination, focussing on the aims of the Member States in the course of European integration. That is in line with the concept of the common good, which takes shape and political meaning through shared practices over time. Having identified internal free movement and humanitarian protection in line with international law as the dual common purpose of European migration management, the book goes on to use these historical insights as well as the conceptual and theoretical framework to (re-)interpret existing EU asylum and migration law. As to the internal dimension, Chapter 4 thus asks in how far EU law is in fact empowering, zooming in on both elements of the European common good: the protection of refugees and the Schengen Area. Instead of being pursued in parallel to each other, these aims are often to be balanced when, for instance, Member States reintroduce internal border controls. The chapter suggests how, in that case, EU law can be ordered to the common good, which gives due consideration to each of these aims. Regarding the external dimension, Chapter 5 deals with the EU-Turkey Statement, one of the most controversial measures the EU and its Member States have taken during the 'refugee crisis' to reduce irregular migration to Europe. It has been criticised for, inter alia, violating the ERTA doctrine, which prohibits Member States from concluding international agreements where these are liable to affect or alter the scope of Union law. In fact, this comes down to precluding the Member States from representing the Union. However, the chapter reconstructs the ERTA doctrine so that it enables the Member States to act on behalf of the common purpose while still subjecting their actions to the rule of law. Seen in that light, the EU-Turkey Statement is a useful (albeit imperfect) instrument of European migration management. The book ends with a conclusion, summarising the findings and reflecting on the potential of the 'European spheres' to help *represent* other common policies.

PART 1

The Theory of the European Spheres

CHAPTER 1

Representing the Union and the Nation State

1 Introduction

The hallmark of the ruling in *Van Gend & Loos* is the empowerment of individuals who, as subjects of the EU legal order, have the right to enforce directly effective provisions of EU law before national courts.[1] In particular, the free movement rights have emancipated individuals from national societies, promoting economic liberalism and scepticism towards state intervention. Ever since, collective self-determination in matters as diverse as social welfare, education and taxation has been limited in the name of individual freedom. However, *Van Gend & Loos* has also empowered the Member States. The crucial passage reads as follows:

> The conclusion to be drawn (…) is that the Community constitutes a new legal order of international law for the benefit of which *the* [*Contracting*] *States* have limited their sovereign rights, albeit within limited fields, and the subjects of which comprise not only *the Member States* but also their nationals.[2]

Back then, the European Court of Justice recognised the transformation of the Six into Member States who became the subjects of the new legal order alongside their nationals. The Six established the European Economic Community for the benefit of which they accepted a sector-specific limitation of their 'sovereign rights'. Nowadays, in *Opinion 2/13*, the Court represented the foundation of the EU in subtly different terms:

> As the Court of Justice has repeatedly held, *the founding Treaties of the EU*, unlike ordinary international treaties, *established* a new legal order, possessing its own institutions, for the benefit of which *the Member States* have limited their sovereign rights, in ever wider fields, and the subjects of which comprise not only those States but also their nationals

1 Case 26/62 *Van Gend & Loos* EU:C:1963:1, p 13.
2 Ibid p 12 (emphasis added).

 | DOI:10.1163/9789004695733_003

> (see in particular the judgments in van Gend & Loos, 26/62, EU:C:1963:1, p.12 (…)).[3]

It seems as if the Contracting States were not involved in the constitution of the EU.[4] The Court appears to suggest that the Treaties established a self-sustaining legal order without a constituent power, even though the limitation of sovereign rights is logically prior to the status of Member State. Hence, it were the *Contracting States* who transferred some of their powers to the EU. This is not to deny that significant legal developments have taken place since the 1960s, in particular the maturing of the early Communities into an autonomous, quasi-constitutional legal order.[5] However, law alone cannot explain why the Court purported to continue a seemingly consistent line of jurisprudence since *Van Gend & Loos*.

Part of the explanation rests in the practice of representation. As mentioned in the Introduction, representing is 'the making present of something which is nevertheless not literally present'.[6] Something is presented anew, like a narrative that is passed on from generation to generation.[7] And like a narrator, a representative can mould what is being represented. Hence, he or she is empowered to include and exclude, to do away with other, competing representations. Resistance is likely to emerge if the object of the representation is deemed to be misappropriated. But if successful, the representative will integrate the audience around that object similar to a narrator who is capable of gathering people around a campfire.

The Court represents the foundation of the EU legal order from a particular point of view. In *Opinion 2/13*, it appears to have exercised its power of representation by excluding the Contracting States from the foundation. What remains are the Member States, the subjects of the EU legal order who exercise rights and obligations in accordance with EU law. Embedded in a well-known line of case law, the narrative went unnoticed.[8] For our purposes, it is

---

3 *Opinion 2/13* (*Accession to the ECHR*) EU:C:2014:2454, para 157 (emphasis added).

4 See Hans Lindahl, 'The Paradox of Constituent Power: The Ambiguous Self-Constitution of the European Union' (2007) 20(4) Ratio Juris 485, who reads *Van Gend & Loos* as the constitution of 'market citizens'.

5 See Chapter 2.

6 Hanna Fenichel Pitkin, *The Concept of Representation* (University of California Press 1967) 144.

7 See Albrecht Koschorke, 'Auf der Suche nach dem verlorenen Europa-Narrativ' in Claudius Franzius et al. (eds), *Die Neuerfindung Europas: Bedeutung und Gehalte von Narrativen für die europäische Integration* (Nomos 2019) 21, 23.

8 At least, case notes did not address this issue, see Daniel Halberstamm, '"It's the Autonomy Stupid!" A Modest Defense of Opinion 2/13 on EU Accession to the ECHR, and the Way Forward' (2015) 16(1) German Law Journal 105; Buno de Witte & Šejla Imamovic, 'Opinion

a representation of the inner sphere of the Treaties, whereas the intermediate sphere of the 27 surfaced in the abandoned passage in *Van Gend & Loos*.

It is the aim of this book to elucidate the intermediate sphere in EU migration management, and to analyse the interrelation with the inner sphere of the Treaties. The present chapter will be the first step, submitting that action in the intermediate sphere implies a representation of unity from the angle of a particular Member State. As it occurs in the intermediate sphere, we need to account for the multiple identities of the 27 who are both members of the Union and nation states. The practice of representation is never just a response to events like a sudden inflow of asylum seekers. It also expresses the political underpinnings of a legal order, its 'constitutional imagination'. This refers to 'sets of ideas and beliefs that help to motivate and justify the practice of government and collective self-rule (…) They provide political action with an overarching sense and purpose recognized as legitimate by those governed.'[9] There is a close relationship between constitutional imaginations and sovereignty. For the latter can be unpacked into a 'claim' or an outward expression of power, and into a 'frame' that generates or produces the 'claim' because it furnishes political meaning.[10] A 'claim' to sovereign power in order to address a certain problem can thus not be made without a deeper sense of what it means to act in common in the first place. The 'claim' is then situated within the lifeworld of those on whose behalf it is made, enabling them to attribute the exercise of power to themselves. Apart from generating the exercise of power, the 'frame' thus serves to evaluate the 'claim'. Self-attribution or 'self-creation'[11] is a prerequisite to distinguish (brute) exercise of power from legitimate authority. In this book, the concepts of 'constitutional imagination' and 'sovereignty frame' are treated synonymously.

The chapter proceeds as follows. To start with, it explains the constitutional imagination of the 27, before zooming in on the German ideas of constitutionalism for illustration purposes. Explaining then what underlies the EU legal order paves the ground for the third, crucial step: how can a Member State represent the Union while remaining loyal to its national identity? The present chapter cannot give a complete answer. But as representation is a practice, this

2/13 on Accession to the ECHR: Defending the EU Legal Order against a Foreign Human Rights Court' (2015) 40(5) European Law Review 683.

9 Jan Komárek, 'European Constitutional Imaginaries: Utopias, Ideologies, and the Other' in Jan Komárek (ed), *European Constitutional Imaginaries: Between Ideology and Utopia* (OUP 2023) 1, 2.

10 See Neil Walker, 'Sovereignty Surplus' (2020) 18(2) I·CON 370, 381–382.

11 Ibid 386.

stage of the inquiry will explain the role of EU law in empowering the Member States to act on behalf of the Union. Two recent rulings of the Court demonstrate that the EU legal order has to mediate the exercise of national powers in order for the latter to be recognised, in a formal sense, as a representation on behalf of the Union.

2 Representing the Nation State

2.1 *Political Reflexivity in the Constitutional State*

Every legal order is the institutionalisation of collective agency. It emanates from the will of individuals or groups to be part of a collective whose common affairs require a legal-institutional form. In modern Western democracies, the constituent power of the people is deemed to have given itself a constitution which constitutes the legal order. This process of constitutional ordering is encapsulated by the notion of popular sovereignty.[12] Once the people has constituted the legal order, it is considered to recede and to be represented by the constituted powers, the trias politica of legislature, executive and judiciary. The background against which the powers of the constitutional state operate is side-stepped.[13] The Court in *Opinion 2/13* seemed to follow this line of thought because it merged the constituent power of the 27 into the constituted Member States. The alternative is to postulate a strict dualism between the powers. The constituent power, the unity of the people, can at any time reappear to overthrow the existing order and to constitute itself anew. It is thus, as it were, outside the legal order waiting for the rupture.[14]

On yet another understanding, which is supported here, the relationship between constituted and constituent power is reflexive.[15] That is to say, it is

12 This, and related notions of sovereignty, are explained in historical perspective in Dieter Grimm, *Sovereignty: The Origin and Future of a Political and Legal Concept* (Columbia University Press 2015) 33–75.

13 In legal theory, this view is attributed to Hans Kelsen. See, for example, Martin Loughlin, 'On Constituent Power' in Michael W Dowdle & Michael A Wilkinson (eds), *Constitutionalism Beyond Liberalism* (CUP 2017) 151, 156–159.

14 In legal theory, this view is attributed to Carl Schmitt. See, for example, Loughlin (n 13) 159–165 and Hans Lindahl, *Authority and the Globalisation of Inclusion and Exclusion* (CUP 2018) 169ff and 288ff.

15 Based mainly on the works of Hans Lindahl and Martin Loughlin. However, these authors do not have exactly the same understanding of political reflexivity. That is because Lindahl considers the difficulties of a national community to relate itself to the multiple sites of authority beyond the state and vice versa, see Lindahl (n 14) 378, 401, 406, 417. Compare Martin Loughlin; *Foundations of Public Law* (OUP 2010) 226–232, 310–311.

approached from the first-person perspective of a collective self, a national political community in particular. It takes an internal perspective on what we (ourselves) have in common, contrary to an external observer who attributes certain characteristics to a people.[16] The chapter will gradually unfold the nature of political reflexivity; for the time being, it suffices to outline that it implies an interrelationship between the powers of constitutional ordering. There is no collective absent any, even minimal, constituted power. Individuals are ready to push aside whatever divides them when someone represents them as a bounded community of values, faith or beliefs. But as symbolic representation alone cannot overcome actual differences between individuals, a legal-institutional order is necessary to reconcile competing interests. The outcome of any balancing exercise cannot but favour some individuals more than others. And yet, at least a majority will feel represented because an unfavourable law, decree or court ruling cannot outweigh the long-term benefits of membership in a political community. It follows that the constituted power is not self-sustaining. A representative needs the recognition of the represented in order to fulfil its tasks. If it is responsive to their interests, the represented are likely to regard the legal order as their own. In this sense, they exercise power over themselves through their representatives.

That is a brief outline of the authority of the constitutional state. It is based on a school of European legal thought called political jurisprudence. Martin Loughlin is the most influential contemporary scholar of a field rooted in the works of Hobbes, Rousseau, Burke, Schmitt and others.[17] It is essentially concerned with the political, separate but related to law. The meaning of the political is not exhausted by ordinary political decision-making in and outside of parliament. It refers to the legitimacy of legal and political authority. Legitimate power over citizens by means of law-making, application and enforcement (*potentia*) hinges on the power to represent a unity of purpose (*potestas*). This is to say, the institutions constituted by the legal order must justify the exercise of power in view of the common good. The representation of unity has been successful if a majority of the citizenry attributes it to itself. Hence, the exercise of *potentia* is legitimate. Conversely, power will be illegitimate if a majority does not feel represented, which implies that it refuses to

16 See Bert van Roermund, *Law in the First Person Plural: Roots, Concepts, Topics* (Elgar 2020) ch 4 in particular.

17 This paragraph is based on Martin Loughlin, *Political Jurisprudence* (OUP 2017) 1–4; see also Van Roermund (n 16) for a detailed analysis of the work of Rousseau.

attribute the exercise of power to itself. In that moment, the political community has dissolved because it cannot exist without a representative legal-institutional order.[18]

This explains why the common good is not just a political objective determined in part by the exigencies of time such recuing the climate, managing migration or the fighting a pandemic.[19] Measures taken on these and other contemporary challenges serve the existence of the polis,[20] which is the final purpose of sovereign statehood.[21] What defines a political community other than the everyday decision-making on matters of common concern? Common decision-making within a nation state is only possible because of mutual trust and loyalty. It finds expression in the acceptance of, for example, taxation and military service. Citizens are thus willing to make sacrifices[22] for the benefit of the community, confident that they will profit from the loyalty of their fellow citizens in the future.[23] Mutual trust and loyalty are generated by the will to concerted action. The nation state fosters a stronger bond than other associations since the former makes it possible to transcend one's individual existence beyond time and space.[24] That is due to the imagination and representation of a national identity.

David Miller outlines five elements that distinguish a national identity from other identities: (1) it is a matter of belief; (2) it embodies historical continuity; (3) it is an active identity; (4) it is connected to a particular territory and (5) to a distinct public culture encompassing, for example, common political principles, social norms and cultural ideals.[25] Based on our theoretical framework, we can explore each element in turn. Regarding the first, subjective belief is a substitute for the objective impossibility to relate personally to every member of the nation. Even though trust and loyalty may grow from actual shared experience such as a national crisis, they cannot do without a credible political

18 That is not to say that the old is replaced by a new order. Rather, someone (a constituted power) will represent the unity anew. Hence, it will include and exclude on the basis of the extant order. It is an evolution as opposed to a revolution, see Lindahl (n 14) 404.

19 See Lindahl (n 14) 50.

20 See Marco Goldoni & Michael A Wilkinson, 'The Material Constitution' (2018) 81(4) The Modern Law Review 567, 592.

21 See Ulrich Haltern, *Europarecht und das Politische* (Mohr Siebeck 2005) 75ff.

22 Ibid 87: 'Die Macht eines Gemeinwesens liegt vielmehr in einem Einstehenwollen, das sich durch Drohung nicht erreichen läßt und das über jede vertraglich festgeschriebene Verpflichtung hinausgeht. In dem Maße der Anerkennung dieses Einstehenwollens als Opfer ist die Macht eines Staates präsent.'

23 See David Miller, *On Nationality* (OUP 1995) ch 3.

24 See Haltern (n 21) for a detailed discussion of the political in the EU.

25 Miller (n 23) 21–27.

imagination. Second, political jurists underline that a legal order is the product of a particular history.[26] That is why a representation of unity will face the risk of non-recognition if it cannot be situated within a historical context. However, the meaning of national identity inevitably evolves when the authorities must represent a unity in the face of sudden events or, generally, a changing environment.[27] To increase the legitimacy of their response, they represent a unity against the background of a shared history. Third, it is an active identity because the belief in what we have in common is empowering. Finally, the remaining elements indicate that a national polity is bounded in terms of space and the background conditions that inform the common action.

This sense of belonging is decisive for collective agency. By contrast, political jurists deny the integrative and motivating force of rational thought guided by universal principles. Scepticism is due to a realist worldview and the inclination of human beings to follow their interests rather than a universal morality.[28] As mentioned, one of these interests is to surpass one's individual existence and to be part of a community not bound by time. Communities who are said to represent universal principles like the EU are confronted with a conceptual and empirical challenge. Conceptually, even the premise of universality is difficult to uphold because every representation of unity by definition includes and excludes.[29] That is the case when, for example, common values like solidarity or the rule of law are given a certain meaning to the exclusion of others. A representation is thus always particular, never truly universal. That is not to say that an international organisation like the EU may not try to be more inclusive. Empirically, however, citizens are likely to reject attempts to replicate the political imagination of the nation state, as the Dutch and the French did in referendums on the Constitutional Treaty.[30] The next section explains the political imagination of the EU legal order, which is of a different quality than the sovereignty frame of the 27.

We have thus seen that a legal order cannot exist without a shared identity. At the same time, the will to concerted action cannot find expression other than in legal-institutional form. In political jurisprudence, the nature of legal order is both limiting and empowering. On the one hand, and in line with liberal constitutionalism, the separation of powers and fundamental rights reduce

---

26 See Loughlin (n 17) 8–9.

27 See Lindahl (n 14) 52; Loughlin (n 15) 226ff.

28 See Loughlin (n 17) 7.

29 See Lindahl (n 14), ch 5 and pp 398ff.

30 See Haltern (n 21) 199ff concerning the symbolism culminating into the Constitutional Treaty.

the risk of domination by a majority in the name of a mythical unity. On the other hand, an idea of what we, as a political community have in common generates political power mediated through representative institutions. Indeed, a legal order is unlikely to be empowering if individuals cannot presume that the competent institutions will, as a last resort, enforce the reciprocity on which the polis is based. The institutions themselves have been empowered by the legal order. Of particular importance in this respect is the constitution. It is at the same time the source and the limit of any legal power. That is why it also has an expressive function, for any exercise of power is to serve the common good of the (imagined) collective to which it gives expression. It is thus the reservoir (*Sinnspeicher*) of the political imagination.[31] Law – the constitution in particular – is essential for the reflexive relationship between *potentia* and *potestas*. It mediates between the source of power and its manifestation, which is significant for the following reasons. The constitution guarantees relative stability by virtue of the procedural hurdles for constitutional amendment. It thus facilitates orientation in the face of everyday politics. In addition, evolution in time is possible because constitutional norms are rather vague and thus open to interpretation. Finally, the latter explains why the source of power is always represented.[32] If it appeared directly, it would be nothing but naked power.[33]

A valid critique observes that the reflexive relationship between *potentia* and *potestas* seems to presuppose the centrality of the nation state as if national decision-making was immune to other sites of authority of which the EU is but one prominent example.[34] To be precise, political jurisprudence is concerned with the authority of the sovereign state. Internal and external sovereignty denotes, following the most basic definition, the final authority over all public matters without external interference. The holder of sovereignty is

31 Instead of many, see in particular Haltern (n 21) 92ff; Martin Loughlin, 'The Constitutional Imagination' (2015) 78(1) The Modern Law Review 1; Goldoni & Wilkinson (n 20); Wim Voermans, *Het Verhaal van de Grondwet: Zoeken naar Wij* (Prometheus 2019) pt 5.

32 But see Van Roermund (n 16) ch 6.

33 See, a contrario, Haltern (n 21) 100 in the footnote: 'Sobald Erscheinung und Quelle getrennt sind, eröffnet sich für die Erscheinung ein Interpretationsraum mit der Folge, daß über die Bedeutung der Erscheinung gestritten werden kann. Der Wille des Souveräns ist nicht mehr eins mit dem Willen des Monarchen. Es entsteht die paradoxe Situation, gegen die Person des Monarchen im Namen des wahren Monarchen opponieren zu können.'

34 See Neil Walker, 'Foundations of Public Law and Postnational Constitutionalism' in Michael A Wilkinson & Michael W Dowdle (eds), *Questioning the Foundations of Public Law* (Hart 2018) 133–142.

the state who upholds the unity of the represented and the representatives acting on their behalf.[35] Obviously, such a dense unity no longer exists since international organisations, agencies and bodies have exercised powers in matters falling beyond the purview of individual states. Moreover, those authorities have become more autonomous and, correspondingly, the ability of states to exert influence over them is reduced.[36] The rise of new authorities and the relative demise of the nation state lead to several overlapping, competing representations of unity. The former are more inclined to represent functional properties like better climate or migration governance, whereas the representatives of the nation state seek to maintain their influence over the attendant cultural, economic and social contexts. As every legal order is inherently contingent,[37] citizens are likely to alienate from their nation state without feeling fully represented by global legal orders.[38]

Lindahl proposes a normative account to deal with the contingency of legal orders, based on his explanatory model of institutionally authorised collective action.[39] As mentioned, a legal order is emerging when somebody is representing a unity that cannot include without excluding, and it cannot exclude without including. The political, according to Lindahl, is characterised by conflicts about who we really are and what we have in common.[40] Conflicts occur because a representation of unity is either over-inclusive or under-inclusive. They deal with demands for recognition either of difference or of sameness. The question is thus whether the boundaries of the legal order can be redrawn to account for the demand. Although a political community may adapt to changing circumstances, it will have limits or 'fault lines' that cannot be crossed without losing self-recognition. In other words, there is a point at which a polity can no longer identify itself as such, and the institutions of the legal order who dare to make the leap will lose their legitimacy. This worst-case scenario can be avoided if the mentioned contingency is acknowledged. Lindahl promotes a model of restrained collective self-assertion. Confronted with a demand for recognition, a collective asserts itself by representing itself as a unity who recognises the other as one-of-us. That is accompanied by collective self-restraint recognising the other as other-than-us. The logic of inclusion and exclusion

35 See Loughlin (n 15) 186: 'Sovereignty is vested neither in the ruler, nor in the office of government, nor in the people: sovereignty vests in the relationship itself.'

36 See Lindahl (n 14) 417; Walker (n 11) 411ff ('rationing' of sovereignty).

37 See Lindahl (n 14) 224ff.

38 Ibid 161: the risk of 'multiple alienations'.

39 Ibid ch 2.

40 The remainder of the paragraph is based on Lindahl (n 14) ch 6.

allows self-recognition on either side: we still recognise ourselves as a political community while being responsive to the identity of the other. That is not only of theoretical relevance because a legal order accepted as our own is likely to be effective in the sense of inducing law-abiding behaviour.[41]

In practical terms, there are several forms and mechanisms of restrained collective self-assertion such as the margin of appreciation in the case law of the European Court of Human Rights.[42] Lindahl takes the case of *Lautsi* as an example, in which the Strasbourg Court ruled that the mandatory display of crucifixes in Italian public schools did not violate the applicants' rights to education and freedom of religion.[43] Hence, the Italian authorities did not exceed their margin of appreciation to perpetuate a tradition connected to the historical development of the country.[44] For our purposes, it is important to note that a technique like the margin of appreciation postpones the self-assertion of, in this case, the Council of Europe.[45] It defers to the other (Italy) to represent a unity from its point of view, determined by the same logic of inclusion and exclusion. By justifying its particular education policy in accordance with the ECHR, Italy recognised itself as one-of-us and as other-than-us. It follows that the invocation of difference is not only exclusionary; it is also to recognise the other-in-ourselves.

This theoretical insight makes it possible to bridge the divide between the inner and the outer sphere. Reference to national identity is not only a defence against EU interference. Likewise, it is not only a representation addressed to a national audience. By recognising the other (the EU) as one-of-us, any of the 27 is motivated to promote that part of itself by making a claim to represent the Union. But the latter is also other-than-us, so any exercise of power triggered by the will to be a member of the Union will be informed by a particular imagination of the political. To illustrate such an imagination, the next step is to outline the German frame of sovereignty, followed by an explanation of what underlies the EU legal order. After all, Member States cannot be one-of-us unless they also represent the fundamentals of European integration.

41 Lindahl (n 14) 356.
42 Ibid ch 7.
43 *Lautsi and Others* v *Italy* App no 30814/06 (ECtHR, 18 March 2011).
44 Ibid paras 67–68.
45 Lindahl (n 14) 375–376.

2.2 *How the German Federal Constitutional Court Represents European Integration*

The foregoing demonstrated that sovereignty is not only the surface level of legal powers, with constitutions at the apex; it is also a deeper frame of asserting oneself as a member of a political community acting through its legal order. Other than the Court, who represents an autonomous, apparently self-sustaining system of norms, the German *Bundesverfassungsgericht* (FCC) and other national constitutional courts derive the authority of the EU legal order from the will of the national people, expressed in the constitution. This jurisprudence exposes the reflexivity of the sovereignty frame.

In the *Lisbon* judgment, the Second Senate of the FCC ruled on the constitutionality of the German Act Approving the Treaty of Lisbon.[46] The standard of review was the right to vote, laid down in Article 38 of the Basic Law (*Grundgesetz*, henceforth: GG), in conjunction with the principles of democracy, constitutional identity and openness towards European integration.[47] In Germany, the right to vote is considered equivalent to a fundamental right, establishing a right to democratic self-determination which is exercised through elections and other votes. Article 20(2) GG stipulates the principle of representative democracy: 'All state authority is derived from the people. It shall be exercised by the people through elections and other votes and through specific legislative, executive and judicial bodies.' Eijsbouts explains the duality of the original (constituent) and the electoral (constituted) people in, respectively, the first and the second sentence.[48] Similar to political reflexivity, the function of the duality is to preserve a balance between permanence and change. Unlike an ethno-cultural homogeneity, the electoral people is composed of individuals who have to sort out their differences through representative institutions. At the same time, the mediation allows for the representation of unity in time, for the evolution of the polity as opposed to sudden, abrupt change instigated by the unmediated appearance of the constituent power. With regard to the *Lisbon* judgment, Eijsbouts argues that the German Court conflated the duality in favour of an active people who exercises the right to vote inside the Constitution, by voting for the *Bundestag*, and in a pre-constitutional state where it may vote for a re-constitution in, for example, a European federal state.[49] In each case, the expression of the will is apparently

46 BVerfG, Judgment of the Second Senate of 30 June 2009, 2 BvE 2/08 ('Lisbon Judgment').

47 These principles are codified in, respectively, articles 22, 79(3), 23 GG.

48 Tom Eijsbouts, 'Wir sind das Volk – Notes about the Notion of "The People" as Occasioned by the *Lissabon-Urteil*' (2010) 6(2) EuConst 199, 212–215.

49 Ibid 218–219.

immediate, not mediated by the constituted powers. Eijsbouts' critical analysis demonstrates the dependency of collective agency on representative institutions like the FCC.[50]

That said, the German Court was not completely indifferent to the reflexivity of representation. The principle of representative democracy would be violated if, as a result of European integration, the *Bundestag* can no longer effectively shape the will of the people. It went on to elaborate the constitutive principles of the German state:

> The order constituted by the Basic Law *rests on* the self-esteem and dignity of the individual in free determination. This order is power under the rule of law *founded on* the self-determination of the people in freedom and equality according to the will of the respective majority. (...) Consequently, citizens are not subject to an inescapable political power which they are fundamentally incapable of freely determining, with equal regard to persons and subject matter.
>
> Self-determination of the people according to the majority principle, achieved through elections and other votes, is constitutive of the state order as constituted by the Basic Law.[51]

The constituted power thus presupposes the readiness of the individual to subject his or her liberty to the majority of the people. If it were otherwise, the constituted power would be an illegitimate alien power. Conversely, if the premise holds, the legal order is a vehicle of individual and collective liberty. Now, what makes individuals accept majority rule? The closest we can get is the understanding of sovereign statehood:

> [T]he Basic Law codifies the maintenance of peace and the overcoming of destructive antagonism between European states as outstanding political objectives of the Federal Republic of Germany. This means that sovereign statehood stands for a pacified area and the order guaranteed therein on the basis of individual freedom and collective self-determination. The state is neither a myth nor an end in itself but the historically grown and globally recognised form of organisation of a viable political community.[52]

---

50 Ibid 221–222.

51 Lisbon Judgment (n 46) paras 212–213 (emphasis added).

52 Ibid para 224.

The German legal order thus represents a final (though not exclusive) purpose of democratic self-determination, which goes beyond individual freedom: peace and security, no longer against but together with other European states. Hence, the sovereignty frame is embedded into a particular context, mindful of history and national responsibility. Individuals subject themselves to the legal order because the Basic Law is the reservoir of their political existence, and the guardian of their individual and collective liberty. Indeed, the Basic Law 'not only presumes sovereign statehood for Germany but guarantees it'.[53]

This entails limitations on the surrender of sovereign rights to the EU. The FCC identified five areas which belong to the 'inviolable core content'[54] of Germany's constitutional identity.[55] These are (1) criminal law; (2) the use of force; (3) the budget; (4) the social state; (5) and decisions of particular cultural importance, for example on family law, the school and education system and on dealing with religious communities. EU legal acts will be inapplicable in Germany if they intervene into these areas to such a degree that the organs of the German state no longer have 'sufficient space [...] for the political formation of the economic, cultural and social living conditions'.[56] The FFC is relatively silent about any theory or argument behind this seemingly arbitrary list.[57] At least, political formation requires meaningful democratic discourse which, according to the FCC, is primarily a national discourse because of the close connection to 'patterns of identification related to the nation-state, language, history and culture'.[58]

The *Lisbon* judgment marked the beginning of a new stage in the constitutional relationship between the EU and Germany, with impact well beyond Brussels, Luxembourg and Karlsruhe. Delivered at the dawn of a decade of

53 Ibid para 216.

54 Ibid para 240.

55 On a combined reading of Articles 23 and 79(3) GG. Under the Basic Law, Germany shall not participate in European integration to the extent the division of the Federation into *Länder*, their participation on principle in the legislative process, or the principles laid down in Articles 1 and 20 are affected. For details, see Christian Calliess, 'Constitutional Identity in Germany – One for Three or Three in One?' in Christian Calliess & Gerhard van der Schyff (eds), *Constitutional Identity in a Europe of Multilevel Constitutionalism* (CUP 2019).

56 Ibid para 249.

57 See Daniel Halberstamm & Christoph Möllers, 'The German Constitutional Court Says "*Ja zu Deutschland!*"' German Law Journal (2009) 10(8) 1241, 1250; Daniel Thym, 'In the Name of Sovereign Statehood: A Critical Introduction to the Lisbon Judgment of the German Constitutional Court' (2009) 46(6) CML Rev 1795, 1800–1801.

58 Lisbon Judgment (n 46) para 251.

multiple crises, the German Court since had several opportunities to specify the mentioned constitutional caveats. In particular, ruling on various emergency measures in the sovereign debt crisis, the FCC developed the concept of constitutional identity with respect to the budgetary responsibility of the *Bundestag*.[59] The jurisprudence culminated into the recent *PSPP* judgment[60] on whether the German state organs violated their responsibility with regard to European integration (*Integrationsverantwortung*) either by implementing the so-called Public Sector Purchasing Programme (PSPP) of the European Central Bank (ECB), or failing to actively take steps to ensure that conformity with the European integration agenda (*Integrationsprogramm*) is re-established. For the first time, the FCC declared an EU legal act to be ultra vires. As if that was not enough, it also found that the Luxembourg Court acted outside its Treaty mandate by upholding the legality of the PSPP under the EU legal order. The majority of the reactions were overtly critical of the German Court, especially of what some deemed a schoolmasterly attitude towards Luxembourg.[61]

The ruling further illuminates the sovereignty frame of the German legal order (and, broadly, of many other legal orders founded on liberal democracy). The FCC held that neither the ECB nor the Luxembourg Court, in exercising judicial review over the former, sufficiently weighed in the actual effects of the programme on the economic, fiscal and social policies of the Member States. This affects the division of competences insofar as the mandate of the ECB is restricted to monetary policy; economic, fiscal and social policies remain with the Member States, only subject to a coordinating role of the EU institutions. Facilitated by the low intensity of judicial review at EU level, the ECB could effectively decide on the scope of its competences. This struck at the heart of how the FCC conceives of European integration: the EU is 'a union based on the multi-level cooperation of sovereign states',[62] where the

59 BVerfG, Judgment of the Second Senate of 18 March 2014, 2 BvR 1390/12 (on the Treaty establishing the European Stability Mechanism and the Treaty on Stability, Coordination and Governance in the Economic and Monetary Union).

60 BVerfG, Judgment of the Second Senate of 5 May 2020, 2 BvR 859/15 ('PSPP').

61 Instead of many, see Jan Dietze et al., 'Europa – Quo Vadis? Ein kritischer Kommentar zum EZB-Urteil des BVerfG' (2020) Europäische Zeitschrift für Wirtschaftsrecht 525; Daniel Kelemen et al., 'National Courts Cannot Override CJEU Judgments: A Joint Statement in Defense of the EU Legal Order' (2020) Verfassungsblog <https://verfassungsblog.de/national-courts-cannot-override-cjeu-judgments/> accessed 1 March 2024. In June 2021, the Commission initiated infringement proceedings against Germany, see European Commission, 'Primacy of EU Law: Commission Sends Letter of Formal Notice to Germany for Breach of Fundamental Principles of EU Law' (Press release 9 June 2021) <https://ec.europa.eu/commission/presscorner/detail/en/inf_21_2743> accessed 1 March 2024.

62 PSPP (n 60) para 111.

Member States (or rather the 27) decide in how far they limit their sovereign rights. They are, in other words, the 'Masters of the Treaties' who retain the *Kompetenz-Kompetenz*.[63]

PSPP is thus seemingly but another conflict over the limitation of sovereign rights, albeit with an unprecedented outcome. However, the dispute cuts deeper into the legitimacy of EU monetary policy. The judgment is fundamentally about defending the principle of democracy against the ECB, a non-representative institution who operates, at least, at the margins of its mandate.[64] It is at the heart of the ruling to preclude a distortion in the reflexive relationship between the powers of the German constitutional state:

> The democratic legitimation by the people of public authority exercised in Germany belongs to the essential contents of the principle of the sovereignty of the people and thus forms part of the Basic Law's constitutional identity protected in Art. 79(3) GG; it is therefore beyond the reach of European integration in accordance with Art. 23(1) third sentence in conjunction with Art. 79(3) GG.
>
> Art. 38(1) first sentence, Art. 20(1) and (2) and Art. 79(3) GG protect, in particular, the budgetary powers of the German *Bundestag* (…) and its overall budgetary responsibility as indispensable elements of the constitutional principle of democracy.[65]

This excerpt corroborates the impression that the identity review is concerned with democracy and popular sovereignty. In the same vein, the ultra vires review upholds not only the division of competences but also the democratic legitimisation of any public authority exercised in Germany. Any such exercise must be traced back to the citizens, who would be otherwise subject to an alien political authority 'they cannot escape'.[66]

Overall, the jurisprudence of the FCC illustrates the model of political reflexivity. As long as European integration adheres to the principles of conferral and constitutional identity, the EU legal order is a vehicle for national self-determination. Reflexivity implies that the powers of the constitutional state relate to one another (constituent/constituted). In plain terms, the German people recognises the EU legal order as its own by, for example, accepting the

63 Ibid paras 102, 111.

64 See Ulrich Haltern, 'Ultra-vires-Kontrolle im Dienst europäischer Demokratie' (2020) Neue Zeitschrift für Verwaltungsrecht 817.

65 PSPP (n 60) paras 101, 104.

66 Ibid para 99.

primacy of EU law in all but the most exceptional circumstances. The limit or fault line of the German legal order is the principle of democracy whose purpose is to maintain individual freedom in a political community bound together by language, history and culture. It remains to be seen in how far the EU legal order recognises the constituent power of the 27 and their underlying sovereignty frame. Recognition is possible only in accordance with the frame of the *Rechtsgemeinschaft*, which will be explained in the next section.

3 Representing the *Rechtsgemeinschaft*: The Common Purpose of Mutual Non-interference

Following the *PSPP* judgment, the Court in Luxembourg issued, unexpectedly, a press release. It elucidates the frame of the EU legal order in the following words:

> In order to ensure that EU law is applied uniformly, the Court of Justice alone – which was created for that purpose by the Member States – has jurisdiction to rule that an act of an EU institution is contrary to EU law. Divergences between courts of the Member States as to the validity of such acts would indeed be liable to place in jeopardy the unity of the EU legal order and to detract from legal certainty. Like other authorities of the Member States, national courts are required to ensure that EU law takes full effect. That is the only way of ensuring the equality of Member States in the Union they created.[67]

This is a particular representation of unity, intended for media use. That is why EU legal language expressed in words like autonomy or primacy, is absent. However, in terms of substance, there is no deviation from the Court's well-established reasoning on the authority of EU law except as regards the principle of primacy. Assuming that the press release implicitly refers to primacy (for otherwise EU law cannot take 'full effect'),[68] the Court states that primacy

67 Court of Justice of the EU, 'Press Release Following the Judgment of the German Constitutional Court of 5 May 2020' (Press Release No 58/20, 8 May 2020) <https://curia.europa.eu/jcms/upload/docs/application/pdf/2020-05/cp200058en.pdf> accessed 1 March 2024.

68 See Justin Lindeboom, 'Is the Primacy of EU Law Based on the Equality of the Member States? A Comment on the CJEU's Press Release Following the *PSPP* Judgment' (2020) 21(5) German Law Journal 1032, 1034ff (with further references to the views of CJEU President Lenaerts).

'is the only way of ensuring the equality of Member States'. This additional justification has, in the meantime, become part of the Court's jurisprudence.[69] It is similar to Fabbrini's argument submitting that a unilateral derogation from EU law, in violation of the principle of primacy, has negative effects for other Member States.[70] It is thus an argument of justice between Member States, quite different from the rather abstract defence of the EU legal order in *Costa*.[71]

It is, to be precise, a particular conception of justice, rooted in the history of European integration. The European Coal and Steel Community was founded to remove the control over the production of coal and steel from individual nation states who could no longer exploit these resources for waging a war. This logic of mutual non-interference has survived the foundational period.[72] It continues to inform the Court's interpretation of the EU legal order and, as will be discussed later on, the rules on EU migration management in particular.[73] The decision to shift migration control to the external borders exposed the majority of the Member States to the political will and administrative capacity of the frontline Member States to fulfil the requirements of EU border, asylum and immigration laws. That is but one reason why national sovereignty frames cannot be underestimated. If the Member States can no longer recognise the EU legal order as their own, they are unlikely to meet their obligations and the rest of the Union will have to bear the costs of non-compliance.

However, legal equality is a bar to the recognition of actual differences. A representation of unity informed by a particular national identity must be in line with the primacy of EU law, so the argument goes, for primacy is the

69 See Joined Cases C-357/19, C-379/19, C-547/19, C-811/19 and C-840/19 *Criminal proceedings against PM and Others* EU:C:2021:1034, para 249: 'It must be added that Article 4(2) TEU provides that the Union is to respect the equality of Member States before the Treaties. However, the Union can respect such equality only if the Member States are unable, under the principle of the primacy of EU law, to rely on, as against the EU legal order, a unilateral measure, whatever its nature.' For criticism, see Ferdinand Weber, 'The Identity of Union Law in Primacy: Piercing Through *Euro Box Promotion and Others* (2022) 7(2) European Papers 749, 765–766.

70 Federico Fabbrini, 'After the OMT Case: The Supremacy of EU Law as the Guarantee of the Equality of the Member States' (2016) 16(4) German Law Journal 1003.

71 Case 6/64 *Costa* v *ENEL* EU:C:1964:66, p 594: 'It follows (...) that the law stemming from the Treaty, an independent source of law, could not, because of its special and original nature, be overridden by domestic legal provisions, however framed, *without being deprived of its character as Community law and without the legal basis of the Community itself being called into question*' (emphasis added).

72 See Floris de Witte, 'Interdependence and Contestation in European Integration' (2018) 3(2) European Papers 475.

73 In particular, see Chapters 2 and 3.

only way of ensuring the equality of the Member States before the Treaties. To accept this argument is to reduce equal legal status to equal application of EU law in the Member States.[74] Indeed, primacy is necessary to ensure the uniform application of the common rules, subject to EU judicial review. But it cannot affect the legal status of Member States who are deemed to have equal rights and obligations under EU law.[75] The meaning of membership is not exhausted by EU legal principles and doctrines. On the contrary, it is heavily informed by the constitutional imagination of every Member State; the interpretation of the principle of democracy by the Court in Karlsruhe is one of them. If equal legal status was collapsed into equal application of EU law, Member States would be nothing but law-applying agents of the EU. Indeed, the press release represents a familiar view on the instrumentality of EU law, whose intellectual roots go back to the 'Integration through law' (ITL) project in the 1980s.[76]

ITL is the product of a certain period in European integration characterised by cumbersome decision-making and implementation deficits, not to mention the economic difficulties. It was a time of passage since the Maastricht Treaty, giving rise to major institutional innovation, was already being prepared. However, ITL has been influential until the present day.[77] The General Introduction to the project outlines the aims and the methodology.[78] On the one hand, ITL analyses integration *of* law or, in other words, the construction of the EU legal order driven by the Luxembourg Court. On the other hand, it is interested in integration *through* law, that is, the role of law in shaping the political and social contexts in which it operates. Hence, the methodology is neither limited to legal positivism, nor does it try to retreat into abstract principles of natural law. It is rather informed by a federal principle, the normative vision of the project. ITL thus promotes an equilibrium between the unity of the EU legal order and national diversity. It is reluctant to characterise

---

74 See Lindeboom (n 68) 1034–1040; similarly, see Weber (n 69) 766.

75 Obviously, Member States do not have exactly the same rights and obligations because of opt-outs and other forms of differentiated integration. This is more comprehensible if one considers that the EU equality principle is related to and yet different from the principle of the sovereign equality of states under international law, see Claus Dieter Classen, 'Die Gleichheit der Mitgliedstaaten und ihre Ausformungen im Unionsrecht' (2020) Europarecht 255.

76 Mauro Cappelletti et al., *Integration through Law: Europe and the American Federal Experience* (De Gruyter 1986).

77 See the contributions in Daniel Augenstein (ed), *"Integration through Law" Revisited: The Making of the European Polity* (Ashgate 2012); Loïc Azoulai, '"Integration through Law" and Us' (2016) 14(2) I·CON 449.

78 See Mauro Cappelletti et al., 'Integration through Law: Europe and the American Federal Experience – A General Introduction' in Cappelletti et al. (n 75) 5–15.

power-shifts in favour of the Member States as disintegration. On the contrary, in line with the federal vision, the value of integration has to be assessed against the loss of liberty or democracy.

Joseph Weiler, one of the editors of the ITL project, is most outspoken in this regard. His seminal paper 'The Transformation of Europe' used the model of Exit, Voice and Loyalty to explain the history of European integration.[79] A crucial moment was the introduction of Qualified Majority Voting in the Council since an outvoted Member State has less Voice, and the risk of non-compliance or selective Exit increases.[80] Majority voting is also a threat to the social legitimacy of European integration insofar as a national political community will not accept to become the minority in a larger European polity.[81] Weiler goes on to argue that a challenge to something fundamental like the boundaries of the polity cannot be addressed by institutional reform. The typical proposal in this regard is to increase the powers of the European Parliament. It is rather a matter of social convergence over time: integration *through* law.[82]

On this basis, Weiler presents his normative vision of community or his development of the federal principle.[83] In negative terms, it is a rejection of unity in the sense of a United States of Europe, so Member States will not become sub-level entities in a full political union with strong central institutions. In positive terms, the idea of community amounts to a kind of self-limitation or a redefined self-interest, aware of 'the autonomous self and the self as part of a larger community'.[84] If Weiler is correct, integration through law contributes to the civilisation of Europe and the taming of nationalism after a violent past. The driver of change is the individual who will, over time, develop a basic European identity owing to internal free movement. This new identity will replace the identification with the nation state as far as cross-border interaction is concerned.[85] However, national identities will not vanish in total. It seems as if Weiler accepts them as a private matter behind the front door.[86] In his later writings, Weiler complements this liberal individualism with a more

79 Joseph H H Weiler, 'The Transformation of Europe' in Miguel Poiares Maduro & Marlene Wind, *The Transformation of Europe: Twenty-Five Years On* (CUP 2017). The essay was first published in 1991.

80 Ibid 71–73.

81 Ibid 73–82.

82 Ibid 80 ('adjustment period').

83 Ibid 82–93.

84 Ibid 90.

85 Ibid.

86 For a critical reading, see Jan Komárek, 'Why Read *The Transformation of Europe* Today? On the Limits of a Liberal Constitutional Imaginary' in Komárek (n 9) 119, 139–140.

communitarian outlook, contending that the principle of constitutional tolerance governs inter-state relationships in the Union.[87] On this view, the Member States do not accept the primacy of EU law as a matter of legal doctrine. It is rather an 'autonomous voluntary act',[88] driven by the political will to tolerate each other not as one-of-us but as other-than-us. This, according to Weiler, is the 'originality [and] nobility'[89] of European integration. Pretending as if there was a single European people is to subvert this historical achievement.

That is not to suggest that national identities are immaterial in terms of EU legal doctrine. On the contrary, in accordance with Article 4(2) TEU, the Union is obliged to respect the national identities of the Member States and their essential State functions.[90] Since the Lisbon revision introduced Article 4(2) TEU in its present form, EU legal scholarship has debated about its scope and legal effects. It is disputed whether an element of national identity needs to be of constitutional rank,[91] and whether it has to be common to the EU and the Member States in order to be worthy of protection.[92] Indeed, there are valid reasons for protecting constitutional rather than national identities. The national constitution expresses the fundamentals of a polity mostly in written form, and the textual basis reduces, though not eliminates, the risk of capture by political ideologies. That is why several authors have warned about the

87 Joseph H H Weiler, 'In Defence of the Status Quo: Europe's Constitutional *Sonderweg*' in Joseph H. H. Weiler & Marlene Wind (eds), *European Constitutionalism beyond the State* (CUP 2003).

88 Ibid 21. See also Franz C Mayer, 'Die Europäische Union als Rechtsgemeinschaft – ein überholtes Narrativ?' in Franzius et al. (n 7) 123ff ('Freiwilligkeitsgemeinschaft').

89 Joseph H H Weiler, 'Prologue: Global and Pluralist Constitutionalism – Some Doubts' in Graínne de Búrca & Joseph H H Weiler, *The Worlds of European Constitutionalism* (CUP 2012) 13.

90 The Article reads as follows: 'The Union shall respect the equality of the Member States before the Treaties as well as their national identities, inherent in their fundamental structures, political and constitutional, inclusive of regional and local self-government. It shall respect their essential State functions, including ensuring the territorial integrity of the State, maintaining law and order and safeguarding national security. In particular, national security remains the sole responsibility of each Member State.'

91 Pro: Thomas Wischmeyer, 'Nationale Identität und Verfassungsidentität. Schutzgehalte, Instrumente und Perspektiven' (2015) 140(3) Archiv des öffentlichen *Rechts* 415, 430–432. Contra: Elke Cloots, 'National Identity, Constitutional Identity, and Sovereignty in the EU' (2016) 45(2) Netherlands Journal of Legal Philosophy 82.

92 Pro: Sacha Garben, 'Collective Identity as a Legal Limit to European Integration in Areas of Core State Powers' (2020) 58(1) JCMS 41, 51. Contra: Anita Schnettger, 'Article 4(2) TEU as a Vehicle for National Constitutional Identity in the Shared European Legal System' in Calliess & Van der Schyff (n 55) 15, who essentially argues that each Member State has the right to specify the meaning of national constitutional identity subject to EU primary law.

notion of constitutional identity.[93] While appropriate in principle, the sceptical voices underestimate that every political community needs to imagine what it has in common, for otherwise it cannot peacefully exist. Recourse to constitutional identity will be abusive only if it is used to undermine politics in the name of a mythical unity. Hence, the identity of a political community should be expressed through the medium of national democracy. This also explains why efforts to arrive at a shared European constitutional identity tend to fail.[94] Some issues are so particular to a specific polity that 'Europeanisation' would amount to a violent capture. In such cases, the particular should prevail over the universal.

Having said that, this chapter is not primarily interested in conflicts between EU law and national constitutional identities. In terms of legal effects, Member States have invoked Article 4(2) TEU to justify derogations from EU law. They were successful in free movement law.[95] But in asylum and migration law, the Court found that Member State cannot rely on Article 4(2) TEU, in conjunction with Article 72 TFEU, because EU legislation took into account their interests in maintaining law and order and safeguarding national security.[96] Constitutional identity is thus protected in the process of EU law-making and application. It is balanced against competing interests recognised by EU law, in accordance with the principle of proportionality. It is not an exception to the absolute primacy of EU law, as far as the Court and the majority in legal scholarship are concerned.[97] For our purposes, constitutional identity is less a defence[98] against than a gain for the EU legal order. By interpreting and applying EU law in view of their constitutional identities, Member States contribute to the Union's objectives 'in their way'. The Germans, the Dutch or

93 Instead of many, see Monika Polzin, 'Constitutional Identity as a Constructed Reality and a Restless Soul' (2015) 18(7) German Law Journal 1595.

94 For a successful doctrinal reconciliation, see Case C-36/02 *Omega* EU:C:2004:614. For a sceptical conceptual argument, see Dieter Grimm, 'Three Meanings of Constitutional Identity and Their Prospects in the European Union' in Jurgen de Poorter et al. (eds), A Constitutional Identity for the EU?' (2022) 4 European Yearbook of Constitutional Law 13.

95 For example, see Case C-208/09 *Sayn-Wittgenstein* EU:C:2010:806; Case C-391/09 *Runevič-Vardyn* EU:C:2011:291; Case C-202/11 *Anton Las* EU:C:2013:239.

96 Joined Cases C-715/17, C-718/17 and C-719/17 *Commission* v *Poland, Hungary, Czech Republic* EU:C:2020:257, paras 134–172; Case C-808/18 *Commission* v *Hungary* EU:C:2020:1029, paras 261–265.

97 See Schnettger (n 92) 32–34, for a nuanced view arguing that Article 4(2) TEU is a ground for derogating from EU legislation. However, it is not conceptualised as an exception to the primacy of EU law.

98 See Walker (n 10) 416ff ('reinforcement' of sovereignty); Grimm (n 94) 15.

the Hungarians will not simply be tolerated as other-than-us, as Weiler would have it, but their power to make the Union a success will be recognised. They become one-of-us *because of* their particularities. The next section develops the argument further.

4 Representation, EU Law and the Empowerment of the Member States

4.1 *What Makes a (Good) Representative?*

When Member States use their power for the benefit of the Union, they are the latter's representatives. This proposition calls for an exploration of what a representative is or rather is doing, and the relationship to law-making and application. Rehfeld has developed a general theory of representation, carefully distinguishing description from normativity.[99] He defines a representative as someone who is accepted by an audience, formally or socially, to stand in for another individual or group in order to fulfil a certain task. In representative democracy, for example, a member of parliament is representing her constituency when voting on a legislative proposal. The members of her constituency recognise her being a representative because she came into office in accordance with formal democratic procedures. However, formal authorisation is not a necessary condition to become a representative. Especially in non-democratic contexts, a would-be representative will make a claim to act in the name of somebody's interests. Acceptance will hinge not on formal but on substantive criteria such as the actor's reputation in the relevant matter. In that regard, representation is always context-dependent and targeted at a social role like voting in parliament. Rehfeld gives the striking example of a member of parliament who is not actively[100] representing when swimming in Barbados. Hence, a person is only representing when acting on matters and for purposes associated with her role or status.

Conversely, still according to Rehfeld, the quality of what she is doing is immaterial in this regard.[101] The member of parliament who is voting for a legislative proposal contrary to the wishes of her constituency is representing. Being responsive to the interests of the represented is not constitutive of

99 This paragraph is based on Andrew Rehfeld, 'On Representing' (2018) 26(2) The Journal of Political Philosophy 216.

100 She is passively representing in the sense that the audience will associate her with her official function even when she is spending her free time.

101 Rehfeld (n 99) 221ff.

qualifying as a representative. It is rather a normative criterion, which deserves separate treatment. Edmund Burke made the following distinction in his famous speech to the electors of Bristol:

> Parliament is not a *congress* of ambassadors from different and hostile interests; which interests each must maintain, as an agent and advocate, against other agents and advocates; but parliament is a *deliberative* assembly of *one* nation, with *one* interest, that of the whole; where, not local purposes, not local prejudices, ought to guide, but the general good, resulting from the general reason of the whole. You choose a member indeed; but when you have chosen him, he is not member of Bristol, but he is a member of *parliament*. If the local constituent should have an interest, or should form an hasty opinion, evidently opposite to the real good of the rest of the community, the member for that place ought to be as far, as any other, from any endeavour to give it effect.(…) Your faithful friend, your devoted servant, I shall be to the end of my life: a flatterer you do not wish for.[102]

Thus, a good representative is someone who exercises independent judgment about the common good. Particular interests are weighed against other interests to arrive at a mutually acceptable compromise in the course of democratic procedures. By contrast, a member of parliament who is but the mouthpiece of her constituency qualifies, according to Burke, as an 'agent and advocate' rather than as a representative. This book follows Rehfeld in this respect, classifying such a person as a representative, provided she is formally or socially recognised to act on behalf of somebody. Nonetheless, that is a notion of representation stripped off the political, closer to administrative accountability with less room for manoeuvre.

Finally, representative democracy in a normative sense hinges on the rule of law and vice versa. The rule of law would be nothing but a formal standard if the meaning of the good life was not determined in democratic procedures. Conversely, democracy would be inherently fragile if it was not stabilised by the rule of law. Representative law-making is to deliberate and to abstract from the particular interests of individuals who happen to live on the same territory.[103]

---

102 Edmund Burke, 'Speech to the Electors of Bristol' in Philip B Kurland & Ralph Lerner (eds), *The Founders' Constitution* (volume 1, web edition, University of Chicago Press) ch 13, document 7 <https://press-pubs.uchicago.edu/founders/documents/v1ch13s7.html> accessed 1 March 2024 (emphasis in original).

103 See Jeremy Waldron, *Political Political Theory: Essays on Institutions* (Harvard University Press 2016) ch 6.

Their belonging to a political community is expressed in a generally applicable law, reconciling the diverse interests involved, stabilising expectations and allowing every member of the polity to feel represented or recognised as one-of-us. To be more precise, a generally applicable law complying with the principle of equal treatment, a fundamental requirement of the rule of law, is a necessary but not a sufficient condition. In terms of content, the norms should be rather abstract,[104] empowering the members of the executive and judiciary to do justice in a wide range of circumstances. Fairness among members of a polity can be secured through administrative discretion, exemptions and derogations provided for in the piece of legislation. Hence, interpretation and application of the law are the other concrete expressions of representation in a constitutional state, apart from law-making.[105] To be a good representative, the official has to be independent and responsive to all relevant interests within the confines of the separation of powers. For example, a constitutional judge is only bound by the constitution, whereas a civil servant may have more or less discretion depending on the legislation in question. Less discretion implies that the notion of representation will be less political. However, that is inherent in liberal constitutionalism under the rule of law. The civil servant will only be a poor representative if he abuses his discretion by, for example, sacrificing the common good for partisan interests.

4.2 *What Makes Member States (Good) Representatives of the Union?*

Based on the foregoing, Member States can be conceptualised as representatives of the Union. In the first place, they formally have that status when implementing the obligations derived from EU law in accordance with the principle of loyalty, codified in Article 4(3) TEU. In the quasi-federal system of the EU, they are responsible for giving effect to EU law through decentralised administration and adjudication.[106] In line with our definition, this formal empowerment to stand in for the EU institutions to achieve the Union's objectives suffices to qualify as a representative. However, in order not to lose the social recognition of the domestic population, each Member State can only be a good

104 See Dimitris Tsarapatsanis, 'Representative Legislatures, Grammars of Political Representation, and the Generality of Statutes' (2018) 31(4) Ratio Juris 444; Donald Bello Hutt, 'Political Representation as Interpretation: A Contribution to Deliberative Constitutionalism' (2020) 33(4) Ratio Juris 351.

105 That is not to say that every institution is equally representative. According to Waldron (n 103) 141, parliaments in Western liberal democracies, rather than courts, best represent the common good.

106 Since the Lisbon revision, art 291(1) TFEU has been the lex specialis of art 4(3) TEU.

representative if the duties flowing from EU membership do not undermine its national identity. Ideally, the particular should be represented at the level of the Union. This is legally possible because the principle of loyalty empowers each Member State to assert itself as a member of the Union with a particular identity. Burke would thus contest that Member States are nothing but delegates of the EU. In modern terminology, they are not agents but trustees of the Union interest.[107]

As regards legal design, discretionary provisions facilitate the task of the Member States to reconcile their double bind. In EU law, there are various types of national discretion.[108] On the one hand, the EU legislature may decide to confer discretion on the Member States. Instead of a right, Member States have the obligation to act on behalf of the Union. This is called 'assessment discretion' because Member States may realise Union policies by different means. Depending on the margin of discretion, they may represent their nation at the same time. On the other hand, the EU legislature may recognise a right of the Member States, which corresponds to a national competence. A typical legal tool to exercise what is called 'policy discretion' are optional clauses, which Member States may choose to apply. A national competence can be retained, meaning the Union has not yet fully harmonised a field of shared competences. To the extent the EU legislature did adopt common rules, autonomous national action is precluded.[109] National competence can also be reserved, meaning that the Treaties exclude a few policies from direct EU intervention. According to well-established case law based on the principle of loyalty, Member States must not violate their duties owing to Union membership when exercising their retained or reserved competences.[110] It is submitted that in this type of discretion, Member States are not prima facie representing the Union.

---

107 See Giandomenico Majone, 'Two Logics of Delegation: Agency and Fiduciary Relations in EU Governance' (2001) 2(1) European Union Politics 103, 116ff; Christoph Möllers, 'Durchführung des Gemeinschaftsrechts: Vertragliche Dogmatik und theoretische Implikationen' (2002) Europarecht 483, 499–500.

108 See Joined Cases C-609/17 and C-610/17 *TSN and AKT* EU:C: 2019:981, paras 49–50, for a differentiation by the Court itself; Ton van den Brink, 'National Discretion in EU Legislation' in Sacha Garben & Inge Govaere, *The Division of Competences Between the EU and the Member States: Reflections on the Past, the Present and the Future* (Hart 2017) 256ff elaborating a typology of national discretion, which is similar to the one presented here.

109 Art 2(2) TFEU.

110 See Bruno de Witte, 'Exclusive Member State Competences – Is There Such a Thing?' in Garben & Govaere (n 108).

We need to make a further distinction as regards policy discretion. First, when a right of the Member States is explicitly laid down in EU law, they are at least authorised to represent the Union. Hence, they have a choice to exercise their competence either on their own behalf or for the benefit of the common whole. In any case, it is a voluntary choice only subject to the mentioned duty not to breach the principle of loyalty. Second, EU law may be silent as to whether Member States have a right to autonomous action. Under certain conditions, the principle of loyalty precludes national measures even where there is no explicit prohibition.[111] The frame of the *Rechtsgemeinschaft* explains why that is the case. The purpose of European integration is to tame power politics as much as possible, namely through law. If the EU legislature has explicitly recognised a right of the Member States, the invocation of that right will rather not lead to domination. At least, the EU courts have the residual responsibility to monitor how Member States exercise their competences. Where no such right has been explicitly recognised, it is not yet clear whether it is compatible with the EU legal order in the first place. In both of these situations, a Member State will have to make a claim to become a representative. It will be a substantive claim aiming less at formal than at social recognition from the domestic population and the EU institutions. Compared to assessment discretion, it is this type of policy discretion that is most conducive to national sovereignty frames. Therefore, each of the mentioned sub-categories will be illustrated in turn.

In the *Ritual Slaughter Case*,[112] the Constitutional Court of Belgium asked the Court of Justice to rule on the interpretation and validity of Article 26(2)(c) of Regulation No 1099/2009,[113] which allows Member States to adopt national rules aiming at more extensive protection of animals when they are being killed for the purpose of, inter alia, food production. In particular, Member States may adopt stricter national rules than those laid down in Article 4(4) of the Regulation derogating from the obligation to stun animals prior to killing. The derogation applies when the animals are killed in accordance with religious rites and the killing takes place in a slaughterhouse. The national proceedings were brought by Jewish and Muslim organisations complaining about a decree of the Flemish Government that imposed a ban on (religious) slaughter without prior stunning. While aiming at eliminating all avoidable animal suffering,

---

111 See Chapter 5.

112 Case C-336/19 *Centraal Israëlitisch Consistorie van België and Others* v *Vlaamse Regering* EU:C:2020:1031 ('Ritual Slaughter').

113 Regulation No 1099/2009/EC on the protection of animals at the time of killing [2009] OJ L303/1.

the decree also tried to find ways of limiting the interference with the fundamental right of religious freedom. It stipulated a reversible, non-lethal method of stunning (electronarcosis). 'If the animal's throat is cut immediately after stunning, its death will be purely due to bleeding', in accordance with Jewish and Islamic rites as far as the Flemish Government was concerned.[114] The religious organisations disagreed and sought the annulment of the decree before the referring court.

At the outset, the Court of Justice observed that the obligation of prior stunning reflects the value of animal welfare, enshrined in Article 13 TFEU according to which the Union shall pay full respect to the welfare requirements of animals in formulating common policies while respecting national diversity relating in particular to religious rites, cultural traditions and regional heritage.[115] Next, according to the Grand Chamber, slaughter without prior stunning is authorised only by way of derogation and solely in order to ensure observance of freedom of religion as required by Article 10(1) of the Charter.[116] Since previous EU rules about religious slaughter have been transposed differently 'depending on national contexts and considering that national rules take into account dimensions that go beyond the purpose of this Regulation',[117] the EU legislature decided to maintain the derogation contained in Article 4(4) while leaving 'a certain level of subsidiarity to each Member States'.[118] That is the purpose of Article 26(2)(c) of the Regulation according to the Court,[119] who concludes this first part of the analysis by qualifying the Regulation as a 'framework'.[120] Hence, it is the task of the Member States to reconcile the opposing interests, subject to judicial review by the Court.

Having found an interference with the right to freedom of religion,[121] the Grand Chamber examined whether measures adopted on the basis of Article 26(2)(c) of the Regulation, such as the decree of the Flemish Government, may be justified under Article 52(3) of the Charter. For our purposes, the standard of review is more relevant than the separate steps in the legal analysis. In the first place, it follows from Article 13 TFEU that the protection of animal welfare is a general interest recognised by the Union.[122] In the second place, as

114 The quote is from the preparatory documents for the decree, see Ritual Slaughter, para 13.
115 Ibid para 41.
116 Ibid para 43.
117 Regulation No 1099/2009/EC, recital (18).
118 Ibid.
119 Ritual Slaughter (n 112) para 45.
120 Ibid para 47.
121 Ibid para 55.
122 Ibid para 63.

regards compliance with the principle of proportionality, the Court adopted a low intensity of judicial review following the approach of the European Court of Human Rights on matters of general policy concerning, inter alia, the relations between the State and religions. That is because national authorities are, in principle, better placed than international courts to resolve those sensitive issues 'on which opinions within a democratic society may reasonably differ widely'.[123] The Court went on to state that it was this lack of consensus about ritual slaughter that led to the adoption of Articles 4 and 26 of the Regulation.[124] Attitudes towards animals depend on national perceptions and there is thus a demand in some Member States for welfare requirements going beyond the standards of EU law, which is explicitly acknowledged in the preamble of the Regulation.[125] Accordingly, the Court found that 'the EU legislature intended to preserve the specific social context of each Member State in that respect and to give each Member State a broad discretion in the context of the need to reconcile Article 13 TFEU and Article 10 of the Charter'.[126] This interpretation was supported by EU primary law. Since the Charter is a 'living instrument'[127] to be interpreted in light of present-day conditions, it is legitimate to attach greater weight to animal welfare than in previous times. In view of these considerations, the Court arrived at the following conclusion:

> Thus, in an evolving societal and legislative context, which is characterised (…) by an increasing awareness of the issue of animal welfare, the Flemish legislature was entitled to adopt, following a wide-ranging debate organised at the level of the Flemish Region, the decree at issue in the main proceedings, without exceeding the discretion which EU law confers on Member States as regards the need to reconcile Article 10(1) of the Charter with Article 13 TFEU.[128]

The *Ritual Slaughter Case* is thus an example of national policy discretion. The Flemish Region was entitled to make a political choice about the value it ascribes to animal welfare. In taking that political decision, it did not exceed the wide margin of discretion conferred by EU law. The Court accepted that Member States need to balance competing requirements of EU primary law,

123 Ibid para 67.
124 Ibid para 68.
125 Regulation No 1099/2009/EC, recital (57).
126 Ritual Slaughter (n 112) para 71.
127 Ibid para 77.
128 Ibid para 79.

namely animal welfare and religious freedom. By representing the dispute only in terms of EU law, the Court recognised Belgium and specifically the Flemish Region as one-of-us while, at the same time, respecting that the Flemish are other-than-us insofar as they attach greater importance to animal welfare. That is a welcome reasoning, for it avoids a confrontation of legal orders without trying to universalise the particular. And yet, it would have been more appropriate to recognise the power of Member States to realise the common value of animal welfare, in line with the above conceptualisation of national discretion.[129] The Regulation falls within the common agricultural policy, a competence shared between the EU and the Member States. It is contended that the Member States have retained the power to provide for more extensive protection of animals. Their capacity to represent a unity around the value of animal welfare is thus recognised rather than conferred by the EU legislature. In other words, the EU legal order has empowered the Member States to move from the inner to the intermediate sphere, where it their responsibility to strike a fair balance between two common values.

4.3 *How the Formal Representation of the Union May Become Contentious*

In stark contrast, it may not even be certain that the Member States are representing the Union. Section 2 explained that a national constitution, and the legal acts adopted on that basis, represent a unity. Every legal act validly adopted in accordance with the constitution gives expression to what a polity has in common and how it intends to reconcile opposing interests. The institutions responsible for making, interpreting and applying the law are prima facie representatives of the legal order. In the EU, the Treaties are at least a 'functional'[130] constitution in the sense of attributing the task of representation to the EU institutions and the Member States when they are implementing Union law. But what is implementation, and what is Union law?

The EU increasingly makes recourse to a plethora of instruments other than those mentioned in Article 288 TFEU. Since the sovereign debt crisis, the Member States have adopted international agreements outside the

129 To concede, the Court is indeed a representative of the EU legal order whose task it is to ensure that in the interpretation and application of the Treaties the law is observed (art 19(1) TEU). Considering also the traditionally concise reasoning, it is rather unlikely that the Court will elaborate on the empowerment of the Member States.

130 Lisbon Judgment, para 231.

EU institutional framework,[131] and the EU has coordinated national fiscal, economic and social policies through a combination of legally binding and non-binding tools.[132] EU migration management is characterised by a similar development, as we will see in the following chapters. One of the atypical instruments is the Memorandum of Understanding (MoU). In the context of the sovereign debt crisis, it was a contract between the Member State facing financial difficulties and the Commission. Depending on the legal basis, the ECB and the International Monetary Fund were contracting parties as well. The Member State in question received financial assistance in exchange for implementing reforms with a view to a balanced budget. It affected matters of national competence such as social security and pensions. That was the case in *Florescu*,[133] one of several judicial proceedings about the social hardship of austerity policies.[134] It concerned the interpretation of the MoU between the Commission and Romania in accordance with Article 143 TFEU, governing balance-of-payments assistance to non-Eurozone Member States.

For the first time, the Court declared an action seeking the interpretation of a MoU to be admissible. It found that the MoU is an act of an EU institution within the meaning of Article 267 TFEU because the legal basis lies in certain provisions of EU law.[135] Hence, the Grand Chamber gave judicial blessing to the argument of legal scholars claiming that the pedigree of atypical instruments is to be found in the EU legal order because of substantive and institutional links.[136] In theoretical literature, the pluralisation and intertwinement of typical and atypical instruments is called 'hybridity'. The next

131 See the categorisation in Bruno de Witte & Thibault Martinelli, 'Treaties between EU Member States as Quasi-Instruments of EU Law' in Marise Cremona & Claire Kilpatrick (eds), *EU Legal Acts: Challenges and Transformations* (OUP 2018).

132 Integrated under the European Semester, see Sonja Bekker, 'The European Semester: Understanding an Innovative Governance Model' in Paul James Cardwell & Marie-Pierre Granger (eds), *Research Handbook on the Politics of EU Law* (Elgar 2020).

133 Case C-258/14 *Florescu* EU:C:2017:448.

134 Other leading judgments are Joined Cases C-8/15 P to 10/15 P *Ledra Advertising* EU:C:2016:701 and Joined Cases C-105/15 P to C-109/15 P *Mallis* EU:C:2016:702. They concerned the legal responsibility of the EU institutions. Like in *Florescu*, the Court in part closed the gaps in legal protection against atypical instruments, see René Repasi, 'Judicial Protection Against Austerity Measures in the Euro Area: *Ledra* and *Mallis*' (2017) 54(4) CML Rev 1123.

135 *Florescu* (133) para 35.

136 Instead of many, see Claire Kilpatrick, 'Are the Bailouts Immune to EU Social Challenge Because They Are Not EU Law?' (2014) 10(3) EuConst 393; Anastasia Poulou, 'Financial Assistance Conditionality and Human Rights Protection: What is the Role of the EU Charter of Fundamental Rights?' (2017) 54(4) CML Rev 991, 995–1003.

chapter will return to this theme in more detail. Further, the Court was asked to determine whether national measures taken under the MoU were compatible with the EU Charter. The latter is addressed to the Member States only when they are implementing EU law.[137] The Court had interpreted the meaning of 'implementation' widely, covering (1) any measure to give effect to EU law in line with Article 291(1) TFEU; (2) derogations from EU law; and (3) any measure falling within the scope of EU law following the *Åkerberg Fransson* line of jurisprudence.[138] In the given case, the Court quoted from the national law to underline that the Romanian legislator intended to fulfil the obligations arising under the Memorandum, which is part of EU law.[139] Arguably, it was the purposeful, obligatory implementation of EU law within the meaning of the first situation. Other findings of the Court support that proposition. Romania had a certain margin of assessment discretion to meet the 'mandatory'[140] requirements of the MoU. Indeed, the specific pension cuts at issue were the outcome of national law-making; they were not at such required by the Memorandum. Confirming well-established case law, the Court recalled that the exercise of discretion conferred by EU law triggers the application of the Charter.[141] It then added the following puzzling statement: 'the objectives set out in [the Decision pursuant to Article 143 TFEU], as well as those set out in the Memorandum of Understanding, are *sufficiently detailed and precise* to permit the inference that the purpose of the [national law] is to implement both the memorandum and that decision, and thus EU law, within the meaning of Article 51(1) of the Charter'.[142]

Comparing the provisions involved in terms of their level of detail and precision, the Court found that the national legislation providing for pension cuts implements EU law and thus falls within the scope of application of the Charter. However, that legal standard will beg the question in similar cases in the future.[143] It suggests that EU legal acts, especially their objectives, may be so open-ended as to render it difficult to determine whether national law actually intends to give effect to them. Accordingly, it is difficult to determine whether

137 Art 51(1) Charter.

138 Case C-617/10 *Åkerberg Fransson* EU:C:2013:105; Angela Ward, 'Article 51' in Steve Peers et al. (eds), *The EU Charter of Fundamental Rights: A Commentary* (Hart 2021) 1577ff.

139 *Florescu* (n 133) paras 45–47.

140 Ibid para 41.

141 Ibid para 48.

142 Ibid (emphasis added).

143 See Menelaos Markakis & Paul Dermine, 'Bailouts, the Legal Status of Memoranda of Understanding, and the Scope of Application of the Charter: *Florescu*' (2018) 55(2) CML Rev 643, 664–667.

a Member State like Romania is still acting on behalf of the Union. The Treaties have constituted the 27 qua Member States, so they owe that particular existence to EU law. When a Member State is acting at the fringes of the EU legal order, it jeopardises its formal recognition as a representative of the Union. By claiming to implement EU law, a Member State gives expression to EU membership. It asserts itself as one-of-us and as other-than-us by implementing EU law in a manner most conducive to its particular identity. To assert itself as a Member State brings the matter under the frame of the *Rechtsgemeinschaft*. That is relevant insofar as representation involves the construction of unity around a common purpose for which the actor assumes responsibility. If the representation succeeds, joint responsibility will follow. That is to say, the EU institutions and the Member States will be co-responsible. In the present context, Romania took austerity measures due to the mandatory conditionality requirements contained in the Memorandum of Understanding, which is an act of EU law. Hence, the EU had to assume responsibility for the ensuing social hardship by safeguarding respect for EU fundamental rights. However, that had been anything but settled before *Florescu*,[144] and other related issues continue to await legal resolution.[145] Disputes about the boundaries of the EU legal order disturb the ideals of rationality, coherence and systemic integrity associated with that frame, and efforts of the Court to provide legal certainty are only partial.[146]

The representation of unity might fail if, in the meantime, other EU institutions and Member States represent the outer sphere of international relations. That is characterised by power politics and bargaining. On this view, the MoU was a contract freely entered into by the lending Member State and subject to national democratic approval. Proponents of this position either neglect the political pressure on the debtor country or openly foster it by invoking the frame of the *Rechtsgemeinschaft* to argue that excessive budgetary deficits were detrimental to financial stability in the Eurozone. Consequently, every Member State had to comply with EU budgetary rules. That is a valid argument in case it refrains from suppressing the political at national level.[147] Then,

144 See Poulou (n 136) 1015–1024, for a critical appraisal of the law pre-*Florescu*.

145 Apart from the mentioned application of the Charter to national measures, the legal status of Memoranda of Understanding is far from settled, see Markakis & Dermine (n 143) 657ff (with further references).

146 See Claire Kilpatrick, 'The EU and its Sovereign Debt Programmes: The Challenges of Liminal Legality' (2017) 70(1) Current Legal Problems 337, 344, 359–360.

147 Compare Mark Dawson & Floris de Witte, 'From Balance to Conflict: A New Constitution for the EU' (2016) 22(2) European Law Journal 204, who argue for political conflict at EU level.

it would no longer be in line with the *Rechtsgemeinschaft* as understood in this book. EU law empowers the Member States to assume responsibility for the Union, subject to legal control to guarantee a minimum level of fairness among Member States (and vis-à-vis the EU institutions). In *Florescu* at least, the Court corrected the balance in favour of closer judicial scrutiny.

5 Conclusion

The present chapter made a first step in answering the research question of this book. It explored what makes joint action possible in the first place: an idea of a purpose or, in a richer sense, a common good, ingrained in a polity's 'constitutional imagination' or its 'frame' within which the exercise of sovereign powers (the 'claim') acquires deeper political meaning. Member States are not unencumbered selves when acting according to the Treaties; they continue to be informed by their national identities. That is the basis for understanding the EU legal order as a site of empowerment. Relying on legal theory and philosophy, the chapter argued that the limitation of power to protect individual liberty is but one aspect of legal order next to the facilitation of power generated by the will to collective action. However, the EU legal order has a frame of its own, albeit not characterised by the same deep sense of mutual trust and loyalty historically grown in the nation state. It is a juridical frame informed by the belief in law to civilise the European continent and to substitute rule-based multilateralism for unilateralism. No Member State should be legally permitted to dominate and to interfere with the rights of EU citizens.

It follows that the Member States have to navigate a fine line between both frames. That occurs in the intermediate sphere where they represent a unity around a common purpose. Indeed, Member States are representing the Union when giving effect to EU law in their national legal systems. The more discretion conferred or recognised by EU law, the more they can do justice to their sovereignty frame. However, the more they act at the margin of the EU legal order, the more they lean towards the outer sphere of international relations. It may thus not even be certain that a Member State is representing the Union. The Court clarifies whether a particular representation of unity is to be recognised as one-of-us, as it did in *Florescu*. The latter illustrates a wider trend to express belonging to the Union in forms other than the typical EU legal acts. That is why the demand for social instead of formal recognition is becoming increasingly important, as the next chapter will demonstrate. The demand cannot be accommodated by replacing the frame of the *Rechtsgemeinschaft*.[148] Irrespective of the developments in European integration, it is impossible to represent the Union from a view of nowhere. This chapter tried to explain that the practice of representation fluctuates between permanence and change.

Taking the contingency of every legal order for granted, the next step in our inquiry is the fight for recognition. Whereas the main purpose of the present chapter was to expose each sovereignty frame, it only hinted at the possibility of conflict. On the one hand, the very notion of empowering a Member State to represent the Union seems to be in tension with the autonomy of the EU legal order. On the other hand, a competing self-assertion by the EU institutions could entail the suppression of national particularities, tempering the will to assume responsibility for the common whole. That is all the more important in the field of migration management, as we will see in due course.

148 But see Armin von Bogdandy, 'Jenseits der Rechtsgemeinschaft: Begriffsarbeit in der europäischen Sinn- und Rechtsstaatlichkeitskrise' (2017) Europarecht 487.

CHAPTER 2

Acting on Behalf of the Common Purpose

1 Introduction

Chapter 1 explained the frame underlying every legal order. A Member State claiming to act on behalf of the Union will inevitably be informed by a certain understanding of the national identity and by what it means to be a member of the European Union. The purpose of this chapter is to argue how the Member States may reconcile their multiple identities or, in other words, under what conditions it is permissible to move from the inner into the intermediate sphere. This is a challenge since the Court claims a monopoly over the final interpretation of what EU membership requires.

The aim of the first part is to analyse and evaluate interaction at the systemic level or, in less neutral terms, conflicting claims to ultimate legal authority. Section 2 will use constitutional pluralism for this purpose. However, both the meaning of interaction or conflict and ways to accommodate it differ widely in EU legal scholarship.[1] The analysis in this chapter is not comprehensive since it is interested in a normative theory that is mindful of the frames of legal ordering. There are three candidates, which will be presented in turn: (1) radical, (2) cosmopolitan and (3) epistemic pluralism. While each of them generates important insights, none of them facilitates the expression of the political in the nation state. Hence, some conceptual refinement will be necessary.

Section 3 analyses the conditions a Member State must fulfil in order to be permitted to move into the intermediate sphere. After all, the expression of the national political imagination must not be contrary to EU membership obligations. The principle of autonomy requires the Member States to respect the independent capacity of the EU legal order to defend the common purpose of mutual non-interference. However, under certain conditions, the Member States may also assume responsibility for the common purpose because the autonomy of the EU legal order is not absolute. Section 4 will demonstrate the relevance of this theoretical inquiry for the field of EU migration management. It will explain how the principle of solidarity guides the Member States in moving between the spheres.

1 See the Introduction in Matej Avbelj & Jan Komárek (eds), *Constitutional Pluralism in the European Union and Beyond* (OUP 2012).

 | DOI:10.1163/9789004695733_004

The second part of the chapter shifts the attention to the instrumental dimension. This is necessary because Chapter 1 has already explained that Member States rely on specific norms to move 'inside-out'. Those norms are not only contained in EU law but also in various modes of governance. Section 5 will explain the relationship between EU law and governance in conceptual terms, illustrated with the Memorandum of Understanding concluded between Italy and Libya to address irregular migration on the Central Mediterranean. The section will submit that governance should be part of the inter-systemic interaction if certain conditions are met. Section 6 will conclude by wrapping up what it means to be a representative of the Union.

2 Moving between the Spheres (1): The Systemic Dimension

2.1 *Radical Pluralism: Each to Their Own*

Radical pluralism has been at the roots of constitutional pluralism since Neil MacCormick defended his thesis of post-sovereignty.[2] In his view, the sector-specific pooling or fusion of powers beyond the state entails the loss of state sovereignty without leading to sovereignty of the EU or any other international organisation. While provocative at first, the thesis gained traction following the ruling of the German *Bundesverfassungsgericht* on accession to the Maastricht Treaty.[3] It was on this occasion that the German Court developed the ultra vires review of which the *PSPP* judgment, analysed in Chapter 1, is the most recent manifestation.[4] Any ultra vires review brings up the fundamental question of who holds ultimate legal authority to determine the limits of EU competences (*Kompetenz-Kompetenz*). The German Court reserves that power for itself because, from its point of view, the competences of the EU are derived from the German Basic Law which is the legal basis for its own power of adjudication. It is thus entitled to determine the legal effects of EU law within the German legal system, yet it does not rule on the validity of EU law as such. This view is contrary to the position of the CJEU holding that the EU Treaties have established an autonomous legal order with primacy over national law.[5] Hence, the authority of the EU legal order is independent of national constitutional law. The Luxembourg Court has the monopoly on the authoritative

2 Neil MacCormick, 'Beyond the Sovereign State' (1993) 56(1) The Modern Law Review 1.

3 Neil MacCormick, 'The Maastricht-Urteil: Sovereignty Now' (1995) 1(3) European Law Journal 259.

4 See Chapter 1.2.

5 See Chapter 1.3.

interpretation of EU law, including the limits of EU competence, yet it does not rule on the validity of national law. This impasse of (judicial) sovereignty claims is what MacCormick famously calls constitutional pluralism:

> Where there is a plurality of institutional normative orders (...), it is possible that each acknowledge the legitimacy of every other within its own sphere, while none asserts or acknowledges constitutional superiority over another. In this case, 'constitutional pluralism' prevails.[6]

The premise of this argument is a concept of legal order that is closed in principle.[7] According to MacCormick, every legal order has criteria of validity by which the competent institutions determine which norms form part of the legal order. The constitution or the functional equivalent thereof attributes powers to those institutions, subject to criteria of validity concerning form and substance. However, MacCormick acknowledges that valid norms are not automatically effective. The exercise of power must be legitimate in the eyes of the addressees, and the legal order must have the means to enforce compliance. This view exposes the contingency of every legal order, and constitutional pluralism is the logical corollary. On the one hand, EU membership would be pointless without recognising that EU law is valid, in principle, in every national legal order. On the other hand, the effectiveness of EU law hinges on domestic institutions whose authority is derived from national rules and procedures.

It follows that constitutional pluralism is essentially a theory of mutual recognition premised on an internal point of view of ultimate legal authority. The normativity of the theory is to recognise every internal perspective and to find ways of mutual accommodation for the benefit of those who happen to be confronted with inconsistent norms stemming from more than one legal order. In the words of MacCormick:

6 Neil MacCormick, *Questioning Sovereignty: Law, State and Nation in the European Commonwealth* (OUP 1999) 104.

7 ibid 102ff. The concept described in this paragraph corresponds to MacCormick's theory of law as normative institutional order. It is advisable to consider constitutional pluralism a development of his theory of law. Both theories are related but separate. Hence, after MacCormick, a contribution to constitutional pluralism is not necessarily a contribution to the institutional theory of law. However, this paragraph has been included here because any contribution to the school of constitutional pluralism presupposes a system-internal understanding of law. Obviously, the system can be rather closed or rather open.

> The ECJ ought not to reach its interpretative judgments without regard to their potential impact on national constitutions. National courts ought not to interpret laws or constitutions without regard to the resolution of their compatriots to take full part in European Union and European Community. If conflicts despite this come into being through judicial decision-making and interpretation, there will necessarily have to be some political action to produce a solution.[8]

At this point, politics takes over from law – if it were not MacCormick himself who is not ready to fully endorse what he calls 'radical pluralism'. If national courts unilaterally determined the legal effects of EU law, the EU legal order would unravel slowly but surely. At the same time, they are not required to defer to whatever ruling of the CJEU. MacCormick thus seems to be aware of the frames of every legal order involved. In the event of irreconcilable conflicts, he promotes recourse to international arbitration or adjudication ('pluralism under international law'). However, this back door reveals a pitfall of the theory that would henceforth preoccupy every scholar working in the field. By falling back on international law, MacCormick substitutes monism for pluralism.

It would be impossible to reconcile the underlying sovereignty frames if radical pluralism or its softer variant determined the interaction of legal orders. That is first due to the juridical classification of constitutional conflict. On the one hand, radical pluralism manages to take an internal perspective by regarding conflict through the lens of the highest national courts who, by definition, act as the guardian of a particular legal order. On the other hand, a court-centred legal theory cannot fully embrace the national sovereignty frame. The powers of supreme courts usually stem from the national constitution, yet radical pluralism fails to account for the legitimacy of the latter. Although MacCormick is aware of the need for social legitimacy, he underestimates the integrative capacity of a national political imagination since, in his view, even a university or a church can have a 'constitution'.[9] It is therefore more appropriate to speak of legal rather than constitutional pluralism in this case.[10] Second, the relationship between law and politics is underdeveloped. On the one hand, it is understandable that the late MacCormick prefers pluralism under international law. It is indeed not satisfactory for any lawyer to concede that law is giving way to politics and pragmatism. In addition, what

8 Ibid 120.

9 Ibid 104.

10 See also Martin Loughlin, 'Constitutional Pluralism: An Oxymoron?' (2014) 3(1) Global Constitutionalism 9, 14–19.

MacCormick has in mind is not a zero-sum relationship since the EU and the Member States should observe the duty of cooperation under international law. That is another, milder way of insisting on the principle of loyalty under EU law. Instead of just labelling his redefined theory as monist, it is therefore more appropriate to examine the room for political manoeuvre within a legal framework. On the other hand, law is not only a limit on the exercise of power; it is also a catalyst for the political. Hence, as we will see, principles like cooperation in good faith or loyalty also guide behaviour in a way most conducive to our political existence in the nation state, integrated into the European Union.

2.2 *Cosmopolitan Pluralism: Principles Anywhere*

Mattias Kumm is one of those scholars who have developed constitutional pluralism on the basis of legal and political principles. The common normative premise of this line of research is to solve constitutional conflicts not by power politics but by universal principles that validate a claim to hierarchy in any particular case. Such a claim is likely to be accepted because the principle on which it is based is common to all legal orders involved. Human rights, democracy and the rule of law are the constitutional principles on which all legal orders in the West ground their legitimacy. Their commitment is thus essentially the same: 'the idea of free and equal persons governing themselves through law'.[11] That is why a principled legal discourse is possible among judicial authorities from several legal orders. However, Kumm concedes that even rational lawyers and judges will not necessarily agree on the interpretation and application of principles to any concrete case.[12] It is the moral point of constitutional pluralism to determine when one or the other claim to authority is justified.[13]

There is a presumption of hierarchy in favour of the more comprehensive legal order, that is, a legal-institutional framework capable of solving collective action and coordination problems.[14] In particular, Kumm considers the EU legal order to institutionalise the rule of law beyond the state. Instead of following the functional reasoning in *Costa*, the Member States should accept

---

11 Mattias Kumm, 'Constituent Power, Cosmopolitan Constitutionalism, and Post-Positivist Law' (2016) 14(3) I·CON 697, 710.

12 Ibid 709.

13 Mattias Kumm, 'The Moral Point of Constitutional Pluralism: Defining the Domain of Legitimate Institutional Civil Disobedience and Conscientious Objection' in Julie Dickson & Pavlos Eleftheriadis (eds), *Philosophical Foundations of European Union Law* (OUP 2012).

14 Ibid 232–233.

the primacy of EU law because it guarantees respect for the principle of legality, which is an element of the rule of law.[15] Kumm develops this argument in later writings on public international law.[16] The rule of law beyond the state protects from 'justice-sensitive externalities', meaning the negative cross-border impact of state action. Examples are as many as they are varied: military interventions; the use of nuclear energy; carbon-dioxide emissions; and the fight against transnational organised crime. All these example leave room for reasonable disagreement about what justice requires. Kumm argues that states must not unilaterally determine what is just in these circumstances, for it entails the risk of domination contrary to the self-determination of affected outsiders.[17] Therefore, states must subject themselves to independent conflict resolution in accordance with international or EU law. Instead of completely avoiding any mutual interference ab initio, the purpose of law beyond the state is to give due consideration to all affected interests and to settle conflicts in a peaceful and authoritative manner.

Conversely, a state continuous to have sovereign authority over matters not generating justice-sensitive externalities.[18] Kumm readily makes a concession on this point, for it may be necessary to weigh the rule of law beyond the state against other principles. The difficulty lies in drawing a red line. Kumm argues that external harm is unjust if it has been caused by a failure to comply with legal obligations voluntarily entered into.[19] State consent thus gives rise to a duty of good faith, quite similar to what the late MacCormick argues. Anything outside the remit of state consent falls, in principle, within the right to national self-determination even if it inflicts damage outside the own territory. However, Kumm clarifies that state consent is sufficient but not necessary to bring up a legitimate claim to justice. He tries to draw the line in the following general terms:

> Self-governing entities are not under a general duty to *enable* others to do something they otherwise would not be able to do without them, even

15 Ibid 228–231, 238–241.

16 See Kumm (n 11) and 'Sovereignty and the Right to Be Left Alone: Subsidiarity, Justice-Sensitive Externalities, and the Proper Domain of the Consent Requirement in International Law' (2016) 79(2) Law and Contemporary Problems 239, 244ff.

17 Kumm (n 16) 248.

18 Ibid 253.

19 Ibid 254.

> though they are under a *prima facie* duty *not to disable* them, make them worse off than they would be if there was no other self-governing entity.[20]

This normative baseline will be violated if, for example, states are complicit in the perpetration of internationally wrongful acts by authorising the export of weapons to non-democratic regimes. It is immaterial, for that matter, whether they are held accountable under the rules of international law.[21] Similarly, membership in an international organisation may give rise to a duty to share the benefits of the cooperation fairly beyond the actual terms of the agreement.[22] In other words, behaviour may be perfectly in line with the rules of the organisation and yet entail a demand for justice. In such cases, states are held responsible in moral rather than legal terms. But as soon as we are on moral grounds, it will not be difficult to imagine other telling examples showing the harmful effects of unilateralism in an interdependent world.

That is why Kumm seems to favour principled multilateralism. Returning to the European context, he recognises a right of Member States to disapply EU law under certain conditions.[23] That is permissible if the highest national courts come to the conclusion that a principle like subsidiarity or democracy has greater weight in the relevant context than the uniform application of EU law. They arrive at such a verdict from an 'intermediate position':[24] committed to the rule of law beyond the state, they are nonetheless ready to rebut the presumption in favour of applying EU law if countervailing principles carry sufficient weight in any individual case. The outcome of their balancing might not meet universal approval. But any principle-based, morally worthy resistance to EU law will only occur exceptionally since the EU made great progress in upholding the principles of liberal constitutionalism.[25] Member States may resist EU law to correct remaining structural imbalances of European

20 Mattias Kumm, 'Constituent Power, Boundaries and Identity: On the Justificatory Depth of Constitutionalism – A Rejoinder to Neil Walker' (2016) 14(4) I·CON 914, 919 (emphasis in original).

21 Kumm (n 16) 255–256: 'Arguably one of the scandals of existing international law is the extent to which complicit states are shielded from accountability under prevailing rules of state responsibility.'

22 Ibid 256 and Kumm (n 20) 919–920: 'States claiming that injustice is being done to them would have to argue that, *notwithstanding* the actual terms of the agreement and the fact that states have entered them voluntarily, there are structural features of the agreements that preclude benefits of the joint cooperative endeavors to be shared fairly' (emphasis added).

23 Kumm (n 13) 232ff.

24 Ibid 234.

25 Ibid 240.

integration, or to accommodate individual concerns related to a national constitutional identity.[26] Any such resistance is legitimate only if it is based on common constitutional principles. Their authority is in turn derived from the European constitutional tradition not limited to either the EU Treaties or any national constitution.[27]

To sum up, cosmopolitan pluralism is essentially about a fair balance between principles associated with the authority of EU law on the one hand, and the authority of the sovereign state on the other. It is thus tempting to conclude that we may accommodate the frame of the *Rechtsgemeinschaft* and that of the national legal orders within one conceptual framework. That is compelling to the extent that principles constitute common ground for a constitutional discourse. It is indeed common to presume the existence of a shared core of constitutional principles in liberal democracies.[28] However, it is challenging to delimit the range of such principles, rendering final judgment as to whether, for instance, all values listed in Article 2 TEU are to be recognised, and to interpret them so as to facilitate dialogue across legal orders.[29] This connects also to the institutional question who has the power to decide about the terms of the debate.

Leaving aside this thorny issue, we have a useful basis for meaningful engagement from different internal points of view. To underline, the theory presupposes divergent interpretations of constitutional principles, and it is not the purpose to solve legal conflicts in each and every respect. But in spite of disagreement, it is possible to fall back on a common core meaning of what, for example, the rule of law requires at EU level and to evaluate other interpretations on that basis. Indeed, Kumm's theory is compatible with the frame of the EU legal order, demanding that the uniform application of EU law should in principle prevail to guarantee a minimum level of fairness in inter-state relations. Furthermore, Kumm prefers final judgments over enduring judicial

26 Ibid 234–238 ('institutionalised civil disobedience' and 'conscientious objection', respectively).

27 Ibid 239.

28 As has been highlighted in debates about alleged abuses of (national) constitutional identity, see eg Julian Scholtes, 'Abusing Constitutional Identity' (2021) 22(4) German Law Journal 534, 551; Gary Jeffrey Jacobsohn, 'How to Think About the Reach of Constitutional Identity' (2023) 1(1) Comparative Constitutional Studies 6.

29 This connects to the recent discourse about an EU constitutional identity, see Jurgen de Poorter et al. (eds), A Constitutional Identity for the EU?' (2022) 4 European Yearbook of Constitutional Law.

dialogue about the issue of *Kompetenz-Kompetenz* (even though conflicts may turn out to be irreconcilable).[30]

At first sight, the theory also seems to be in line with the national sovereignty frame since the 27 have 'a right to be left alone' insofar as they justify any unilateral measure that is liable to cause harm elsewhere by reference to common principles. However, this well-intentioned concession is but one aspect of constitutional interaction. Another one is the (voluntary) submission to the authority of EU law, as required by the CJEU. And yet, the blind spot in Kumm's analysis is the intermediate sphere of the 27 even though his theory could in part account for it. Any of them can represent a unity on common ground, demonstrating that it is one-of-us but also other-than-us. Hence, principles are the shared language of the 27 to express, in their own words, what EU membership means to each of them from the internal perspective of a collective self. Kumm fails to consider this because, in his view, constitutional principles have their basis in natural law.[31] He is thus not interested in how a particular interpretation of a principle came about or what motivates a political community to commit itself to one or the other principle.[32] Political will is sidestepped in favour of rational discourse. To clarify, this is not an argument for the opposite in view of the close connection between both motives for collective action. Hence, any exercise of power will be informed by principles constitutive of the legal order concerned, and authorities violating them will lose their legitimacy. And although authorities cannot represent a unity from nowhere, they do reinterpret principles with regard to changing circumstances in and beyond the state. Consequently, the prevailing interpretation may evolve, yet falling short of a complete disembedding from time and space.[33]

2.3 *Epistemic Pluralism: The Elusive Common Whole*

The third line of research takes distinct epistemic sites as its starting point. On this view, it is only possible to analyse the interaction of legal orders if one reckons with the contexts in which law is operating. How law is understood and applied is in part determined by political, economic and cultural-historical

30 Kumm (n 13) 243.

31 Kumm (n 11) 699–703, 709–711.

32 See also the critique in Neil Walker, 'The Return of Constituent Power: A Reply to Mattias Kumm' (2016) 14(4) I·CON 906.

33 See Kumm (n 20) 920, who affirms 'the constitutive and constraining role of principle for establishing and contesting the boundaries of the political community', illustrated by German unification and other historical examples. In my understanding, he thereby admits that any recourse to principles is also necessarily particular.

circumstances.[34] Factors like these are always located somewhere, mainly but not exclusively within the nation state. Unlike cosmopolitan pluralism, it is thus not difficult to accept that every claim to authority is relative. Indeed, there is prima facie no reason to settle the question of hierarchy if every legal order involved owes its authority to certain social facts and beliefs. In this sense, the conclusions of radical pluralism are extended beyond the courtroom because neither a judge nor anybody else will manage to abstract himself completely from the surrounding environment that, as we shall see, is likely to correspond to the borders of the nation state.

From this point forward, it is not a long way to the acceptance of plain power relations. Even if epistemic pluralism is descriptively accurate and realist, it has no normative ambitions unless it tries to bridge the divide of insular epistemic sites communicating in the language of power. Matej Avbelj has taken up the challenge with his principled legal pluralism.[35] The principle of equal human dignity is at the heart of the theory.[36] It is not a cosmopolitan but a foundational principle of every European legal order. This explains why it may govern cross-border legal discourse while remaining rooted in distinct epistemic sites. It facilitates legal interaction because it is the common point of reference, notwithstanding value diversity. In addition, it constitutes the limit to diversity, the bottom line every legal order must adhere to. However, a common substantive foundation alone would not be sufficient if every legal order used it in a purely self-referential manner. Principled legal pluralism is therefore premised on self-reflexivity as well, the capacity to identity oneself with regard to the other. Preserving the status quo is thus not an end in itself. By claiming to be different, a legal order engages with the addressee of the claim, opening to a process of contestation, learning and – finally – adaptation.

Avbelj argues that these virtues presuppose a separation of pluralism and constitutionalism. That is to say, the very notion of *constitutional* pluralism is a misnomer because you cannot have both at the same time.[37] After all,

34 Regarding constitutional law, see Signe Rehling Larsen, 'Varieties of Constitutionalism in the European Union' (2021) 84(3) Modern Law Review 477.

35 This paragraph is based on Matej Avbelj, *The European Union under Transnational Law: A Pluralist Appraisal* (Hart 2018) ch 2.

36 For details, see Matej Avbelj, 'Human Dignity and EU Legal Pluralism' in Gareth Davies & Matej Avbelj (eds), *Research Handbook on Legal Pluralism and EU Law* (Elgar 2018).

37 For details, see Matej Avbelj, 'Can European Integration Be Constitutional and Pluralist – Both at the Same Time?' in Avbelj & Komárek (n 1). However, more recently, he calls for a revised pluralist constitutionalism deviating from the predominant American federalist model, see Matej Avbelj, 'Revitalisation of EU Constitutionalism' (2021) 46(1) European Law Review 3.

constitutionalism implies that pluralism would be subject to a higher authority. If we followed Kumm for example, a judicial authority would interpret universal principles to determine, ideally, the extent to which pluralism is permissible. Avbelj limits the substantive foundation of his theory to the principle of equal human dignity, the meaning of which is eventually determined at each epistemic site including, in particular, the constitutional state.[38]

It might seem puzzling why constitutionalism is accepted in the nation state, characterised in nature (though not in degree) by the same tension between universality and particularity. We find answers in the work of Nico Krisch who has been the most adamant proponent of radical pluralism since MacCormick became more inclined towards the constitutionalist camp.[39] Krisch observes that society is postnational, meaning that national identity is complemented by, for example, a European identity. Thus, the nation state is still the most salient but no longer the exclusive site for identification. But in contrast to the nation, it is impossible to unite postnational society under a constitution, understood as the foundation of collective self-government. It would require major institutional and certainly social transformation, which is utopian at this point in time. Any attempt in this regard would face a dilemma. Constitutionalism would either suppress social diversity, or it would become meaningless in efforts to accommodate it. So instead of global constitutionalism, it is a pluralist postnational order Krisch has in mind. It is evolving in line with the changing social practices in and beyond the nation state. And similar to inter-state relations, the emerging new collectives should mutually respect each other's right to self-government. Obviously, the meaning of collective self-government is more fluid than in the constitutional state. But as mentioned, this is considered a virtue of pluralism, and institutional processes and mechanisms need to adapt to the pace of social change. For example, checks and balances are important to prevent one collective from violating the right to self-government of another– a risk already underlined by Kumm. But according to Krisch, the existing forms of accountability need to adapt to the new modes of governance beyond the state.

In practice, what Krisch and Avbelj contemplate is the rise of authorities beyond the state. This legal space is filled with authorities as diverse as the Basel Committee on Banking Supervision and the terrorist organisation ISIS. The previous chapter explained that such authorities claim to represent a unity to an audience of, for example, bank employees and terrorists. If the claim is

38 Avbelj (n 35) 34–38.

39 This paragraph is based on Nico Krisch, *Beyond Constitutionalism: The Pluralist Structure of Postnational Law* (OUP 2010) chs 2 and 3.

accepted, new epistemic communities are emerging who may interact with one another and with the more established sites like the EU and the Member States. In this context, Avbelj refuses to think in constitutional terms because it would fuel discussions about the EU becoming a state.[40] In his conception based on principled legal pluralism, the EU is a non-hierarchical compound of three elements: the Member States, the supranational EU and a 'common whole' (or the EU sensu lato).[41] The latter is the normative anchor connecting the national and supranational elements. It indicates a double commitment to plurality and to the common whole, which is more than the sum of the individual parts. The substantive objective is to guarantee perpetual peace and individual liberty in conformity with the overarching principle of equal human dignity. But other than that, the meaning of the common whole cannot be specified in advance:

> Unlike the monist framework, the grand structure of a union is in a constant and permanent search for the best coordinative equilibrium between the independent participating states and the self-standing supranational level. In this way (…) the union is condemned to a continuous state of 'in-between' (*ein Zwischen*), marked by inherent dynamics, instability, conflicting objectives and antinomies.[42]

That is not to say that pragmatic accommodation happens in a legal void. Apart from the substantive principle of equal human dignity, there are structural principles of EU law like primacy and loyalty.[43] Since any claim to authority is relative, these principles are best suited to preserve the ensuing plurality. The principle of loyalty obliges the Member States to contribute to the objectives of the EU while respecting their constitutional identity. The principle of primacy requires the disapplication of conflicting national law under certain conditions, without stipulating the supremacy of EU law as a matter of principle.[44]

40 Avbelj (n 35) 42–43. But see supra n 37 and Matej Avbelj, 'Values, Constitutionalism and the Viability of European Integration' in Matej Avbelj (ed), *The Future of EU Constitutionalism* (Hart 2023) 48–50.

41 Avbelj (n 35) ch 3.

42 Ibid 51 (references omitted).

43 Ibid 56–57.

44 For details, see Matej Avbelj, 'Supremacy or Primacy of EU Law? – (Why) Does It Matter?' (2011) 17(6) European Law Journal 744. This view is in accordance with the case law of the CJEU, see eg Case C-573/17 *Popławski* EU:C:2019:530, paras 61–62; Joined Cases C-357/19, C-379/19, C-547/19, C-811/19 and C-840/19 *Criminal proceedings against PM and Others* EU:C:2021:1034, para 252.

This broadly corresponds to the view of the national constitutional courts. It may then be possible to solve concrete cases by deferring, if necessary, to the authority of another legal order without engaging with the grand question of who the final arbiter of constitutional conflicts is (or the holder of *Kompetenz-Kompetenz*). Most importantly, any attempt at conflict resolution must be in a principled legal manner.

Summing up, epistemic pluralism tries to arrange distinct sites of legal ordering into a common normative whole. The effort to construct a unity from different starting points is precarious, for it might destroy the plurality it purports to cherish. That is why, in terms of substance, the common monist framework only consists of the minimum requirement to respect equal human dignity, complemented by strong(er) procedural duties of cooperation. Having regard to the discussion so far, we can conclude that this line of research combines the best of what radical and cosmopolitan pluralism have to offer. This is encompassed in the principle of equal human dignity which has a universal scope but particular meanings. In addition, it is not only a limit of power but also a source of empowerment because, according to Avbelj, it is constitutive of the way legal collectives 'explain the object and purpose of their existence'.[45] Indeed, human dignity is at the heart of the liberal democratic promise of individual liberty. This is the foundation of, for example, the German legal system.[46]

On this basis, it would be consequential to embrace the constitutional register. For as soon as the principle of equal human dignity is the object of inter-systemic interaction, it will be used to represent a unity from the internal perspective of a collective self. The room for interpretation will be filled with the political imagination of the institution responsible for conflict resolution. As Chapter 1 explained, the constitutional state is the largest reservoir in this respect. Therefore, insofar as the interaction among the EU and the Member States is concerned, principled legal pluralism will at least involve a plurality of political imaginations. A certain hesitation of the constitutional language is understandable to caution against the transformation of the EU into anything close to a federal state. However, it is still possible and appropriate to speak of the interaction between various constitutional sites and, if necessary, to distinguish between the EU and the Member States with regard to the underlying sovereignty frames.

45 Avbelj (n 36) 110.

46 See Chapter 1.2.2.

There are, in addition, normative arguments for not throwing the baby out with the bathwater. In the first place, it is unlikely that human dignity alone is sufficient to bridge the legal and political cleavage in Europe. It may even aggravate tensions since it is not only a tool to include but also to exclude. Those acting contrary to the principle of equal human dignity may not participate in legal interaction, according to Avbelj. While terrorist organisations like ISIS are clear candidates for exclusion,[47] other cases are less straightforward.[48] This not to suggest that we need another basis for principled legal pluralism. On the contrary, it is worthwhile keeping human dignity as a minimum requirement for a more encompassing constitutional discourse. The latter would have to reckon with the political imagination as to who and what we are in the nation state and beyond. That means that respect for equal human dignity and any principles or rules derived therefrom is but one (fundamental) part of the equation to the wider common good.[49] State constitutionalism is traditionally the frame within which the equation is formed. Confronted with emerging authorities at EU and international level, it is under pressure but no less important. It is indispensable for giving effect to norms elaborated beyond the state, and in so doing, it makes sure that the exercise of power is legitimate in the eyes of those to whom it is addressed. In fact, no other entity has either the right or the capacity to integrate functional ends like banking supervision or border management into a common political endeavour. New epistemic sites are indeed emerging, yet they are still functionally limited and thus in need of an audience. In fact, it will be a national audience that determines in how far the new sites may be recognised as one-of-us. Instead of retreating from change, a legal-political order is adapting to it against the background of existing social practices and beliefs. That is not only inevitable but also desirable, for the alternative would be a fragmented legal universe prone to instability and friction.[50] The latter cannot be ruled out in a rapidly changing

47 Avbelj (n 35) 143.

48 Ibid 144, illustrated by EU migration management. He seems to suggest that national and EU policies, especially those concerning the distribution of people, are contrary to the principle of equal human dignity. If that is correct, those who clearly adopt an unjust position would be excluded from the discourse. Here, the already mentioned problem returns with a vengeance: who decides about the terms of the debate?

49 For a discussion, see Christopher McCrudden, 'Alasdair MacIntyre's Critique of Human Dignity: A Response' (2022) 189 Law & Justice: The Christian Law Review 110.

50 But see Krisch (n 39) ch 7, for whom instability is a virtue because it allows persons to break free from the rigid structures of the nation state. It is interesting to note that even Krisch starts from a systemic perspective, see supra n 7.

world. But political, economic or cultural change is not just happening; it has to become part of the political imagination to have a lasting impact.

In the second place, constitutionalism facilitates legal and political conflict resolution. It has been explained that a legal order is only empowering if the addressees can rely on legal protection and other requirements of the rule of law.[51] Only then is it sensible to consider the exercise of power as expression of collective self-determination. For example, according to the German Federal Constitutional Court, EU powers are only legitimate if they emanate from the will of the German people. But this political reflexivity is difficult to realise if authority is exercised at a growing distance from national polities. One way to address the ensuing conflicts is to qualify their importance, arguing that any law-polity nexus is neither plausible nor appealing in times of fragmented societies.[52] Law would rather follow authority than polity. In other words, forms of accountability would equally move beyond the state, with the consequence of drastically reducing the influence of national parliaments and courts. This is not only a theoretical possibility but a practical reality. Avbelj concludes his monograph by observing a 'tendency (…) of avoiding direct legal conflicts and their judicial resolution, and pushing the frictions into the domain of experts whereby, following the prescriptions of principled legal pluralism, these are resolved through a self-reflexive dialogue'.[53] Hence, his theory explains and defends technocratic rather than political reflexivity. Conflicts are tamed down by shifting them to sites detached from national polities, thereby avoiding the question in how far the new authorities affect our political existence. If that is correct, the elusive 'common whole' seems to be nothing but an a-political space. Perhaps Avbelj intends otherwise, for in his view, the EU common whole is occupied by administrative, judicial and political authorities alike.[54] However, it is submitted that he cannot fully reckon with them because he excludes constitutionalism from his transnational account.[55]

2.4 *Synthesis: The Common Purpose in Constitutional Pluralism*

It follows from the foregoing that none of the three lines of research fully explores the frame of legal ordering. All of them concentrate on claims to legal authority, and less so on the underlying frames. If the latter does get attention, it is limited to the legal order stricto sensu without considering that legal

51 See Chapter 1.2.
52 Nico Krisch, 'Law and Polity: Contingency, Fiction, Loss' (2018) 16(4) I·CON 1223.
53 Avbelj (n 35) 154–155.
54 Avbelj (n 35) 57–59.
55 But see supra n 40.

order is an expression of political will (radical pluralism). In the alternative, the emergence of epistemic sites is seen as detached from the political imagination in the nation state (epistemic pluralism). To concede, even cosmopolitan pluralism is not indifferent to the question of what legitimises the exercise of power. But principles derived from natural law are not as such sufficient to generate political will; they are mainly the product of rational thought. For conflict resolution, rationality is required as much as an idea of the political. Hence, conflicting claims will not be destructive if the addressees believe that authority is being exercised on their behalf. They have to relate the exercise of power to *themselves*, to their political existence in the nation state and beyond.

Neil Walker has been arguing for a long time not to lose sight of the political in constitutional pluralism.[56], [57] To this end, he promotes a meta-constitutional discourse of epistemic sites, with the following characteristics.[58] First, it draws from the statist discourse of constitutionalism and extends it to new sites of authority. But it is not a conceptual extension writ large from the nation state as this would face serious obstacles. Second, the purpose is to derive legitimacy for the exercise of power from a meta-constitution. This is neither a (written or unwritten) constitution nor a new monist source external to states. It is rather the frame underpinning the constitution, which we have encountered in the previous chapter. In times of constitutional pluralism, power is no longer legitimate if it is exercised in a purely self-referential manner. More precisely, the collective self is no longer confined to a national political existence. 27 European nation states are, at the same, EU Member States. Therefore, the legitimate exercise of power hinges on recognition by those affected, that is, all other Member States of the EU, whose very purpose is to preclude mutual interference. That is, however, a matter of degree. To what extent may a Member State assert itself without interfering with the analogous right of other Member States as protected within the frame of the EU legal order? Walker has no clear answer to this.[59] But he is unambiguous in his conviction that reducing the constitution to a question of institutional design will fall short, although the multiple crises of the past decade have triggered that question and might

56 Neil Walker, 'The Idea of Constitutional Pluralism' (2002) 65(3) The Modern Law Review 317.

57 Neil Walker, 'Constitutional Pluralism Revisited' (2016) 22(3) European Law Journal 333.

58 Walker (n 56) 356–359. See also Neil Walker, 'Flexibility Within a Metaconstitutional Frame' in Gráinne de Búrca & Joanne Scott, *Constitutional Change in the EU: From Uniformity to Flexibility?* (OUP 2000) 14ff.

59 For a recent interpretation, see Amnon Lev, 'The Imaginary and the Unconscious: Situating Constitutional Pluralism' in Jan Komárek (ed), *European Constitutional Imaginaries: Between Ideology and Utopia* (OUP 2023) 180, 188ff.

even call for a new attempt at drafting a 'big C' EU Constitution.[60] The main appeal of the latter would be the constitution-making process as such, requiring us the Europeans to debate the proper balance between EU and national constitutionalism.[61] Apart from an institutional question, that is thus also an exercise in collective self-reflection as to 'the degree of common cause that it is possible and desirable for the European states and citizenry to find'.[62] The following makes a modest effort to situate the quest for that 'common cause' or common purpose at the intersection of the three European spheres.[63]

In the first place, the common whole (or the intermediate sphere) has a substantive content composed of a surface and a deep layer. The former encompasses the objectives; the latter the final purpose of the Union.[64] Measures taken in pursuit of crime prevention, sustainable development or social justice serve the final purpose to promote peace, the common values and the well-being of the European peoples, according to Article 3(1) TEU.[65] This interpretation suggests that the elements of neither the surface nor the deep layer belong exclusively to the EU stricto sensu (or the inner sphere of the EU legal order). The latter must only act within the scope of the competences conferred on it, in view of the common objectives.[66] However, the competence norms delimit the powers of the EU institutions only, with indirect legal effects on the Member States who shall not jeopardise the attainment of the common goals through autonomous action.[67] This does not rule out measures to promote a matter of common concern, as demonstrated by the

60 See Neil Walker, 'The Burden of the European Constitution' in Avbelj (n 40).

61 Walker (n 57) 352: '[W]hat is needed as a distinguishing factor is an explicit recognition that this [EU] constitution, and its constituent authority, is only concerned with transnational institutions and competences, and that national jurisdiction over unpooled capacity remains rooted in national acts and systems of constitutional authority. What requires to be delivered, then, is a new kind of constitutional dualism, one that guards against opposite forms of slippage in order to track the deeper dualism of the political system'; Walker (n 60) 24.

62 Walker (n 60) 23–24.

63 For a more institutional account, see Marco Goldoni, 'Constitutional Pluralism and the Question of the European Common Good' (2012) 18(3) European Law Journal 385.

64 The distinction between objective and purpose is based on Josef Isensee, *Gemeinwohl und öffentliches Amt: Vordemokratische Fundamente des Verfassungsstaates* (Springer 2013) 25 (with further references).

65 Compare Matthias Ruffert, 'Art. 3 (ex-Art. 2 EUV) [Ziele der Union]', in Christian Calliess & Matthias Ruffert (eds), *EUV/AEUV: Das Verfassungsrecht der Europäischen Union mit Europäischer Grundrechtecharta [Kommentar]* (5th edition, C H Beck 2016) 46ff. He distinguishes general from specific objectives ('Ziele').

66 Art 1 TEU.

67 Art 4(3) TEU; Ruffert (n 65) 43, 46.

coordination of, for example, financial and military support for Ukraine after the Russian invasion in February 2022. In this sense, the EU is different from a traditional international organisation whose very existence is predetermined by its tasks.[68] Similarly, the Union and the Member States alike are founded on the common values listed in Article 2 TEU.[69] In terms of content, some values have corresponding legal principles.[70] The mentioned principle of equal human dignity is thus an integral part of the common purpose (just like freedom, democracy, equality, the rule of law and respect for human rights). This multi-layered structure of the common whole has important consequences for legal and political reasoning because any measure in pursuit of a common objective must qualify as an expression of the common purpose. The latter therefore legitimises political decision-making, both in the EU stricto sensu and lato sensu.[71] Justification by reference to the common whole is thus one requirement to gain recognition as a representative of the Union.

In the second place, justification follows the concept of representation, which is essential to avoid that the present proposal falls prey to power politics. To start with, the previous chapter explained that the concept as such is concerned with (indirect) agency and responsibility. It is the flip side of the predominant negative understanding of unilateralism, associated with a retreat from the EU framework. Obviously, a claim to pursue the common purpose is not by itself sufficient. But the concept of representation increases the burden to corroborate the claim both internally and externally. It requires an exercise in political reflexivity, demanding from Member States to justify measures taken in a European context in front of their national audience. One of the most pertinent questions is whether the exercise of power is a legitimate expression of our political existence in the nation state and in the European Union. Ideally, the answer will be given in parliament, by far the most representative institution. Whether a national democratic debate has taken place is, at the same time, a relevant standard to gain external recognition. It is indeed difficult to maintain that other Member States should recognise action on their behalf if not even domestic support is certain. Next, the outcome of internal

68 See Joris Larik, 'From Speciality to a Constitutional Sense of Purpose: On the Changing Role of the Objectives of the European Union' (2014) 63 ICLQ 935.

69 This follows from the text of art 2 TEU, see also Christian Calliess, 'Art. 2 [Die Werte der Union]' in Calliess & Ruffert (n 65) 32–34.

70 Ibid 32.

71 Ibid 33: 'In diesem Kontext vermitteln Werte freilich nicht nur Legitimation, sondern sie können – vermittelt über ihren Prinzipiengehalt – als Auslegungsleitlinie und Normenkontrollmaßstab dienen.'

democracy furnishes substantive arguments to justify action on behalf of the Union, going deeper than the mere invocation of a shared political objective. Chapter 1 explained that the national sovereignty frame is composed of a reflexive relationship between *potentia* and *potestas*, essentially between the capacity and the right to govern. While the institutions of the state are vital to collective agency, any exercise of power will be illegitimate if the citizens cannot attribute it to themselves. Self-reflexivity is a virtuous circle, involving the iterative representation of unity stimulated from the outside. Hence, external challenges force a polity to re-assure itself of the meaning of the common good. For practical purposes, a claim on behalf of the Union presupposes several considerations from the internal perspective of a collective self. Are we in fact capable of assuming responsibility for the Union in political, economic or administrative terms, and would it be legitimate? However, once the question of legitimacy arises, the inevitable contingency of the collective self is likely to be a problem. It is submitted that even the most sincere effort in political reflexivity cannot overcome the limited capacity to imagine oneself as a member of a larger European polity. Chapter 1 argued that the political imagination is mainly a national one. That is why another collective might not feel represented, and tensions might not ease but intensify.

In the third place, we therefore need more clarity about dispute resolution. This is all the more necessary when the force of the political is to return centre stage. The argument is that it should despite the undeniable risks. The theoretical basis is the understanding that any representation of unity involves the claim to be one-of-us and other-than-us – both at the same time. There is therefore no need to find universal approval of a national political imagination if the latter generates the will to act in line with the common purpose of the Union. This is still no guarantee for recognition since the Member State concerned may be accused of misrepresenting the common purpose. Who then decides about recognition as one-of-us? It is self-evident that the CJEU has the task of ruling over national action within the scope of EU law. However, this as such cannot be the final answer, for any exercise of power on behalf of the EU legal order requires self-restraint in order to also recognise Member States as other-than-us. But self-restraint cannot go so far as to undermine the identity or the purpose of the EU legal order. The latter will only recognise itself if it continues to assume responsibility for mutual non-interference. This common purpose is, at the same time, the ground on which the Member States can recognise each of them as one-of-us. It thus all comes down to the issue of how to defend the fundamentals of European legal integration, which is the prerequisite for national action on behalf of the Union.

At this stage, we need to return to the findings of the previous chapter. Common rules of EU law serve the purpose of mutual non-interference, and Member States giving effect to them act as formal representatives of the Union. More specifically, there is a rebuttable presumption of formal representation when Member States intend to give effect to EU law. The Court may rebut the presumption, or remain silent if it is not even certain whether a claim has been expressed. The empowerment of the Court is ultimately based on the will of the 6 (founding members) to settle their disputes in a peaceful, independent and authoritative manner. However, on its own account, the Court is more than a forum for intergovernmental conflict resolution: it is the guardian of a new legal order that is autonomous or independent from the Member States. Hence, the common purpose is pursued from within the autonomous structures of EU law and the EU legal order, and national action is assessed in this light. The next section will explore the meaning of the principle of autonomy according to case law and legal doctrine. In addition, the limits of that principle are just as important to supplement the internal with an external perspective. The latter ensures that the 27 continue to recognise the EU legal order as their own. This is the basis for their own empowerment, for assuming responsibility for the Union.

3 The Principle of Autonomy in EU Law: Meaning and Limits

Autonomy is a judge-made principle of EU law. In the most general sense, its purpose is to protect the EU legal order from external influences. It is no surprise that the Court is wary of international law and, in particular, alternative dispute settlement liable to threaten its own jurisdiction.[72] Yet, also the Member States may pose an 'external' risk when exercising their right to self-determination. This is the subject matter of the present inquiry, developing an argument for the relative nature of the principle of autonomy: it has foreseen normative closure *and* opening since the Court interpreted it in constitutional terms.[73] It therefore guides Member States in moving from the inner to the

72 For details, see Jed Odermatt, 'The Principle of Autonomy: An Adolescent Disease of EU External Relations Law?' in Marise Cremona (ed), *Structural Principles in EU External Relations Law* (Hart 2018).

73 This argument is not as such original. The following section describes the work of René Barents, a former judge at the Court, whose take on European integration different from the one developed in this book. Still, he accepts the relative autonomy of the (then) Community legal order. The question obviously is: relative as to what and why? According to Barents, the Community legal order is in principle open to norms from other

intermediate sphere, reconciling their double bind between the EU and their independent political existence.

3.1 *The Original Justification*

In the foundational jurisprudence, the notion of autonomy justified the principles of direct effect and primacy. Already in *Van Gend & Loos*, the Court expressed a modest claim to autonomy by finding that Community law[74] governs the legal affairs of citizens independently of the law of the Member States.[75] For this reason, it was incumbent upon the Court to determine whether a particular rule of the supranational legal order is capable of being enforced before national courts. *Costa/ENEL* became known for establishing the autonomous nature of that legal order as such.[76] Community law must take precedence over national law, for otherwise the binding force and uniform application of the former would be jeopardised. The Court concluded that primacy guaranteed the very character of Community law common to the Member States as well as the legal basis of the Community itself.[77]

It was left unclear where the Court derived the notion of autonomy from. One might assume that Community law is autonomous because it stems from a new legal order established by the Treaty. According to Barents, it is the opposite: Community law is inherently autonomous by virtue of the substance of European integration, so it can be described as a single legal order.[78] When Barents was writing, the main objective was to establish an internal market by removing inter-state barriers to trade. That is why, in his submission, Community law has an 'inherent unity',[79] and autonomy is necessary to protect it against unilateral state action.[80] Hence, Member States may only derogate

---

jurisdictions. It can therefore develop in light of developments in its legal environment. I am not interested in the development but in the limits of the EU legal order. At some point, I contend, the EU legal order cannot legitimately claim authority and it is up to the 27 to assume responsibility for a viable Union.

74 This section uses the pre-Lisbon legal terminology.

75 Case 26/62 *Van Gend & Loos* EU:C:1963:1, p 12: 'Independently of the legislation of Member States, Community law [...] not only imposes obligations on individuals but is also intended to confer upon them rights which become part of their legal heritage.'

76 Case 6/64 *Costa* v *ENEL* EU:C:1964:66, p 594.

77 Ibid: 'It follows (...) that the law stemming from the Treaty, an independent source of law, could not, because of its special and original nature, be overridden by domestic legal provisions, however framed, without being deprived of its character as Community law and without the legal basis of the Community itself being called into question.'

78 René Barents, *The Autonomy of Community Law* (Kluwer 2004) 251–253.

79 Ibid 211.

80 Ibid 211–215.

from the fundamental freedoms where explicitly permitted by Community law and subject to the Court's supervision. The preliminary ruling procedure is the mechanism by which the Court protects the autonomy and unity of the legal order. In Barents' opinion, Community law is best described as a self-referential system: the Treaty established a new legal order, characterised by an inherent substantive and institutional unity, and that legal order maintains itself through its own rules, principles and mechanisms such as the preliminary ruling procedure and under the control of a final arbiter: the Court in Luxembourg.[81]

Perpetual self-preservation might, however, prevent the development of the system. Barents concedes that a purely functional concept of law revolving around the integration process in general and the internal market in particular cannot justify the principle of autonomy.[82] Standards of the rule of law became part of Community law as soon as the Court recognised them as general principles derived from the common constitutional traditions of the Member States and the ECHR in particular. In exercising the power to ensure that in the interpretation and application of the Treaties the law is observed,[83] the Court may determine which rules and principles form part of Community law. According to Barents, it follows that the EC legal order is open insofar as the gatekeeper – the Court – permits.[84] Community law is thus an autonomous system with a constitutional character, subject to the inherent unity of the legal order. Constitutional principles may only become part of EU law to the extent the very nature of that law permits. On this view, subsidiarity and flexibility are concepts to be rejected.[85]

From a historical perspective, Barents' account explains why, in the field of international relations, the Court held that concurrent powers on the part of the Member States 'would be incompatible with the unity of the common market and the uniform application of Community law'.[86] If it is correct that substantive and institutional unity was intrinsic to the autonomy of the new legal order, the Member States could not conclude an international agreement falling with the scope of Community law unless the latter had contained an express authorisation to that effect. But in the contemporary EU, it is difficult to justify autonomy on the basis of unity understood in that sense. The

81 Ibid 262–265.
82 Ibid 283ff.
83 Art 220 EC Treaty (now art 19 TEU).
84 Barents (n 78) 296–298.
85 Ibid 298.
86 Case 22/70 *Commission* v *Council* (*ERTA*) EU:C:1971:32, para 31; see also Chapter 6.

establishment and functioning of the internal market is no longer the predominant objective of the EU since the Court elevated the Area of Freedom, Security and Justice (AFSJ) to one of the 'fundamental provisions'[87] of EU law, each of which has 'particular characteristics'.[88] Whereas the internal market is premised on overcoming national differences, the AFSJ has to harness them in order to develop common policies on asylum, immigration and border controls. Those differences are essentially rooted in national societies who differ as regards their humanitarian traditions, their demand for legal migration or their security interests. Much more than the internal market, the AFSJ has to cope with political interests and value choices.

3.2 *Today: Upholding the Common Values and Mutual Trust*

The abolition of the pillar structure, at the latest, called for a new justification of the autonomous nature of EU law. The Court ruled that the EU itself is founded on common values, long before the failed Constitutional Treaty.[89] And yet, as we shall see, the recognition in primary law of common values has spurred a new line of jurisprudence on the autonomy of the EU legal order. *Opinion 2/13* on the accession to the ECHR constitutes the building block in this regard. The Court ruled on the foundations of the EU legal order of which 'a structured network of principles, rules and mutually interdependent legal relations'[90] is but the outward expression.

> This [autonomous] legal structure [of the EU and EU law] is based on the fundamental premiss that each Member State shares with all the other Member States, and recognises that they share with it, a set of common values on which the EU is founded, as stated in Article 2 TEU. That premiss implies and justifies the existence of mutual trust between the Member States that those values will be recognised and, therefore, that the law of the EU that implements them will be respected.[91]

In essence, legal autonomy is justified by the common values on which the EU is founded, and those values imply and justify the existence of mutual trust between the Member States. It thus seems as if the unity of common values has substituted the unity of the internal market. However, the economic and

87 *Opinion 2/13* (*Accession to the ECHR*) EU:C:2014:2454, para 172.
88 Ibid.
89 Case 294/83 *Les Verts* EU:C:1986:166, para 23.
90 *Opinion 2/13* (n 87) para 167.
91 Ibid para 168.

political constitution of the EU are not comparable because the former encompasses both the objective and the means: according to the 27, the EU institutions shall establish an internal market by removing national obstacles to trade. Substantive and institutional independence from the Member States is required for this purpose.[92] In comparison, the recognition of common values on which the EU is founded has no effect whatsoever on the meaning attributed to them in different epistemic contexts. It therefore appears questionable to justify autonomy by reference to common values.

However, the quoted passage suggests that mutual trust is justified only to the extent the Member States, in their capacity as members of the Council, have implemented the common values in the form of legally binding rules of EU law.[93] The common values thus find expression in and through the autonomous characteristics of the EU and of EU law. In this sense, the principle of autonomy is justified by the common values on which the EU is founded. But as much as legislative rules are a political compromise, so are the values on which they are based. In other words, the Member States have surmounted the pluralism of values only insofar as necessary to adopt rules on matters of common concern. This implies that they do not owe a duty of mutual trust to one another in the absence of common rules.[94] Similarly, mutual trust is at least under pressure where EU law leaves ample room for expressing national values. But insofar as there are limits to mutual trust, there are limits to the autonomy of the EU legal order as well. The latter is thus relative rather than absolute. The following will test this hypothesis, focussing on the value of the rule of law. The reasons for this are twofold: the rule of law encompasses the principles of legality and effective judicial protection, and these are essential to the frame of the *Rechtsgemeinschaft* as explained in the previous chapter. Hence, the EU legal order is not empowering unless it also limits the exercise of power so as to preclude mutual interference. In addition, the rule of law has been the subject of a series of leading judgments on, in particular, controversial reforms of the Polish and Hungarian judicial systems. While a full

92 In this regard, Barents' argument is still valid.

93 See also Cecilia Rizcallah, *The Principle of Mutual Trust in European Union Law* (Bruylant 2022) 205.

94 A contrario, where common rules do exist and the presumption of equivalent fundamental rights protection is in fact met, mutual trust will be a 'driver of integration' because of the obligations it entails, see Cristina Sáenz Pérez, 'Mutual Trust as a Driver of Integration: Which Way Forward?' in Katja S Ziegler et al. (eds), *Research Handbook on General Principles in EU Law: Constructing Legal Orders in Europe* (Elgar 2022) 530, 534ff.

discussion of this topic is beyond the scope of this book,[95] some aspects of it tell a lot about the meaning of EU membership.

As a preliminary point, one may validly ask why something so fundamental like the value of the rule of law gives rise to controversies. The prior question is why we the Europeans consider the rule of law to be fundamental in the first place. It is because of the way it is represented by the authorities acting on our behalf. Asked whether he ever contemplated leaving the EU, the Hungarian Prime Minister Viktor Orbán gave the following answer to a German newspaper:

> No never. Thirty years ago there was a dictatorship here, and Hungary was part of the Soviet Union's sphere of influence. My companions and I sacrificed years of our lives to change that. We brought down the communists. *Rule of man*, which is communism, has been replaced by *rule of law*. We are the street fighters, the revolutionaries of the rule of law. And we thought that if we overthrew the communists, then we would enter into an alliance with the western countries that were united in the EU. This is not a political programme, this is our life. How could I step out of my own life?[96]

In a few sentences, the Hungarian Prime Minister represents a unity based on the rule of law. He attributes it to post-communist Hungary and implicitly to the (Western) Member States and to the EU. The rule of law is even said to define his personal identity. On his own account, he is now the embodiment (*Verkörperung*) of the rule of law after having made sacrifices in the fight against communism. Orbán represents a particular material conception of the rule of law, closely related to his understanding of justice. Despite potential overlap, it is useful to distinguish such a material (thick) from a formal (thin) understanding.[97] Under a formal conception, it is commonplace to subject every exercise of public authority to law. The risk of arbitrariness is reduced where the holder of official authority is bound by legal rules and procedures whose content is informed by general principles of law such as legality, legitimate expectations and legal certainty. The purpose of the formal conception is to effectuate the law in accordance with the legal order, even if the contents

95 Instead of many, see Mark Tushnet & Bojan Bugaric, *Power to the People: Constitutionalism in the Age of Populism* (OUP 2022) ch 4.

96 Giovanni di Lorenzo, 'Meine kleine Handgranate reicht dafür nicht' *DIE ZEIT* (25 November 2020) 7 (own translation).

97 See Teng-Chieh Yang, 'Eine starke oder eine schwache Konzeption der Rechtsstaatlichkeit? – Auch zur Problematik der Universalität der Rechtsstaatlichkeit' (2015) 54 Der Staat 375.

are immoral or unjust. This is what a material understanding seeks to avoid. On this view, the rule of law is closely connected to justice, solidarity, human rights and democracy. These are values underlying the legal order, which is thus a body of rules with an ethos. Every exercise of public authority requires justification in substantive terms.

Recent case law clarifies the meaning of the rule of law in the EU legal order. Of particular importance is the ruling in *Associação Sindical dos Juízes Portugueses* (*ASJP*) because the Court has, for the first time, asserted itself over the judicial system of a Member State in a matter potentially outside the scope of EU law.[98] In a preliminary reference from the Portuguese Supreme Administrative Court, the Court was asked to ascertain whether the principle of judicial independence, enshrined in the second subparagraph of Article 19(1) TEU and Article 47 of the Charter, precludes general salary-reduction measures from being applied to the members of a national judiciary. In the case at hand, Portugal temporarily reduced the remuneration of judges and other employees working in the public sector in order to comply with EU financial assistance conditionality. The Trade Union of Portuguese Judges (the ASJP) brought the national proceedings on behalf of the members of the Court of Auditors.

Following the Opinion of the Advocate General, it was expected that the ruling would further clarify the applicability of the Charter to austerity measures connected to EU law.[99] To this end, it would have been necessary to determine whether the salary reduction measures were a purposeful implementation of EU austerity policies, despite the leeway afforded to Portugal to reduce its excessive budgetary deficit. There are additional factors which help to establish a link between a national measure and a particular provision of EU law.[100] However, the Court reformulated the preliminary question,[101] focussing exclusively on the second subparagraph of Article 19(1) TEU which reads: 'Member States shall provide remedies sufficient to ensure effective legal protection in the fields covered by Union law.' Surprisingly, the Court found this obligation to be applicable irrespective of whether the Member States are implementing Union law within the meaning of Article 51(1) of the Charter.[102] The Court

98 Case C-64/16 *Associação Sindical dos Juízes Portugueses* EU:C:2018:117 (henceforth: 'ASJP').

99 Opinion of AG Saugmandsgaard Øe in *ASJP* EU:C:2017:395, paras 43–53; see also Chapter 1.4.3.

100 Case C-198/13 *Julian Hernández and Others* EU:C:2014:2055, para 37.

101 See Matteo Bonelli & Monica Claes, 'Judicial Serendipity: How Portuguese Judges Came to the Rescue of the Polish Judiciary' (2018) 14(3) EuConst 622, 628ff, who explain the Court's unexpected reasoning with the rule of law crisis in Poland and Hungary.

102 *ASJP* (n 98) para 29.

eventually concluded that Member States are obliged to ensure that any court or tribunal who may rule on the interpretation or application of EU law meets the requirements of effective judicial protection including judicial independence.[103] In this way, matters concerning the organisation of the judiciary will be subject to EU judicial review, whilst not falling with the scope of EU law as traditionally understood. Hence, it is sufficient if there is a functional as opposed to a substantive link with EU law.[104] Accused of interfering with the national administration of justice, the Court classified *ASJP* into a well-established line of case law requiring that any exercise of national competences must not violate EU law.[105] This should not detract from the remarkable reasoning, with the principle of autonomy at the very basis.[106]

The Court began by reformulating the principle from *Opinion 2/13*: mutual trust, in particular among national courts and tribunals, is based on the fundamental premiss that Member States share common values including the rule of law. The latter finds 'concrete expression'[107] in Article 19 TEU, according to which both the CJEU and national courts and tribunals are responsible for ensuring judicial review. Member States are therefore obliged, by virtue of Article 4(3) TEU, to establish a system of legal remedies and procedures ensuring effective judicial review in the fields covered by EU law. This obligation is not only contained in Article 19 TEU but also in the general principle of effective judicial protection, stemming from the constitutional traditions common to the Member States, from the ECHR and which is now reaffirmed in Article 47 of the Charter. After having underlined that effective judicial review is essential to the rule of law, the Court held that any court or tribunal who may be called on to interpret or apply EU law must fulfil the requirements of effective judicial protection. These are 'courts or tribunals' within the meaning of Article 267 TFEU, who thus form part of the EU judicial system. Judicial independence is indeed one of the conditions a national court or tribunal must satisfy in order to send preliminary questions to Luxembourg. However, so far EU law had not attached any consequence to a failure to meet this condition other than the exclusion of the relevant court or tribunal from the preliminary ruling procedure. The ruling in *ASJP* transformed judicial independence into a primary law obligation derived from Article 19 TEU.[108] Indeed, according to the

103 Ibid paras 40–41; clarified in Case C-619/18 *Commission* v *Poland* (Independence of the Supreme Court) EU:C:2019:531, para 51.

104 See Bonelli & Claes (n 101) 631.

105 *Commission* v *Poland*, para 52.

106 *ASJP* (n 98) paras 30ff.

107 Ibid para 32.

108 See Bonelli & Claes (n 101) 633–634.

Court, Article 47 of the Charter merely confirms that a national court or tribunal must be independent in order for judicial protection to be effective. That is to say, Article 47 of the Charter is merely ancillary to the reasoning. The Court rather underlined that judicial independence is essential to the proper working of the preliminary ruling procedure. This explains why the precise meaning of independence is to be found in previous case law on Article 267 TFEU.

The reasoning is succinct and complex, not making it readily apparent why Article 19(1) TEU enshrines the requirement of judicial independence without express wording to that effect. Indeed, the Advocate General argued that the obligation to provide remedies sufficient to ensure effective legal protection is procedural in nature, different from the material requirement of judicial independence expressly contained in Article 47 of the Charter.[109] It is submitted that the value of the rule of law, in conjunction with other provisions, underpinned the systematic-teleological reasoning of the Court. This was possible precisely because the rule of law lies at the foundation of the EU legal order. Hence, the procedural obligation in Article 19(1) TEU was supplemented with a material one, and the scope was extended to include any national court or tribunal who could de facto act as a court of the Union. While not explicitly stated, Article 4(3) TEU is another expression of the rule of law, obliging Member States to ensure that EU law is applied and enforced. The value-based interpretation in turn led to a specification of the value of the rule of law. It is a particular formal-material conception, meaning that both dimensions are interrelated. Judicial independence is not only a fundamental right of individuals necessary to effectively rely on rights or interests conferred by EU law; it is also a tool to ensure the functioning of the preliminary ruling procedure.

At a higher level of abstraction, it is useful to unpack the formal-material conception into a rule of EU law and the EU rule of law,[110] each of which is informed by the principle of autonomy. The rule of EU law relates back to Barents' analysis. It is essentially concerned with the autonomous structure of the EU legal order vis-à-vis the Member States. In particular, the preliminary ruling procedure ensures the uniform interpretation and application of EU law over conflicting national law. It is also a mechanism to develop EU law in and through the autonomous structure of that system. Hence, the provisions

---

109 Opinion of AG Saugmandsgaard Øe in *ASJP* (n 87), paras 57–67.

110 Compare the classification in Monica Claes & Matteo Bonelli, 'The Rule of Law and the Constitutionalisation of the European Union' in Werner Schroeder (ed), *Strengthening the Rule of Law in Europe: From a Common Concept to Mechanisms of Implementation* (OUP 2016) 269–279 (the rule of EU law; the rule of law at the EU level; the rule of law in the Member States).

of EU law mutually reinforce each other from within, like Baron Munchausen who was pulling himself out of the swamp by his own hair. *ASJP* is but one example of self-referential reasoning,[111] which is prone to foreclose external scrutiny.[112] But whereas the EU is still not subject to the ECHR and the jurisprudence of the Strasbourg Court, the Luxembourg Court has been developing an internal material conception of the EU rule of law, spurred by the Charter of Fundamental Rights. Again, it is contingent on the autonomous structure of the EU legal order, corresponding to the internal perspective of a collective self. The general principle of effective judicial protection, now reaffirmed in Article 47 of the Charter, is a case in point. It is closely related to the principle of effectiveness, the purpose of which is not the protection of individual rights but the effective enforcement of EU law before national courts.[113] More generally, the purpose of EU fundamental rights protection is to avoid a situation in which the level of protection afforded by the Member States varies in such a way as to undermine 'the unity, primacy and effectiveness of EU law'.[114]

It follows that material conceptions are (purely) idealist if they are not (also) functional to the EU legal order. In other words, the frame of this particular legal order explains the meaning attributed to the rule of law. It was not by coincidence that the Court in *ASJP* began by recalling that common values imply and justify the existence of mutual trust between the Member States. Fulfilment of the requirements of effective judicial protection generates mutual trust since it is essential to the uniform and effective application of Union law. And the latter is the guarantee of mutual non-interference, which constitutes the very purpose of the EU legal order. Conversely, courts or tribunal outside the EU judicial system may be a source of distrust. This is the case when other legal orders exclude the Court of Justice from dispute settlement on matters relating to the interpretation or application of Union law. The

111 See Armin Von Bogdandy & Luke Dimitrios Spieker, 'Countering the Judicial Silencing of Critics: Article 2 TEU Values, Reverse Solange, and the Responsibilities of National Judges' (2019) 15(3) EuConst 391, 413ff. More in general, see also Marcus Klamert, 'The Autonomy of the EU (and of EU Law): Through the Kaleidoscope' (2017) 42(6) European Law Review 815, 817–819 (with further references).

112 See Dimitry Kochenov, 'EU Law Without the Rule of Law: Is the Veneration of Autonomy Worth It?' (2015) 34(1) YEL 74, 83ff. However, in view of the recent case law discussed in this section, it can no longer be maintained that art 2 TEU is neither specific (specifiable) nor enforceable.

113 See Michael Dougan, 'The Vicissitudes of Life at the Coalface: Remedies and Procedures for Enforcing Union Law before the National Courts' in Paul Craig & Gráinne de Búrca, *The Evolution of EU Law* (OUP 2011).

114 *Julian Hernández and Others* (n 100) para 47.

exclusion of the Court undermines the autonomy of the EU legal order and, by implication, mutual trust between the Member States.[115] The same applies, mutatis mutandis, when the EU legal order excludes national courts and tribunals not meeting the requirements of effective judicial protection. The Court reaffirmed the principles from *ASJP* in the context of judicial cooperation in criminal matters.[116] Hence, judicial independence is necessary to maintain mutual trust, without which the system of judicial cooperation would break down.[117]

---

115 See *Opinion 2/13* (n 87) paras 193–194. The ECHR would have required Member States to check each other's compliance with fundamental rights in situations where EU law imposes an obligation of mutual trust. In order to preclude an external legal regime from becoming a source of distrust, the relations between the Member States as regards matters falling with the scope of EU law must, in principle, be governed exclusively by the EU legal order. See also Case C-284/16 *Achmea* EU:C:2018:158, concerning the compatibility with arts 267 and 344 TFEU of an arbitration clause in a bilateral investment treaty (BIT) between the Netherlands and Slovakia. Disputes falling within the scope of the BIT were to be referred to an arbitral tribunal who could, according to the Court, rule on the interpretation and application of EU law without being a 'court or tribunal' within the meaning of that law. It could therefore not make a reference to the CJEU, and judicial review at national level was severely limited by the applicable law. This was liable to frustrate the 'full effectiveness of EU law' (para 56). The Court indicated that violating the principle of autonomy has adverse effects on mutual trust between the Member States (para. 58). See, in this regard, Jens Hillebrand Pohl, 'Intra-EU Investment Arbitration After the *Achmea* Case: Legal Autonomy Bounded by Mutual Trust?' (2018) 14(4) EuConst 767, 788–789. In his view, paragraph 58 of the judgment supports the argument that the principle of autonomy is delimited by the principle of mutual trust (ibid 781). In other words, an interpretation or application of EU law by a body outside the EU judicial system is contrary to the principle of autonomy only insofar as the principle of mutual trust is thereby called into question. I fully agree and add that *ASJP* lends further support to this argument outside the context of investment arbitration. But see Cristina Contartese & Mads Andenas, 'EU Autonomy and Investor-State Dispute Settlement under *Inter Se* Agreements Between EU Member States: *Achmea*' (2019) 56(1) CML Rev 157, 165–168, who argue that the interpretation or application raises a concern if, inter alia, it is binding on the EU institutions, with no mention of mutual trust.

116 Case C-216/18 PPU *LM* EU:C:2018:586, paras 49–58.

117 But note that art 47 of the Charter rather than art 19 TEU was the standard of review in *LM* (para 62). This is not to refute the present argument. Article 47 of the Charter was instrumental to maintain the individual risk assessment a national court must carry out when executing a European Arrest Warrant (EAW) if there are substantial grounds for believing that the person concerned would run a real risk of breach of the fundamental right to a fair trial on account of general or systemic deficiencies concerning the independence of the judiciary in the Member State that issued the EAW. Without art 47 and the individual risk assessment, the Court would have lowered significantly the threshold for refusing the surrender of criminal suspects to Member States with a deficient justice system. This could have amounted to the collapse of the EAW system, see Mattias Wendel, 'Mutual

This interpretation has been confirmed in the more recent *Conditionality Judgments* on the legality of a regulation establishing a horizontal conditionality mechanism that subjects the disbursement of EU funds to respect for the value of the rule of law in the Member States.[118] In examining if Article 322 TFEU is the appropriate legal basis for the contested regulation, the CJEU addressed the argument that requiring respect for the value of the rule of law, rather than for a more specific condition such as respect for EU financial programs, falls outside the scope of 'financial rules' as referred to in that Article.[119] Rejecting the argument, the Court recalled – citing, amongst others, its ruling in *ASJP* – that the autonomous legal structure of the EU is based on the fundamental premiss that the Member States share a set of common values on which the EU is founded, as stated in Article 2 TEU. That premiss implies and justifies the existence of mutual trust between the Member States that those values will be recognised and, therefore, that the law of the EU that implements them will be respected. As respect for the common values is not just a condition of accession to the Union but must be ensured also thereafter, the EU must be able to defend, subject to the principle of conferral, the common values which 'define the very identity of the EU as a common legal order'.[120] The EU is competent to defend the value of the rule of law by means of its financial rules since breaches of the rule of law are liable to compromise the financial interests of the Union and, in a more fundamental sense, mutual trust among the Member States and thus the foundation of the EU as such.[121]

Nonetheless, determining the scope of a competence norm by reference to an open-ended foundational norm such as Article 2 TEU bears the risk of overstretching the limits of EU competences. In this regard, the Court held that the possibilities for EU interference are limited to certain situations and measures specified in the contested regulation, ensuring a sufficiently direct relationship between the alleged breach of the rule of law and the sound financial management of the Union budget or the financial interests of the EU.[122]

Trust, Essence and Federalism – Between Consolidating and Fragmenting the Area of Freedom, Security and Justice after *LM*' (2019) 15(1) EuConst 17, 26–32, 45.

118 Case C-156/21 *Hungary* v *European Parliament and Council* EU:C:2022:97; Case C-157/21 *Poland* v *European Parliament and Council* EU:C:2022:97. The following references are based on the Hungarian case.

119 Ibid paras 123–133.

120 Ibid para 127.

121 For criticism of this systematic-teleological reasoning, see Ferdinand Weber, 'The Pluralism of Values in an Identity-Framed Verbund: Federal Belonging in the European Union after the Rule of Law Conditionality Judgments' (2022) 47(4) European Law Review 514.

122 Ibid paras 134–153.

Furthermore, the regulation refers to CJEU jurisprudence deriving certain legal principles from the value of the rule of law, containing specific legal obligations Member States are bound to respect.[123] Like in *ASJP*, the Court thus confirmed that the value of the rule of law has been specified within the autonomous structure of the EU legal order. However, it seemed to be interested in overcoming its self-referential reasoning to a certain extent, holding that 'the obligation relating to respect for the rule of law (...) is a specific expression of the requirements *resulting, for the Member States, from their membership of the European Union*, pursuant to Article 2 TEU.'[124] Hence, the Court connected respect for the rule of law as a common EU value to the sovereign decision to join the Union.[125] This opens theoretical space for a membership lens that is broader than legal compliance alone, encompassing responsibilities for the Union and the distinct European nation states.[126] As will be argued in the next sub-section, it is thus legal to interpret the common values according to the national political imagination, provided the specific requirements flowing from EU law are respected. But these are rather rigid because of their embeddedness into an autonomous legal order with its own (functional) logic.[127]

3.3 *Interim Conclusion*

This section defended the hypothesis that the principle of autonomy is not justified insofar as there are limits to mutual trust between the Member States, and mutual trust is limited to the degree by which the values listed in Article 2 TEU have been specified by principles and rules of EU law. Following the ruling in *ASJP*, the requirement of judicial independence is one (though not the only) specification of the value of the rule of law. It is a formal-material specification since the material rights dimension is inextricable from the functioning of the EU legal order. The Member States must trust each other in upholding the independence of their judiciary and ensuring, more generally, the functioning

123 Ibid para 236.

124 Ibid para 231.

125 See also Case C-621/18 *Wightman* EU:C:2018:999.

126 Similarly, see Alun Gibbs, 'Common Values, Europe's Indeterminate Nature and Enduring Sovereignty' in Avbelj (n 60) 27.

127 See Armin Cuyvers, 'The Legal Space for Structural Differentiation in the EU: Reciprocity, Interconnectedness and Effectiveness as Sources of Constitutional Rigidity' (2022) 7(3) European Papers 1165; Weber (n 121) 527ff.

of the decentralised EU judicial system. This is the prerequisite for the uniform and effective application of EU law, making sure that Member States do not unilaterally exercise power over one another. The principle of autonomy is thus justified insofar as the EU institutions specify the conditions for mutual non-interference. Specification is inevitable, for it would be otherwise impossible to ensure the uniformity and effectiveness of EU law, and mutual trust between the Member States would vanish. It is mutual trust in and through the autonomous structure of the EU legal order. It has been demonstrated that the value of the rule of law maintains, to a certain degree, the self-referentiality of the system: it justifies the autonomy of the EU legal order insofar as it has been operationalised through rules and principles of EU law, which are enforced in the name of the rule of law.

That is not to say that the value of the rule of law in Article 2 TEU has no legal effect unless it has been somehow implemented. It has legal effects in the intermediate sphere where the Court no longer enjoys a monopoly on its autonomous interpretation. The Court itself seemed to suggest this in the *Conditionality Judgments*, recognising that the Member States are (also) sovereign nation states who once had the political will to accede to a Union founded on the rule of law. This value may thus be the point of reference for a European constitutional discourse among 27 collective selves. The purpose is not to overcome the differences and to strengthen the EU rule of law. This may be the outcome if the Court rejects a certain representation in the intermediate sphere and forces the Member State concerned back into the sphere of the Treaties. The purpose is rather to promote political reflexivity in the Union. Knowing that the EU legal order will defend the common purpose of peaceful co-existence, the 27 will be more ready to accept that each of them may assume responsibility for the common whole. The EU legal order is a site of empowerment precisely because it upholds mutual trust between the Member States. Mutual trust is even likely to grow when the 27 act on behalf of the Union. They will realise that different value conceptions are not necessarily a ground for exclusion, but for inclusion into a wider, political notion of EU membership.

The foregoing paves the way for exploring solidarity in EU migration management. The next section will argue that solidarity is not a cosmopolitan principle but a component of the EU rule of law. In addition, it is a political principle informing national contributions to the common purpose of migration management. This will be illustrated, in the section thereafter, with the cooperation between Italy and the EU on the one part, and Libya on the other.

4 Solidarity and the Common Purpose of Migration Management

4.1 *The Concept of Solidarity*

The Treaties give expression to solidarity in several provisions, most fundamentally in the preamble[128] and in the second sentence of Article 2 TEU according to which the common values, listed in the first sentence, are common to the Member States in a society in which, inter alia, solidarity prevails. This provision neither clarifies whether the scope is national or transnational, nor whether the nature of solidarity is ethical, political or legal. One could argue that the entire Article 2 TEU lays down the fundamental values of the EU, constitutive of a European identity,[129] and solidarity is thus an integral part thereof.[130] Or one could unpack the provision into several categories of values. Cliteur argues that democracy and the rule of law are the constitutional tools to realise freedom and equality, which serve the final purpose of human dignity; whereas solidarity, alongside the other values listed in the second sentence, is a contemporary ideal of justice.[131] This comes close to considering solidarity as a political principle. It is thus the source of political rather than legal obligations. Klamert argues that the former contain an ideal of what Union membership should entail, whereas legally binding, enforceable obligations are derived from other principles and rules of EU law.[132] In stark contrast, Moreno-Lax approaches solidarity through a cosmopolitan lens, submitting that it structurally underpins the EU legal order as a meta-principle or general principle of law.[133] This classification implies that, in her opinion, solidarity

128 It reads: 'Desiring to deepen the solidarity between their peoples while respecting their history, their culture and their traditions.'

129 See Jan Wouters, 'Revisiting Art. 2 TEU: A True Union of Values?' (2020) 5(1) European Papers 255, 258–259.

130 This is what the preamble of the EU Charter of Fundamental Rights says: '[T]he Union is founded on the indivisible, universal values of human dignity, freedom, equality and solidarity.' See also Eglė Dagilytė, 'Solidarity: A General Principle of EU Law? Two Variations on the Solidarity Theme' in Andrea Biondi et al. (eds), *Solidarity in EU Law – Legal Principle in the Making* (Elgar 2018) 71–75.

131 See Paul Cliteur, 'Strengthening the Rule of Law Within the Union: Some Advice to Break the Deadlock' in Afshin Ellian & Raisa Blommestijn (eds), *Reflections on Democracy in the European Union* (Eleven 2020) 167, 169.

132 Marcus Klamert, *The Principle of Loyalty in EU Law* (OUP 2014), 35–41; more detailed and with regard to recent case law in EU energy law, see Marcus Klamert, 'Loyalty and Solidarity as General Principles' in Ziegler et al. (n 94) 122, 128–129.

133 Violeta Moreno-Lax, 'Solidarity's Reach: Meaning, Dimension and Implications for EU (External) Asylum Policy' (2017) 24(5) Maastricht Journal of European and Comparative Law 740.

has legal effects on the validity, interpretation and application of the entire body of EU law.[134] However, according to the majority of doctrinal writings, solidarity is indeed a legal principle, yet falling short of general application.[135] The various expressions of solidarity in EU law differ in terms of their nature, scope and legal effects. It is indeed difficult to infer a general principle of EU law from specific (legal or political) solidarity obligations in fields as diverse as citizenship, foreign policy and migration management. The latter is of particular interest for our purposes. Article 80 TFEU stipulates:

> The policies of the Union set out in this Chapter [on border checks, asylum and immigration] and their implementation shall be governed by the principle of solidarity and fair sharing of responsibility, including its financial implications, between the Member States. Whenever necessary, the Union acts adopted pursuant to this Chapter shall contain appropriate measures to give effect to this principle.

This or any other variation cannot be understood unless one reflects upon the concept of solidarity as such. Indeed, it seems impossible to elucidate the inter-state dimension as foreseen by Article 80 TFEU, without appreciating the national contexts in which solidarity has been flourishing. And any kind of national solidarity as we know it today, for example in sharing the costs and benefits of social security, is partially rooted in political thought prior to the emergence of the nation state. Elaborating on the rich history of political thought, Borger concludes that solidarity mediates between the collective and the individual.[136] The modern mechanisms or meanings attributed to solidarity obviously differ from the more ancient ones insofar as each account has to be located in historical time. But thinkers like Aristotle and Rousseau share the

---

134 Ibid 747.

135 See Peter Hilpold, 'Understanding Solidarity Within EU Law: An Analysis of the "Islands of Solidarity" with Particular Regard to Monetary Union' (2015) 34(1) YEL 257; Jürgen Bast, 'Deeping Supranational Integration: Interstate Solidarity in EU Migration Law' (2016) 22(2) European Public Law 289, 293–294, 302 (who seems to observe the emergence of a general principle); Esin Küçük, 'Solidarity in EU Law – An Elusive Political Statement or a Legal Principle with Substance?' (2016) 23(6) Maastricht Journal of European and Comparative Law 965; Daniel Thym & Evangelia Tsourdi, 'Searching for Solidarity in the EU Asylum and Border Policies: Constitutional and Operational Dimensions' (2017) 24(5) Maastricht Journal of European and Comparative Law 605, 608; Dagilytė (n 130) 75ff; Klamert, 'Loyalty and Solidarity as General Principles' (n 132) 132–134.

136 Vestert Borger, *The Currency of Solidarity: Constitutional Transformation During the Euro Crisis* (CUP 2020), 50–52. The remainder of this paragraph is based on ch 1 of his monograph.

belief in the social embeddedness of every individual. The collective presupposes individuals to exist; and individuals presuppose the collective in order to be free. Hence, individuals owe one another an obligation to maintain the collective to which they all belong. This obligation emanates from the collective whose existence is sui generis, so it cannot be collapsed into that of the individual members. The duty corresponds, at the same time, to their self-interest in realising personal freedom. Reciprocity and the common good are the forces that keep the mediating mechanisms going. In modern differentiated societies, individuals enter into reciprocal relationships in which each and every one has to contribute his or her share to the common good. In other words, individuals owe solidarity to one another because the common good is unattainable unless everyone (or the overwhelming majority) is committed to it.

Borger further explains that the mentioned obligation is political in nature.[137] Once persons (or states) act in concert, they incur a political obligation to maintain their association irrespective of whether they have, in addition, entered into any legally binding commitment. That is to say, a political obligation is derived from membership and not from contract. In conceptualising solidarity between the EU Member States, Borger makes a distinction between normative and factual solidarity. If reason requires a Member State to subordinate selfish interests to the common good, solidarity is normative. In comparison, factual solidarity accounts for the fact that even selfish interests may motivate action for the common good. This is particularly the case when Member States share a common destiny and the level of interdependence is high. His conceptualisation has significant implications for our understanding of EU law. Member States may incur a political obligation even when EU law is not formally enacted or amended, for example when the European Council issues strategic guidelines. The content of a political obligation cannot be reduced to the legal obligation to follow the rules. On the contrary, it might be necessary to stretch the boundaries of what the law permits in order to defend the common purpose of the Union. To recall a term used earlier in this chapter, a political obligation is a commitment to the Union lato sensu, and not just to the laws governing it. In other words, a political obligation is implemented in the intermediate sphere of the 27.

4.2 *Solidarity in the Inner Sphere*

Moving on to EU migration management, the remainder of this section will demonstrate how solidarity guides the Member States in moving from the

137 This paragraph relies on Borger (n 136) ch 2.

inner to the intermediate sphere. To understand what solidarity requires in the inner sphere of the Treaties, we need to consider the Court's ruling on the legality of mandatory relocation,[138] one of the few cases in which the Court attributed meaning to that principle in the field of EU asylum law. Brought by Slovakia and Hungary, the annulment actions concerned the validity of Council Decision 2015/1601/EU establishing a temporary relocation scheme for the benefit of Italy and Greece.[139] Adopted on the basis of Article 78(3) TFEU, the legal basis for emergency measures in case one or more Member States are confronted with a sudden inflow of third-country nationals, the Decision provided for the mandatory distribution of 160.000 protection seekers among the other Member States (except for those with an opt-out: the United Kingdom, Ireland and Denmark). It complemented Council Decision 2015/1523 which was based on the voluntary commitment of 22 Member States to relocate 40.000 persons in need of international protection.[140] In view of the migratory pressure at that time, voluntary relocation was soon considered insufficient, and Decision 2015/1601 was adopted by Qualified Majority Voting – against the will of the Czech Republic, Hungary, Romania and Slovakia (Finland abstained). Although the Court upheld the validity of the Decision, the Czech Republic, Hungary and Poland persistently refused to implement it. This led to infringement proceedings and to a declaration that these Member States failed to fulfil their obligations.[141] These lengthy rulings deal with diverse issues pertaining to EU asylum and institutional law, not all of which are relevant to the present inquiry.[142] Hence, the subsequent analysis will be selective, focussing on the annulment actions since it was in these proceedings that the Court interpreted the principle of solidarity.[143]

---

138 Joined Cases C-643/15 and C-647/15 *Slovakia and Hungary* v *Council* EU:C:2017:631.

139 Council Decision (EU) 2015/1601 of 22 September 2015 establishing provisional measures in the area of international protection for the benefit of Italy and Greece [2015] OJ L248/80.

140 Council Decision (EU) 2015/1523 of 14 September 2015 establishing provisional measures in the area of international protection for the benefit of Italy and of Greece [2015] OJ L239/146.

141 Joined Cases C-715/17, C-718/17 and C-719/17 *Commission* v *Poland, Hungary and Czech Republic* EU:C:2020:257.

142 For details, see Bruno de Witte & Evangelia Tsourdi, 'Confrontation on Relocation – The Court of Justice Endorses the Emergency Scheme for Compulsory Relocation of Asylum Seekers Within the European Union: *Slovak Republic and Hungary* v. *Council*' (2018) 55(5) CML Rev 1457.

143 Merely reaffirmed in the infringement proceedings, see *Commission* v *Poland, Hungary and Czech Republic* (n 141) para 80.

The first plea which is worth considering alleged that Article 78(3) TFEU was not a proper legal basis for the Decision. Slovakia and Hungary essentially argued that this legal basis provision does not entitle the Council to adopt a non-legislative act derogating from a legislative act under Article 78(2) TFEU. The applicants were referring to Article 13 of the Dublin Regulation stipulating that the Member State of first entry will be responsible for processing asylum applications. The Decision derogated from this rule by shifting responsibility from Greece and Italy to all the other Member States. This was arguably one of the more challenging pleas since it is indeed not unproblematic to use an emergency procedure, conferring on the European Parliament only a consultation right, to derogate from a rule adopted in accordance with the ordinary legislative procedure. Having found that Article 78(3) TFEU allows for the adoption of non-legislative acts,[144] the Court conducted a systematic-teleological interpretation of the term 'provisional measures' that may be adopted on that basis. The Court concluded that the term must be sufficiently broad, enabling the EU institutions to respond 'effectively and swiftly'[145] to a specific migration crisis. In comparison, the second paragraph of Article 78 TFEU empowers the EU institutions to take effective structural measures in the field of international protection, so both provisions are 'complementary'.[146] With that in mind, a non-legislative act derogating from a legislative act is in principle valid if the material and temporal scope of the derogation is limited.[147] A permanent or general derogation or amendment would circumvent the requirements of the ordinary legislative procedure. The contested Decision expired after two years, and it provided for the relocation of a limited number of asylum seekers. Therefore, the Court rejected this plea as unfounded.[148]

The second noteworthy plea alleged a breach of the principle of proportionality, according to which the content and form of Union action shall not exceed what is necessary to achieve the objectives of the Treaties.[149] The Court meticulously addressed the applicants' legal arguments as to whether the contested Decision was suitable and necessary, and whether it had disproportionate effects on Hungary. In the first place, the Grand Chamber relied on the principle of solidarity when adjudicating on Slovakia's plea that mandatory relocation was not necessary since the objective of relieving pressure on

144 *Slovakia and Hungary* v *Council* (n 138) para 66.
145 Ibid para 77.
146 Ibid para 74.
147 Ibid para 78.
148 Ibid paras 79–84.
149 Art 5(4) TEU.

Italy and Greece could have been attained by measures interfering less with national sovereignty: voluntary relocation as well as financial and operational support. As a preliminary observation, the intensity of judicial review was low because measures adopted under Article 78(3) TFEU involve complex political assessments that justify a wide margin of discretion. The Court will invalidate a measure only if it has been shown that the political institutions conducted a 'manifest error of assessment' in the sense that a less restrictive but equally effective measure could have been taken within the same period. The migratory pressure at the relevant time led the Court to find that mandatory relocation was proportionate. The principle of solidarity informed the reasoning as follows:

> In that regard, the Council, when adopting the contested decision, was in fact required, as is stated in recital 2 of the decision, to give effect to the principle of solidarity and fair sharing of responsibility (…) between the Member States, which applies, under Article 80 TFEU, when the EU common policy on asylum is implemented.[150]

In the second place, solidarity functioned as an interpretation guide when the Court was confronted with a plea submitted on behalf of Hungary, alleging that the contested Decision had disproportionate effects on the Hungarian asylum system in particular. That Member State should have been excluded from the scope of the Decision because it was facing an emergency itself. Having reiterated its previous case law according to which the EU legislature is not required to take into account the particular situation of individual Member States,[151] the Grand Chamber deduced the following rule from the principle of solidarity:

> When one or more Member States are faced with an emergency situation within the meaning of Article 78(3) TFEU, the burdens entailed by the provisional measures (…) must, as a rule, be divided between all the other Member States, in accordance with the principle of solidarity and fair sharing of responsibility between the Member States, since, in accordance with Article 80 TFEU, that principle governs EU asylum policy.[152]

The principle of solidarity is thus the source of a legally binding obligation, namely to share responsibility among all Member States when one of them

150 *Slovakia and Hungary* v *Council* (n 138) para 252.

151 Ibid para 290 (with a further reference).

152 Ibid para 291.

is confronted with a sudden inflow of third-country nationals in the sense of Article 78(3) TFEU. The Council gave effect to this primary law obligation through the adoption of the contested Decision. To choose the controversial burden-sharing instrument of mandatory relocation was in line with the wide margin of policy discretion. However, the Court only pronounced itself regarding the implementation of the solidarity principle under Article 78(3) TFEU. In how far that principle structurally governs the exercise of public authority in EU asylum and migration law is yet to be specified.[153]

Reviewing the jurisprudence about the situation in 2015/2016, Thym criticises the Court for not justifying its rulings in constitutional terms.[154] More specifically, the reasoning was rather administrative, seeking to uphold the integrity of EU law 'as an instrument of governance'[155] while being relatively silent on the normative values underpinning the common rules. Thym has analysed one of the reasons before, demonstrating the partial overlap of solidarity with other EU legal principles such as loyalty.[156] Codified in Article 4(3) TEU, loyalty has been called the principle of sincere cooperation since the Lisbon revision. It concerns the vertical as opposed to the horizontal dimension in Article 80 TFEU. The Member States have a positive obligation to fulfil their EU law obligations and a negative obligation to refrain from any measure which could jeopardise the attainment of the Union's objectives. Thym and Tsourdi argue that both principles are related but conceptually distinct. Solidarity is less an objective of EU integration than a safety net against the unravelling of the common European asylum system.[157] It thus complements the loyalty-based duty to effectively implement EU law in the sense of informing any solution to implementation problems such as financial and operational support.[158] Similarly, Küçük submits that loyalty corresponds with solidarity where the Member States give effect to their EU legal obligations, suggesting that in other cases, the nature and scope of solidarity is broader.[159] In any event, solidary obligations will remain ineffective if they are not accompanied by self-interest.[160] She seems to suggest that the EU legislature, in reforming the Dublin Regulation, should better reflect national interests, especially the

153 See also De Witte & Tsourdi (n 142) 1477–1480, 1493.

154 Daniel Thym, 'Judicial Maintenance of the Sputtering Dublin System on Asylum Jurisdiction: *Jafari*, *A.S.*, *Mengesteab* and *Shiri*' (2018) 55(2) CML Rev 549, 561–563.

155 Ibid 562.

156 Thym & Tsourdi (n 135) 612ff.

157 Ibid 606, 610; see also Bast (n 135) 296, 302–304.

158 Thym & Tsourdi (n 135) 614–615.

159 Küçük (n 135) 974.

160 Ibid 968–970, 973.

actual capacity of Member States to the exclusion of arbitrary criteria like geographical location.[161] Goldner Lang disagrees when writing that the worst case scenario for the future of EU asylum law would be if self-centred national interests dominated EU decision-making.[162] At the same time, she calls for solidarity which is apparently generated by EU law. She takes the view that a Member State violating the principle of loyalty weakens the incentive of other Member States to show solidarity, for example by assuming responsibility for refugee protection.[163] The former principle is not conceptually distinct but rather encompassed by what seems to be a wider spirit of solidarity.[164] "There can simply be no EU solidarity without loyalty to EU law."[165]

All these scholars approach solidarity from the internal perspective of the EU legal order. This is justified in view of the autonomous nature of that system. To recall, the autonomous structure of EU law and the EU legal order ensure that the common values are capable of having effect in the Member States insofar as they have been implemented through legally binding rules of EU law. This serves the final purpose of the Union: to safeguard peace and mutual non-interference. It has been demonstrated that the Court cannot represent just any ideal of the rule of law without losing sight of the common purpose. Hence, the formal dimension of the rule of law is strong, demanding that EU law in fact produces legal effects in every Member State. Solidarity is capable of adding a material dimension, still oriented towards the mentioned common good. The Court's relocation ruling demonstrates that, even though the reasoning is so succinct that the constitutional dimension is difficult to uncover. However, it can be argued that, in a migration crisis, all Member States are required to contribute their fair share (not per se limited to relocation), upholding a well-functioning common asylum system. Consequently, none of the Member States may decline to show solidarity in an emergency within the meaning of Article 78(3) TFEU without, at the same time, violating the legal duty to maintain the integrity of the EU legal order, as required by the principle of loyalty. Here, the obligation is both of a legal and political nature because defending the EU legal order is to uphold the common purpose. The former is

161 Esin Küçük, 'The Principle of Solidarity and Fairness in Sharing Responsibility: More Than Window Dressing?' (2016) 22(4) European Law Journal 448, 459–463.

162 Iris Goldner Lang, 'No Solidarity Without Loyalty: Why Do Member States Violate EU Asylum and Migration Law and What Can Be Done?' (2020) 22(1) European Journal of Migration and Law 39, 59.

163 Ibid 41.

164 Ibid (loyalty as an 'essential and inherent part of the principle of solidarity').

165 Ibid 58.

after all the structure through which the latter is represented, and the principle of solidarity is not a cosmopolitan principle requiring assistance to a Member State in need, but an integral part of that structure. In other words, it is a tool or a mechanism to uphold the common purpose of migration management.[166]

4.3 *Solidarity in the Intermediate Sphere*

The common purpose is, at the same time, the basis for moving into the intermediate sphere. Solidarity in the inner sphere, as explained in the previous sub-section, is indeed to some degree generated by the legal obligations flowing form the principle of loyalty. Furthermore, it gives expression to the political obligation derived from EU membership and the interdependence thereby maintained and promoted. This partially explains the 'spirit of solidarity'[167] to which, for example, Slovakia referred when arguing that mandatory relocation was not necessary in view of Decision 2015/1523, which gave effect to previous European Council conclusions stating that the Member States may honour their joint commitment by means of voluntary relocation as well as operational and financial support.[168] Some of these measures had been taken without being legally required by EU law, as we will see in the next section. In such moments, solidarity is coming 'from the heart',[169] at least according to the then President of the Commission.[170] Without ruling out altruism altogether, it is still more realistic to assume national self-interest as motivating force alongside the bond of Union membership. These elements of the collective self partially overlap insofar as Union membership has significantly increased the power of the 27 to defend their political existence. However, managing cross-border interdependence does not exhaust what it means to be German, Dutch or Slovakian. To better understand the common purpose of migration management, one has to look at it from another angle as well: external to the EU legal order but internal to the national collective self.

166 For a similar inward-looking interpretation, see Eleni Karageorgiou & Gregor Noll, 'What is Wrong with Solidarity in EU Asylum and Migration Law?' (2022) 4 Jus Cogens 131.

167 See the Opinion of AG Bot in in *Slovakia and Hungary* v *Council* EU:C:2017:618, para 249.

168 European Council, 'Conclusions' (Meeting of 25 and 26 June 2015) EUCO 22/15, para 4.

169 European Commission, 'State of the Union Address 2016: Towards a Better Europe – a Europe That Protects, Empowers and Defends' (Speech 14 September 2016) <https://ec.europa.eu/commission/presscorner/detail/en/SPEECH_16_3043> accessed 1 March 2024.

170 But see Moreno-Lax (n 133) 751, submitting that solidarity 'from the heart' is contrary to Art. 80 TFEU. This proposition is problematic for two reasons. First, it does not thoroughly consider what the Court actually ruled in the annulment actions about mandatory solidarity. Second, it is indifferent as to what motivates a Member State to act for the common European purpose.

Like any other public interest, migration management has a surface and a deep layer. The former encompasses the power of the state authorities to regulate migration. It has a political and a technocratic dimension. The political process determines the aims, rules and procedures, which form the legal basis for administrative decision-making on, for example, admission into the territory, the merits of asylum applications, and the negotiation and conclusion of international agreements regarding return and readmission. This broad definition underlines that the management of migration is – despite the semantics – a deeply political question in the sense that the state institutions need to weigh various competing interests.[171] On the one hand, there is the interest to free movement and individual protection as far as forced migration is concerned. It is true that international, European and national law protect persons fleeing from persecution or warfare, so national policy discretion is not absolute. But one would miss the important dimension of political will if the argument did not go further than stating that ratio and interdependence require a nation state to embed sovereignty into international cooperation.[172] On the other hand, one must therefore account for the interests of the political community into which immigration is taking place. Those interests are manifold; yet with regard to the surface layer, the continuous functioning of the state institutions is the most important one. Chapter 1 explained that the legal order is the guarantee of freedom and equality as long as it has the actual capacity to act for the common good. In other words, the correct application and enforcement of the law is empowering insofar as it stabilises expectations, which is the basis for individual liberty. This explains why, in every respect, migration requires regulation. The border of the state fulfils the most fundamental regulatory function.[173] Immigration may put pressure on the financial and administrative capacity of the state, with broader implications for the infrastructure, the social welfare system and the economy. Hence, regulating migration flows at the border or elsewhere seeks to uphold the capacity of the state to govern for the common good. However, this practical argument seems less convincing when considering the wide-spread policy of containing migration flows at

171 Daniel Thym, 'Steuerung der Migration im öffentlichen Interesse', in Georg Jochum et al.; *Grenzüberschreitendes Recht – Crossing Frontiers: Festschrift für Kay Hailbronner* (C F Müller 2013) 255–259; Klaus Ferdinand Gärditz, 'Die demokratische Gestaltungsverantwortung durch Recht in einer Einwanderungs-gesellschaft' (2017) 44(17–20) Europäische Grundrechte-Zeitschrift 516.

172 But see Anuscheh Farahat & Nora Markard, 'Forced Migration Governance: In Search of Sovereignty' (2016) 17(6) German Law Journal 923, 944–947.

173 This argument is based on Paul Scheffer, *De Vorm van Vrijheid* (De Bezige Bij 2018).

their source, far away from the European Union which is characterised by internal free movement anyway. While empirically correct, this counter-argument underestimates the political imagination. The border literally forms the polity by delineating an inside from an outside. It is therefore the precondition for any representation of unity to succeed. To recall, power will be legitimate if the addressees manage to attribute it to themselves. The border – though barely visible inside the EU – facilitates the identification of a polity, and the location of oneself in time and space.

It follows that the authorities are responsible for maintaining the functioning of the state, apart from honouring their international and European legal obligations. That is all the more necessary in times of crisis when they have to react to migration flows. Then it is a matter of regulating the inflow at the border, accommodating persons who have a right to enter the territory, allocating funds, and so forth. In normal circumstances, responsibility is to represent the deep layer of migration management. Law-making and application as such is not sufficient. In addition, it is inevitable to imagine and to represent a polity 'behind' the law.[174] Apart from affecting the functioning of the legal order, immigration is capable of influencing its political underpinnings, that is, anything which is deemed essential for the political existence. It has been mentioned that individual liberty is constitutive of liberal democracies, but not sufficient to explain the national bond.[175] Every person also wishes to belong somewhere, to be part of a common endeavour which surpasses his or her individual existence. Culture, tradition and social practices are both a vehicle for individual liberty and an intrinsic value of the political. Cultural defence is, according to Orgad, a legitimate justification for restrictive immigration law,[176] subject to a number of conditions.[177] One of them is to require that a certain cultural aspect is so fundamental that it belongs to the national constitutional identity.[178] This ties in with the argument made earlier according to which the national constitution is the political reservoir of the polity

174 See Martin Nettesheim, 'Migration im Spannungsfeld von Freizügigkeit und Demokratie' (2019) 144(3) Archiv des öffentlichen Rechts 358, 367–369, 407–411, who compares how different 'frames' (international, EU, German) imagine the migrating person. This presupposes an idea of the political community, which is underdeveloped in each frame.

175 See Chapter 2.2.

176 Liav Orgad, *The Cultural Defense of Nations – A Liberal Theory of Majority Rights* (OUP 2015) ch 5.

177 Ibid ch 6.

178 Ibid 217–218.

and, at the same time, the point of reference for evolution.[179] The purpose here is not to argue for or against a certain policy. It is rather to underline that immigration is an external trigger for an exercise in political reflexivity. The polity has to re-assure itself of who and what we are together, and to what extent the meaning of membership may evolve. At the very least, the policy should 'internalise' the interests of the migrating person who thereby becomes part of the political imagination. Only then will it be possible to govern migration and to design specific policies, whatever their political colour. It will mainly be current majorities in parliament who will represent the common good in light of international migration, and who are responsible for any decisions taken. Representation implies that policy-making is taking place with a prior understanding of the political. Consequently, immigration will and may bring about change as long as it does not undermine the self-recognition of the polity.[180] In other words, the wide policy discretion in managing migration will be exceeded if the majority cannot attribute the policy to itself.

Once identified in national democratic decision-making, the self-interest may correspond to the European common purpose or, more positively, the latter may be regarded as an integral part of the national collective self. In any event, a Member State may conclude that acting on behalf of the Union is what political will requires. In the judicial proceedings about mandatory relocation, any other form of solidarity was 'plainly irrelevant'[181] since the contested Decision simply did not provide for the option to substitute other contributions for relocation. This does not rule out the possibility that the same Member States – Hungary, Slovakia, Poland and the Czech Republic – fulfil what they consider to be a *political* obligation. The cooperation between Italy and Libya is a prominent example, which will be described in more detail below. The Visegrad Group, composed of the four mentioned Eastern European states, issued a letter to then Prime Minister of Italy, containing a particular representation of migration management:

> V4 countries are ready to meaningfully contribute in the spirit of solidarity to all European and national efforts aiming at alleviating the burden

179 See Chapter 2.2. and Daniel Thym, 'Verfassungspatriotismus in der Einwanderungsgesellschaft – Über die gesellschaftliche Breitenwirkung des Verfassungsrechts und kulturelle Parteinahme unter dem Grundgesetz' (2020) 145(1) Archiv des öffentlichen Rechts 40.

180 Similarly, Orgad (n 176) 198; Thym (n 179) 61–62, 67–70.

181 Opinion of AG Sharpston in *Commission* v *Poland, Hungary and Czech Republic* EU:C:2019:917, para 236.

> on frontline Member States such as Italy with financial and other contributions, in line with our general approach and our national capacities, with the exclusion of actions and instruments that may create further and stronger pull factors for migration, especially in relocation and compulsory and automated redistribution mechanism.[182]

The V4 countries in fact contributed 35 million euros to finance the Libyan Border and Coast Guard. The then President of the Commission, Jean-Claude Juncker, politically accepted their claim when stating that the contribution was proof 'that the Visegrad countries are fully aligned when it comes to solidarity with Italy and with others'.[183] However, political recognition does not necessarily imply social recognition in view of severe criticism from civil society.[184] In addition, legal recognition is equally uncertain because, in this context, the V4 countries did not support Italy in implementing EU law. On the contrary, Italy and Libya informally concluded a legally non-binding Memorandum of Understanding, which the Italian Parliament approved ex post facto. The following section will explain under what conditions (if at all), the 27 should be permitted to act on behalf of the Union as representatives in the intermediate sphere.

5 Moving between the Spheres (II): The Instrumental Dimension

This chapter has so far elaborated a *concept* according to which the Member States act on behalf of the common purpose of migration management. The next step is to explain the *means* which give practical relevance to the concept. In other words, if the Member States are to be conceptualised as representatives of the Union, it is inevitable to account for what they are doing and how. In the inner sphere, Member States are required to give effect to EU law as enacted in accordance with the Treaties. This obligation may encompass the entire policy-cycle of transposition, application and enforcement.

182 Visegrad Group, 'V4 Letter to the Prime Minister of Italy' (Letter 19 July 2017) <https://www.visegradgroup.eu/documents/official-statements/v4-letter-to-the-prime> accessed 1 March 2024.

183 Nikolaj Nielsen & Caterina Tani, 'Slovak PM: Human Rights are not a Travel Pass to EU' *EUobserver* (14 December 2017) <https://euobserver.com/migration/140291> accessed 1 March 2024.

184 With this caveat in mind, I continue to use the language of 'social recognition' consistent with Chapter 1.

A loyal, law-abiding Member State is at the same time a formal representative of the Union. But what if an action related to the common purpose of migration management has not been formally authorised by EU law? The Memorandum of Understanding between Italy and Libya is such a case. It concerns migration management in various dimensions including border controls and reception-capacity. The Italian Parliament authorised the mobilisation of financial resources after the then Prime Minister Paolo Gentiloni signed the Memorandum in February 2017. The members of the European Council endorsed the initiative and expressed their willingness, on behalf of the EU, to support Italy in implementing the MoU.[185] On this basis, the Commission set up a programme on integrated border and migration management in Libya, financed under the EU Trust Fund for Africa.[186] In accordance with EU law, the Commission delegated the task of implementing the programme to the Italian Ministry of Interior.[187]

The Memorandum thus illustrates the dispersal of power, potentially across all European spheres. Italy acts in the inner sphere insofar as it complies with all the requirements attached to the implementation of the EU-funded programme. But as far as the Memorandum as such is concerned, it is not prima facie certain whether the action is worthy of recognition in the intermediate sphere or whether it is just an expression of the national self-interest in the outer sphere. In any event, governance is the term used to describe, analyse and evaluate the interrelationship of various power-sites. The following will give an overview of how the literature conceptualises EU law and governance, which thus impacts on the relationship and movements in-between the European spheres. Generally, governance may be external or internal to EU law and the inner sphere of the Treaties.[188] In case of the former, it will entail shortcomings in terms of democracy and the rule of law (the gap thesis). In case of the latter, it may either change the traditional understanding of EU law

185 European Council, 'Malta Declaration by the Members of the European Council on the External Aspects of Migration: Addressing the Central Mediterranean Route' (Press Release 43/17, 3 February 2017) <https://www.consilium.europa.eu/en/press/press-releases/2017/02/03/malta-declaration/> accessed 1 March 2024, point 6(i).

186 European Commission, 'Action Fiche of the EU Trust Fund to be Used for the Decisions of the Operational Committee: Support to Integrated Border and Migration Management in Libya' (2017), T05-EUTF-NOA-LY-04 for the first phase ('Action Fiche 1') and T05-EUTF-NOA-LY-07 for the second phase ('Action Fiche 2').

187 Action Fiche 1 (n 186) 16 referring to art 58(1)(c) Regulation of 25 October 2012 on the financial rules applicable to the general budget of the Union [2012] OJ L298/1.

188 Based on Mark Dawson, 'New Modes of Governance' in Dennis Patterson & Anna Södersten (eds); *A Companion to European Union Law and International Law* (Wiley 2016).

(the transformation thesis) or it will remain conceptually distinct but actually complementary to Union law (the hybridity thesis). Each of these conceptualisations will be addressed in turn, with the MoU as a practical example and against the background of wider trends in EU migration management.

5.1 *The Relationship between Law and Governance*

According to the *gap thesis*, governance is a departure from EU law as traditionally understood.[189] The latter is typically seen as a hierarchical system of universally applicable rules, enacted in accordance with the Treaties and subject to the jurisdiction of the CJEU. Governance is at least a variation of EU law- and policy-making insofar as the Member States have more leeway to elaborate substantive standards. This means that EU law stipulates open-ended norms to be specified and implemented at national, regional or local level. Those standards are flexible and revisable to account for changing circumstances such as new knowledge of environmental degradation, economic development or migration flows. Governance is a deviation from EU law- and policy-making insofar as it replaces the procedures foreseen by the Treaties. Public international law is one prominent fallback option, allowing Member States to conclude international agreements of a political or technical nature.[190] Italy opted for this instrument when it concluded the Memorandum of Understanding with Libya.

The MoU reveals a gap insofar as the Treaties do not provide for the negotiation and conclusion of a non-binding international agreement by a Member State. The gap thus refers to the nature and status of the Memorandum whereas, in terms of substance, Italy has assumed similar commitments under the MoU and the EU Trust Fund. In practice, Italy might manage EU funds under the bilateral arrangement with Libya, as suggested by a complaint brought before the EU Court of Auditors.[191] Hence, the gap implies a serious accountability challenge because mechanisms to hold executive actors to account are not necessarily available at every site where authority is exercised. The Memorandum reflects a wider trend in EU migration management, especially in the external

189 The following is based on Joanne Scott & David M Trubek, 'Mind the Gap: Law and New Approaches to Governance in the European Union' (2002) 8(1) European Law Journal 1.

190 See Chapter 1.4.3.

191 Global Legal Action Network et al., 'Complaint to the European Court of Auditors Concerning the Mismanagement of EU Funds by the EU Trust Fund for Africa's "Support to Integrated Border and Migration Management in Libya" (IBM) Programme' <http://aa76854664da4e33.filesusr.com/ugd/14ee1a_ae6a20e6b5ea4b00b0aa0e77ece91241.pdf> accessed 1 March 2024, point 39.

dimension. In this context, legally non-binding instruments have been criticised for their lack of transparency, the exclusion of the European Parliament and the shortcomings in securing effective judicial protection for the benefit of third-country nationals.[192]

The *transformation thesis* tries to fill the gap by re-thinking legal concepts like accountability, participation and judicial review.[193] Scholars of experimental governance reconfigure law as providing a procedural framework for the elaboration of substantive norms. Law could also function as a negative incentive, meaning that prescriptive rules follow in case of non-compliance (penalty default). Accountability transforms into a dynamic variant in the sense that the principal evaluates how well the agent is reacting to changing circumstances. What is less relevant is to monitor compliance with detailed substantive requirements because on this view, it is doubtful whether hierarchical, pre-defined rules meet the demands of policy complexity, strategic uncertainty and political contestation. Overall, the transformation thesis underlines the instrumental function of law, which is a means to a 'common, albeit somewhat indeterminate project'.[194]

Since 2015/2016, the public discourse on migration management has been characterised by a similar emphasis on effective outcomes. For example, the increasing number of arrivals via the Central Mediterranean prompted the members of the European Council to step up cooperation with Libya and other transit countries. One of their priorities was to train, equip and support the Libyan Coast Guard and to complement the efforts of individual Member

---

192 See eg Jorrit Rijpma, 'External Migration and Asylum Management: Accountability for Executive Action Outside EU-Territory' (2017) 2(2) European Papers 571; Thomas Spijkerboer, 'Bifurcation of People, Bifurcation of Law: Externalisation of Migration Policy before the Court of Justice' (2017) 31(2) Journal of Refugee Studies 216; Paul James Cardwell, 'Tackling Europe's Migration "Crisis" Through Law and "New Governance" (2018) 9(1) Global Policy 67; Pauline Melin, 'The Global Compact for Migration: Lessons for the Unity of EU Representation' (2019) 21(2) European Journal of Migration and Law 194; Juan Santos Vara, 'Soft International Agreements on Migration Cooperation with Third Countries: A Challenge to Democratic and Judicial Controls in the EU' in Sergio Carrera et al., *Constitutionalising the External Dimensions of EU Migration Policies in Times of Crisis* (Elgar 2019); Evangelia Tsourdi et al. (eds), 'The EU's Shifting Borders Reconsidered: Externalisation, Constitutionalisation, and Administrative Integration' (2022) 7(1) European Papers 87; Juan Santos Vara et al. (eds), 'The Externalisation of EU Migration Policies in Light of EU Constitutional Principles and Values' (2023) 8(2) European Papers 901.

193 The following is based on Charles F Sabel & Jonathan Zeitlin, 'Learning from Difference: The New Architecture of Experimentalist Governance in the EU' (2008) 14(3) European Law Journal 271.

194 Ibid 305.

States like Italy in that respect.[195] Hence, the then President of the European Council appreciated Italy's 'decisive action'[196] that has proven to be 'effective'[197] in reducing irregular migration on the Central Mediterranean route. Regarding Italy's task to implement the EU-funded programme, EU law imposes a number of procedural obligations to avoid the misappropriation of funds.[198] In fact, compliance with the rule of law is difficult to monitor since the aims of the programme are defined in very broad terms.[199] Once again, such difficulties are not limited to the cooperation with Libya. Indeed, legal scholarship in the field of asylum and migration has generally not shared the enthusiasm for experimentalism, new forms of accountability, and the like. On the contrary, the alleged managerial attitude of law- and policy-making has been the subject of criticism. It has been argued that efficiency is attributed more weight than individual rights, and technocratic decision-making is a way to evade political responsibility.[200] On this view, Member States do not necessarily replace EU law with governance. The former rather becomes a tool to legitimise the latter. Hence, Member States will hollow out the law from within by claiming to act in accordance with the applicable rules and procedures, but that is in fact a politicised, perverted interpretation.[201]

Finally, according to the *hybridity thesis*, EU law and governance are conceptually distinct, but they do interrelate in various ways.[202] On the one hand, there may be parallelism in the sense that governance may be experimental without prejudice to minimum legal requirements (baseline hybridity). On the other hand, there may be interaction in the sense that governance is a means

195 European Council (n 162) points 6(a) and (i).

196 European Council, 'Migration: Way Forward on the External and Internal Dimension' (Leaders' Agenda December 2017) <https://www.consilium.europa.eu/media/32143/en_leaders-agenda-note-on-migration_.pdf> accessed 1 March 2024.

197 Ibid.

198 Regulation (EU, Euratom) 2018/1046 of the European Parliament and of the Council of 18 July 2018 on the financial rules applicable to the general budget of the Union [2018] OJ L193/1; Council Regulation (EU) 2018/1877 of 26 November 2018 on the financial regulation applicable to the 11th European Development Fund [2018] OJ L307/1.

199 Global Legal Action Network et al. (n 191) points 15ff.

200 See eg Anne Neylon, 'Producing Precariousness: 'Safety Elsewhere' and the Removal of International Protection Status under EU Law' (2019) 21(1) European Journal of Migration and Law 1.

201 See generally Marc de Leeuw & Sonja van Wichelen, 'Un-signing Geneva: Legal Pragmatics in the Management of Asylum' (2019) 15 International Journal of Law in Context 20.

202 See Graínne de Búrca & Joanne Scott, 'Introduction: New Governance, Law and Constitutionalism' in Graínne de Búrca & Joanne Scott (eds), *Law and New Governance in the EU and the US* (Hart 2006) 6–9.

of developing or applying existing legal norms (instrumental hybridity). Like the other conceptualisations, hybridity is also normative since it assumes a positive-sum relationship between law and governance in which each outweighs the deficits of the other.[203] If law rather tends to universalise particular cases into a normative order, governance is more inclined to respond to what is to be done here and now. Neither the stability associated with law nor the flexibility connected to governance is absolute, because stability may also be rigid and flexibility may also be arbitrary. Instead, hybridity is interested in productive encounters.

Compared to the other conceptualisations, hybridity is essentially a middle way trying to handle policy complexity and uncertainty without sacrificing certain qualities of law like stability, clarity and uniformity. Consequently, it is the mirror image of constitutional pluralism on the instrumental dimension. And similar to constitutional pluralism, it has to walk a fine line with the constant risk of privileging one side over the other. In the context of migration management, executive actors tend to circumvent the law with new governance techniques, and legal actors try to close the gap. For example, it still has to be determined whether Italy is subject to the jurisdiction of the European Court of Human Rights on grounds of exerting influence on Libya, a non-contracting party to the ECHR accused of violating human rights.[204] To legalise migration governance is not necessarily hybridity in a normative sense if governance is a tool to circumvent law, and law is then used to undercut governance. It is submitted that hybridity is normative if it means inquiring what the present state of the law is (not what it ought to be), and if it includes governance into the equation of how the law may be applied or improved. For example, in line with baseline hybridity, the principle of non-refoulement is a safety net against permissive migration governance. The minimum core content is not to return a person to a country where he or she faces a real risk of torture, inhuman or degrading treatment.[205] At the time of writing, Libya is not a safe place because of well-documented human rights violations at detention centres.[206] However, in line with instrumental hybridity, governance is

203 See Neil Walker and Graínne de Búrca, 'Reconceiving Law and New Governance', (2007) 13 Columbia Journal of European Law 519, 533ff.

204 See the pending case of *S.S. and Others v Italy* App no 21660/18 (communicated on 26 June 2019); Violeta Moreno-Lax, 'The Architecture of Functional Jurisdiction: Unpacking Contactless Control—On Public Powers, *S.S. and Others v. Italy*, and the "Operational Model"' (2020) 21(3) German Law Journal 385.

205 See Vincent Chetail, *International Migration Law* (OUP 2019) 124.

206 See Human Rights Watch, 'Libya: Events of 2023' (World Report 2024) <https://www.hrw.org/world-report/2024/country-chapters/libya#1d4050> accessed 1 March 2024.

useful to monitor and improve the situation on the ground. On the one hand, the cooperation with Libya has been correctly criticised for the absence of a human rights impact assessment.[207] According to the European Ombudsman, an ex post impact assessment requires continuous and systematic treatment of (1) the impact (direct and indirect) of implementing measures on the human rights of individuals directly affected by it; (2) the extent to which EU agencies and Member States involved are able to fulfil their human rights obligations; (3) any necessary mitigating measures.[208] In a nutshell, an impact assessment increases the explanatory burden of any alleged representative in view of the applicable legal obligations. On the other hand, the Commission is right to underline that the success of the Libyan programme hinges on knowledge of the political, economic and social context and a bottom-up approach to problem-solving.[209] Governance through persuasion and social learning makes sure that the Libyan population takes ownership of the assistance with a view to becoming, in a distant future, a people capable of governing itself through functioning institutions.[210]

5.2 *Political Hybridity as Part of the Meta-constitutional Discourse*

So far, it has been shown that hybridity is a tool to describe, analyse and evaluate the relationship between law and governance. It is suggested supplementing this surface layer with the deep layer and introducing an additional category: political hybridity. It has been explained that law validly enacted in accordance with the constitution or the functional equivalent thereof expresses who we are as a political community. Governance too has such an expressive function, and it should be recognised as such under certain conditions.

In the first place, governance gives expression to a different kind of power than law. Krisch makes a distinction between solid and liquid authority.[211] The former means that the power to adopt legally binding rules is vested in a certain governing institution who may instruct other institutions to apply and enforce the law.[212] In our model, the latter institutions correspond to the

207 See Global Legal Action Network et al. (n 191) points 21ff.

208 Decision of the European Ombudsman in the joint inquiry into complaints 506-509-674-784-927-1381/2016/MHZ against the European Commission concerning a human rights impact assessment in the context of the EU–Turkey Agreement, 18 January 2017, para 30.

209 See Action Fiche 1 (n 186) 12–14.

210 See generally Sabel & Zeitlin (n 193) 312ff.

211 Nico Krisch, 'Authority, Solid and Liquid, in Postnational Governance', in Roger Cotterrell & Maksymilian Del Mar (eds), *Authority in Transnational Legal Theory: Theorising Across Disciplines* (Elgar 2016).

212 Ibid 27–32.

competent authorities of the Member States who claim formal recognition for representing the Union. According to Krisch, liquid authority has several elements.[213] First, it is characterised by informal, legally non-binding instruments such as soft law, recommendations, indicators, and the like. Second, it is grounded in substantive criteria such as expertise, moral principles and values, or problem-solving capacity. Third, it is dispersed across various actors who defer to the authority of one another according to the mentioned substantive criteria. Authority is thus relative, focussing on what an actor can invoke to gain legitimacy and to arrive at an optimal allocation of responsibility.[214] Fourth, it is dynamic since legitimacy gained may soon fade away if it turns out that the actor cannot solve a certain problem or another actor has more expertise. In our model, liquid authority is what Member States are claiming when trying to get social recognition as representatives of the Union. Krisch takes the view that both types of authority relate to one another on a continuum, so it is rather common to have a combination of solid and liquid elements.[215] Likewise, the theory of acting on behalf of the Union submits that Member States move inside-out from the inner into the intermediate sphere, seeking formal *and* social recognition.

In the second place, this movement 'inside-out' indicates that recourse to governance is not unconditional. As far as formal recognition is concerned, governance is of limited relevance for legal and practical reasons. First, it is well-known that the Court depends on cases being referred to it, and in the politically salient context of migration management, some unresolved legal issues have simply not reached the Court's docket.[216] Second, even when the Court has the opportunity to rule on political issues like the meaning of solidarity, it tends to defer to the authority of the other EU institutions and some of them, including the Commission, often rely on the political authority of the Member States. Third, the jurisdiction of the Court may pose a challenge, as we will see later concerning the EU-Turkey Statement. That is not to say that governance is irrelevant for the inner sphere of the Treaties – on the contrary. However, it is not certain that the Member States will receive formal

213 Ibid 39–43.

214 See also Ingo Venzke & Joana Mendes, 'The Idea of Relative Authority in European and International Law' (2018) 16(1) I·CON 75.

215 Krisch (n 211) 39; see also Krisch (n 52) 1229–1230.

216 For example, the Court has not yet interpreted the concept of safe third country, see Angeliki Tsiliou, 'When Greek Judges Decide Whether Turkey is a Safe Third Country Without Caring Too Much for EU Law' (2018) EU Immigration and Asylum Law and Policy <https://eumigrationlawblog.eu/when-greek-judges-decide-whether-turkey-is-a-safe-third-country-without-caring-too-much-for-eu-law/> accessed 1 March 2024.

recognition if they express their belonging to the Union in terms not captured by the EU legal order.

In such a case, governance is a way to claim social recognition. It is submitted that Member States must in any event argue that they are fulfilling a political obligation to the Union. Hence, they must justify their action by reference to the common purpose of mutual non-interference.[217] The EU institutions, in particular the European Council, should decline a claim if the action is liable to impact negatively on other Member States or, as the next chapter will explain, on third-country nationals. Therefore, the fact that a certain practice has not yet been endorsed by the European courts does not absolve a Member State from making a credible commitment to human rights. More specifically, even though Italy may not be legally responsible for human rights violations committed by the Libyan Coast Guard, it is at least politically responsible and so it should take practical steps in this regard. Finally, a claim for social recognition must state the reasons why that particular Member State is well placed to act on behalf of the Union. Italy refers to 'the common historical and cultural heritage and the strong bond of friendship'.[218] Indeed, according to the Commission, the well-established bilateral relationship with Libya justifies the prominent role of Italy in the implementation of the EU-funded programme. In practice, Italy gained experience in training the Libyan Coast Guard, so there have been institutional and personal connections between these countries.[219] Regarding the common commitment to human rights, the Commission continues as follows: 'In the face of the deteriorating situation in Libya, it is (...) clear that the risks of inaction largely outweigh the risk of action. Entrusting the project and its monitoring to the responsible authorities of the Member State that are most knowledgeable about and concerned with the situation is possibly the primary risk mitigating measure.'[220]

In the third place, political hybridity as outlined here is part of a meta-constitutional discourse in the intermediate sphere. Unlike in the inner sphere, there is thus no final arbiter for dispute resolution. Hence, even though the political institutions of the EU, especially the European Council, reject a claim, the Member State concerned might still carry out the action if it is of the opinion that it does qualify as action on behalf of the Union. But without recognition, it will slide into the outer sphere of international relations. The

217 Similarly, Neil Walker, 'EU Constitutionalism and New Governance' in de Búrca & Scott (n 202) 29–36.

218 Preamble of the Memorandum of Understanding.

219 See Action Fiche 1 (n 186) 5.

220 Ibid 14.

meta-constitutional discourse is about what ought to be done and how common values and principles should guide the joint action. Disagreement is more likely than not. Governance should be part of the discourse because it is capable of widening the possibilities for Member States to express their belonging to the Union. Whereas the EU institutional framework seeks to aggregate the interests of the Member States and to align them with the interests of the Union and the EU citizens,[221] governance in the intermediate sphere is a means to articulate what a particular Member State has to offer for the benefit of all. To some degree, governance may transform or broaden the role of the Member States who are more than just implementing agents of the EU. They are, in addition, sovereign but responsible, reflexive nation states who explain and justify their decisions in front of a European audience.[222]

6 Conclusion

The aim of this chapter was to explain constitutional conflict and to justify that Member States may represent the Union in certain circumstances. The chapter adopted the angle of both the national and the EU collective self. Constitutional conflict is in part due to the limited chance to express the national political imagination when interacting with the EU legal order. At least, the present concepts do not sufficiently account for it. Radical pluralism does not go further than interaction among courts who cannot on their own represent the political. Cosmopolitan pluralism is interested in rational thought based on undefined principles and less so in political will. Epistemic pluralism is indeed rooted in the contexts in which law operates, yet it is more concerned about emerging sites of authority than about the historically grown nation state. It was therefore suggested to refine the existing concepts by paying more attention to the political underpinnings of a legal order. A claim to represent the Union should not be accepted if a Member State only refers to its national identity. In addition, it will have to justify the action by reference to the common purpose of the Union. Article 2 TEU enumerates the founding values of the EU, which promote the final purpose of mutual non-interference.

The leeway for national responsibility is defined by the degree to which the EU legislature has implemented the common values. The adoption of

221 Art 13(1) TEU.

222 See Mark Dawson, 'Integration through Soft Law? New Governance and the Meaning of Legality in the European Union' in Daniel Augenstein (ed), *"Integration through Law" Revisited: The Making of the European Polity* (Ashgate 2012) 148ff.

legally binding rules of EU law amounts to a representation of unity in and through the autonomous structure of the EU legal order. The representation is in part addressed to the Member States who are obliged to give effect to EU law in their national legal systems. In doing so, Member States are not just law-applying agents of the EU deprived of their political will. On the contrary, they are representatives of the Union in a formal sense insofar as they exercise their discretion according to EU legislation. More discretion corresponds to more responsibility for the Union *and* for their independent political existence.

Representation is of a different nature insofar as the EU institutions have not yet specified the legal duties, or when Member States invoke a national competence. This chapter used the principle of solidarity as an example. The Court ruled that solidarity is mandatory when a Member State is faced with a sudden inflow of third-country nationals within the meaning of Article 78(3) TFEU. In other words, any measure adopted on that legal basis is binding on every Member State. National implementation is above all informed by the frame of the EU legal order. Solidarity is thus an integral part of the EU rule of law demanding the uniform and effective application of the common rules. But regarding assistance unrelated to an emergency, neither the Court nor the EU legislature has determined the meaning of solidarity. In those circumstances, the 27 owe not a legal but a political obligation to each other in order to uphold the purpose of their joint action. Here, the action is above all informed by the national political imagination. Member States claim to be a representative in a social sense, pursuing the common interests in accordance with national political will and capacity. It will not be the Court but, in particular, the European Council as the top political institution who may or may not recognise a claim for social recognition.

Recognition is logically premised on cognition. In other words, those to whom a claim is addressed need to hear or otherwise take notice of it to evaluate whether it is to be recognised as one-of-us. However, the Member States often exercise authority through various modes of governance that are less noticeable than law because of their informal nature. By way of example, this chapter used the Memorandum of Understanding between Italy and Libya concerning irregular sea arrivals. As governance is often connected to the EU legal order, it should in principle count as an expression of belonging to the Union (political hybridity). There are, however, a number of conditions: (1) the Member State concerned must justify the action by reference to the common purpose of the Union; (2) it must explain why it is well placed to act and, in this context, why common action within the EU institutional framework is not suitable or necessary; (3) most fundamentally, the Court is in principle competent to declare the action incompatible with the inner sphere of the Treaties. That said, judicial review of governance cannot be taken for granted. This is a serious problem since independent and impartial adjudication is a necessary though not sufficient condition to regard a legal order as a site of empowerment. Social representation with only a weak connection to the EU legal order, for example to a general norm like a value or objective, should be limited because the lack of a final arbiter is liable to reduce mutual trust. Consequently, the 27 might slip into the outer sphere of power politics, undermining the common purpose of mutual non-interference. But if governance is treated with caution, it will assist Member States in finding pragmatic solutions to the common challenge of migration management.

This concludes the theoretical part of this book. The next chapter goes to describe what, according to the 27, is the specific purpose of EU migration management. Mutual non-interference has a particular meaning in an area of internal free movement demarcated by a common external border. In recent years, since many thousand persons in need of international protection crossed the external border, Member States have been called upon to assume responsibility for collective security and individual protection.

PART 2

The Practice of the European Spheres

CHAPTER 3

The Common Purpose of EU Migration Management

1 Introduction

The foregoing chapters made the case for understanding the EU legal order as a site of empowerment insofar as the Member States have ample room to represent their national identity alongside the common purpose of the Union. In the most general sense, the raison d'être of the EU is to safeguard mutual non-interference and to attain the common objectives by means of legal integration. It is the aim of this chapter to identify the specific common purpose of EU migration management. More precisely, instead of outlining policy preferences at the time of writing, the aim is to reveal the political purpose underneath the surface of law and policy. Indeed, as mentioned, migration management potentially affects the political existence or self-recognition of a polity.

But because of the contingency of every legal order, it is assumed that the policy of the day is to some degree informed by that underlying purpose. Hence, the present chapter will give more clarity about the so-called comprehensive approach to migration, which features in almost every EU policy document since the crisis in 2015/2016. The Introduction pointed out that under the comprehensive approach, the Member States have been called upon or unilaterally claimed to assume responsibility for the Union. This chapter will show that the approach has not just been a hasty crisis response but an established way to express the self-identity of the 27.

For this purpose, the chapter will conduct a historical interpretation of EU primary law. This method is unusual in EU law due to the unprecedented impact of systematic-teleological interpretation in the jurisprudence of the Court. However, it is still appropriate for our purposes because in EU migration management, the Court has been more deferential to the wording of the legislation and thus, at least implicitly, to the intention of the Member States qua Council of Ministers. In addition, our aim is to identify the common purpose that is capable of connecting the inner and the intermediate sphere. To study the evolution of EU primary law will be helpful because in this context, the 27 take an intermediate position by renegotiating their EU membership according to a procedure that is heavily informed by public international law. Apart from the EU Treaties, it will be useful to close read the conclusions of the

 | DOI:10.1163/9789004695733_005

European Council, in which the 27 are also in a state of in-between qua members of an EU institution who owe that membership to a national democratic mandate.

The first section will outline the basic tenets of international refugee law since the Member States, when acting in the context of the EU, will be informed by their consent to the international protection system. The second section will conduct the mentioned historical interpretation of Article 78 TFEU in particular, clarifying the relationship between the common policy and the Common European Asylum System (CEAS). The section thereafter will explain that developments in international migration governance have had a lasting impact on European cooperation and the responsibility of individual Member States for the common purpose. Before summarising the main findings, this chapter will, in section 5, explain that the 27 intended to use the single institutional framework at least in part as a support structure, for example in order to discuss the meaning of solidarity.

2 The Basic Tenets of International Refugee Law

The main source of international refugee law is the 1951 Geneva Convention and the 1967 Protocol Relating to the Status of Refugees.[1] The former was drafted against the background of the Second World War and therefore contained geographical and temporal limitations, restricting the scope of application to events occurring in Europe before 1951. The intention was to protect persons from persecution through the Communist regime. Although the 1967 Protocol removed these limitations, the historical background of the Convention is European. This might explain why the EU and in particular the founding Member States have continuously reaffirmed the rules of the Geneva Convention, as the following sections will describe in more detail.

Having regard to the rules of the Convention from a bird's eye view, the main principle is the responsibility of individual states for the protection of refugees. A refugee within the meaning of the Geneva Convention is entitled to protection from a host state due to a well-founded fear of being persecuted for a limited number of grounds in the country of origin.[2] The right to seek

1 Convention Relating to the Status of Refugees, signed at Geneva on 28 July 1951, UNTS, vol 189, p 137 (henceforth: 'Geneva Convention' or 'GC'); Protocol Relating to the Status of Refugees, done at New York on 31 January 1967, UNTS, vol 606, p 267 (henceforth: 'Protocol').

2 Art 1(A)(2) Geneva Convention. These grounds are: race, religion, nationality, membership of a particular social group or political opinion.

asylum does not, however, correspond with a duty to grant asylum. Rather, since the Geneva Convention confers a considerable margin of discretion on states, it is more appropriate to speak of the duty to assume responsibility for every refugee falling within the jurisdiction of the state. The limits of that discretion are the right to temporary protection,[3] and the principle of non-refoulement.[4] Both are necessary to uphold the useful effect of the protection regime as such. If refugees were not entitled to temporary protection from that state in whose jurisdiction they arrive, they would risk of being constantly on the run without any state assuming responsibility for their safety. Since refugee status is presumed until the completion of an examination on the merits, the mere claim to be a refugee triggers a first set of entitlements vis-à-vis the host state.[5] The essential core is the right not to be returned or expelled to a country where the basic human rights of the refugee are jeopardised (non-refoulement). These minimum obligations provide a framework within which the host state is responsible for refugees. Temporary protection may be the initial step towards permanent residence or even naturalisation.[6] In other cases, it may not go beyond the provision of basic needs pending the transfer to a safe third country where the refugee's protection claim will be finally examined on the merits.[7]

Burden-sharing principles or mechanisms are missing under the Geneva Convention. On the contrary, only the preamble contains a general reference to the need for international cooperation because 'the grant of asylum may place unduly heavy burdens on certain countries'.[8] Indeed, most refugees live in the global South, that is, in developing countries who struggle to meet the obligations under the Geneva Convention. In a strict sense, many are not refugees within the meaning of international refugee law but protection seekers in a broader sense. They flee not from individual persecution but from structural

---

3 According to art 1(C) Geneva Convention, the latter ceases to apply, inter alia, as soon as it is safe for the person concerned to return to his or her country of nationality.

4 Art 33 Geneva Convention.

5 Fundamentally, the right to non-discrimination (art 3 GC) and various rights intended to protect the refugee's safety (see, inter alia, arts 27, 32, 33 GC). Other rights depend on lawful stay or residence. James Hathaway rationalised the complex legal framework of the Geneva Convention into an 'assimilative path', ie refugee rights increase relative to the bonds with the host country, see James C Hathaway, *The Rights of Refugees under International Law* (2nd edition, CUP 2021) ch 3; for criticism, see Vincent Chetail, *International Migration Law* (OUP 2019) 181.

6 Art 34 Geneva Convention.

7 See UNHCR, 'The Concept of Protection Elsewhere' (1995) 7(1) International Journal of Refugee Law 123.

8 Preamble to the Geneva Convention.

shortcomings in fragile states such as economic misery, famine or the impact of climate change. However, host states are still under a legal obligation to assume responsibility for their safety since the principle of non-refoulement is part of customary international law and thus commits states also outside the scope of the Geneva Convention.[9] Without international cooperation, both the overburdened states in the global South and the privileged states in the global North have an incentive to shift the burden rather than to share it. Faced with economic decline and social unrest, the former are inclined to facilitate or at least to tolerate secondary movements of their refugee population. The latter have instead relied on non-entry policies, considering that in most cases territorial jurisdiction triggers the application of international refugee law. Hence, affluent states have invested considerable efforts and resources in trying to prevent refugees from reaching their territory in the first place. For example, they have used their political power to 'outsource' migration control to third countries, located far away from their own territory, and employed new technologies for border controls.[10] Migration flows are eventually contained in the global South through unilateral burden-shifting. Such policies consolidate the 'accidents of geography',[11] on which the whole protection regime is based.

3 The Dual Common Purpose: Individual Protection and Collective Security

Bearing in mind the hurdles of international cooperation, it is pertinent to ask why EU Member States did opt for closer mutual relationships. Reading the Treaties is not particularly instructive with a view to identifying a higher purpose for cooperation.[12] A seminal provision is Article 3(2) TEU, which is worth quoting in full:

> The Union shall offer its citizens an area of freedom, security and justice without internal frontiers, in which the free movement of persons

9 Chetail (n 5) 120.

10 See eg Evangelia Tsourdi et al. (eds), 'The EU's Shifting Borders Reconsidered: Externalisation, Constitutionalisation, and Administrative Integration' (2022) 7(1) European Papers 87; Juan Santos Vara et al. (eds), 'The Externalisation of EU Migration Policies in Light of EU Constitutional Principles and Values' (2023) 8(2) European Papers 901.

11 James C Hathaway & R Alexander Neve, 'Making International Refugee Law Relevant Again: A Proposal for Collectivized an Solution-Oriented Protection' (1997) 10 Harvard Human Rights Journal 115, 141.

12 See Daniel Thym, *European Migration Law* (OUP 2023) 34–37.

> is ensured in conjunction with appropriate measures with respect to external border controls, asylum, immigration and the prevention and combating of crime.

Going to the substantive policies contained in the TFEU, Title V deals with the Area of Freedom, Security and Justice (AFSJ). The General Provisions begin with Article 67 TFEU stipulating in paragraph (2):

> [The AFSJ] shall ensure the absence of internal border controls for persons and shall frame a common policy on asylum, immigration and external border control, based on solidarity between Member States, which is fair towards third-country nationals.

Finally, Article 78(1) TFEU, contained in the Chapter 2 about policies on border checks, asylum and immigration, reads as follows:

> The Union shall develop a common policy on asylum, subsidiary protection and temporary protection with a view to offering appropriate status to any third-country national requiring international protection and ensuring compliance with the principle of non-refoulement. This policy must be in accordance with the Geneva Convention of 28 July 1951 and the Protocol of 31 January 1967 relating to the status of refugees, and other relevant treaties.

Having regard to these provisions, a few observations and open questions readily come to mind. First, it follows clearly from the wording of Article 78(1) TFEU that asylum policy has a humanitarian purpose. It is striking, however, that instead of aiming at a high level of protection, the provision seeks to ensure 'appropriate' status, adding that only third country nationals 'requiring international protection' are entitled to such status. Second, as confirmed by the enumerations in Article 3(2) TEU and Article 67 TFEU, it is therefore necessary to read the mentioned humanitarian purpose in light of migration management as a whole. Indeed, Article 79 TFEU mandates the development of a common immigration policy that includes 'the prevention of, and enhanced measures to combat, illegal immigration'. Similarly, Article 77 TFEU is the legal basis for the management of the external borders. In view of mixed migration flows, measures in these fields might justify non-entry policies, with the effect of putting into perspective the humanitarian purpose of Article 78 TFEU. Finally, the quoted provisions suggest a close relationship between asylum policy and internal free movement. But any details remain inconclusive by just reading the Treaties. On the one hand, one might argue that asylum policy is but a tool to ensure the free movement of persons because the latter is formulated as an obligation of result and the indeterminate adjective 'appropriate' should be interpreted as enabling the EU to take any measures necessary to achieve that result. On the other hand, the goal to develop a 'common policy on asylum, subsidiary protection and temporary protection' indicates that it is a self-standing policy.[13] Moreover, neither the conjunction 'and' nor the phrase 'in conjunction with' suggest a relationship of subordination.

As a textual and systematic interpretation has not clarified the purpose(s) of EU asylum policy, this section outlines the historical evolution of what is now Article 78 TFEU. Because the next section will examine who, according to the drafters of the Treaties, should act on which elements of the maturing comprehensive approach to migration, this section takes the separate elements listed in Article 78(2) TFEU as a starting point (though in a different order). It reads as follows:

> For the purposes of paragraph 1 [quoted above], the European Parliament and the Council, acting in accordance with the ordinary legislative procedure, shall adopt measures for a common European asylum system comprising:
> (a) a uniform status of asylum for nationals of third countries, valid throughout the Union;
> (b) a uniform status of subsidiary protection for nationals of third countries who, without obtaining European asylum, are in need of international protection;
> (c) a common system of temporary protection for displaced persons in the event of a massive inflow;
> (d) common procedures for the granting and withdrawing of uniform asylum or subsidiary protection status;
> (e) criteria and mechanisms for determining which Member State is responsible for considering an application for asylum or subsidiary protection;
> (f) standards concerning the conditions for the reception of applicants for asylum or subsidiary protection;

13 See also Thym (n 12) 29.

(g) partnership and cooperation with third countries for the purpose of managing inflows of people applying for asylum or subsidiary or temporary protection.

It will be shown that most of these elements are intended to facilitate internal free movement. Hence, they seek to avoid externalities from differences in national asylum systems by means of harmonisation. Because harmonisation may preclude autonomous national measures, it is important to understand that some elements are more important for internal free movement than others. The most important pillar of the CEAS read in light of the goal of internal free movement is Article 78(2)(e) TFEU, the legal basis for the current Dublin Regulation that originated in the intergovernmental agreements of Schengen (1985) and Dublin (1990).[14] The main purpose is to assign responsibility for asylum applications to a single Member State according to a set of criteria. If the asylum seeker arrives in another Member State, the person would in principle be returned to the Member State responsible in line with the rules and procedures of the Dublin system. Hence, at the time of intergovernmental cooperation, the fixed allocation of responsibility mitigated the negative implications of secondary movements and thereby created favourable conditions for the abolition of internal border controls.[15] In other words, confining third country nationals within jurisdictional borders facilitated the transition to a borderless area for nationals of the Member States. While never explicitly mentioned in the Treaties, common security interests lurked behind the objective of internal free movement and the perceived need to cooperate on flanking policies.[16] Specifically, individual persons who pose a security risk may benefit from open borders, and uncontrolled cross-border movements, if on a significant scale,

14 Agreement between the Governments of the States of the Benelux Economic Union, the Federal Republic of Germany and the French Republic on the gradual abolition of checks at their common borders ('Schengen Agreement') [2000] OJ L239/13; Convention implementing the Schengen Agreement of 14 June 1985 between the Governments of the States of the Benelux Economic Union, the Federal Republic of Germany and the French Republic on the gradual abolition of checks at their common borders ('Implementing Convention') [2000] OJ L239/19; Convention determining the State responsible for examining applications for asylum lodged in one of the Member States of the European Communities ('Dublin Convention') [1997] OJ C254/1.

15 According to the preamble to the Dublin Convention (n 14), assigning responsibility for asylum claims was necessary to pursue the 'joint objective of an area without internal frontiers'.

16 See Eiko Thielemann & Carolyn Armstrong, 'Understanding European Asylum Cooperation under the Schengen/Dublin System: A Public Goods Framework' (2013) 22(2) European Security 148.

may have destabilising security effects by themselves. In that sense, the Dublin system of allocating responsibility on a stable, permanent basis has aimed at common security interests.

Those elements addressing *substantive* asylum law have been mainly intended to serve the functioning of the Dublin/Schengen regime and, by implication, the goal of internal free movement. The legal bases for protection statuses, procedures and reception conditions fall within this category. They all follow the same compensatory logic according to which differences are likely to encourage secondary movements, undermining the permanent responsibility of a single Member State and inciting other Member States to reintroduce internal border controls. It is noteworthy that the envisaged level of harmonisation differs. The EU legislature should arrive at *common* procedures for the granting and withdrawing of *uniform* protection status. Moreover, it should agree on indeterminate standards concerning reception conditions. This leaves considerable discretion to harmonise reception conditions as far as possible, having regard to divergent national socio-economic conditions. In similar vein, the harmonisation of asylum procedures is confronted with legal-cultural differences. By contrast, the harmonisation of refugee status was a national priority from the beginning because the Member States could build on the fact that each of them was a party to the Geneva Convention.[17] In 1996, they decided to apply a harmonised understanding of the term 'refugee' in Article 1 of the Convention.[18] Contained in an instrument whose legal effects were limited, this common understanding failed to achieve the level of harmonisation necessary to manage interdependence in a borderless area.[19] Hence, over time the Member States accepted the need for more comprehensive harmonisation within the framework of the EU legal order. The same applied to asylum procedures and reception conditions, subject to the mentioned structural limits.

One might object that the broader scope and higher level of harmonisation are intended to advance humanitarian policies. That view is, however, not

17 See Coordinators' Group on the Free Movement of Persons, '"The Palma Document" Free Movement of Persons. A Report to the European Council by the Coordinators' Group' (Key texts on justice and home affairs 1976–1993) <https://www.statewatch.org/media/documents/semdoc/assets/files/keytexts/ktch1.pdf> accessed 1 March 2024, point III. B. See also European Council, 'Conclusions' (Meeting of 26 and 27 June 1989) SN 254/2/89, p 6.

18 Joint Position 96/196/JHA defined by the Council on the basis of Article K.3 of the Treaty on European Union on the harmonized application of the definition of the term "refugee" in Article 1 of the Geneva Convention relating to the status of refugees [1996] OJ L63/2.

19 See infra section 5.

supported by a historical interpretation of the Treaties. Instead of introducing an autonomous humanitarian purpose of the EU, the successive Treaty revisions have required compliance with international refugee and human rights law. Moreover, the Maastricht Treaty established an institutional structure for more systematic, less informal cooperation than before (the so-called pillar structure), falling short of a transfer of competence to the then European Community. The Treaty stipulated that Member States shall regard policies pertaining to the Third Pillar of justice and home affairs as matters of 'common interest'.[20] In particular, the Member States prioritised the harmonisation of selected aspects of asylum policy: not as an end in itself but as a means to realising internal free movement.[21] Evaluating whether the Third Pillar should be communitarised, the Commission and Council agreed on the desirability of substituting framework objectives for the empty 'common interest' formulae.[22] While the Commission wanted to subject the policies of the entire Third Pillar to the legal basis for the internal market,[23] the Member States were more cautious. Although deciding, at Amsterdam, to transfer asylum policy from the Third to the First Pillar, they inserted a provision to distinguish between flanking measures directly related to the free movement of persons, and other measures in the fields of asylum, immigration and safeguarding the rights of third country nationals.[24] But it remained unclear what those 'other measures' should aim at other than compliance with international refugee and human rights law. In addition, the category of 'directly related flanking measures to the free movement of persons' refers to the legal basis for temporary protection.[25] Although the latter quite clearly serves protective ends, a systematic interpretation of the Amsterdam Treaty indicates that temporary protection followed the said compensatory logic insofar as a large influx of refugees or displaced persons was liable to cause the reintroduction of internal border controls.

---

20 Art K.1 TEU, signed at Maastricht, [1992] OJ C191/1.

21 Report from the Ministers Responsible for Immigration to the European Council Meeting in Maastricht on Immigration and Asylum Policy, SN 4038/91 (WGI 930), 3 December 1991, point A.II.

22 European Commission, 'Communication on the Possible Application of Article K.9 of the Treaty on European Union COM(95) 566 final; Secrétariat Général du Conseil de l'Union Européenne, *Conférence Intergouvernementale en vue de la Révision des Traités – Semestre de la Présidence Néerlandaise* (*Recueil de Textes*) (Secrétariat Général du Conseil de l'Union Européenne 1997), 27.

23 European Commission (n 22) 3.

24 Art 61(a) and (b) TEC, as amended by the Treaty of Amsterdam, [1997] OJ C340/173 (consolidated version).

25 Art 61(a) in conjunction with art 63(2)(a) TEC, as amended by the Treaty of Amsterdam, [1997] OJ C340/173 (consolidated version).

This last point merits further attention. Although not an independent rationale for European cooperation, humanitarian policies were informed by collective security interests. More precisely, the Member States devised humanitarian policies in reaction to emergencies in their immediate neighbourhood or further afield. First, in the 1990s the wars in the former Yugoslavia and in Kosovo exposed Member States to large refugee movements. Noting that migratory pressure potentially has destabilising effects on host societies, the Member States defined principles governing external aspects of migration, including policies intended to tackle the root causes of refuge while also providing temporary protection in the Member States.[26] Second, since international terrorism on 9/11 and thereafter, Europeans used to live with diffuse but real security threats. This explains why the fight against 'illegal immigration' became a top political priority,[27] with the underlying (but controversial) assumption of a migration-security nexus. In sum, the EU first developed comprehensive approaches in reaction to the changing nature of security, turning from an internal into an external interest and from an abstract into an imminent risk.

But using humanitarian policies for security interests might jeopardise the collective commitment to international refugee and human rights law. To recall, Article 78 TFEU actually has a humanitarian purpose insofar as it mandates the EU to develop a common policy with a view to international protection, and the 27 have actually 'reaffirmed' their joint responsibility on several occasions in the past.[28] Although reaffirmation does not necessarily imply a high level of protection, this is not the crux of the matter. The Member States might rather try to evade international refugee law in practice, for the deeper the conviction of having to tackle root causes abroad, the greater the risk of obstructing the exercise of rights under the Geneva Convention. That would be incompatible with a truly comprehensive approach.

Article 78(2)(g) TFEU – the legal basis for partnership and cooperation with third countries – is noteworthy in this regard. It allows measures to manage 'inflows of people applying for asylum or subsidiary or temporary protection'. This purpose should not be interpreted narrowly in the sense of only

---

26 European Council, 'Conclusions' (Meeting of 11 and 12 December 1992) SN 456/1/92 Rev 1, 41ff. (Annex 5: Declaration on Principles Governing Aspects of Migration Policy).

27 European Council, 'Conclusions' (Meeting of 19 and 20 June 2003) 11638/03, point 19.

28 For example, see supra n 21, and more recently, European Council, 'Conclusions' (Meeting of 10 and 11 December 2009) EUCO 6/09, Annex: 'The Stockholm Programme – An Open and Secure Europe Serving and Protecting the Citizen', point 6.2.1 ('full and inclusive application of the Geneva Convention (…) and other relevant international treaties').

encompassing measures capable of managing inflows into the EU.[29] Otherwise, it would follow the well-known compensatory logic of internal security. It should rather be regarded as the legal basis for principled and forward-looking humanitarian policies, complementing the security-related policies as part of a truly comprehensive approach. As we will see next, this interpretation is supported by historical developments at international level, and their reception by the EU and the Member States.

Having contributed to comprehensive approaches in reaction to refugee crises,[30] the United Nations High Commissioner for Refugees (UNHCR) started pursuing a more predictable path at the beginning of this millennium. The so-called Convention Plus initiative aimed at developing norms about burden-sharing to fill the gaps of the Geneva Convention.[31] The norm-generating work strived for agreements on resettlement, secondary movements, and development aid to make international cooperation more principled and less ad hoc and discretionary. At the same time, it built on previous experience with emergency measures in order to ensure that the norms would be context-sensitive. Despite the limited output, the initiative bolstered the norms of the Geneva Convention insofar as it insisted on upholding the right to seek asylum even when migratory challenges and the ensuing comprehensive approaches got increasingly complex.

Having been involved in the work of the Convention Plus initiative, it was no surprise that the Commission received it well.[32] When the United Kingdom made a controversial proposal for externalising the examination of asylum applications, the Commission insisted on the integrity of the CEAS,[33] and portrayed a more prominent role for the EU in offering durable solutions for refugees.[34] Apart from facilitating voluntary returns to the countries of origin, these are integration in the EU for those already present and resettlement of recognised refugees from third countries. This policy orientation met with

29 See Thym (n 12) 571–575; for a more narrow interpretation, see Malte Graßhof, 'Artikel 78 AEUV' in Jürgen Schwarze (ed), *EU-Kommentar* (3rd edition, Nomos 2012) 1029.

30 For example, see UN Secretary General, 'Draft Declaration and Comprehensive Plan of Action Approved by the Preparatory Meeting for the International Conference of Indo-Chinese Refugees on 8 March 1989' A/CONF 148/2, 26 April 1989.

31 See Alexander Betts & Jean-François Durieux, 'Convention Plus as a Norm-Setting Exercise' (2007) 20(3) Journal of Refugee Studies 509.

32 European Commission, 'Communication on the Common Asylum Policy and the Agenda for Protection COM(2003) 152 final, 5.

33 European Commission, 'Towards More Accessible, Equitable and Managed Asylum Systems' COM(2003) 315 final, 12–13.

34 European Commission (n 32) 10–12.

approval at the European Council, expressing its commitment to grant asylum in the EU and to promote the norms of international refugee law in the external relations of the Union.[35] Leaving aside actual policies, it is worth noting that in the face of mounting security challenges, the 27 reaffirmed their common humanitarian purpose. At the same time, it is equally crucial that as part of a comprehensive approach, humanitarian aims continued to be embedded in the common security agenda. To illustrate, the Commission supported a strategic use of resettlement following the example of UNHCR.[36] Resettlement should be used as a leverage to foster international cooperation on other elements of the comprehensive approach, in particular the fight against irregular migration.

A systematic interpretation of Article 78(2)(g) TFEU confirms this dual purpose. Listed among the elements of the CEAS, partnership and cooperation with third countries must not undermine the integrity of that system. International cooperation must therefore not jeopardise the objective of internal free movement. At the same time, the CEAS forms part of a common policy that shall adhere to international refugee and human rights law. It follows that it would be wrong to reduce the security-humanitarian nexus to a painful balancing act or even to a zero-sum relationship. Both are an integral part of the common purpose, so any actor claiming to act on behalf of the Union must assume responsibility for each in order to be recognised as a legitimate representative.

4 Responsibility-Sharing under a Comprehensive Approach

The foregoing has identified collective security and humanitarian protection as higher purposes of EU asylum policy. The 27 have come a long way to recognise the interdependence of these objectives. While security interests followed naturally from European integration and external events, humanitarian protection was initially not more ambitious than reaffirming existing international legal obligations. Influenced by international migration governance, the Member States accepted that proactive protection policies contribute to the common security interests. That is the basis for developing a truly comprehensive approach under Article 78 TFEU. The next question is who should act on the various elements of a comprehensive approach. When should an issue

35 The Stockholm Programme (n 28) point 6.2.3.

36 European Commission (n 33) 19.

be regulated at EU level, and when might it be more appropriate to leave it to the Member States individually or collectively? To recall, this section examines this question solely from the angle of the 27, with regard to their intention as expressed in the context of primary law-making.

It has been explained that the common aim to establish an internal area of free movement was the impetus for cooperating on asylum and related policies. However, according to the early views of the Member States, European cooperation was not to pre-empt national action in these areas.[37] The tension between the need for collective action on the one hand, and the preservation of national sovereignty on the other, characterised the period between the Single European Act and the Maastricht Treaty. This is best illustrated by the disputed scope of Article 8a EEC, stipulating that '[t]he Community shall adopt measures with the aim of progressively establishing the internal market over a period expiring on 31 December 1992'.[38] It was contested whether the permissible 'measures' encompassed asylum and immigration policies.

The Court soon clarified the matter,[39] ruling on the validity of Commission Decision 85/381/EEC setting up a prior communication and consultation procedure on migration policies in relation to non-member countries.[40] It was adopted on the basis of Article 118 EEC, allowing the Commission to promote close cooperation between Member States in the social field. Since the latter was a flanking policy of the internal market, consultation on migration from third countries was considered necessary to achieve the free movement of workers within the EU. However, the five Member States who brought the case before the Court complained about the broad scope of migration policy under the Decision. In particular, they were of the opinion that cultural integration fell outside the scope of Article 118 EEC. The Court agreed, holding that migration policy fell within the scope of Article 118 EEC only insofar as it had an impact on the free movement of workers within the meaning of Article 48 EEC.[41] But of even greater concern to the Member States was the requirement to communicate national draft measures to the Commission to ensure

---

37 Compare Declaration on art 8a of the EEC Treaty and the General Declaration on arts 13 to 19 of the Single European Act [1987] OJ L169/24; see also Eileen Denza, *The Intergovernmental Pillars of the European Union* (OUP 2002) ch 3.

38 Art 8a EEC Treaty, as amended by the Single European Act, [1987] OJ L169/1.

39 Joined Cases 281, 283 to 285 and 287/85 *Germany, France, the Netherlands, Denmark, United Kingdom* v *Commission* EU:C:1987:351.

40 Commission Decision 85/381/EEC setting up a prior communication and consultation procedure on migration policies in relation to non-member countries [1985] OJ L217/25 (no longer in force).

41 *Germany and Others* v *Commission* (n 39), para 23.

conformity with common policies. The applicant Member States argued that, since the legal basis only conferred procedural powers on the Commission, the latter was not entitled to require Member States to refrain from implementing the draft measures communicated to it under the Decision. Accepting this argument, the Court declared the Decision void for lack of competence with respect to the scope and legal effects of the consultation procedure.[42]

At first sight, the legal dispute seemed to reflect a familiar fault line in European integration. On the one hand, the broad scope of the consultation procedure exemplified the functional logic of internal market harmonisation, trying to increase the scope of central intervention for the purpose of economic integration. On the other hand, the resistance from the applicant Member States underlined the ensuing anxiety about the slow but gradual erosion of national self-determination. But underneath the competence quarrels, there was the willingness to cooperate on 'problems of common interest', as the contested Decision itself indicated.[43] And yet, each side compromised the success of cooperation. The Commission felt compelled to adopt a binding consultation procedure 'against a background of frustration',[44] given that the Member States had previously refused to consult each other informally on their migration policies but ironically called on the Commission to organise such consultations. The Commission contributed to the dispute by adopting the contested Decision without awaiting the outcome of a Council meeting where its initial proposal would be discussed. Furthermore, the 'excessive detail'[45] of the measure paid insufficient attention to the national concern of losing control over immigration, as expressed in a Declaration to the Single European Act.[46]

The dispute had ramifications beyond the subject matter at stake. As we will see, it marked the beginning of a period in which pragmatic cooperation was gradually prioritised over a precise division of competences. The Maastricht Treaty was the first sign of this development. The Member States decided to establish the mentioned pillar structure to better cooperate on matters of 'common interest',[47] without being ready to sacrifice the power of autonomous action. While the Maastricht Treaty was being negotiated, the European Council adopted the so-called Palma Document by the Coordinators' Group,

42 Ibid paras 35–36.
43 Art 3 Commission Decision 85/381/EEC (n 40).
44 Opinion of AG Mancini in *Germany and Others* v *Commission* EU:C:1987:169, p 3241.
45 Ibid p 3229.
46 General Declaration on arts 13 to 19 of the Single European Act (n 37).
47 Art K.1 TEU, signed at Maastricht, [1992] OJ C191/1.

an informal gathering of national representatives. Taking note of the different opinions as to the interpretation and scope of Article 8a EEC, the Coordinators' Group agreed to sidestep those differences for the purpose of taking 'practical steps upon which all could agree'.[48] Likewise, shortly after the Maastricht Treaty had entered into force, the Commission neglected the question of competence in favour of working with the Member States in an intergovernmental forum on asylum.[49]

The foregoing is not to suggest the absence of competence disputes in the post-Maastricht period. On the contrary, the Court was regularly called upon to clarify the competence division in visa policy.[50] This was due to the artificial spread of visa policy across the First and the Third Pillar. The Community was competent to determine the third countries whose nationals must be in possession of a visa, and to adopt measures relating to a uniform format of visas.[51] Conditions governing the crossing of the external borders and the entry, movement and residence on the territory of the Member States remained within the Third Pillar.[52] This unfortunate fragmentation eventually led to the integration of border, asylum and immigration policies into the First Pillar.[53] Having realised the ineffectiveness of non-binding intergovernmental cooperation in bringing about the degree of harmonisation considered necessary to safeguard internal free movement, the Member States accepted the vertical transfer of powers on the occasion of the Amsterdam revision.[54]

Nonetheless, Amsterdam did not mark the end of the period of pragmatic cooperation. On the contrary, pragmatism gained new momentum against the background of security threats. In 2004, the European Council declared that '[t]he citizens of Europe rightly expect the European Union (…) to take a more effective, joint approach to cross-border challenges such as illegal migration'.[55] More than ten years later, then Commission President Juncker

48 See supra n 17, point I.3.

49 European Commission, 'Report to the Council on the Possibility of Applying Article K.9 of the Treaty on European Union to Asylum Policy' SEC(93) 1687 final/3, point 3.

50 For example, Case C-392/95 *European Parliament* v *Council* EU:C:1997:289.

51 Art 100c TEC, as amended by the Treaty of Maastricht, [1992] C224/1 (consolidated version).

52 Art K.1 TEU, signed at Maastricht, [1992] OJ C191/1.

53 Arts 61–63 TEC, as amended by the Treaty of Amsterdam, [1997] OJ C340/173 (consolidated version). For an assessment of the previous legal regime, see Antonio Cruz, 'Visa Policy under the First Pillar: A Meaningless Compromise', in Monica den Boer (ed), *Schengen, Judicial Cooperation and Policy Coordination* (European Institute of Public Administration 1997).

54 Regarding the instruments, see infra section 5.

55 European Council, 'Conclusions' (Meeting of 4 and 5 November 2004) 14292/04, point 14.

expressed the same idea in more concise terms: the EU 'should be big on the big things'.[56] However, the bigger the thing is getting, the more difficult it will be to determine who *the* EU actually is. The development of the comprehensive approach to migration illustrates the point. It was initially confined to the external dimension, according to the Tampere European Council where the first multi-annual programme for justice and home affairs was agreed upon.[57] The EU and the Member States were to act within their respective competence, conducting external policies and ensuring coherence with the internal dimension. The CEAS was not explicitly part of the comprehensive approach but a separate goal to be realised through the adoption of common rules.[58] In comparison, the next multi-annual framework (The Hague Programme) expanded the scope of the comprehensive approach so as to involve 'all stages of migration, with respect to the root causes of migration, entry and admission policies and integration and return policies'.[59] This marked the beginning of a development where internal and external policies intertwined more and more, culminating in the present Article 78 TFEU. As mentioned, the latter integrated partnership and cooperation with third countries into the internal dimension. In other words, international migration governance (the common policy) had a growing impact on the rules of the common asylum system. Indeed, the gradual integration seems to suggest that the Member States should defer to the EU for the exercise of competence under Article 78 TFEU in its entirety because national action could adversely affect the common rules.

However, the 27 attributed a prominent role to themselves. The 2008 European Pact on Immigration and Asylum was clear in this respect. It is worth quoting the relevant paragraph in full:

> Convinced that a consistent approach is essential so as to include the management of migration among the European Union's global objectives, the European Council considers that the time has come, *in a spirit of mutual responsibility and solidarity between Member States and of partnership with third countries*, to give a new impetus to the definition of a common immigration and asylum policy that will take account of *both*

56 European Commission, 'President Jean-Claude Juncker's State of the Union Address 2017' (Speech 13 September 2017) <https://ec.europa.eu/commission/presscorner/detail/en/SPEECH_17_3165> accessed 1 March 2024.

57 European Council, 'Conclusions' (Meeting of 15 and 16 October 1999), point A.I.

58 Ibid point A.II.

59 See supra n 55, Annex I: 'The Hague Programme – Strengthening Freedom, Security and Justice in the European Union', 16.

> *the collective interest of the European Union and the specific needs of each Member State.*[60]

Within a framework of joint responsibility, each Member State was to take up parts of the common challenge. It was for example obvious that the frontline Member States exercised external border controls, 'giving access to a common area of free movement, (...) in a spirit of joint responsibility on behalf of all Member States'.[61] However, the Pact was not limited to reiterating existing legal obligations. It also called upon Member States to supplement common rules with autonomous action. They should inter alia conclude bilateral readmission agreements and offer opportunities for legal migration to third country nationals, depending on labour market needs.[62] Where competence was shared, the EU would have to show 'value added in relation to projects carried out by the Member States'.[63]

Other than labour market needs, the Pact did not refer to particular national needs or interests. On the one hand, it was not surprising given the insistence on full implementation of existing EU legislation, which in principle gave rise to the same obligations across the Union. On the other hand, this omission was noteworthy since international migration governance, with the participation of the Member States, was developing a principle of common but differentiated responsibility in international refugee law. The mentioned Convention Plus initiative was an effort in that direction, yet without leading to a horizontal framework agreement. There is no longer a gap in that respect since the adoption in 2018 of the Global Compact on Refugees[64] and the related Global Compact on Migration.[65] These legally non-binding declarations express the willingness of a large majority of UN members to better cooperate on international migration. The Global Compact for Refugees states the following in respect of national contributions:

> It will be operationalised through voluntary contributions to achieve collective outcomes and progress towards its objectives, [i.e. to ease

60 Council of the EU, 'European Pact on Immigration and Asylum' 13440/08, 4 (emphasis added).

61 Ibid 9.

62 Ibid 7, 13.

63 The Hague Programme (n 59) 42.

64 UN General Assembly, Global Compact on Refugees (2018) A/73/12 (Part 2).

65 UN General Assembly, Global Compact for Safe, Orderly and Regular Migration (2018) A/RES/73/195.

> pressure on host countries; enhance refugee self-reliance; expand access to third country solutions; and support conditions in countries of origin for return in safety and dignity]. These contributions will be determined by each State and relevant stakeholder, *taking into account their national realities, capacities and levels of development, and respecting national policies and priorities.*[66]

The Global Compact is thus more explicit in recognising the differences between states than the European Pact on Immigration and Asylum and any other EU policy document. Despite the different context, the Global Compact should inform EU policy-making because all Member States, except for Hungary, voted in favour of its adoption at the UN General Assembly. It is therefore pertinent to reflect on why taking into account national differences is crucial for a truly comprehensive approach. To recall, the previous section has explained that common security interests were the main stimulus for EU Member States to cooperate on asylum and other flanking policies of the internal market. Refugee protection is a public good because everyone benefits in terms of a higher level of security.[67] However, joint responsibility is prone to free-riding because each Member State could rely on contributions by others without fearing exclusion from the ensuing benefits. It is therefore necessary to call on Member States not only as members of the Union but also as distinct nation states. To this end, the public good should be broken up into separate elements that correspond with national interests.[68] In a matter as sensitive as immigration, states are more inclined to cater for their own interests than for altruistic concerns. Hence, cooperation requires incentives to get off the ground.[69] Comprehensive approaches are a tool to weave incentives into a framework of mutual give-and-take so that everyone assumes responsibility as part of a common whole. Each Member State would thus act on those elements it considers to be a private interest or norm. It would expect an excludable benefit while the other contributors to the comprehensive approach would profit indirectly. In terms of the theory developed in the previous chapters, each

66 Global Compact on Refugees (n 64), para 4 (emphasis added).

67 See Thielemann & Armstrong (n 16); contra: Randall Hansen, 'Making Cooperation Work: Interests, Incentives, and Action' in Randall Hansen et al. (eds), *Migration, Nation States and International Cooperation* (Routledge 2011) 17.

68 See Alexander Betts, 'Public Goods Theory and the Provision of Refugee Protection: The Role of the Joint Product Model' (2003) 16(3) Journal of Refugee Studies 274.

69 See Betts (n 68); Eiko Thielemann, 'Between Interests and Norms: Explaining Burden-Sharing in the European Union' (2003) 16(3) Journal of Refugee Studies 253; Hansen (n 67).

Member State would act so as to express its national collective self. National differences are not an obstacle to cooperation but a necessary condition since each Member State can identify itself with the common challenge.

To illustrate the argument, it is useful to recall that the humanitarian goal of providing access to durable solutions significantly informed the Union's comprehensive approach. One such durable solution is resettlement. The 27 qua European Council consistently expressed their preference for voluntary action in this field because they differ regarding their commitment to humanitarian policies.[70] For example, due to historical reasons, Germany decided to confer constitutional status on the right to seek asylum.[71] On the one hand, the German state caused refugee movements during the Second World War, while benefitting, on the other hand, from humanitarian policies elsewhere after the liberation from the Nazi regime. A historically developed sense of national responsibility may thus explain why Germany is one of the largest refugee-hosting and -supporting countries worldwide,[72] where resettlement and humanitarian admission programmes are structural policies.[73] It is acting in line with its humanitarian ideals *and* on behalf of the Union, especially of those Member States who are reluctant to participate in this element of the comprehensive approach.

5 European Cooperation and Support from the EU Institutions

This section goes on to describe how, according to the 27, the comprehensive approach should be organised in institutional terms. As we will see, the Member States promoted the institutionalisation of asylum policies to prevent negative externalities, and to create a forum for debating the terms of their

70 For example, European Pact on Immigration and Asylum (n 60) 12; The Stockholm Programme (n 28) point 6.2.3.

71 Art 16a German Basic Law; see also Tanja Podolski, 'Ein Symbol der Humanität' (2019) Legal Tribune Online <https://www.lto.de/recht/hintergruende/h/grundgesetz-70-jahre-art-16a-interview-seegmueller/#:~:text=70%20Jahre%20Grundgesetz%20%2D%20das%20Asylrecht,GG%20%22Ein%20Symbol%20der%20Humanität%22&text=Das%20Grundrecht%20auf%20Asyl%20ist,erklärt%20Robert%20Seegmüller%20im%20Interview.> accessed 1 March 2024.

72 See UNHCR, 'Germany: Fact Sheet' (February 2023) <https://www.unhcr.org/sites/default/files/legacy-pdf/640747697.pdf> accessed 1 March 2024.

73 See Federal Office for Migration and Refugees, 'Resettlement and the NesT Programme' (14 February 2023) <https://www.bamf.de/EN/Themen/AsylFluechtlingsschutz/ResettlementRelocation/Resettlement/resettlement-node.html> accessed 1 March 2024.

cooperation. The Amsterdam Treaty was the major step towards 'communitarisation' because it transferred asylum and immigration policies from an intergovernmental forum to the EU legal order (at that time, to the First Pillar). After a transitional period of five years, it formed the basis for the present-day institutional framework governed by what is still called the Community Method. The European Council determines the overall strategic guidelines; the Council of Ministers and the European Parliament co-legislate on a proposal from the Commission; and the Court of Justice subjects the EU institutions and the Member States to judicial control.

In the first place, the single institutional framework supported the common purpose of mutual non-interference. Chapter 1 already gave theoretical arguments why a legal order carried by institutions is a prerequisite for collective action. From a descriptive historical point of view, the Member States wanted to increase the effectiveness of their joint action through common institutions.[74] The proxy of effectiveness was legal certainty and uniformity in the sense that substantive harmonisation was deemed ancillary but inevitable with a view to internal free movement. That is why the Member States gradually replaced international soft law with legally binding instruments of Community and later Union law.[75] These instruments had the capacity to harmonise the laws of the Member States since the Court, especially via the preliminary ruling procedure, contributed to their uniform and effective interpretation. In this regard, common institutions should also ensure consistency and continuity of the common policy.[76] Hence, the pillar structure was gradually abolished, administrative support was rationalised,[77] and the European Council became an official EU institution responsible for the political directions of the EU as a whole and specifically within the AFSJ.[78]

In the second place, the single institutional framework has been a forum for intergovernmental cooperation. Since it might seem unusual (or for some undesirable) to think of the EU in such terms, a comparison to international

74 Secrétariat Général du Conseil de l'Union Européenne; *Conférence Intergouvernementale en vue de la Révision des Traités – Semestre de la Présidence Irlandaise* (*Recueil de Textes*) (Secrétariat Général du Conseil de l'Union Européenne 1997) 29.

75 Council of the EU, 'Action Plan of the Council and the Commission on How Best to Implement the Provisions of the Treaty of Amsterdam on an Area of Freedom, Security and Justice' [1999] OJ C19/1, point 8.

76 Art C TEU, signed at Maastricht, [1992] OJ C191/1.

77 For example, the General Secretariat of the Council took over the tasks of the Schengen General Secretariat.

78 Arts 13, 15 TEU and art 68 TFEU.

migration governance might clarify what it means to act within a forum.[79] In the first place, it is useful to distinguish between operational (agency) and political cooperation. The former was long the dominant characteristic of international migration governance. UNCHR and IOM are the relevant forums acting respectively in the fields of refugee protection and migration. UNHCR developed from a normative organisation, who issued non-binding interpretations of the Geneva Convention, into a provider of humanitarian aid. IOM has traditionally been service-oriented through information collection and operational support for the purpose of capacity-building in third countries, for example. It is self-evident that for a comprehensive approach to succeed, both knowledge and operational capacity are crucial. Suffice it to point out that return and readmission policies requires information about partner countries in order to preclude violations of the principle of non-refoulement. But ultimately, each state has to decide for itself if and in how far it makes use of the support from UNHCR and IOM. Both suffer from a lack of legal and political power because of their dependency on national financial contributions. Expertise and experience are the main pillars of their legitimacy.

Having regard to the political level, cooperation was long characterised by the absence of a multilateral framework. The UN gained greater recognition in that respect since the adoption of the mentioned Global Compacts. Regarding the Global Compact for Refugees, the main institutional innovation is the Global Refugee Forum.[80] Every four years, states take stock of progress towards the common objectives, exchange good practices and – with the support of UNHCR – review each other as far as the implementation of national pledges and contributions is concerned. While the institutional arrangements are not ideal,[81] the Global Compacts epitomise the main concern of international migration governance: falling short of centralisation, it is an effort of 'plurilateralism',[82] meaning the coordination of various initiatives within a multilateral framework.

Against that background, it is possible to reflect on the EU as a forum for intergovernmental cooperation. The aspect of operational cooperation has been less controversial among the Member States than political cooperation. Indeed, agency governance has been an important part of EU migration

79 The following is based on Chetail (n 5) pt III.

80 Global Compact on Refugees (n 64) paras 17–19.

81 See Gillian D Triggs & Patrick C J Wall, '"The Makings of a Success": The Global Compact on Refugees and the Inaugural Global Refugee Forum' (2020) 32(2) International Journal of Refugee Law 283.

82 Betts & Durieux (n 31) 519.

management, not least since the crisis in 2015/2016. However, it falls outside the scope of this book.[83] In comparison, political cooperation is not only more sensitive from the angle of national sovereignty; it is also liable to evade the single institutional framework. In this regard, political scientists described the practice of 'venue-shopping' as a deliberate strategy to circumvent institutional safeguards such as democratic control and judicial review.[84] These legal and political concerns were accompanied by a sense of abnormality because historical accounts tend to describe European integration as a continuous, irreversible process.[85] However, this ignores the relevance of the pillar structure and its legacy in the post-Lisbon institutional framework (despite the formal abolition). Before the entry into force of the Maastricht Treaty, the Member States,[86] later supported by the Commission,[87] noted the potential of the pillar structure for a comprehensive approach to migration. With hindsight, Guild formulated that potential as follows:

> Another legal analysis of the divided competence problem would entail rejecting the division of powers approach between the two Pillars in favour of a division between policy and law making which is co-extensive. "Common interest" (…) may mean a number of different things. Rather than being understood as a competence, it could just as easily mean that there is *a forum outside the Community for Member States to discuss and reach common agreement on policy without such a procedure impinging on the right of the Community to propose and adopt legislation.*[88]

On this view, the Second and Third Pillar were complementary venues for cooperation, without prejudice to the legal order of the then Community and, in particular, the law- and decision-making powers of the common

83 See generally Thym (n 12) chs 7 and 8.

84 See generally Virginie Guiraudon, 'European Integration and Migration Policy: Vertical Policy-Making as Venue-Shopping' (2000) 38(2) Journal of Common Market Studies 251; and more recently, Sandra Lavenex, 'Failing Forward' Towards Which Europe? Organized Hypocrisy in the Common European Asylum System' (2018) 56(5) Journal of Common Market Studies 1195, 1207.

85 For example, see Christian Kaunert & Sarah Léonard, 'The European Union Asylum Policy after the Treaty of Lisbon and the Stockholm Programme: Towards Supranational Governance in a Common Area of Protection?' (2012) 31(4) Refugee Survey Quarterly 1.

86 European Council (n 26) 43.

87 European Commission, 'Communication on Immigration and Asylum Policies' COM(94) 23 final, point 39.

88 Elspeth Guild, *Immigration Law in the European Community* (Kluwer 2001) 278–279 (emphasis added).

institutions. That is compatible with the view defended in this book, arguing that the 27 must in any case respect the autonomous function of the EU legal order to uphold the common purpose, which is the normative connecting factor between the European spheres.[89] The EU institutions are connecting in structural or organisational terms despite the abolition of the pillar structure. Hence, the single institutional framework shall ensure that flexible cooperation within a 'common policy' flourishes without the integrity of the CEAS being undermined .

Of central importance in this respect is the European Council. Initially only recognised under the TEU,[90] since Lisbon it has been responsible for ensuring coherence between all policies of the former pillars.[91] Composed of the Heads of State or Government, it is better placed than the Commission to ensure coherence in a sensitive domain like migration management because it represents the common EU interest, including compliance with the Treaties, and the individual national interests. In other words, the European Council can bridge the sphere of the EU legal order and the sphere of the Member States.[92] In the area of asylum, the European Council facilitates national contributions on behalf of the common interests, for example in the areas of resettlement, readmission or development aid. At the same time, it tries to safeguard the regime of internal free movement, without prejudice to the powers of the other EU institutions.

To substantiate this proposition, the origins of the principle of solidarity will be explained. It follows from the analysis in Chapter 2 that the EU legal principle as codified in Article 80 TFEU is an integral part of the EU rule of law insofar as it requires Member States to assist one another with the correct implementation of EU law in the field of migration management (at the very least when emergency measures under Article 78(3) TFEU have been taken). Apart from the EU legal principle, tailored to the functional demands of the EU legal order and especially the Schengen regime, there are 27 national understandings of solidarity, socially and culturally constructed in different national contexts. The European Council offers a forum where those varying interpretations are discussed in a 'spirit of solidarity'. Hence, following the

89 See Chapters 1 and 2.

90 Art D TEU, signed at Maastricht, [1992] OJ C191/1.

91 Together with the other EU institutions acting under the single institutional framework. The latter shall 'ensure the consistency, effectiveness and continuity of [the Union's] policies and action' (art 13 TEU).

92 For a detailed historical study, see Luuk van Middelaar, *The Passage to Europe: How a Continent Became a Union* (Yale University Press 2013).

conceptualisation in the previous chapter, the 27 fulfil a political obligation vis-à-vis the Union. Without being subject to a positive legal obligation, they are responsible for the common purpose of migration management according to political will and actual capacities. Their actions must not be contrary to the EU legal order, specifically the CEAS and related instruments.

The theoretical argument corresponds with solidarity as a practice over the course of recent integration history,[93] which is not surprising given the realist pretensions of the theory. Solidarity was intended to counterbalance the inequitable distribution of burdens under the rules of the CEAS. As mentioned, the Dublin regime assigning responsibility for asylum applications to a single Member State has always been the cornerstone of European asylum harmonisation. To mitigate the disproportionate burden on the countries at the external borders, the European Council relied primarily on financial and material support whereas relocation is a more recent and less explored form of solidarity.[94] In any case, mechanisms were devised not to overcome but to sustain the principle of individual national responsibility upon which EU-level cooperation is founded.[95] The same applied to solidarity with refugees outside the EU and with third countries. An early example is the Council Resolution of 1995 on burden-sharing with regard to the admission and residence of displaced persons on a temporary basis.[96] Against the background of the war in the former Yugoslavia, displaced persons should get temporary protection from the Member States acting 'in a concerted fashion and in a spirit of solidarity'.[97] Considering the different national capacities, the Resolution accepted contributions other than temporary protection such as crisis-mitigating measures.[98] In addition, it is important to note that action under the Resolution had to be compatible with the Dublin rules.[99] It is true that the latter was, at that time, governed by public international law just as the Resolution was cast in

93 For details, see Eleni Karageorgiou & Gregor Noll, 'What is Wrong with Solidarity in EU Asylum and Migration Law?' (2022) 4 Jus Cogens 131, who are however critical of the idea of 'common but differentiated responsibility'.

94 For example, see European Council (n 27) points 22–23.

95 The Stockholm Programme (n 28) point 6.2.2., which required that 'the principles of the CEAS are not undermined'.

96 Council of the EU, 'Resolution on Burden-Sharing with Regard to the Admission and Residence of Displaced Persons on a Temporary Basis' [1995] OJ C262/1.

97 Ibid preamble.

98 Ibid point 4.

99 Ibid preamble: 'Whereas, in the case of persons who have applied to a Member State for protection under the Geneva Convention on the Status of Refugees of 28 July 1951, this resolution must not stand in the way of the rules laid down by the Dublin Convention of 15 June 1990.' See also point 6.

international soft law. However, in view of the later integration of Dublin into the First Pillar, the Resolution could be interpreted as an early sign of the double commitment towards the Union and the common legal order. In similar vein, the Member States long favoured resettlement within the framework of regional protection programmes.[100] Hence, they prioritised voluntary repatriation and local integration in third countries over resettlement to the EU. This policy orientation was arguably due to a concern for orderly immigration into the Schengen area, and the prevalence of legally non-binding instruments that could not guarantee compliance with the common purpose. Consequently, a common institutional framework is crucial to discuss flexible national contributions and to build mutual trust in adhering to the political obligation of Union membership.[101]

6 Summary

This chapter argued that the 27 drafted the Treaties so as to enable a comprehensive approach to migration within the framework of the EU. Heavily influenced by developments at the international level, the Member States realised that the principle of international cooperation, laid down in the 1951 Geneva Convention, is best put into effect through a comprehensive approach. International cooperation as such was considered necessary in view of the unfair distribution of burdens following the application of the Geneva Convention, whose underlying principle of individual state responsibility placed a disproportionate burden on certain countries. But a mere call for international cooperation or joint responsibility is prone to collective action failure. That is why comprehensive approaches were embraced. Based on the principle of common but differentiated responsibilities, they harness the differences between states for the public good of refugee protection and the underlying security interests. States can contribute to the common challenge by using a large toolbox in various related policy areas.

The EU is well suited for a comprehensive approach to migration. The fundamental political aim to realise and safeguard a free and secure area without internal border controls is the glue holding the Member States together. This is the specific common purpose of the Union in the field of migration management, apart from the (highest) goal of perpetual peace. Moreover, the origins

100 The Hague Programme (n 59) 21.

101 See Chetail (n 5) 294ff regarding the trust-building role of soft law.

of the Geneva Convention underline the humanitarian tradition of Europe, which is anything but mere political rhetoric. More mundane, Schengen and European integration as such have created strong interdependencies and thus the need for common rules and enforcement mechanisms. At the same time, the EU is composed of diverse Member States, each having particular interests, norms and capabilities that can be put to the benefit of all under a comprehensive approach. The single institutional framework promotes mutual understanding and prevents free-riding behaviour.

Nonetheless, it is difficult to put this potential into practice. While some accuse the EU of being too permissive of national restrictive policies, others are of the opinion that it interferes too much into national sovereignty under the pretext of European values. As uncomfortable as it might seem, this is not a tension to be avoided. On the contrary, the Treaties require it to be managed. Article 78 TFEU obliges the EU to establish a common European asylum system within the framework of a common policy. It has been explained that the former developed against the backdrop of common security interests while it also forms part of a common policy with a humanitarian purpose. Article 78(2)(g) TFEU is the legal basis for external policies like resettlement that must operate within the confines of the rules of the CEAS and the underlying security rationale. Collective security and individual protection depend on each other. Without protecting refugees in third countries, the common policy would lose its humanitarian purpose, whereas neglecting the security dimension would go against the predominant rationale for European cooperation. Moreover, it would be incompatible with the principle of individual state responsibility upon which the CEAS and the Geneva Convention are founded. Each Member State is responsible for those asylum seekers and refugees it admits into its territory. Hence, entry into the common Schengen area needs to be well managed to preclude the shifting of responsibility from one Member State to another. The flipside of (passive) non-interference into the responsibility of each Member State is to assume (proactively) national responsibility on behalf of the Union. The 27 have at least expressed a greater sense of responsibility since the complexity of migration management increased and pragmatism gained momentum.

CHAPTER 4

Acting on the Internal Dimension: Implementing EU Migration Management

1 Introduction

The previous chapter made the first step into the second, more practice-oriented part of this book. Preserving public security in an area of internal free movement while protecting persons in need of international protection was identified as the specific common purpose of EU migration management. Internal rule-making is one element of the comprehensive approach just as international migration governance to which the 27 want to contribute on behalf of the Union, at least that is their intention. It is the aim of this chapter to examine the role of EU law in facilitating or obstructing movements 'inside-out', for acting on behalf of the common purpose is subject to compliance with Union law. Chapters 1 and 2 provided the theoretical background, explaining that norms of EU law are empowering if they leave sufficient room to represent the common purpose of the Union and the national political imagination.

The chapter will conduct a legal doctrinal examination into the degree of national discretion, analysing in particular the case law of the Court of Justice of the EU (CJEU) since the 'crisis' in 2015/2016. At the same time, it will construct the identified remaining national powers as a chance to represent the Union and to contribute to the comprehensive approach to migration. It will thus offer a novel lens of responsible Member States, to be distinguished from (extreme) views seeing Member States either as agents of the EU, so that implementation is nothing but a quasi-automatic legal process, or as sovereign nation states, reducing the interpretation and application of Union law to a matter of political will. That said, this chapter does not suggest that the Member States whose behaviour was subject to judicial review in fact claimed to act on behalf of the common purpose. Nor does this chapter postulate that their behaviour ought to be recognised as a legitimate representation of the Union. The scope of the inquiry is instead limited to what the Member States are legally allowed to do and that is, at the same time, a justification and a frame to assume responsibility (which may or may not be used). Although dealing with the legislation applicable pending the entry into force of the New Pact on Migration and Asylum, the reconstruction will be of continued

 | DOI:10.1163/9789004695733_006

interest, considering that the new laws will increase the degree of national discretion and thereby the room to represent the Union.[1]

The examination will cover several internal policies of the comprehensive approach, showing in each case the dynamic movements between the spheres. The first section will demonstrate how the Member States may assume responsibility for individual protection, followed by a section dealing with the common purpose of public security. The third section will analyse the rules on the reintroduction of internal borders, complemented with a case study from German practice. The concluding section will give an overview of the limiting and empowering potential of EU law in the field of migration management.

2 Responsibility for Individual Protection

2.1 *Allocating Responsibility under the Common European Asylum System* (*CEAS*)

Since EU asylum law only applies within the territorial jurisdiction of the Member States, a person seeking international protection has to enter the EU via the external borders. The Schengen Borders Code stipulates that third country nationals who do not fulfil the entry conditions for an intended stay of no more than 90 days within any 180-day period, shall be refused entry at the external borders, unless the person concerned asks for asylum.[2] As the Schengen Borders Code shifted border controls from the internal to the external borders, a third country national who has crossed the external borders can, as a matter of fact, move freely within the Schengen Area. Thus, the frontline Member States act on behalf of the other Schengen States.[3] 'Strict compliance'[4] with the rules of the Schengen Borders Code is imperative in order not to create negative externalities. Failing that, the frontline Member States must assume responsibility in accordance with the Dublin Regulation (assuming that, indeed, the third country national was registered as an asylum seeker). According to the first entry/stay rule, that Member State who failed to prevent the irregular border crossing is responsible for examining the application for international protection.[5] The other criteria for determining responsibility

---

1 See Conclusions, sub-s 2.1.

2 Arts 6, 14 Regulation 2016/399/EU of 9 March 2016 on a Union Code on the rules governing the movement of persons across borders ('Schengen Borders Code') [2016] OJ L77/1.

3 Recital (6) Schengen Borders Code.

4 Case C-606/10 *ANAFE* v *Ministre de l'Intérieur* EU:C:2012:348, para 26.

5 Art 13 Regulation No 604/2013/EU of 26 June 2013 establishing the criteria and mechanisms for determining the Member State responsible for examining an application for

follow the same logic: having conferred a right of legal stay or residence to the asylum seeker or to his or her family members triggers responsibility under the Dublin Regulation.[6] Similar to the rules on external border controls, the Dublin system aims to assign the Member State that is supposed to act on behalf of the others. Whereas the Member States are collectively responsible for granting access to the asylum procedure, a single Member State determined according to the said criteria will be in charge of the examination in any individual case.[7] Procedural rules, including strict time limits, regulate the intergovernmental cooperation in rather great detail to avoid the phenomenon of 'refugees in orbit', meaning that Member States shift the burden to one another without anyone of them assuming responsibility.[8]

The determination of the Member State responsible has legal consequences beyond the rules of the Dublin Regulation. More specifically, lodging an application for international protection triggers, apart from the intergovernmental Dublin procedure, a set of individual rights under various instruments of the CEAS. Although the Member State where the application was lodged is, inter alia, obliged to comply with certain procedural obligations and material reception conditions, the main burden falls on the Member State responsible. Provided the national asylum procedure does not suffer from major deficits and the number of applications is not exceptionally high, the period after status determination constitutes the biggest challenge. If the applicant is recognised as a beneficiary of international protection, the Member State responsible is obliged to grant socio-economic rights such as access to employment, education, accommodation and social welfare benefits.[9] If the applicant's protection claim is rejected, the stay becomes in principle illegal, requiring the Member State responsible to remove the person from EU territory.[10] In either case, the Member State designated in accordance with the Dublin Regulation

international protection lodged in one of the Member States by a third-country national or a stateless person ('Dublin Regulation') [2013] OJ L180/31.

6 Arts 7–12 Dublin Regulation.

7 Art 3(1) Dublin Regulation.

8 Preamble of the Convention determining the State responsible for examining applications for asylum lodged in one of the Member States of the European Communities ('Dublin Convention') [1997] OJ C254/1 ('to ensure that applicants for Asylum are not referred successively from one Member State to another without any of these States acknowledging itself to be competent to examine the application for asylum').

9 Arts 14–19 Directive 2013/33/EU of 26 June 2013 laying down standards for the reception of applicants for international protection ('Reception Conditions Directive') [2013] OJ L180/96.

10 Arts 6, 8 Directive 2008/115/EC of 16 December 2008 on common standards and procedures in Member States for returning illegally staying third-country nationals ('Return Directive') [2008] OJ L348/98.

remains responsible because the third- country national does not benefit from free movement rights within the Schengen area.[11]

Furthermore, Member States have to apply the said rules of EU asylum and migration law in line with fundamental rights as derived from the EU Charter, the European Convention on Human Rights (ECHR) and international law.[12] In particular, the scope of the principle of non-refoulement, originally circumscribed by the narrow refugee definition under international refugee law, was widened to cover instances of inhuman or degrading treatment within the meaning of Article 4 of the Charter (Article 3 ECHR), including various forms of mistreatment ranging from torture to inhuman living conditions. In the EU, the CEAS is based on the principle of mutual trust, that is, on a presumption of compliance with fundamental rights.[13] Indeed, the CEAS in its entirety is based on that presumption, so Member States are responsible for protecting fundamental rights at *all* stages of the asylum procedure and thereafter. This follows from the recent judgment in *Jawo*, in which the Court found that even though the Dublin Regulation only applies to applicants for international protection, a transfer is prohibited if in case of recognition, the status holder would suffer from inhuman or degrading treatment on account of the living conditions in the Member State responsible.[14]

This begs the questions when the risk of inhuman or degrading treatment is such as to merit the prohibition of transfer, and who is then responsible for the asylum application. These questions are important for the present inquiry, for they refer to deviations from the principle of mutual (or blind) trust. More precisely, under certain conditions, the Member State responsible is not considered able to act on behalf of the common humanitarian purpose. But in discharging their joint responsibility, the Member States have to allocate the task to any one of them (or to a third country).

---

11 A contrario art 7(1) Reception Conditions Directive.

12 Member States are bound by the Charter of Fundamental Rights whenever they are implementing Union law, according to art 51 of the Charter. All Member States are parties to the ECHR and the Convention Relating to the Status of Refugees ('Geneva Convention'), UNTS vol 189, p 137.

13 Joined Cases C-411/10 and C-493/10 *N.S. and Others* v *Secretary of State for the Home Department and Others* EU:C:2011:865, para 83.

14 Case C-163/17 *Jawo* v *Germany* EU:C:2019:218, paras 87–89; see also Mattias Wendel, 'Die Pflicht zur Berücksichtigung von anerkannt Schutzbedürftigen im EU-Ausland' (2019) 74(20) Juristenzeitung 983.

2.2 *Responsibility and Exceptions to Mutual Trust*

To answer the first question, it is necessary to examine the jurisprudence of the CJEU since the seminal ruling in the *N.S.* case. Following that judgment, a Dublin transfer is precluded 'if there are substantial grounds for believing that there are systemic flaws in the asylum procedure and the reception conditions for asylum applicants in the Member State responsible, resulting in inhuman or degrading treatment, within the meaning of Article 4 of the Charter'.[15] The threshold of systemic deficiencies turned out to be difficult to square with the test of the European Court of Human Rights (ECtHR) requiring a 'thorough and individualised examination of the situation of the individual concerned'.[16] In the case of *CK*, the Luxembourg Court adopted the lower threshold of the Strasbourg Court to a limited extent, meaning that an individual risk is in principle capable of giving rise to a violation of Article 4 CFR.[17] However, the former Court highlighted the exceptional circumstances of that case where the transfer in itself of the mentally ill applicant could have amounted to inhuman or degrading treatment.[18] At the same time, it did not modify its position on the principle of mutual trust.[19]

The nature of the risk, individual or systemic, is not by itself conclusive as to whether it may result in inhuman or degrading treatment. Whether or not the required threshold for suspending a Dublin transfer is reached, depends on all the circumstances of the case. If the breakdown of the national asylum system affects the essence of the right to seek asylum, a Dublin transfer is precluded.[20] The same applies to cases of extreme vulnerability, for example where families with small children are concerned.[21] After recognition, the threshold of inhuman or degrading treatment will only be reached if the beneficiary of international protection finds himself 'in a situation of extreme material poverty that does not allow himself to meet his most basic needs'.[22] In all these cases, the threshold is high, excluding minor infringements of EU legislation.[23] Mostly, the Member State where the applicant or the status holder is present, is thus not obliged to absolve the Member State designated under the Dublin

15 *N.S.* (n 13) para 86.
16 *Tarakhel* v *Switzerland* App no 29217/12 (ECtHR, 4 November 2014), para 104.
17 Case C-578/16 PPU *C.K. and Others* v *Slovenia* EU:C:2017:127, paras 91–92.
18 Ibid para 94.
19 Ibid para 95.
20 The situation in *N.S.* (n 13).
21 The situation in *Tarakhel* (n 16).
22 *Jawo* (n 14) para 92.
23 Ibid para 93; *N.S.* (n 13) para 85.

Regulation from its responsibility. In other words, the principle of mutual trust stands, except for the most serious violations of fundamental rights.

Despite the exceptional nature of inter-state scrutiny, national courts should be aware of the circumstances when exactly an interference with the responsibility of another Member State is justified. Put differently, when is a violation of EU law 'minor' and when is it so serious as to justify a deviation from the principle of mutual trust? To start with, since fundamental rights are at stake, it is necessary to consider the individual circumstances of each case, so a general, abstract risk is never conclusive. With this in mind, it is possible to derive limits to mutual trust from the inter-state relationships in the legal and political order of the EU. The Member States decided to take joint responsibility for a comprehensive approach to migration that includes, as a minimum, temporary protection against persecution and indiscriminate violence. Each Member State must participate in that element of the comprehensive approach by virtue of the Geneva Convention and the EU Treaties. If a Member State is unable to fulfil its obligations, the others must step in. The situation in Greece, which gave rise to the judgments in *M.S.S.* and *N.S.*, is a clear example because the authorities were unable to realise the right to seek asylum. Because of the systemic nature of the deficiencies, Dublin transfers were temporarily suspended. Without European support, Greece was simply not able to rectify the shortcomings. By contrast, if a Member State *can* restore the rule of law, it will not be absolved of its responsibility. In *Ibrahim*, the Court had to clarify whether a Member State (Germany) was precluded from declaring asylum applications inadmissible if the applicants were granted subsidiary protection in another Member State (Bulgaria) where the latter systematically refuses to grant refugee status.[24] Although the Court held that the Bulgarian practice was contrary to Article 18 of the Charter, Germany was not obliged to declare the applications admissible. Instead, the persons concerned had to return to Bulgaria where the authorities were required to resume the procedure for the obtaining of refugee status.[25]

Next, it is part of the comprehensive approach to offer durable solutions for persons with a recognised protection status. For those already present in the EU, there are two options: return to the country of origin as soon as the situation permits, or long-term integration into the Member State of lawful stay. Because of the policy discretion involved, exceptions to mutual trust are highly circumscribed. Article 34 of the Qualification Directive requires Member States to

---

24 Joined Cases C-297/17, C-318/17, C-319/17, C-438/17 *Ibrahim and Others* v *Germany* EU:C:2019:219; see also Wendel (n 14).

25 *Ibrahim* (n 24) paras 99–100.

ensure access to 'appropriate' integration programmes in order to facilitate the integration of beneficiaries of international protection into society.[26] In *Jawo*, which concerned a Dublin transfer from Germany to Italy, the Court held that an infringement of this rule does not amount to inhuman or degrading treatment in the sense of Article 4 of the Charter, notwithstanding the situation in Italy whose underdeveloped social system causes a particular disadvantage to beneficiaries of international protection who, unlike the Italian population, cannot rely on personal support networks.[27] By contrast, the Advocate General echoed the concerns of the referring court observing that insufficient language skills render more difficult the exercise of the (other) rights laid down in the Qualification Directive.[28] Following this reasoning, a failure to ensure access to integration programmes, especially language courses, is liable to undermine the useful effect of the right to social welfare. Having regard to all relevant facts, this may amount to inhuman or degrading treatment. It is submitted that this effects-based reasoning constitutes a disproportionate limitation on the principle of mutual trust. First, recognition as a beneficiary of international protection entails a right to equal treatment with the nationals of the Member State of lawful residence.[29] This rule, which is in line with the Geneva Convention, reflects the different legal status during and after the asylum procedure. But save for exceptional circumstances, an interpretation in light of fundamental rights must not lead to a situation where beneficiaries of international protection are treated more favourably than the nationals of the host state.[30] Second, the policy discretion in the said Article 34 empowers each Member State to determine in how far integration is desirable with a view to a durable solution for the individual concerned. In order not to interfere with this responsibility, a dynamic interpretation in light of fundamental rights should be treated with caution. However, the EU legislature should specify the minimum content of integration programmes necessary for restoring the person's autonomy with a view to both sustainable re-integration into the society of the home country and, if the former option is not feasible, permanent residence in the host Member State.

---

26 Art 34 Directive 2011/95/EU of 13 December 2011 on standards for the qualification of third-country nationals or stateless persons as beneficiaries of international protection, for a uniform status for refugees or for persons eligible for subsidiary protection, and for the content of the protection granted ('Qualification Directive') [2011] OJ L337/9.

27 *Jawo* (n 14) paras 94–97.

28 Opinion of AG Wathelet in Case C-163/17 *Jawo* v *Germany* EU:C:2018:613, paras 140–142.

29 For example, art 29 of the Qualification Directive on social welfare.

30 See Daniel Thym, 'Rücküberstellung von anerkannten Schutzberechtigten innerhalb der EU' (2018) 37(9) Neue Zeitschrift für Verwaltungsrecht 609, 612ff.

In case a transfer is precluded, the issue arises who should instead assume responsibility for the person seeking international protection. Article 17 of the Dublin Regulation, the so-called sovereignty clause, allows a Member State to examine an application for international protection lodged with it even if such examination is not its responsibility according to the criteria laid down in the Regulation.[31] The Court has consistently held that the application of the sovereignty clause is not subject to any conditions because it was introduced to allow for autonomous decisions 'for political, humanitarian or practical considerations'.[32] Hence, the Member State concerned has the choice between examining the application itself or continuing the procedure for determining the Member State responsible under the criteria in the Dublin Regulation. Only if the procedure takes an unreasonable length of time, the Member State concerned must itself examine the application.[33] Although the Court has not found any other instance where the voluntary option turns into an obligation, the mere fact that Article 17 of the Dublin Regulation is subject to compliance with fundamental rights has inspired doctrinal constructions.[34] This again leads to the mentioned objections, especially because the text of the sovereignty clause does in no way constrain national discretion. An interpretation in light of fundamental rights should not unnecessarily reduce the power to act on behalf of the Union. For example, Member States applied the sovereignty clause to avoid the cumbersome procedures of the Dublin Regulation,[35] and thereby contributed to the rapid processing of asylum applications – serving both asylum seekers and the functioning of the CEAS because it reduces the risk of secondary movements. Similarly, Member States should not be deprived of a flexible application of the so-called humanitarian clause, permitting them to request each other to take charge of an applicant with a view to re-uniting him or her with family members on humanitarian grounds.[36]

2.3 *Responsibility in Light of Interdependence*

Furthermore, the question as to where responsibility should lie is determined by the inter-state relationships in the Union. If EU rules such as Article 17

---

31 Art 17 Dublin Regulation.

32 Case C-528/11 *Halaf* EU:C:2013:342, para 37.

33 *N.S.* (n 13) para 98.

34 For example, see Constantin Hruschka & Francesco Maiani, 'Dublin III Regulation' in Kay Hailbronner & Daniel Thym (eds), *EU Immigration and Asylum Law: A Commentary* (2nd edition, Beck 2016) 1499–1500.

35 See Agnès G Hurwitz, *The Collective Responsibility of States to Protect Refugees* (OUP 2009) 106–111.

36 Art 18 Dublin Regulation.

of the Dublin Regulation are silent in this respect, an interpretation in light of the principle of sincere cooperation will be necessary. When Germany announced the 'suspension' of the Dublin procedure in respect of Syrian refugees in autumn 2015, it put an end to the humanitarian crisis in Hungary where thousands of people got stranded. They could travel onwards to Germany in order to lodge an application for international protection there. Moreover, the announcement stimulated asylum seekers who were staying in camps outside Europe to travel to Germany. Wendel convincingly argues that the large-scale application of the sovereignty clause overstretched the limits of administrative discretion, contrary to the principle of sincere cooperation that would have required, at least, 'intensive and ongoing coordination and the greatest possible consideration for the interests of fellow Member States'.[37]

Certain rules of EU legislation do contain limits on the exercise of national discretion in order not to upset the constitutional relationships in the Union. According to Article 6(5)(c) of the Schengen Borders Code, a Member State may derogate from the entry conditions laid down in paragraph 1 of that provision in order to allow a third-country national 'to enter its territory on humanitarian grounds, on grounds of national interest or because of international obligations'.[38] Conversely, entry into the territory of one Member State for transit purposes is prohibited, unless the third country national holds a residence permit from another Member State. A violation of the entry conditions amounts to irregularly crossing the border into the first Member State within the meaning of Article 13 of the Dublin Regulation. The Court confirmed this systematic interpretation in *Jafari*.[39] The applicants sought international protection in Austria after having crossed the EU external border in Croatia. They argued that the Croatian 'waving through policy' was covered by Article 6(5)(c) of the Schengen Borders Code. The Court rejected the argument by setting out a systematic reasoning. Recalling the 'direct link' between the Dublin Regulation and border management, the Court went on to find that 'each Member State is answerable to all the other Member States for its actions concerning the entry and residence of third-country nationals and must bear the consequences thereof in a spirit of solidarity and fair cooperation'.[40] Hence, a Member State will have to assume responsibility for the asylum application in

37 Mattias Wendel, 'The Refugee Crisis and the Executive: On the Limits of Administrative Discretion in the Common European Asylum System' (2016) 17(6) German Law Journal 1005, 1028.

38 Art 6(5)(c) Schengen Borders Code.

39 Case C-646/16 *Jafari* EU:C:2017:586.

40 Ibid para 88.

accordance with Article 13 of the Dublin Regulation if it failed to ensure that the power recognised by Article 6(5)(c) of the Schengen Borders Code does not produce negative spill-over effects in the sense of secondary movements.

From a constitutional perspective, that Member State must consider the implications for the Union when authorising entry into its territory. In that regard, the Court specified that it is immaterial whether the border crossing 'was tolerated or authorised in breach of the applicable rules or whether it was authorised on humanitarian grounds by way of derogation from the entry conditions generally imposed on third-country nationals'.[41] On the one hand, in a legal system based on the rule of law, even the best intentions cannot excuse a violation of the applicable rules. On the other hand, intention does matter from the angle of the national collective self. Instead of creating adverse external effects, a Member State may just as well make a positive contribution to the common interests.

The case of *X and X* v *Belgium* is an instructive example.[42] It was brought by a Syrian family living in Aleppo during the civil war. At the Belgian embassy in Lebanon, they applied for a humanitarian visa with limited territorial validity on the basis of Article 25(1)(a) of the Visa Code stipulating that a Member State may derogate from the entry conditions in the Schengen Borders Code in order to grant a visa on, inter alia, humanitarian grounds that is valid for the territory of that State.[43] Belgium refused the request on grounds of, first, Article 32(1)(b) of the Visa Code requiring Member States, without prejudice to Article 25(1), to refuse a visa if there are reasonable grounds as to the applicant's intention to leave the territories of the Member States before the expiry of the visa. Second, Belgium argued that fundamental rights, notably the prohibition of inhuman or degrading treatment, do not impose a positive obligation on Member States to grant a humanitarian visa. The Court agreed with Belgium on the first issue, holding that since the applicants in fact aimed at long-term residence in Belgium, the subject matter fell outside the scope of EU law.[44] It was then no longer necessary to rule on the second, more disputed question. Some commentators suggested that the Court deliberately avoided a ruling on the substance out of concern for the systemic integrity of the CEAS, which could be undermined if visa applications were used to get access to procedures

---

41 Ibid para 92.

42 Case C-638/16 PPU *X and X* v *Belgium* EU:C:2017:173.

43 Art 25(1)(a) Regulation No 810/2009/EC of the European Parliament and of the Council of 13 July 2009 establishing a Community Code on Visas ('Visa Code') [2009] OJ L243/1.

44 *X and X* (n 42) para 45.

for international protection.[45] However, the Court should have addressed the matter because a refusal to grant a visa *is* an application of the Visa Code that triggers the application of EU fundamental rights.[46]

It is interesting to consider how the Court *could* have ruled on the substantive question as to whether Member States may have a positive obligation to grant a humanitarian visa. The obligation to refuse a visa if the applicant is unlikely to leave the EU in due time is without prejudice to the right of Member States to grant a humanitarian visa.[47] While the former rule is intended to reduce the risk of secondary movements, the latter respects the national competence to decide on entry and residence in individual cases. But instead of carving out an 'island' of national sovereignty, the legislature established a systematic link to the common purpose as specified in Article 32(1)(b). Consequently, while not explicitly stated in the Regulation, it is submitted that once a Member State exercises its policy discretion to grant a humanitarian visa, it incurs legal obligations upon expiry of the visa: to either issue a new residence document or to return the person concerned in accordance with the Return Directive. The initial decision to issue a humanitarian visa is then rather a political obligation vis-à-vis the Union insofar as persons in need of protection get shelter in a regular manner as opposed to uncontrolled arrivals that put pressure on national asylum systems. The exercise of that power obviously depends on political will informed by the national identity.

However, according to Advocate General Mengozzi, the obligation to issue a humanitarian visa was of a legal nature by dint of Article 25(1)(a) of the Visa Code and it was triggered when the humanitarian grounds put forward by the applicant are well founded.[48] The discretion in the latter respect was circumscribed by EU law and the Charter of Fundamental Rights in particular. Hence, a Member State had a positive obligation to issue a humanitarian visa if it knew or ought to have known that the person concerned is exposed to a genuine risk of inhuman or degrading treatment in the sense of Article 4 of

45 See Margarite Zoeteweij & Sarah Progin-Theuerkauf, 'CJEU Case C-638/16 PPU, X and X – Dashed Hopes for a Legal Pathway to Europe' (2017) European Law Blog <https://europeanlawblog.eu/2017/03/10/cjeu-case-c-63816-ppu-x-and-x-dashed-hopes-for-a-legal-pathway-to-europe/#:~:text=on%20EU%20law-,CJEU%20Case%20C%2D638%2F16%20PPU%2C%20X%20and%20X,a%20legal%20pathway%20to%20Europe&text=On%207%20March%202017%2C%20the,EU%20Charter%20of%20Fundamental%20Rights.> accessed 1 March 2024; Shu-Perng Hwang, 'Humanitäre Visa für Flüchtlinge: Einfallstor für ein unbeschränktes Asylrecht?' (2018) 53(3) Europarecht 269.

46 Ibid.

47 Art 32(1) in conjunction with art 25(1) Visa Code.

48 Opinion of AG Mengozzi in Case C-638/16 PPU *X and X* v *Belgium* EU:C:2017:93, para 120ff.

the Charter (and Article 3 ECHR). In his opinion, the threshold was reached in the context of the Syrian civil war, so he advised the Court to find a violation of Belgium's positive obligation under Article 4 of the Charter. His reasoning and conclusion are comprehensible in view of the situation in Syria. But in more general terms, it is submitted that the (legal or political) obligation to grant a humanitarian visa under exceptional circumstances is not only a constraint but also an opportunity for Member States to create the conditions that preclude the application of the obligation in the first place. Under a comprehensive approach, the Member States have more than one option to take humanitarian responsibility. For example, they could contribute to temporary protection close to the refugees' countries of origin. A group of willing Member States could also use the procedure for enhanced cooperation to promote legal certainty about humanitarian visas. In any event, the Member States should have discretion to determine on a case-by-case basis how to best realise individual protection. Article 4 of the Charter is in that sense both an incentive and a safety net.

No or a limited margin of discretion can instead lead to a suboptimal allocation of responsibility. In the case of *X*,[49] the Court had to deal with the phenomenon of multiple applications submitted by the same person in two Member States. The applicant lodged two applications for international protection in the Netherlands, the first had the force of res judicata at the material time. Pending appeal proceedings against the rejection of the second application, the applicant was accused of a sexual offence which led him to abscond to Italy where he lodged a new application. Although Italy surrendered the person to the Netherlands on the basis of a European Arrest Warrant, the Dutch authorities requested Italy to take him back on grounds of the new application pending in that country. For their part, the Italian authorities argued that the Dublin Regulation required the Netherlands to take the person back, yet they failed to submit the take back request within the prescribed time limit. That is why Italy became responsible under Article 23(3) of the Dublin Regulation. The Dutch court asked the CJEU whether a transfer is precluded where the transferring Member State (the Netherlands) had previously examined asylum applications of the person concerned and where appeal proceedings were still pending.

Based mainly on a literal interpretation of the rules, the Court held that responsibility shifts to the Member State where the new application was lodged (Italy) as soon as the time limit for a take back request has expired.[50] In

49 Case C-213/17 *X* v *Staatssecretaris van Veiligheid en Justitie* EU:C:2018:538.

50 Ibid paras 35–40.

contrast to this sober reasoning, Advocate General Bot suggested derogating from the clear wording of Article 23(3) of the Dublin Regulation, which in his view resulted in 'absurd consequences'[51] for the individual who is subject to 'a game of ping-pong'[52] contrary to his human dignity. In view of the ongoing proceedings in the Netherlands, the Dutch authorities were 'best placed'[53] to assume responsibility for the person concerned. The AG sought to justify the proposed derogation by reference to the objectives of the Dublin Regulation and the principles underpinning the CEAS. Having regard to the objective of rapidly processing asylum applications by a single Member State, the automatic transfer of responsibility would deprive the procedure of 'the rationality, objectivity and fairness pursued by the EU legislature'.[54] In that regard, AG Bot gave arguments related to the legitimacy of the Dublin system.[55] First, the automatic transfer of responsibility was tantamount to imposing a penalty on Italy, even though the third application lodged in that country was probably abusive. Second, there was the risk of inconsistent decision-making where two Member States rule on asylum applications by the same person on a similar if not identical matter. The Member States would in fact call into question each other's decisions, which increased the risk of secondary movements. Regarding the foundations of the CEAS, the Advocate General referred to the principles of sincere cooperation and solidarity. He argued that the Member States could not have been unaware of the migratory pressure on Italy at the material time, which rendered it difficult for the Italian authorities to comply with the strict time limits. Relying on the bare rules without regard to the circumstances on the ground was contrary to the principles of sincere cooperation and solidarity. He concluded by suggesting a derogation from Article 23(3) of the Dublin Regulation 'in order to preserve the effectiveness of that regulation'.[56]

This interpretation of the principles of sincere cooperation and solidarity stands in stark contrast to the Court's ruling in *Jafari*, holding that these principles command strict compliance with the rules of the Schengen Borders Code and the Dublin Regulation. And strict compliance in turn safeguards the common purpose of mutual non-interference, in line with the frame of the EU legal order. In comparison, AG Bot suggested that the Member States, albeit in

---

51 Opinion of AG Bot in Case C-213/17 *X* v *Staatssecretaris van Veiligheid en Justitie* EU:C:2018:434, para 8.
52 Ibid para 97.
53 Ibid para 84.
54 Ibid para 10.
55 Ibid para 78ff.
56 Ibid para 101.

the special circumstances of the *X* case, will only observe the said principles if they *deviate* from the rules. He offered another solution from within the EU legal order. The Member States should mutually recognise negative asylum decisions, a principle that is contained in Article 33(2)(d) of the Procedures Directive.[57] It stipulates that the Member States may declare an asylum application inadmissible if the latter is a subsequent application, where no new elements or findings have arisen or have been presented by the applicant. The Court later clarified that the Member States may apply that provision without first having to use the procedures of the Dublin Regulation.[58] Hence, once Italy had declared the application inadmissible on that basis, the status of the person concerned would become irregular and a return to the Netherlands would have been possible, for example under a bilateral readmission agreement.[59] To give effect to the principle of (negative) mutual recognition is a way to recognise other Member States as one-of-us regarding the goal of preventing secondary movements, and the underlying common purpose of public security.

3 Responsibility for Public Security

This section deals with the return of irregularly staying third-country nationals including rejected asylum seekers and other persons without a legal entitlement to stay on the territories of the Member States. The section thereafter is specifically devoted to the issue of return in the context of reintroduced internal border controls. So far, this chapter has analysed rules on the relationship between the Member States and individual third-country nationals. The rules acquired an inter-state dimension following a constructive interpretation according to the theoretical framework of the European spheres. By contrast, the application of certain rules of the Return Directive a priori has consequences for the entire Union. Each Member State decides on the legality of stay or residence in national procedures. For example, it may concern an applicant for international protection whose application was rejected, or an economic migrant who lost his right of residence after a criminal conviction. The national decision gets a European dimension in two situations: first, a Member State may enforce a return decision issued by another Member State;[60] second,

57 Ibid para 102ff.

58 *Ibrahim* (n 24) paras 75–80.

59 As was the case in *Ibrahim* (n 24).

60 Council Directive 2001/40/EC of 28 May 2001 on the mutual recognition of decisions on the expulsion of third country nationals [2001] OJ L149/34 ('Mutual Recognition Directive').

a Member State may issue a return decision accompanied by an entry ban, which is applicable to the entire Schengen area.[61] The following paragraphs will address these situations in turn.

At the outset, the mentioned situations imply that a third country national is staying illegally in the Member State concerned. For the purposes of the Return Directive, illegal stay means the presence on the territory of a Member State, of a third-country national who does not fulfil or no longer fulfils the entry conditions as set out in the Schengen Borders Code or other conditions of national immigration law.[62] However, since the EU legislature failed to cross-reference the Procedures Directive, several Member States do not systematically issue a return decision following a negative final asylum decision.[63] The latter should automatically lead to an enforceable return decision. In any case, the enforcing Member State must arrange the return and readmission with third countries as regards, inter alia, the identity and travel documents of the person concerned. Obviously, a return must not entail the risk of direct or indirect refoulement.

3.1 *Enforcing a Return Decision on Behalf of Another Member State*

Regarding the first situation, any Member State may enforce a return decision on behalf of the issuing Member State, even though it is in principle only valid in the territory of the latter. The purpose is to deter secondary movements following a negative decision and to remove the illegally staying third-country national as swiftly as possible from EU territory. To make sure that Member States are mutually aware of return decisions, they shall enter alerts on return into the Schengen Information System (SIS), in accordance with Regulation 2018/1860/EU on the use of the SIS for the return of illegally staying third-country nationals.[64] If the person subject to a return decision is apprehended in another, the enforcing Member State, the latter 'shall immediately contact the issuing Member State (…) in order to determine the measures to be taken'.[65] More specifically, the enforcing Member State has three options: (1) it may issue a new return decision after having determined that the person

61 Art 11 Return Directive.

62 Art 3(2) Return Directive.

63 Recital (11) Commission Recommendation of 7 March 2017 on making returns more effective when implementing the Directive 2008/115/EC C(2017) 1600 final. The new Asylum Procedure Regulation contains an obligation to that effect, see European Parliament, Text of the Asylum Procedure Regulation, adopted at 1st Reading, T9-0177/2024, art 37.

64 Art 3(1) Regulation 2018/1860/EU of 28 November 2018 on the use of the Schengen Information System for the return of illegally staying third-country nationals [2018] OJ L312/1 ('SIS Regulation').

65 Art 7(2) SIS Regulation.

concerned has been staying illegally on its territory; (2) it may recognise the decision of the issuing Member State pursuant to Directive 2001/40/EC on the mutual recognition of decisions on the expulsion of third-country nationals; or (3) it may return the person to the issuing Member State if a bilateral readmission agreement is in place. During the law-making procedure, the European Parliament criticised the Commission for not requiring Member States to use Directive 2001/40/EC. Issuing a new return decision would delay the removal of the illegally staying third-country national.[66] The responsible Commissioner at that time clarified that mutual recognition of return decisions was ideal, but the Member States could eventually choose with a view to an effective return policy.[67]

At first, the statement is implausible because mutual recognition seems to be the most effective procedure in almost every case. However, it is anything but automatic since not every Member State recognises that possibility. For example, according to the Netherlands, '[i]t ensues from the scheme of the [Return] Directive that irregular stay in a Member State's territory must be established by that Member State. The Directive does not provide for an exception if the irregular stay has already been established by another Member State'.[68] In case of recognition of return decisions issued elsewhere, the grounds and requirements for return differ across the Union.[69] According to the Mutual Recognition Directive, the duty of mutual recognition applies when a third-country national was sentenced to a term of imprisonment of at least one year or the person is accused of 'serious criminal offences' within the territory of a Member State.[70] The EU legislature neither defined 'serious criminal offences' as far as the Mutual Recognition Directive is concerned, nor did it cross-reference the list of those offences that give rise to mandatory execution

66 European Parliament, 'Mutual Recognition of Return Decisions' (Question for written answer E-002722-17to the Commission, 12 April 2017) <https://www.europarl.europa.eu/doceo/document/E-8-2017-002722_EN.html> accessed 1 March 2024.

67 European Parliament, 'Mutual Recognition of Return Decisions' (Answer to question E-002722/2017, 27 June 2017) https://www.europarl.europa.eu/doceo/document/E-8-2017-002722-ASW_EN.html> accessed 1 March 2024.

68 European Migration Network, 'The Effectiveness of Return in EU Member States: Challenges and Good Practices Linked to EU Rules and Standards – Response from the Netherlands' (European Migration Network 2017) 36.

69 See European Migration Network, 'The Effectiveness of Return in EU Member States: Challenges and Good Practices Linked to EU Rules and Standards – Synthesis Report' (European Migration Network 2018) 35–36.

70 Art 3(1) Mutual Recognition Directive.

of a European Arrest Warrant.[71] In addition, the obligation of mutual recognition applies when the return decision is based on a 'failure to comply with national rules on the entry or residence of aliens'. This rule at least obstructs the will of any Member State to act in the name of another, for it imposes a strict obligation without the option to reject the rules of another Member State as other-than-us. Finally, mutual recognition is rendered more difficult since several Member States systematically fail to issue a return decision after having rejected an application for international protection. The basic problem is the same: the rules refer to national law and fail to induce Member States to use their powers for the common purpose. They reveal a disconnect with the intermediate sphere.

It follows that mutual recognition does not guarantee optimal outcomes. It is still one out of three options to realise the objective of an effective return policy. The SIS Regulation is a welcome reform because it enables Member States, on a bilateral basis, to take an informed decision about the return of an illegally staying third-country national. The duty to find a bilateral solution to any legal or practical problem is praiseworthy, apart from the possibility to take into account the external dimension as well. Since return is dependent on readmission into a third country, the diplomatic relationship to that country should inform the internal decision as to which of the two Member States should assume responsibility for the return. Although not required by EU law, it would contribute to the success of the common policy because under the comprehensive approach, the Member State that is best able to perform a certain task should do so.

3.2 *Issuing an Entry Ban on Behalf of All*

Unlike a return decision, an entry ban has by definition a European dimension because it prohibits entry into and stay on the territory of all Member States.[72] Issuing an entry ban prima facie qualifies as action on behalf of the Union, so it is necessary to inquire when and on what grounds it is mandatory or optional. It is mandatory if no period for voluntary departure has been granted or if the obligation to return has not been complied with.[73] In other cases, Member States may issue an entry ban.[74] Even the first, mandatory ground leaves ample room for national discretion because it depends on whether national

71 Art 2(2) Council Framework Decision 2002/584/JHA of 13 June 2002 on the European arrest warrant and the surrender procedures between Member States [2002] OJ L190/1.

72 Recital (14) and art 3(6) Return Directive.

73 Art 11(1) Return Directive.

74 Ibid.

authorities decide to grant a period of voluntary departure. The latter may be denied if there is a risk of absconding, or if an application for a legal stay has been dismissed as manifestly unfounded or fraudulent, or if the person concerned poses a risk to public policy, public security or national security.[75] 'Risk of absconding' means the existence of reasons in an individual case which are based on objective criteria defined by national law to believe that a third-country national who is the subject of return procedures may abscond.[76]

It is no surprise that Member States have implemented their discretion in various ways.[77] A risk to public policy or national security ranges from administrative infringements in some Member States to convictions for serious criminal offences in others. Likewise, there are no common criteria to determine a risk of absconding. Moreover, several Member States impose entry bans for reasons not listed in the Return Directive. Therefore, it might happen that a Member State does not recognise the entry ban imposed elsewhere. The former may consider the reason for the entry ban too trivial or, in the meantime, humanitarian reasons have arisen that militate in favour of granting a residence permit to the person concerned. Indeed, the Return Directive,[78] complemented by related instruments of EU law,[79] contains a legal basis for issuing a residence permit or another authorisation offering a right to stay to a third-country national who is subject to an entry ban issued by another Member State. In that case, the national authorities are obliged to consult each other to reach a consistent solution. If a residence permit has been issued, the Member State who imposed the entry ban shall withdraw it (and the alert in the SIS), while having the option to retain a national entry ban. Thus, EU law establishes a hierarchy in favour of the right to stay derived from national law. Inter-state frictions may arise if the Member States involved fail to give due account to each other's interests, that is, on the one hand the power over the national territory, and the security interests in the Schengen area on the other.

The recent *E* case is a striking example.[80] Finland issued a return decision, accompanied by an entry ban, against Mr E who was considered a threat to public policy and national security after having been convicted for drug offences.

---

75 Art 7(4) Return Directive.

76 Art 3(7) Return Directive.

77 See European Migration Network (n 68) 77–79.

78 Art 11(4) Return Directive.

79 The consultation procedures are laid down in various instruments. See art 6(4) Return Directive in conjunction with art 25 of the Convention implementing the Schengen Agreement [2000] OJ L239/19, and arts 9–11 Regulation 2018/1860/EU.

80 Case C-240/17 *E* EU:C:2018:8.

Since Mr E held a valid residence permit from Spain, Finland was required, under the Convention Implementing the Schengen Agreement (CISA), to consult the Spanish authorities to determine whether the criminal conviction in Finland was a sufficient ground to withdraw the residence permit. The Court received questions for a preliminary ruling on, inter alia, the failure of the Spanish authorities to respond to the Finish consultation requests. Will the Finish authorities be allowed to enforce the return decision, which would give rise to an entry ban for the entire Schengen area, despite the ongoing consultation procedure?

The Court's answer was ambiguous. On the one hand, it held that Finland may enforce the return decision despite the ongoing consultations.[81] On the other hand, Finland will have to withdraw the alert in the SIS and the entry ban if Spain fails to respond after a reasonable period.[82] Holding otherwise would, according to the Court, amount to inconsistency within the system of common rules.[83] This is what the relevant rule in the CISA aims to avoid, stipulating that the alert (and, in effect, the entry ban) shall be withdrawn if the residence permit is not. Does this mean that Finland cannot act on behalf of the common purpose? It still can, but any claim will be weaker. By issuing and enforcing the return decision, Finland contributes to collective security in the Schengen area because a national security threat may quickly spill-over to other Schengen States.[84] However, in the absence of a European entry ban, the individual concerned may any time return and cross the external borders of the Schengen area, only subject to national entry bans.

In this respect, it is interesting to note that, unlike the Court, Advocate General Kokott proposed that Finland should be entitled to issue an entry ban apart from the national return decision. In her view, 'the security interests of all Member States within the Schengen area and the population living on their territory take precedence over efforts towards coherence and consistency in official decisions in the Schengen area'.[85] Instead of supporting this stronger claim to act on behalf of the Union, it is submitted that Finland would rather not get recognition from Spain to act on its behalf. After all, a Schengen-wide entry ban would render the Spanish residence permit de facto nugatory. And even though the Spanish silence in the consultation procedure may be contrary to Union law, silence concerning a matter directly bearing upon the

81 Ibid para 50.
82 Ibid para 54.
83 Ibid.
84 Opinion of AG Kokott in Case C-240/17 *E* EU:C:2017:963, para 76.
85 Ibid para 77.

sovereign right to decide over entry and residence, cannot be interpreted as tacit acquiescence.

4 Balancing a Fine Line after the Reintroduction of Internal Border Controls

4.1 *The Ruling in Arib: Countering the Temptation to Slip Away into the Outer Sphere*

Since the large influx of refugees and migrants in 2015/2016, certain Member States have (repeatedly) reintroduced internal border controls. Those decisions have been controversial not only because they constitute a derogation from the principle of free movement within the Schengen area, but also by reason of their unilateral nature. It is established case law that derogations from the fundamental freedoms must be interpreted narrowly. The public discourse during the crisis revealed the underlying policy imperative: unilateralism is associated with national self-interests. On the one hand, the criticism seems justified because Article 25 of the Schengen Borders Code allows a Member State to reintroduce internal border controls if *that* Member State faces a serious threat to public policy or internal security. By contrast, where there is a serious threat to the Schengen area or parts thereof, Article 29 of the Code empowers a Member State to defend the common interests based on a Council recommendation. Thus, a contextual reading supports a 'nationalist' interpretation of the said Article 25. On the other hand, the Schengen Borders Code stipulates that the relevant provisions of Title II on external borders shall apply, mutatis mutandis, where internal border controls have been reintroduced.[86] In that case, the Member State concerned thus assumes the task of the peripheral Member States to safeguard collective security while respecting the right to seek international protection.

The Court reminded the Member States that have reintroduced internal border controls of their responsibility for the common whole. *Arib* concerned a Moroccan national who was apprehended close to the Franco-Spanish border at which controls had been reintroduced in accordance with the mentioned Article 25 of the Schengen Borders Code.[87] Mr Arib was detained for the purposes of a criminal investigation on account of illegal entry, punishable under French law with a term of imprisonment (and a fine). Instead of swiftly

86 Art 32 Schengen Borders Code.

87 Case C-444/17 *Préfet des Pyrénées-Orientales* v *Abdelaziz Arib and Others* EU:C:2019:220.

removing him from the EU in accordance with the Return Directive, France thus applied its national criminal law. It relied on Article 2(2)(a) of the Return Directive in conjunction with Articles 25 and 32 of the Schengen Borders Code. According to the former provision, Member States may decide not to apply the Directive to a third-country national who has illegally crossed the *external* borders. France argued that where a Member State has reintroduced controls at the internal borders, the latter should be equated with external borders for the purposes of Article 2(2)(a) of the Return Directive. On a literal interpretation of the rules, the Court had no difficulties in rejecting the argument of the French Government.[88] Article 2(2)(a) of the Return Directive expressly refers to the external borders, so the Directive applies to any illegally staying third-country national intercepted or apprehended on national territory, irrespective of whether that is – according to the Advocate General – 'near the border between France and Spain or on the Champs-Elysées'.[89] The Court went on to state that the reintroduction of internal border controls in accordance with Article 25 of the Schengen Borders Code is immaterial because neither the Directive nor the Code contain express wording to that effect.[90] That is not called into question by a systematic interpretation since Article 32 of the Code does not provide for the application of Article 2(2)(a) of the Return Directive.[91] In any case, the former provision is not intended to modify Member States' obligations under the Directive.[92]

The reasoning is not entirely convincing. Even when the Court used its systematic method of interpretation, it was preoccupied with the express wording of the provisions, which may be problematic where rules from various instruments are closely interconnected. On a combined reading of Articles 13(1) and 32 of the Schengen Borders Code, a Member State that has reintroduced internal border controls is obliged to subject a person who has illegally crossed the *internal* borders to the procedures of the Return Directive. It does not follow from the generic reference to the Directive as such that the derogation in Article 2(2)(a) does not apply. On the contrary, the very reference to the Directive in the Code supports a systematic interpretation according to which, for the purposes of the derogation, the term 'external border' should

88 Ibid paras 44–47.

89 Opinion of AG Szpunar in Case C-444/17 *Préfet des Pyrénées-Orientales* v *Abdelaziz Arib and Others* EU:C:2018:836, para 4.

90 *Arib* (n 87) para 51.

91 Ibid para 62.

92 Ibid para 64.

encompass the internal borders of the Member State that has invoked Article 25 in conjunction with Article 32 of the Code.

The succinct teleological reasoning betters supports the ruling.[93] Referring to the legislative history, the Court observed that Article 2(2)(a) of the Return Directive is intended to permit Member States to apply simplified return procedures at their external borders, without having to follow all procedural steps prescribed by the Directive, in order to be able to remove more swiftly illegally staying third-country nationals. The Grand Chamber went on to find that this purpose can be better achieved at the external than at the internal borders. And yet, a more elaborate constitutional frame would have been desirable. The full application of the Return Directive ensures that the Member State who has reinstated controls at the internal borders does not create negative externalities. This risk is greater within the Schengen area than in the vicinity of the external borders. Hence, unlike simplified return procedures, the procedural stages of the Return Directive, complemented by the SIS, regulate intergovernmental cooperation to avert the risk of inter-state frictions (and to uphold procedural safeguards for the individual concerned).

There is no need to make arrangements outside the scope of the Directive, for the full application of the latter does not deprive the Member States of their discretion while they are assuming responsibility for the Union. Apart from removing an illegally staying third-country national from EU territory in accordance with the Return Directive, the Member States may subject the person to national criminal proceedings. To recall, Mr Arib faced a prison sentence on account of illegal entry into France. It is settled case law that pending the return procedure, detention is only permissible where it serves the purpose of effective removal.[94] However, when the return procedure in line with Directive 2008/115/EC has been applied, a Member State may impose a term of imprisonment if the person concerned is staying illegally in that Member State without a justified ground for non-return (e.g. a risk of refoulement) or the person re-enters the territory of that State in breach of an entry ban.[95] In these circumstances, a Member State exercises its national competence in the area of criminal law in order to deter illegal immigration, one of the objectives of the EU that serves the collective security interests.[96] Acting on behalf of the Union is, however, premised on the prior application of the Return Directive.

93 Ibid paras 52–59.

94 Art 15(1) Return Directive; Case C-47/15 *Sélina Affum* v *Préfet du Pas-de-Calais and Procureur général de la Cour d'appel de Douai* EU:C:2016:408, para 63.

95 Case C-290/14 *Celaj* EU:C:2015:640, paras 29, 30.

96 Art 79(1) TFEU.

But what if a Member State, unlike France in *Arib*, is allowed to rely on the derogation in Article 2(2)(a) of the Directive? It follows from the foregoing that reliance on the derogation is assessed in light of the objective to realise an effective return policy. If recourse to the derogation is permissible, the Member State concerned is no longer bound by the terms of the Directive, without prejudice to some minimum requirements intended to protect fundamental rights.[97] Therefore, the mentioned limits regarding national criminal law do no longer apply. And yet, retained competences must be exercised in compliance with EU law, including the principle of sincere cooperation that obliges the Member States to refrain from any measure liable to undermine, for example, the goals of the common return policy. Having said that, the Member States still have much policy discretion that could be put to the benefit of all. Even a period of detention may be suitable in view of the risk of secondary movements in the Schengen area. At least, before the expiry of that period, the Member State concerned should reduce the possibility of re-entry following the return to the country of origin by, for example, helping that country to reintegrate the returnees.

The foregoing demonstrated the difficulties in defending the collective security interests in the context of migration management within, not at the edges of the Schengen area. Without being deprived of its responsibility for the common interests, a Member State that has reinstated internal border controls must not create negative spill-over effects for neighbouring Member States. Furthermore, the reality of mixed migration flows requires thorough balancing of security and humanitarian concerns. The Court in *Arib* protected the integrity of the EU legal order against a Member State who was moving into the outer sphere by trying to circumvent the scope of EU law. The following deals with policy decisions from Germany, a Member State who possibly wanted to act in the intermediate sphere. However, for reasons discussed below, the other Member States could not hear the claim well.

In the summer of 2018, the Federal Minister of the Interior Horst Seehofer and other prominent members of the ruling Christian Social Union (CSU) spearheaded a debate over secondary movements in the Schengen area. They wanted to return certain third-country nationals at the German-Austrian border where border controls had been reintroduced on the basis of Article 25 of the Schengen Borders Code. The measure concerned third-country nationals subject to an entry ban, irrespective of whether they asked for international

97 Art 4(4) Return Directive.

protection; and asylum seekers who had already been registered in another Member State, as borne out by an entry in the Eurodac database.

While the former was uncontroversial within the German Government, the heavy debate on the latter can be framed in terms of the three European spheres. The position of the CSU was located in the outer sphere because it favoured unilateral action under national law. Chancellor Merkel, a member of the sister party Christian Democratic Union (CDU), insisted on the primacy of EU law over national law, as she explained on German TV.[98] As the Chancellor was referring to the procedures of the Dublin Regulation regulating the transfer of asylum seekers, she defended the inner sphere of the Treaties against her own Interior Minister. Both sides eventually arrived at a compromise in the intermediate sphere – at least, the action could be interpreted as a claim to act on behalf of the Union. Compared to the initial proposal of the CSU, the German authorities may only transfer an asylum seeker to the Member State where the application for international protection was registered if Germany concluded an administrative arrangement with that Member State.[99] The Government considered this to be in line with EU law because Article 36 of the Dublin Regulation allows Member States to conclude administrative arrangements among themselves in order to implement the Regulation. More generally, the planned national measure would lose its unilateral nature because it became dependent on the agreement of the Member States concerned. These are Greece, Spain and Portugal; Italy declined the German offer.

The following will explain in more detail how Germany moved 'inside-out'. The sub-section thereafter will develop a similar argument as regards pushbacks of those third-country nationals subject to an entry ban. This latter scenario was not encompassed by the mentioned political compromise, so the German Federal Police in charge of the internal border controls was instructed to refuse entry unilaterally, without the need for European cooperation.

4.2 *Pushbacks of Asylum Seekers Registered in Another Member State*

To illustrate the new practice, this section discusses a case decided by the administrative court in Munich in August 2019.[100] The urgent procedure

98 Helmut Zermin, 'Nach dem G7 Gipfel Bundeskanzlerin Angela Merkel zu Gast bei ANNE WILL am 10. Juni 2018' (Interview 11 June 2018) minute 54:00 <https://www.youtube.com/watch?v=S5dzCRo6XX4> accessed 1 March 2024.

99 Christian Democratic Union (CDU), 'Beschlüsse des Koalitionsausschusses vom 5. Juli 2018' (Press release 6 July 2018) <https://archiv.cdu.de/artikel/beschluesse-des-koalitionsausschusses-vom-5-juli-2018> accessed 1 March 2024.

100 VG München, M 18 E 19.32238, Order of 8 August 2019.

concerned the transfer of an Afghan national to Greece in accordance with an Administrative Arrangement,[101] concluded in the aftermath of the political compromise in Germany. According to the first part of the Arrangement, any asylum seeker apprehended at the German-Austrian border will be transferred to Greece in an accelerated procedure (within 48 hours) if it was in Greece where the person first lodged his application, as demonstrated by a Eurodac hit.[102] In return, the second part commits Germany to swiftly conclude cases of family reunification from Greece.[103] Finally, the parties agreed to subject the deal to EU law, with the notable exception of dispute settlement that is subject to intergovernmental negotiation.[104] They will discontinue this form of cooperation upon entry into force of the revised CEAS.[105]

The claimant in the mentioned case expressed his wish to ask for international protection in Germany when the Federal Police apprehended him at the border with Austria. A search in the Eurodac database revealed that he had applied for international protection in Greece and later in Austria. He submitted that he left Greece because of the bad reception conditions in that country. At the time of the court order, the claimant was in detention in Greece pending his removal to Afghanistan and after Germany had transferred him in line with the Arrangement. The court ordered the return of the claimant and permission to enter Germany; in the framework of the urgent procedure, it rejected the claim insofar as it demanded from the German authorities the substantive examination of the asylum application (i.e. Germany was not required to declare itself responsible under the Dublin Regulation).

The national court found that the transfer to Greece violated the claimant's right to effective judicial protection under the German Constitution and interpreted in light of EU law, the ECHR and the Geneva Convention. Having regard to the facts of the case, the court understood that upon his arrival from Germany, the Greek authorities treated the claimant as an illegally staying third-country national. More specifically, by leaving Greece during the procedure for determining the Member State responsible, the claimant has

101 Administrative Arrangement between the Ministry of Migration Policy of the Hellenic Republic and the Federal Ministry of the Interior, Building and Community of the Federal Republic of Germany on cooperation when refusing entry to persons seeking protection in the context of temporary checks at the internal German-Austrian border <https://www.frnrw.de/fileadmin/frnrw/media/EU_Asylpolitik/Germany_Greece_Deal_eng.pdf> accessed 1 March 2024.

102 Ibid arts 1ff.

103 Ibid arts 7ff.

104 Ibid preamble and art 14(ii).

105 Ibid art 15(ii).

withdrawn his asylum application and consequently lost his rights under EU asylum law. This essentially included the right to a substantive examination of his asylum application by at least one Member State, according to the German court. While reserving the final verdict for the main proceedings, the Munich administrative court attributed the decision of the Greek authorities to systemic deficiencies in the national asylum system, which had not sufficiently improved since the rulings in *N.S.* and *M.S.S.* The remedy for interim measures was to prevent serious, irreversible harm, which a return to Afghanistan – the country from where the claimant was fleeing – would cause.

Although formally outside the scope of the urgent procedure, the issue of which Member State was responsible for the asylum application was in fact pre-determined by the order. The court acknowledged that following the entry into Germany, the claimant would most likely lodge a new application for international protection, and the procedural rules of the Dublin Regulation could eventually trigger the responsibility of Germany. In other words, the court ordered the German authorities, as it were, to act on behalf of Greece. It is therefore worth reflecting upon the central premise underpinning the order: an asylum seeker was entitled to a substantive examination of the application, so the person could not withdraw it by travelling to another Member State. For this reason, the court rejected the Greek decision to consider the application withdrawn after the applicant had absconded, as laid down in Article 28(1) of the Procedures Directive. Any further application in Greece would be treated as a subsequent application within the meaning of that Directive, allowing the Greek authorities to declare it inadmissible unless new elements or findings had arisen. Hence, the examination would not reach the stage of the merits, as required by the German court's interpretation of the Dublin Regulation. That interpretation was based on Articles 18(2) and 20(5) of the Regulation, which regulate the take back procedures in the event of secondary movements. It is striking that the court neither analysed the said provisions in detail, nor did it explain why the Dublin Regulation, rather than the Procedures Directive, was applicable in the case at hand. It could have gained support from Article 28(3) of the Directive that contains an explicit conflict rule in favour of the Dublin Regulation. Instead, the court's reasoning was above all teleological. After reiterating the objectives of the Dublin Regulation, it went on to state the following:

> Aufgrund der eindeutigen Regelung in Art. 18 Abs. 2 und Art. 20 Abs. 5 Dublin-III-Verordnung kann davon ausgegangen werden, dass der europäische Gesetzgeber eine (wenigstens einmalige) Weiterreise eines Asylantragstellers innerhalb des Hoheitsgebiets der Mitgliedstaaten

> nicht damit sanktionieren wollte, dass diese Weiterreise zu einem weitgehenden Ausschluss der Prüfung der materiellen Asylgründe führt.[106]

The court was thus confronted with the common purpose of EU migration management: individual protection on the one hand, and public security on the other. Within the confines of the urgent procedure, the German court had admittedly little opportunity to balance the two. However, the above reasoning fell short of any balancing whatsoever. It rather prioritised the humanitarian objective, suggesting that measures against secondary movements were subject to the duty to conduct a substantive examination of the asylum application.

Several objections or clarifications are appropriate here. In the first place, the premise concerning the strictly mandatory nature of a substantive examination is incorrect. As mentioned, the Member States have committed themselves to examining any application for international protection by a third-country national who applies on the territory of any of them. To examine within the meaning of EU asylum law covers inadmissibility decisions, which may involve a transfer of responsibility for the substantive examination to a safe third country.[107] In this regard, Article 3(3) of the Dublin Regulation allows Member States to send an applicant to a safe third country at any time, before and after the procedure for determining the Member State responsible has been completed. The CJEU held in *Mirza* that this right is not limited by the obligation in Article 18(2) of the Dublin Regulation to ensure that the examination of the application is 'completed', for it would introduce an exception to Article 3(3) contrary to the wording and the aims of the Regulation.[108] In particular, any other interpretation would encourage secondary movements which the Dublin Regulation precisely seeks to prevent.[109] *Mirza* is but one case in which the CJEU interpreted EU asylum law in light of the goal to prevent secondary movements.[110] Having said this, the principle of non-refoulement may preclude a transfer, irrespective of whether the person concerned is

---

106 VG München (n 100) para 40. 'Based on the unambiguous provision in Article 18(2) and Article 20(5) of the Dublin Regulation, it can be assumed that the EU legislature did not intend to sanction an applicant for international protection for travelling onwards within the territory of the Member States by dismissing an examination of the application on the merits' (author's translation).

107 Art 2(d) Dublin Regulation in conjunction with arts 33(2)(c) and 38 Asylum Procedures Directive.

108 Case C-695/15 PPU *Mirza* EU:C:2016:188, paras 46–50.

109 Ibid para 52.

110 For example, see Joined Cases C-582/17 and C-583/17 *Staatssecretaris van Veiligheid en Justitie* v *H. and R.* EU:C:2019:280, para 77.

entitled to international protection. Hence, in view of the security situation in Afghanistan, it cannot be excluded that the German court reached the correct outcome, albeit following a deficient reasoning.

In the second place, a detailed examination of the meaning of Articles 18(2) and 20(5) of the Dublin Regulation is necessary. Their scope differs as regards the stage of the procedure: Article 20(5) of the Regulation applies when the applicant absconds (or otherwise withdraws the application) before the procedure for determining the Member State responsible has been completed.[111] The facts before the German court confirm the applicability of Article 20(5).[112] It is then for the Member State of first application to take back the applicant with a view to completing the process of determining the Member State responsible. A hit in the Eurodac database confirmed that the applicant first lodged his application in Greece, so Germany was entitled to send him to that country. It was not, according to the case law of the Luxembourg Court, required to check whether Greece was in fact the Member State responsible.[113] But it was obliged to adhere to the take back procedure, especially the time limits as laid down in the Dublin Regulation. This does not preclude bilateral agreements facilitating the application of the Regulation and increasing its effectiveness.[114] The Administrative Arrangement is legal as it reduces the applicable time limits, notwithstanding the confusing submissions in the judicial proceedings. Germany argued that it was permissible not to use the Dublin procedures (‘*Pre-Dublin-Verfahren*’) while claiming, at the same time, to serve the objective of the Regulation to combat secondary movements. What is more, the German side ignored that it was the parties’ choice to subject the agreement to Union law. But above all, it is simply unnecessary to challenge the applicability of the Dublin Regulation because Article 20(5) lays down an appropriate procedure for the intended purpose. Since the task of determining the Member State

111 It reads: ‘An applicant who is present in another Member State without a residence document or who there lodges an application for international protection after withdrawing his or her first application made in a different Member State during the process of determining the Member State responsible shall be taken back, under the conditions laid down in Articles 23, 24, 25 and 29, by the Member State with which that application for international protection was first lodged, with a view to completing the process of determining the Member State responsible.’

112 As the applicant absconded from Greece, the Greek authorities were entitled to consider that he has implicitly withdrawn his application within the meaning of art 28(1)(b) of the Procedures Directive. The latter is applicable because of a cross-reference in art 2(e) Dublin Regulation.

113 *H and R* (n 110) para 80, which is subject to a narrow exception at paras 81–83.

114 According to the wording of art 36 Dublin Regulation.

responsible remains with the State of first application (Greece), an applicant does not have an incentive to travel onwards. At worst, the person could decide to travel, speculating on a transfer of responsibility should the relevant time limits expire. But this is precisely what the bilateral agreement seeks to avoid.

The foregoing does not rule out shortcomings in the design and application of the said Arrangement. Indeed, it has significant gaps, notwithstanding the legality in principle. First, it pays insufficient regard to the principle of joint responsibility, as laid down in Article 3(1) of the Dublin Regulation. Bilateral, tailor-made cooperation is in principle well-suited to give meaning to a common sense of responsibility and mutual trust. On the one hand, the humanitarian purpose finds expression in the personal scope of Part 1 of the Agreement covering persons who 'expressed a desire for international protection'.[115] On the other hand, the parties have left unclear what happens to such a person following the return to Greece. The Greek authorities are merely obliged to 'allow the person to enter',[116] unless he or she has objected to the return within a certain timeframe. The generic reference to Union law, contained in the preamble, is insufficient to close the gap because it is not clear which rule of the large body of EU asylum and migration law applies to a person seeking international protection in more than one Member State, like the claimant before the Munich administrative court. Germany assumed that following the transfer, Greece would resume the procedure for determining the Member State responsible in accordance with the Dublin Regulation. In fact, the Greek authorities discontinued the application based on a restrictive interpretation of the Procedures Directive. If this is general practice, the Arrangement fails to uphold the common humanitarian purpose. After all, according to Greece, asylum seekers become illegal migrants after travelling to another Member State. This misunderstanding could have been avoided if the parties had specified that following the transfer, Greece shall apply the Dublin Regulation.

Second, the parties failed to gain legitimacy for their cooperation in the name of the common purpose. This criticism applies in particular to the German Government, representing the more powerful Member State with the greater political interest in setting up the bilateral cooperation. The parties could have sought legitimacy from (binding and non-binding) sources of EU law. In the first place, the agreement fails to mention Article 36 of the Dublin Regulation as a legal basis. In the second place, it does not include an explicit reference to the Commission Recommendation on the resumption of Dublin

115 See the title of Part 1 of the Administrative Arrangement.

116 Art 3(ii) Administrative Arrangement.

transfers to Greece,[117] even though several provisions do reflect the content of the Recommendation. For example, the Arrangement only covers persons whose entry in the Eurodac system dates back to 1 July 2017 onwards. This mirrors the Commission's Recommendation to resume transfers as regards persons who entered Greece irregularly (or for whom Greece is otherwise responsible) from 15 March 2017 onwards.[118] Although non-binding, the Recommendation is an important source of legitimacy because the Commission qua guardian of the Union interest considers how the common rules should be applied in view of the situation in Greece. This is crucial to realise the comprehensive approach which depends on the political will and actual capacities of the Member States. To clarify, the Arrangement is not incompatible with either the Dublin Regulation or the Recommendation. But it does fail to express the claim to act jointly for the common purpose. In other words, Germany and Greece did not manage to represent a unity. Consequently, the Arrangement is likely to muster less support and engagement, including effective control, from the Commission and fellow Member States.

4.3 *Pushbacks of Third-Country Nationals Subject to an Entry Ban*

On 19 June 2018, the Minister of the Interior ordered the Federal Police to reject, in the framework of reintroduced internal border controls, any third-country national subject to an entry ban, irrespective of whether that person asks for international protection.[119] To clarify, the right to seek asylum is not abolished but restricted in this context. As will be discussed in more detail below, a person rejected at the border is deemed not to have entered German territory in a legal sense.[120] On the basis of this fiction of non-entry, the authorities keep control over the person concerned while examining the asylum application in an accelerated procedure. By way of example, the order was put to the test when Mr Miri managed to ask for international protection in Bremen in

117 European Commission, 'Recommendation Addressed to the Member States on the Resumption of Transfers to Greece under Regulation (EU) No. 604/2013' C(2016) 8525 final.

118 Ibid point (9). The latter also recommends not to transfer unaccompanied minors, which is echoed in art 1(i)(b) of the Arrangement.

119 The text of the order is available at Maximilian Matthies, 'Asylstreit: Bundespolizei soll mit Zurückweisungen an Grenzen beginnen' *SVZ* (19 June 2018) <https://www.noz.de/deutschland-welt/politik/artikel/bundespolizei-soll-mit-zurueckweisungen-an-grenzen-beginnen-23005039> accessed 1 March 2024.

120 § 13(2) Act on the Residence, Economic Activity and Integration of Foreigners in the Federal Territory ('Residence Act').

October 2019, without being caught by border guards.[121] Mr Miri was subject to an entry ban on grounds of several convictions for serious criminal offences including the illegal trade in drugs and weapons. He had served a sentence of six years' imprisonment before being deported to Lebanon, his country of origin from where he returned only 15 weeks later. After his asylum application had been rejected as manifestly unfounded, Mr Miri was again deported to Lebanon. To avoid another such incident, which attracted much attention in the media, the Minister of the Interior intensified the controls at the internal borders in order to prevent persons like Mr Miri from crossing the internal border in the first place.[122]

As we will see, legal scholars refuse the measure, often invoking the primacy of EU law. After all, so the argument goes, the Dublin Regulation requires the German authorities to determine the Member State responsible for examining the application for international protection, thus precluding the outright rejection at the border on the mere basis of an entry ban. The criticism suffers from a selective reference to EU law, characterised by a sympathetic reception of norms intended to protect individual rights while sidestepping rules that reflect security interests. For example, it has been argued that the ministerial order mainly affected the legal situation of so-called 'Dublin returnees', that is, persons who return to Germany following the transfer to the Member State responsible in order to lodge a (new) application for international protection.[123] Rather than turning them back, Germany would have to apply the Dublin rules because in the meantime, they might bring forward new grounds to substantiate their claim for international protection. The ruling in *Hasan* is adduced in support of this argument. It concerned the applicability of the take back procedure in the just described case of 'Dublin returnees'.[124] But one has to distinguish the situation at hand insofar as the ministerial order applies in the context of reintroduced internal border controls, which indicates the relevance of the Schengen Borders Code. Thus, the argument of primacy is

---

121 The events are described in Alexander Haneke, 'Hat Herr Miri sich verrechnet?' *FAZ* (31 October 2019) <https://www.faz.net/aktuell/politik/inland/clan-chef-zurueck-in-bremen-hat-herr-miri-sich-verrechnet-16461341.html> accessed 1 March 2024.

122 See Helene Bubrowski & Alexander Haneke, 'Wie Seehofer auf die Rückkehr des Clanchefs reagiert' *FAZ* (6 November 2019) <https://www.faz.net/aktuell/politik/inland/wie-horst-seehofer-auf-die-rueckkehr-des-miri-clanchefs-reagiert-16472169.html> accessed 1 March 2024.

123 See Pauline Endres de Oliveira & Dana Schmalz, 'Anordnung des (Europa-)Rechtsbruchs' (2018) Verfassungsblog <https://verfassungsblog.de/anordnung-des-europa-rechtsbruchs/> accessed 1 March 2024.

124 Case C-360/16 *Hasan* EU:C:2018:35.

unconvincing if the scope and meaning of EU law is more ambiguous than a selective reference to but one piece of EU legislation seems to suggest.

Indeed, the relevant legislation does not contain general conflict rules in favour of one or the other instrument.[125] A careful legal analysis is necessary given that both the Dublin Regulation and the Schengen Borders Code are potentially relevant to the issue at stake. Thym suggests examining the relationship between the Dublin Regulation and Articles 6(1) and 14 of the Schengen Borders Code, read in conjunction with Article 24 of the Schengen Information System (SIS) as well as Article 11 of the Return Directive.[126] Essentially, these rules stipulate that a person for whom a Schengen alert has been issued on grounds of, inter alia, an entry ban shall be refused entry into EU territory. It is important to note that this obligation is without prejudice to the application of 'special provisions concerning the right of asylum and to international protection'.[127] The following is an effort to make sense of this labyrinth of rules, bearing in mind our theoretical premise: Member States are responsible for both individual protection and collective security. The concrete legal issue to be discussed is whether, following the reintroduction of internal border controls, German border guards may reject a third-country national who is subject to an entry ban and asks for international protection.

To start with, it is necessary to determine the meaning of the mentioned provisions in the context of reintroduced internal border controls. After all, Article 14(1) of the Schengen Borders Code stipulates that a third-country national who does not fulfil the conditions laid down in Article 6(1) shall be refused entry to 'the territories of the Member States'. A pushback at the German-Austrian border would merely prevent entry into Germany while the person concerned would still be present on the territory of Austria. However, Article 32 of the Code says that where internal border controls are reintroduced, 'the relevant provisions' of Title II shall apply mutatis mutandis, which includes Article 14 on refusal of entry. To recall, the Court in *Arib* ruled on the relationship between the Schengen Borders Code and the Return Directive.[128] It found that 'for the purposes of that directive',[129] an internal border at which controls pursuant to Article 25 have been reintroduced cannot be equated

125 See Daniel Thym, 'Für ein „Helsinki" im deutschen Migrationsrechtsdiskurs' (2018) Verfassungsblog <https://verfassungsblog.de/fuer-ein-helsinki-im-deutschen-migrationsrechtsdiskurs/> accessed 1 March 2024.

126 Ibid.

127 Art 14(1) Schengen Borders Code.

128 *Arib* (n 87) and accompanying text.

129 Ibid para 62.

with an external border. The ruling therefore does not support the general inference that an internal border can under no circumstances be equated with an external border.[130] But according to Hruschka, the judgment even rules out the legal fiction of non-entry, which underlies the German ministerial order.[131] It is submitted that *Arib* is still relevant insofar as the obligation to apply the Return Directive in full (instead of the derogation) ensures that the temporary reintroduction of internal border controls causes the least possible interference with the interests of neighbouring Member States.

The same constitutional reasoning applies, mutatis mutandis, in the present context. Where a Member State has reintroduced internal border controls, refusal of entry according to Article 14 of the Code should be interpreted so as to permit that Member State to apprehend a third-country national subject to an entry ban with a view to the removal of that person from the Schengen area. Following entry into the Schengen area via a peripheral Member State like Greece, it is the task of – in this case – Germany to act on the basis of Articles 14 and 32 of the Code. The former provision states that an entry ban is a ground for refusing entry. The SIS Regulation supports this reading, requiring Member States to follow-up an entry ban with a Schengen alert.[132] The latter legitimises measures against a person who is considered a threat to the entire Union (and not just to a single Member State). Subject to EU law, it is for the national authorities to decide about the specific measures to be taken.[133]

However, it is suggested that in the context of internal border controls, their margin of discretion is reduced. Returning to the German case study, the Federal Police must not simply turn back a third-country national at the border, for it would shift the burden to Austria. But whereas a bilateral agreement could have arranged an orderly transfer of responsibility, the unilateral ministerial order is likely to cause a denial of responsibility in respect of the third-country national concerned. Hence, the person could freely travel within the Schengen area despite the enforceable entry ban. It is therefore crucial to apprehend the person following the check at the internal border. Indeed, that is the purpose of the national provision on which the ministerial order is

130 Constantin Hruschka, 'Binnengrenze ≠ Außengrenze: Klärendes vom EuGH zur Wiedereinführung von Grenzkontrollen' (2019) Verfassungsblog <https://verfassungsblog.de/binnengrenze-≠-aussengrenze-klaerendes-vom-eugh-zur-wiedereinfuehrung-von-grenzkontrollen/#:~:text=Der%20deutsche%20Vortrag%2C%20die%20Grenzkontrollen,carrier%20sanctions> accessed 1 March 2024.

131 Ibid.

132 Art 24(1)(b) SIS Regulation.

133 See supra nn 95–96 and the accompanying text regarding the possibility to use national criminal law to deter illegal immigration.

based. In particular, the legal fiction of non-entry is not intended to deprive the third-country national of his fundamental rights, including the right to seek international protection, but to restrict his freedom of movement.[134] The person concerned may thus ask for international protection without being entitled to enter Germany in a legal (rather than physical) sense. This is compatible with the Procedures Directive allowing Member States to decide at the border or transit zone about the admissibility or the substance of an application, subject to a time limit of four weeks.[135] Depending on the reasons for the entry ban in the individual case, there are various grounds for taking a substantive decision at the border. In the present context, the most obvious ground is unlawful entry.[136] Furthermore, assuming that the mentioned Mr Miri had been apprehended at the border, Germany would have been entitled to carry out an accelerated procedure on grounds of him being 'a danger to the national security or public order of [that] Member State'.[137] Since Mr Miri was subject to an entry ban, Germany prima facie acted on behalf of the Union by detaining him, examining his application in an accelerated procedure and finally removing him from the Schengen area in accordance with the Return Directive. However, it should be recalled that the criteria for imposing an entry ban are permissive. For example, it is unclear what a conviction for 'serious criminal offences' means in this context. But given Mr Miri's impressive criminal record, it is likely that the other Member States consider that Germany has legitimately acted on their behalf as well. Finally, the foregoing is in line with the second sentence of Article 14(1) of the Schengen Borders Code, stipulating that a refusal of entry shall be 'without prejudice to the application of special provisions concerning the right of asylum and to international protection'. This conflict rule does not accord primacy to a certain instrument of EU asylum law like the Dublin Regulation but leaves it to the Member States to assume responsibility for the individual concerned, obviously in line with EU and international law.

134 § 13(2) Residence Act ('as long as the said authorities remain able to monitor the foreigner's stay').

135 Art 43 Asylum Procedures Directive. Detention for that purpose is legal, as confirmed in Joined Cases C-924/19 PPU and C-925/19 PPU *FMS and Others* EU:C:2020:367, paras 232–248.

136 Art 31(8)(h) Asylum Procedures Directive.

137 Art 31(8)(j) Asylum Procedures Directive.

5 Conclusion

The aim of this chapter was to show how the Member States navigate between the three European spheres. In particular, the task was to identify the intermediate sphere in the law and practice of EU migration management. It is in the intermediate sphere where the Member States use the leeway in the legal framework to act in the name of the common purpose, that is, humanitarian protection and collective security. Their action is driven rather by a *political* sense of responsibility than by the *legal* obligation to give effect to EU law which, in the inner sphere, leaves a certain margin of national discretion that facilitates movements 'inside-out'. Unlike the outer sphere, the Member States claim to act on behalf of the common whole, which does not rule out the pursuit of national interests at the same time. Based on the foregoing, it is possible to reflect on when and how Member States move into the intermediate sphere and why, in certain situations, they remain in the inner or outer sphere.

As regards asylum seekers, the Member States face a tension between, on the one hand, the commitment to 'a common area of protection'[138] and, on the other hand, the sovereign right to grant asylum, closely linked to national self-determination. The inner sphere tries to resolve the tension by imposing strict obligations, at least concerning the first stage of temporary protection. The subsequent steps, notably the examination of the application, are characterised by a wider margin of discretion. The Member State responsible could, for example, send the individual concerned to a safe third country. In that case, it may claim to represent the Union because it acts on the basis of the Dublin Regulation. However, other Member States might not recognise the claim for want of a common list of safe third countries.[139]

In comparison, a Member State clearly moves into the intermediate sphere when, according to Article 3(2) of the Dublin Regulation and the *N.S.* jurisprudence, it acts in lieu of another Member State who is considered unable to guarantee essential fundamental rights. Two aspects point to the intermediate sphere: first, the case law of the Court explaining which violations are so serious as to merit an exception from the principle of mutual trust is an authoritative source from which the intervening Member State derives a high level of legitimacy; second, that Member State acts voluntarily because the legal basis (Article 17 of the Dublin Regulation) is an optional clause. By contrast, in case of minor infringements of EU law, Member States should in principle

138 Recital (7) Dublin Regulation.

139 Such a list is foreseen under the new legislation, see art 60 of the new Asylum Procedure Regulation as adopted by the European Parliament (n 62).

not apply Article 17 in order not to stimulate secondary movements, which would be contrary to the common purpose of public security. It is then rather for the Member State responsible to rectify the shortcomings – if, indeed, it is correct to speak of violations of EU law. After all, there may be disagreement as to whether a Member State has exceeded the applicable margin of discretion, as demonstrated by the *Jawo* case in which Italy was criticised for not granting systematic access to language courses to beneficiaries of international protection.[140] On the one hand, the criticism is unfounded since the Qualification Directive confers policy discretion on Member States to grant access to 'appropriate'[141] integration programmes. On the other hand, Italy does not necessarily act within the intermediate sphere because if the authorities retreat from responsibility by letting recognised refugees fall outside the social system, they are liable to cause secondary movements. In view of the discretion involved, it will hinge on the assessment by all competent authorities at EU and national level as to whether Italy acts on behalf of all. Having regard to the comprehensive approach, recognition is unlikely because Member States must in any case assume responsibility for refugees even though they have the choice among several so-called durable solutions (with integration into the host society being only one of them).

Another clear example of the intermediate sphere, in respect of asylum seekers, is where the Member States act in the absence of EU law. The chapter discussed the issue of humanitarian visas, which was the subject matter of the case of *X and X*. Member States claim to move from the outer into the intermediate sphere when they make use of their national competence to grant humanitarian visas, and justify their decision by reference to the common goal of reducing pressure on the asylum systems of the peripheral Member States. It has been submitted that even if Member States had a positive legal obligation to grant humanitarian visas by virtue of EU fundamental rights, the threshold for triggering any such obligation should be high in order not to reduce their discretion to find the most appropriate solution in the case at hand.

As regards the common return policy, the tension is between the security interests of the Union on the one hand, and national powers to terminate legal stays and enforce the decisions to that effect on the other hand. Here, the Member States usually do not move into the intermediate sphere, even though legal gaps give them ample opportunity to do so. They do not, for example, systematically issue a return decision after the rejection of an asylum application

140 *Jawo* (n 14) para 47.
141 Art 34 Qualification Directive.

has become final. This omission is likely to increase the risk of secondary movements within the Union, contrary to the objective of an effective return policy. Likewise, an entry ban is rarely accompanied by an alert in the SIS. Without being aware of an entry ban, Member States are simply unable to enforce it. Coherence is thus a pressing challenge, irrespective of the degree of national discretion. One way to mitigate the mentioned problems is cross-referencing to point out the systematic connections between the various instruments.[142] In that regard, it is problematic that the EU legislature has, for the time being, not managed to agree on a reform of the Return Directive.

A different issue arises where a certain claim to act in the intermediate sphere is not recognised. That may happen, first, when a Member State makes use of the wide discretion to issue an entry ban and the Member State where the person concerned is present refuses to recognise it. Here as well, legal design is part of the problem: an entry ban is imposed in accordance with criteria defined in national law, whereas the legal effects span across the entire Schengen area. The likelihood for non-recognition increases where the Member States interpret and apply the criteria differently. The EU legislature plans to harmonise them in order to prevent secondary movements. According to the Commission proposal for a recast Return Directive, the discretion not to grant a period for voluntary departure turns into an obligation where there is a risk of absconding as determined in accordance with common criteria.[143] The decision not to grant a period for voluntary departure triggers the obligation to issue an entry ban.[144] Although Member States still have discretion to determine a risk of absconding, that discretion is reduced with a view to the common objective of avoiding the free movement of illegally staying third-country nationals. Second, action in the intermediate sphere may be precluded by virtue of EU law. The chapter discussed the case of *E* in which the Court upheld the consistency of the common rules. The latter stipulate that a Member State must not impose an entry ban in respect of a third-country national who has a residence permit from another Member State. Since the rules are clear and unambiguous, Finland in that case was precluded from moving into the intermediate sphere. Instead, both Member States remained

---

142 See art 37 of the new Asylum Procedure Regulation as adopted by the European Parliament (n 62); art 24(1)(b) SIS Regulation, which includes a reference to the Return Directive; art 8(6) of the Commission proposal for a recast Return Directive COM(2018) 634 final.

143 Art 9(4) in conjunction with art 6(1) of the Commission proposal for a recast Return Directive COM(2018) 634 final.

144 Ibid art 13(1)(a) which reflects the current art 11(1)(a) Return Directive.

in the outer sphere: Finland could deport the person and issue a national alert for the purpose of preventing re-entry into national territory; Spain was entitled to maintain the residence permit.

Finally, the rules on the reintroduction of internal border controls offer ample opportunity to move into the intermediate sphere. This finding might be counter-intuitive because, on a literal reading of the main provision,[145] internal border controls seem to be a unilateral measure driven by selfish national interests. However, in this context the defence of the common purpose is pressing, for the measure targets irregular migrants who have *already* entered the Schengen area and who might be deserving of international protection, notwithstanding an entry ban for example. Member States have ample opportunity to balance both objectives due to the ambiguity of EU law. Again, the latter is mainly due to a lack of legislative coherence. The chapter selected two measures from German administrative practice to demonstrate how under these circumstances, a Member State could claim to assume responsibility for the common whole. It has been submitted that both measures are legal and manage, at least in many respects, to strike a fair balance between the competing interests involved. The Administrative Arrangement between Germany and Greece succeeds in reducing the risk of secondary movements in line with the Dublin Regulation, but it fails to ensure that Greece assumes responsibility for the protection, rather than the outright removal, of the transferees. In similar vein, Germany is allowed to refuse entry to third-country nationals subject to an entry ban if it does not unilaterally shift the burden to Austria or other neighbouring countries. Hence, it must apprehend the person concerned pending the removal from the common area. If the person asks for international protection, Germany is entitled to carry out an accelerated border procedure without first determining the Member State responsible under the Dublin Regulation.

145 Art 25 Schengen Borders Code.

CHAPTER 5

Acting on the External Dimension: The EU-Turkey Statement

1 Introduction

The aim of this chapter is to refine and apply the theory of the European spheres in the context of the external dimension of EU migration management. Refinement is necessary because at stake is not the implementation of existing EU legal obligations, which has been examined before. The present chapter is interested in the proliferation of international migration governance driven by the 27 acting outside the EU legal order. Governance has been defined as the dispersal of power across more than one legal order, so instead of a binary inside/outside distinction, it is assumed that international migration governance is rather located at the margins of the EU legal order. This would imply overlap of claims for formal and social recognition.

The most prominent example is the EU-Turkey Statement adopted by the Heads of State or Government in the form of a press release issued by the General Secretariat of the Council.[1] It generally aims at containing asylum seekers and migrants in Turkey. The (then) 28 made financial and political commitments, expecting Turkey to step up border protection and to take back persons who nevertheless managed to arrive on the Greek islands. Greece has a prominent role in comparison with the other Member States since it is responsible for applying existing obligations under EU asylum and migration law. Greece would thus claim to formally represent the Union, albeit within a wider cooperative framework not foreseen by any instrument of EU law. The EU-Turkey Statement itself would thus rather be an exercise of retained national competence, which as such is not sufficient to qualify as action on behalf of the Union. However, the 28 did claim social recognition by referring to the common challenge of addressing the migration crisis in 2016.

This begs the question as to whether the Member States are competent to act on the external dimension of EU migration management or in other words: whether international migration governance is compatible with the

1 European Council, 'EU-Turkey Statement' (Press release 18 March 2016) <https://www.consilium.europa.eu/en/press/press-releases/2016/03/18/eu-turkey-statement/> accessed 1 March 2024.

 | DOI:10.1163/9789004695733_007

inner sphere. The Treaties confer an explicit competence on the EU for the conclusion of readmission agreements with third countries.[2] Moreover, the Common European Asylum System (CEAS) shall comprise partnership and cooperation with third countries for the purpose of managing inflows of protection seekers,[3] which can be interpreted as an implied competence on all matters concerning the common asylum system such as resettlement and humanitarian visas.[4] The nature of those competences is in principle shared.[5] However, in certain situations, EU external competence may become exclusive, thereby precluding autonomous action of the 27. Article 3(2) TFEU codifies the Court's *ERTA* jurisprudence;[6] it reads as follows:

> The Union shall also have exclusive competence for the conclusion of an international agreement when its conclusion is provided for in a legislative act of the Union or is necessary to enable the Union to exercise its internal competence, *or in so far as its conclusion may affect common rules or alter their scope* (emphasis added).

The third limb is of particular importance in the present context because common rules on asylum and migration have proliferated and the level of harmonisation has increased. In particular, the EU-Turkey Statement regulates matters falling under common rules such as the processing of international protection claims. To underline, there might not even be an intermediate sphere as far as the external dimension of EU migration management is concerned, if autonomous national action is precluded in the first place.

The chapter proceeds as follows. Section 2 will explain the third limb of Article 3(2) TFEU on the basis of case law and legal doctrine. This will include attention to the reasons for prohibiting international action of the Member States in some circumstances, and what that theoretically means for the intermediate sphere. Section 3 will explore the EU-Turkey Statement in detail, including the context of its adoption and its reception in legal circles. In addition, it will be argued that the existing legal doctrine concerning EU external competence is unable to capture a novel instrument such as the EU-Turkey Statement. Section 4 will, for this reason, propose a doctrinal refinement to

2 Art 79(5) TFEU.
3 Art 78(2)(g) TFEU.
4 See Chapter 3.3.
5 Art 4(2)(j) TFEU.
6 Case 22/70 *Commission* v *Council* (*ERTA*) EU:C:1971:32 and the case law building thereon (see section 2 below).

better evaluate compliance with the EU legal order while not interfering too much with national external self-determination. Section 5 will apply that model to the EU-Turkey Statement, arguing that the latter is indeed compatible with the inner sphere of the Treaties. The actual capacity of Greece and other issues pertaining to the intermediate sphere fall outside the scope of this chapter. Section 6 will draw conclusions for the external representation of the Union.

2 ERTA and the Theory of the European Spheres

2.1 *Finding an ERTA Effect*

The Lisbon Treaty introduced the above-mentioned Article 3(2) TFEU in order to codify the Court's jurisprudence on implied exclusive competences. The *ERTA* judgment of 1971 has been the leading case on that matter. The Commission brought the case against the Council, challenging the competence of the Member States to negotiate and conclude the European Agreement concerning the work of crews of vehicles engaged in international road transport (ERTA or AETR, which is the French acronym). According to the Commission, the EU was exclusively competent because the subject matter of the ERTA fell within the scope of the common transport policy and certain rules of the international agreement were in direct conflict with a Regulation concerning road transport. The Court followed the Commission in establishing the principle of parallelism, meaning that the exercise of an internal competence must give rise to a parallel external power to act on the same subject matter.

It is worth examining the three-step reasoning of the Court. First, it recalled that the EU has legal personality according to the Treaties.[7] To develop the reasoning in that way was logical because the EU could not exercise any external competence if it had not the legal capacity to enter into contractual links with third countries. Second, with regard to the 'whole scheme of the Treaties',[8] an EU external competence may be express or implied, so it may either flow from express legal basis provisions or 'from other provisions of the [Treaties] or from measures adopted, within the framework of those provisions, by the [EU] institutions'.[9] In the case at hand, the competence was derived from (now) Article 91 TFEU, the legal basis for the common transport policy, and Regulation No

7 *ERTA* (n 6) para 13; art 47 TEU.
8 *ERTA* (n 6) para 15.
9 ibid para 16.

543/69/EEC enacted on that basis.[10] The Union could only effectively exercise the competence to regulate international road transport, according to Article 91 TFEU, if it is also competent to enter into international commitments.[11] Hence, an implied external competence improved the useful effect of the competence-norm.[12] Third, on a combined reading of (now) Article 4(3) TEU and the aims of the common transport policy, the Court introduced a duty of abstention triggered by the adoption of internal rules.[13] Member States must not, unilaterally or collectively, enter into international commitments that are liable to affect common rules or alter their scope. As for the ERTA, there was a negative effect insofar as its subject matter fell within the scope of Regulation No 543/69/EEC.[14] Concurrent powers on the part of the Member States had to be excluded for the sake of 'the unity of the [internal market] and the uniform application of [EU] law'.[15] Compared to this rather abstract reasoning, the Commission identified a substantive rule conflict between the ERTA and the Regulation.[16] The only way for the Member States to avoid that conflict was to restrict the scope of the Regulation, thereby undermining the uniformity of the common rules. In other words, the Member States could not, at the same time, honour their obligations derived from international and EU law without compromising the unity of the latter. Therefore, their role had to be confined to that of members of the Union, deprived of the external capacity to act in their own right.

In later case law, the Court further clarified the issue of implied exclusive competence.[17] Falling short of a full examination of the jurisprudence, the following explains the current test and methodology for finding an ERTA effect. In recent case law, the Court sets out the test as follows:

> [I]t is apparent from settled case-law that there is a risk that common EU rules may be adversely affected by international commitments undertaken by the Member States, or that the scope of the rules may be altered,

10 Regulation No 543/69/EEC of 25 March 1969 on the harmonisation of certain social legislation relating to road transport [1969] OJ L77/49 (no longer in force).

11 *ERTA* (n 6) para 27.

12 See Alan Dashwood & Joni Heliskoski, 'The Classic Authorities Revisited' in Alan Dashwood & Christophe Hillion (eds), *The General Law of E.C. External Relations* (Sweet & Maxwell 2000) 7–9.

13 *ERTA* (n 6) paras 20–22.

14 Ibid para 30.

15 Ibid para 31.

16 Ibid p 270.

17 The Court consolidated the pre-Lisbon case law in *Opinion 1/03* (*Lugano Convention*) EU:C:2006:81, paras 114–133.

> such as to justify an exclusive external competence of the European Union where those commitments fall within the scope of those rules. However, a finding that there is such a risk does not presuppose that the area covered by the international commitments and that covered by the EU rules coincide fully. In particular, the scope of EU rules may be affected or altered by international commitments where the latter fall within an area which is already covered to a large extent by such rules.
>
> Furthermore, such a risk of common EU rules being affected may be found to exist where the international commitments at issue, without necessarily conflicting with those rules, may have an effect on their meaning, scope and effectiveness.[18]

To paraphrase, the Court scrutinises whether international commitments of the Member States affect common rules, actually or potentially. A risk may be found to exist where:

- those international commitments fall within an EU policy area, which is 'to a large extent' covered by rules of EU law;
- ... those international commitments may have an effect on the meaning, scope and effectiveness of the common rules, without necessarily amounting to a rule conflict.

The notion of 'affecting' thus encompasses overlap in scope, outright rule conflict and various forms of interference with the practical operation of the common rules. The excerpt suggests that these scenarios are alternatives. If that were correct, the capacity of the Member States to act externally would be significantly reduced because even a mere overlap in scope would be sufficient to find EU exclusivity. The threshold is further lowered by not requiring that the scope of the international agreement and of EU law coincide fully.[19] Hence, the Member States shall not regulate, through international commitments, a specific matter on which the EU has not yet legislated but which forms part of an area covered, to a large extent, by common rules.

For our purposes, the decisive question is whether the scope criterion is sufficient *in itself* to find an ERTA effect or whether a rule conflict or any other interference is an additional necessary requirement. The methodology of the Court, as set out in *Opinion 1/03*, lends support to the second alternative. The

18 Joined Cases C-626/15 and C-659/16 *Commission* v *Council* (*Antarctica*) EU:C:2018:925, paras 113–114 (references omitted).

19 *Antarctica* (n 18) para 113.

Court held that the principle of conferral requires 'a specific analysis'[20] having regard not only to 'the scope of the rules in question but also [to] their nature and content'.[21] Hence, a meticulous analysis is required as to whether individual provisions of the envisaged international agreement are liable to interfere with the practical operation of the common rules. If this approach was followed, it would be more likely to isolate a subject matter on which the EU has not yet legislated or which is not liable to undermine the common rules because, for example, both the international agreement and EU law contain only minimum standards.[22] As a result, the likelihood of a mixed agreement would increase.

However, according to most legal scholars, the Court has departed from this approach in favour of the scope criterion.[23] It is thus sufficient to broadly identify the content and aims of the international agreement on the one hand, and of the relevant instruments of EU law on the other hand. The Member States lose their external power if there is at least a large overlap in scope. By contrast, Chamon takes a different position by conceptualising the ERTA effect as 'obstacle pre-emption'.[24] Apart from outright rule conflict, it precludes Member States from entering into international commitments liable to undermine the purpose or objective of a rule of EU law.[25] Similar to *Opinion 1/03*, it is thus a norm-specific analysis, and a mere overlap in scope is not sufficient. According to Chamon, the test as to whether an area is already covered to a large extent by common rules only determines the consequences of finding an ERTA effect, that is, whether the EU can conclude the international agreement

---

20 *Opinion 1/03* (n 17) para 124.

21 ibid para 126.

22 *Opinion 2/91 (ILO)* EU:C:1993:106, para 18.

23 See Piet Eeckhout, *EU External Relations Law* (2nd edition, OUP 2011) 118; Friedrich Erlbacher, 'Recent Case Law on External Competences of the European Union: How Member States Can Embrace Their Own Treaty' *CLEER Papers 2017/2*, 35 <https://www.asser.nl/media/3485/cleer17-2_web.pdf> accessed 1 March 2024; Andrés Delgado Casteleiro, 'Loyalty in EU External Relations Law: The Fabric of Competence, Autonomy and Institutional Balance' in Eleftheria Neframi & Mauro Gatti (eds), *Constitutional Issues of EU External Relations Law* (Nomos 2018) 406–407; more narrow: Markus Klamert, *The Principle of Loyalty in EU Law* (OUP 2014) 107; less clear: Robert Post, 'Constructing the European Polity: ERTA and the Open Skies Judgments' in Miguel Poiares Maduro & Loïc Azoulai, *The Past and Future of EU Law: the Classics of EU Law Revisited on the 50th Anniversary of the Rome Treaty* (Hart 2010) 246; Andrea Ott, 'EU External Competence' in Ramses Wessel & Joris Larik (eds), *EU External Relations Law: Text, Cases and Materials* (2nd edition, Hart 2020) 85.

24 Merijn Chamon, 'Implied Exclusive Powers in the ECJ's Post-Lisbon Jurisprudence: The Continued Development of the ERTA Doctrine' (2018) 55(4) CML Rev 1101.

25 Ibid 1103–1105.

alone or only together with the Member States.[26] He goes on to criticise the Court for defining the telos of the common rules only in the abstract, namely by reference to the system of EU law as a whole.[27] The Court's reasoning is thus circular insofar as the telos of implied exclusive competence, which is to guarantee the uniformity and effectiveness of EU law, is qualified as the objective of the common rules.

The present chapter does not offer another systematisation of the Court's jurisprudence on exclusivity. Instead, the case of *Green Network*[28] is selected to illustrate, on the one hand, the uncertainty as to finding an ERTA effect and, on the other hand, the intermediate sphere in external relations. As we shall see, the national measure at stake – a law in Italy – might qualify as action on behalf of the common purpose. The national proceedings concerned the application of Directive 2001/77/EC on the promotion of electricity produced from renewable energy sources in the internal electricity market.[29] The Italian implementing legislation required electricity producers or importers to feed into the national grid a certain quantity of electricity produced from renewable energy sources ('green electricity') or, failing that, to purchase green certificates from the national grid manager. Imports from a third country were recognised if Italy had concluded an agreement with that country guaranteeing the 'green' origin of the electricity according to the same arrangements as those laid down in Article 5 of the Directive. Italy and Switzerland concluded such an agreement in 2007, which applied for imports from 2006, the year in which Switzerland adopted legislation in conformity with the EU Directive. As Green Network applied for an exemption in respect of energy imported from Switzerland in 2005, the national grid manager rejected the request. The national court asked the CJEU whether Article 5 of the Directive, in conjunction with Articles 3(2) and 216 TFEU, precludes national legislation that makes the recognition of guarantees of origin issued by a third state subject to the conclusion of an appropriate international agreement with that state.

At the outset, it should be noted that the Court did not examine the agreement between Italy and Switzerland because, when the dispute arose, it had not yet been concluded. However, the mere possibility of a future international agreement, on the basis of the said national law, was sufficient to affect the

26 Ibid 1119.

27 Ibid 1126.

28 Case C-66/13 *Green Network* EU:C:2014:2399.

29 Directive 2001/77/EC of 27 September 2001 on the promotion of electricity produced from renewable energy sources in the internal electricity market [2001] OJ L283/33 (no longer in force).

exclusive external competence of the Union, assuming it to have been established.[30] With that in mind, the Court first applied the scope criterion, comparing the subject matter of the envisaged international agreement with the relevant provisions contained in Directive 2001/77/EC. It found an overlap insofar as each instrument regulates the conditions and mechanisms under which green electricity is to be recognised as such on the Italian and the EU internal energy market, respectively. The Court then explained why the overlap was problematic. While acknowledging that Article 5 of the Directive is silent on imports from third countries, the Court nevertheless found that it was the purpose of the Article in question to completely harmonise the recognition of green electricity.[31] A Member State must therefore not unilaterally extend the scope of the Directive to a third country.[32] Accordingly, the Court was not content with establishing a mere overlap in scope; it further underlined a particular kind of interference. The nature of that interference was functional, oriented towards the harmonised system of certification.

Even though the Court could have established a violation of Article 3(2) TFEU at this stage, it went on to consider that the Italian law planned to exempt importers of green electricity from the obligation to acquire green certificates. The measure was part of a national support scheme, in the absence of a Union-wide framework. In this respect, the Directive requires the Commission to assess whether national support schemes contribute to the national indicative targets for the future consumption of green electricity, as laid down in the Directive.[33] According to the Court, the support schemes serve that purpose if they lead to an increase in national production of green electricity.[34] The international agreement provided for by the Italian law could interfere with that objective because Italian energy companies could discharge their obligations by importing recognised electricity from a third country instead of increasing their own production.[35] The failure to increase the national production of green electricity would in turn negatively affect the main objective of the Directive, namely to increase the production of green electricity in the internal market.[36] Overall, the Court concluded that the international agreement envisaged by the Italian legislation is liable to 'affect the proper functioning of

30 *Green Network* (n 28) paras 37–38.
31 Ibid paras 41–46.
32 Ibid paras 48–49.
33 Recital (14) and art 4(2) Directive 2001/77/EC.
34 *Green Network* (n 28) para 57.
35 Ibid para 59.
36 Ibid paras 55, 59.

the system established by [Directive 2001/77] and the objectives it pursues as well'.[37]

In applying the ERTA doctrine, the Court vested exclusive competence in the EU only after having established a possible interference with specific legislative objectives. It is thus correct to explain that ruling by reference to 'obstacle pre-emption'.[38] At the same time, the judgment begs the question when precisely an international agreement is liable to interfere with an objective of the Union. The Court could have opted for an interpretation less restrictive of the external competence of the Member States if it had accepted that the national support scheme contributed rather to the consumption than to the production of green electricity in Italy. But it opted for an interpretation that *best* served the predominant aim and purpose of the Directive. This teleological interpretation in light of the Directive as a whole stands in contrast to the rather systematic, functional interpretation of the mentioned Article 5.

What are the implications for the intermediate sphere? Indeed, one could interpret the reference in the Italian law to Article 5 of the Directive as a claim to act on behalf of the Union. More specifically, Italy made use of the silence in the Directive as to the external dimension in order to pursue the common goal of promoting renewable energy in cooperation with a third country. The Court rejected the claim and required action in the inner sphere instead. While the Court has the power to do so, it is obviously not free from criticism. Arguably, Italy did not undermine the common purpose of mutual non-interference because the other Member States were not obliged to recognise certificates of origin from a third country.[39] It is therefore questionable why, according to the Court, the system established by the Directive completely harmonised the relevant area. Moreover, the Court tied this harmonised system of rules to a specific, internally-oriented legislative objective. One could object that by opening trade for green electricity from third countries, Italy might boost the industry there and contribute to the global protection of the environment in line with Article 21(2)(f) TEU. Even if Italy had limited its own production of green electricity, it is doubtful whether the less than optimal realisation of a legislative objective is a sufficient justification for a complete denial of national external power that could be used for the benefit of the Union. In any case, whether the bilateral agreement between Italy and Switzerland actually had any adverse effects was immaterial because of the preventive function of the ERTA test.

37 Ibid para 60.
38 See Chamon (n 24) 1125.
39 Art 5(4) Directive 2001/77/EC.

The Court in *Green Network* classified the relevant Directive as a unitary system of rules. Italy could only act through the system to pursue a particular objective as a member of the Union. Moving into the intermediate sphere would frustrate the functioning of that system and the goal of the joint action, at least according to the Court. The reasoning is not convincing for the reasons stated above. 'Obstacle pre-emption' is only a starting point, for it fails to consider the scenario when the 27 assume responsibility for their common interests without causing negative externalities (in line with the common purpose of the Union). Hence, the next section will examine the rationales for duties of abstention in more detail.

2.2 *Rationales for Duties of Abstention, Focussing on* ERTA *Exclusivity*

The case of *Green Network* hinted at a functional and substantive rationale for exclusivity. Both are closely related insofar as the system of EU law strives for certain political goals. Member States contribute to them by implementing EU law in line with their legal obligations as members of the Union. Entering into international commitments adds another source of legal obligations to which a certain Member State is subject. This is of concern for the EU legal order not because international commitments could in any way affect the validity of EU law in the territory of the Member States. They cannot because EU and international law are independent sources of law. However, they could interfere with the practical operation of EU law if the conditions for the application of the ERTA doctrine are fulfilled.[40] *Green Network* exemplifies, according to the Court, actual and potential interferences with the scope of the common rules and their objectives. They are caused by the multiple sources of legal normativity to which Member States are subject. As a result, their role as members of the Union becomes volatile and conditional. This scenario can be avoided where EU law precludes them from exercising their external sovereignty outside the EU institutional framework.

The principle of primacy would be of little help in this regard because it is not able to resolve the double bind of the Member States.[41] After all, it could not prevent them from being bound under international law while rendering those obligations inapplicable as a matter of EU law. As will be explained below, this rationale is less compelling where legally non-binding arrangements such as the EU-Turkey Statement govern international affairs. In any event, a sound constitutional rationale is required for imposing, in particular, an ERTA-type

40 See John Temple Lang, The ERTA Judgment and the Court's Case Law on Competence and Conflict' (1986) 6(1) YEL 183, 201.

41 See Klamert (n 23) 105–106.

duty of abstention.[42] The latter has caused tensions with the principle of conferral since the Court carries out a contextualised assessment of the envisaged international agreement in light of the uniformity and effectiveness of the EU legal order as a whole. A comparison with the doctrine of pre-emption, applicable to the internal dimension, underlines the impact of ERTA exclusivity. The former precludes autonomous national measures only insofar as the EU has acted,[43] whereas the latter precludes such measures when common rules cover the field in question to a large extent. In addition, Member States have the opportunity to justify *internal* measures falling within the scope of EU law in the course of ex post judicial review.[44] In comparison, they may explain – in the course of ex ante judicial review – the likely benefits of their *external* activities for the Union only to hear that the mere fact of acting within the scope of EU law is a potential threat to the EU legal order. It thus requires justification why the adoption of common rules has more far-reaching consequences for external than for internal national sovereignty. This requirement is even more pressing in view of the legal tools at the disposal of the Union: apart from the primacy of EU law, Member States are a under a duty of sincere cooperation. On that basis, they could be required to avoid conflicts beforehand and, in the worst case, to renegotiate or renounce the international agreement which is incompatible with EU law.[45]

In the face of the abstract and concise reasoning of the Court, legal and political[46] science stepped in to construct an international actorness of the EU on the basis of a functioning EU legal order. The key to understanding the ERTA doctrine is the parallelism between internal and external powers. The ERTA doctrine is, according to Post, a tool to 'perfect'[47] the European polity where EU citizens govern themselves through the EU legal order in respect

42 See Christina Eckes, *EU Powers under External Pressure: How the EU's External Actions Alter its Internal Structures* (OUP 2019) 78.

43 Art 2(2) TFEU.

44 See Michael Dougan, 'Judicial Review of Member State Action under the General Principles and the Charter: Defining the "Scope of Union Law"' (2015) 52(5) CML Rev 1201.

45 See Piet Eeckhout, 'Bold Constitutionalism and Beyond' in Poiares Maduro & Azoulai (n 23) 221; Klamert (n 22) 106.

46 Research on 'actorness' generally takes the internal characteristics of the EU legal order as a proxy for influence in the world. Relevant criteria are competences and autonomy from the Member States. For a recent overview of the literature and a critique, see Mark Rhinard & Gunnar Sjöstedt, 'The EU as a Global Actor: A New Conceptualisation Four Decades after Actorness' *Swedish Institute of International Affairs 6/2019* <https://www.ui.se/globalassets/ui.se-eng/publications/ui-publications/2019/ui-paper-no.-6-2019.pdf> accessed 1 March 2024.

47 Post (n 23) 241.

of both internal and external policies. ERTA exclusivity is justified because Member States could undermine mutual trust generated through internal law-making if they were allowed to take external action within the scope of EU law.[48] Hence, exclusivity serves to maintain the constitutional balance in the EU. Eckes goes one step further by arguing that EU citizens can only exercise their right to external self-determination through a functioning and autonomous EU legal order.[49] She presupposes a relative advantage of the EU as far as external representation in times of globalisation is concerned.[50] Hence, the EU is a lever for solving cross-border challenges like immigration and climate change which surpass the control of individual nation states. The exercise of EU external competences is thus a source of direct legitimacy in the eyes of EU citizens. But since the latter remain loyal to national communities, the EU is in need of indirect legitimacy from the Member States.[51] However, still according to Eckes, this cannot mean that the Member States take up the task of external self-determination because it would be contrary to the autonomy of the EU legal order. And the latter is necessary to gain direct legitimacy from EU citizens.[52] She argues that (external) duties of abstention are not detrimental to indirect legitimacy due to institutional channels for internal contestation such as the Council of Ministers.[53] Consequently, exclusivity is justified by the internal possibilities of political contestation governed and facilitated by the EU legal order.

It is submitted that the premises underlying Eckes' argument are not correct as far as migration management is concerned. First, the EU is *empirically* not better placed to act on all dimensions of the comprehensive approach.[54] One such aspect is return and readmission. Member States differ from each other and the EU in terms of their interest and capabilities to conclude bilateral readmission agreements (formal and informal). More specifically, it is not

48 Ibid 243.

49 Eckes (n 42).

50 Ibid 41.

51 Ibid 36–37.

52 Eckes conceptualises the autonomous characteristics of the EU legal order as 'structures of bonding': legal principles, rules and procedures that empower citizens to participate in public life and to experience the benefits of European integration (e.g. the principle of direct effect). EU law can only be effective if the EU legal order is autonomous, and both are necessary conditions for 'structures of bonding', which in turn legitimise the exercise of EU powers, see Eckes (n 42) ch 2.

53 Ibid 76–77.

54 See Chapter 3. For a general critique from political science, see Gjovalin Macaj & Kalypso Nicolaidis, 'Beyond One Voice? Global Europe's Engagement with its Own Diversity' (2014) 21(7) Journal of European Public Policy 1067.

surprising that there are much more national than EU-level agreements, considering that readmission is part of the wider international relations to third countries, which are in turn based on established historical ties.[55] Despite the growing influence of the EU, there is no reason to dispense with the expertise and experience of certain Member States, even though it is challenging to embed bilateralism into a common policy.[56] More in general, allocating responsibilities according to scale or other rational criteria underestimates the dimension of political will. Loyalty to the Union might be 'pragmatic'[57] in rather technical matters, but migration management is a political question affecting national identities. Second, Eckes *conceptually* seems to base her argument on the link between internal and external sovereignty.[58] Thinking in these categories assumes that international recognition depends on the internal capacity of effective and independent control. In the EU context, the ambition to become an international actor justifies limits to the external self-determination of the Member States.[59] Extra-legal factors like the credibility or effectiveness of the EU in a rough international environment may thus inform the scope and effects of EU law. For example, Eckes elevates unity of international representation to a common cause that justifies the 'centralising effect'[60] of loyalty obligations.[61] The latter are stricter on the external dimension because the EU heavily depends on the Member States for international recognition.[62] The result is a yet-to-be-completed polity composed of a legal and political order. Member States must protect this fragile construct by taming their own international ambitions. This constructivist approach is at odds with the European spheres and the concept of representation. The obligation to safeguard European legal integration does not exclude political responsibility in the intermediate sphere where Member States rather than the EU

55 See Jean-Pierre Cassarino, 'Informalizing EU Readmission Policy' in Ariadna Ripoll Servent & Florian Trauner (eds), *The Routledge Handbook of Justice and Home Affairs Research* (Routledge 2018).

56 For a recent reflection, see Jean-Pierre Cassarino & Luisa Martin, 'The Pact on Migration and Asylum: Turning the European Territory into a Non-Territory?' (2022) 24(1) European Journal of Migration and Law 1, 16–24.

57 Eckes (n 42) 76.

58 Based on her previous work, see Christina Eckes, 'The Reflexive Relationship between Internal and External Sovereignty' (2015) 18(1) Irish Journal of European Law 33.

59 See also Thomas Verellen, 'European Sovereignty Now? A Reflection of What is Means to Speak of "European Sovereignty"' (2020) 5(1) European Papers 307.

60 Eckes (n 42) 75.

61 This is arguably not the state of the law, see infra n 154 and the accompanying text.

62 For details, see Christina Eckes, 'Disciplining Member States: EU Loyalty in External Relations' (2020) 22 CYELS 85.

claim to represent the national and the EU collective self. Perhaps their claim will not be accepted because the EU is indeed better placed in respect of a particular subject matter. However, the starting point is the formal-legal question whether international action of the Member States would violate the EU legal order. If that was not the case, then the issue of who should act is to be determined. This approach has the benefit of requiring an open balancing of EU and national powers and capabilities, instead of a priori foreclosing such a debate based on the (implicit) assumption that global affairs call for EU-level action as a matter of course.

Against this background, the next section will re-construct the ERTA doctrine. At the heart of any external competence is the legal capacity to engage in international relations. It was therefore the basis of the three-step reasoning in the original *ERTA* judgment. It hinted at what would become the predominant theme of the jurisprudence: ensuring the independent existence of the EU on the international scene.[63] Independence or autonomy, in this context, refers to a legal actor as opposed to a legal order. Chapter 2 explained how the autonomous characteristics of the EU legal order developed from purely functional to value-based. On that basis, apart from developing the ERTA doctrine vis-à-vis the Member States, the Court has been reluctant to accept the validity of international law in the EU legal order. In other words, the internal characteristics have been a shield against external influences. By contrast, the Court has not postulated a positive concept of international autonomy.[64] Autonomy, alongside other structural principles of EU external relations law, has rather constructed an institutional space where it is the task of the political institutions to make substantive policy choices.[65] As will be explained below, the Court safeguards the external legal capacity of the EU without determining what kind of actor the EU is or should be.

But any re-constructive attempt might backfire if it is poorly justified. This is not the place to restate the theory of the European spheres.[66] Instead, the argument will start from practice, introducing the EU-Turkey Statement and

63 See Loïc Azoulai, 'The Many Visions of Europe: Insights from the Reasoning of the European Court of Justice in External Relations Law' in Marise Cremona & Anne Thies (eds), *The European Court of Justice and External Relations Law: Constitutional Challenges* (Hart 2014) 170–171.

64 See Jed Odermatt, 'The Principle of Autonomy: An Adolescent Disease of EU External Relations Law?' in Marise Cremona (ed), *Structural Principles in EU External Relations Law* (Hart 2018).

65 See Marise Cremona, 'Structural Principles and their Role in EU External Relations Law' in Cremona (n 64).

66 See Chapters 1 and 2.

explaining why such an instrument requires legal tools other than the current ERTA doctrine.

3 ERTA and the Practice of Migration Management: The EU-Turkey Statement

3.1 *Background and Content*

Since the summer of 2015, Turkey had become the main transit country for refugees and migrants arriving in the EU from mostly Syria, Iraq and Afghanistan. In the first three months of 2016, more than 146.000 persons arrived on the Greek islands, several hundred or even thousands on a daily basis.[67] At a time when the 'hotspots' for registration and processing were just in their infancy, a majority managed to reach the mainland to continue the journey to Central Europe along the Western Balkans route. Struggling with the migratory pressure, two informal groups of Member States – partially with the involvement of non-EU countries of the Western Balkans – each pressed ahead before finally reaching a compromise.[68]

On the one hand, there was a group led by Germany and composed of, inter alia, the Benelux countries and Greece. Instead of closing the internal borders, they preferred to strengthen external border protection through cooperation with Turkey. At the same time, these Member States boosted the policy of relocation, which led to the controversial mandatory relocation scheme for the benefit of Italy and Greece.[69] According to German Chancellor Merkel, solidary relocation not only serves the functioning of the Schengen regime,[70] it is also an expression of the common European responsibility for refugees.[71] Protecting universal human rights is, after all, one of the founding myths of the European Union.[72] On the other hand, the Austrian Foreign Minister

---

67 See European Stability Initiative, 'Refugees and Asylum in the Aegean – The Impact of the EU-Turkey Statement' (26 January 2018) 3 <https://www.esiweb.org/publications/refugees-and-asylum-aegean-impact-eu-turkey-statement> accessed 1 March 2024.

68 The following description is based on Robin Alexander, *Die Getriebenen – Merkel und die Flüchtlingspolitik: Report aus dem Innern der Macht* (Siedler 2017) ch 14.

69 See Chapter 2.

70 Federal Government, 'Rede von Bundeskanzlerin Dr. Angela Merkel' (Speech 25 November 2015) <https://www.bundesregierung.de/breg-de/service/newsletter-und-abos/bulletin/rede-von-bundeskanzlerin-dr-angela-merkel-452842> accessed 1 March 2024.

71 Phoenix, 'Sommer-Pressekonferenz der Kanzlerin zu aktuellen Themen (Teil 1) am 31.08.2015' (Press conference 31 August 2015) minute 13:00–15:00 <https://www.youtube.com/watch?v=TQgaXHMMkwM> accessed 1 March 2024.

72 Ibid.

Kurz was at the head of a group composed of, inter alia, Croatia, Slovenia and the countries of the Western Balkans. This group was strongly of the opinion that national immigration control is appropriate to curb irregular migration. Indeed, Kurz convinced the states along the Western Balkans route to close their borders to migrants not in need of international protection. Those who do qualify as refugees should receive protection as close as possible to their countries of origin. Hence, a system of intra-EU relocation is redundant, according to the states belonging to this group.

Driven by events and the pressure of time, both coalitions were keen on making their strategy a success. According to the first group, a closure of the Western Balkans route would not only frustrate the negotiations with Turkey, it would also set a dangerous precedent for Schengen and European integration. Refugees arriving from Turkey would strand in Greece, which was in the midst of an economic crisis and known for a weak administration. However, that possibility was part of the second group's strategy.[73] A few weeks before the EU-Turkey Statement was adopted, ministers from Croatia, Slovenia and Austria together with their colleagues from the Western Balkans informally met in Vienna. They adopted a Declaration focussing on the fight against irregular migration, without mentioning the issue of relocation.[74] They insisted on the full application of the Schengen Borders Code including the rejection at the external border of persons not fulfilling the conditions of entry.[75] In Greece, this was understood as political pressure to comply with EU law despite its political, economic and administrative problems.[76]

On 7 March 2016, the dispute was resolved at an informal summit of the EU Heads of State or Government meeting in their individual capacity (thus not qua European Council).[77] On the one hand, they agreed to update the EU-Turkey Joint Action Plan of October 2015.[78] Financial and operational support for Turkey, which was the subject matter of the Joint Action Plan, was consolidated and supplemented by six principles that would inform the EU-Turkey

73 See Alexander (n 68) 229.

74 Council of the EU, 'Conference "Managing Migration Together"' (Vienna, 24 February 2016) <https://data.consilium.europa.eu/doc/document/ST-6481-2016-INIT/en/pdf> accessed 1 March 2024.

75 Ibid point 8.

76 See Alexander (n 68) 234.

77 Council of the EU, 'Statement of the EU Heads of State or Government, 07/03/2016' (Press release 8 March 2016) <https://www.consilium.europa.eu/en/press/press-releases/2016/03/08/eu-turkey-meeting-statement/pdf> accessed 1 March 2024.

78 European Commission, 'EU-Turkey Joint Action Plan' (15 October 2015) <https://ec.europa.eu/commission/presscorner/detail/de/MEMO_15_5860> accessed 1 March 2024.

Statement adopted shortly thereafter. Suffice it to note that the coalition led by Minister Kurz agreed to a resettlement mechanism for the benefit of Syrian refugees in Turkey, at least 'within the framework of existing commitments'.[79] On the other hand, the German-led coalition accepted the formulation 'Irregular flows of migrants along the Western Balkans route have now come to an end.'[80] Despite the careful wording, the EU leaders acknowledged the closure of the Western Balkans route as a matter of fact. Finally, it was considered necessary to reassure Greece that the challenges caused by irregular migration are 'a collective EU responsibility'.[81] Hence, the EU leaders announced financial and operational support and reiterated their commitment to relocation.

The foregoing has demonstrated that the EU-Turkey Statement was as much a reaction to (external) migratory pressure and (internal) claims to political power. It was adopted on 18 March 2016 in the form of a press release. For the purpose of 'end[ing] the irregular migration from Turkey to the EU',[82] the parties agreed on several action points. The Turkish side committed itself to the following:

- to readmit migrants who have arrived in Greece and who have not applied for international protection or whose application has been found unfounded or inadmissible in accordance with the Asylum Procedures Directive;[83]
- to take any necessary measures to prevent new sea or land routes for illegal migration opening from Turkey to the EU and to cooperate with neighbouring states and the EU to that effect;
- to contribute together with the EU to improve humanitarian conditions inside Syria.

The EU and the Member States made the following commitments:

- to resettle, for every Syrian being returned to Turkey, another Syrian to the EU, within the framework of existing commitments;
- to activate a Voluntary Humanitarian Admission Scheme once irregular crossings between Turkey and the EU are ending or at least have been substantially and sustainably reduced;
- to accelerate visa liberalisation for Turkish nationals, provided that Turkey fulfils all requirements;

79 Council of the EU (n 75) 1.

80 Ibid.

81 Ibid.

82 EU-Turkey Statement (n 1) 1.

83 Directive 2013/32/EU of 26 June 2013 on common procedures for granting and withdrawing international protection ('Asylum Procedures Directive) [2013] OJ L180/60.

- to disburse, in total, 6 billion euro under the Facility for Refugees in Turkey;
- to continue working on the upgrading of the Customs Union;
- to re-energise the accession process;
- to contribute together with Turkey to improve humanitarian conditions inside Syria.

Within the framework of the present analysis, the following focusses on the commitments of the EU and the Member States. Having listed the *collective* commitments, it is worth mentioning the outstanding role of Greece. The latter acts on behalf of the Union when committing itself to returning irregular migrants in line with EU and international law. For that reason and considering the possible effect on EU asylum and migration law within the meaning of Article 3(2) TFEU, the following deals specifically with the so-called 1:1 return/resettlement mechanism.

Having regard, first, to returns from Greece to Turkey, the Statement reads as follows:

> All new irregular migrants crossing from Turkey into Greek islands as from 20 March 2016 will be returned to Turkey. This will take place in full accordance with EU and international law, thus excluding any kind of collective expulsion. All migrants will be protected in accordance with the relevant international standards and in respect of the principle of non-refoulement. It will be a temporary and extraordinary measure which is necessary to end the human suffering and restore public order. Migrants arriving in the Greek islands will be duly registered and any application for asylum will be processed individually by the Greek authorities in accordance with the Asylum Procedures Directive, in cooperation with UNHCR. Migrants not applying for asylum or whose application has been found unfounded or inadmissible in accordance with the said directive will be returned to Turkey.

As mentioned, context is important in order to fully understand the EU-Turkey Statement. Political agreement, dating from 7 March 2016, on the building blocks of the cooperation fed into the technical work of the Commission elaborating, on 16 March 2016, how the former was to be implemented.[84] Hence, the final adoption of the EU-Turkey Statement two days later was also based on the preparatory work of the Commission. In the first place, the Commission has

84 European Commission, 'Next Operational Steps in EU-Turkey Cooperation in the Field of Migration' COM(2016) 166 final.

further specified the legal safeguards as laid down in the Asylum Procedures Directive.[85] Returns are premised on the assumption of Turkey being a 'safe third country' within the meaning of the Directive. That country would thus guarantee effective protection of the returnee's basic human rights, the possibility to request refugee status and, as the case may be, further protection in accordance with the Geneva Convention. Despite the general presumption of safety, the person concerned has a right to an individual examination in conformity with the procedural safeguards of the Directive.[86] It is thus possible to challenge the presumption in administrative and judicial proceedings. In the second place, the Commission set out which changes to domestic law and practice Greece and, to a lesser degree, Turkey would have to adopt.[87] The Commission urged Greece to fully transpose the Asylum Procedures Directive so as to allow for accelerated inadmissibility procedures and speedy judicial review. Moreover, the expected rise in asylum applications required more administrative resources, partially catered for by the European Asylum Support Office (EASO) and the Member States.

The Statement of 18 March 2016 is silent as to the rules and procedures governing returns. It leaves it to Greece and Turkey to 'take the necessary steps and agree any necessary bilateral arrangements, including the presence of Turkish officials on Greek islands and Greek officials in Turkey as of 20 March 2016, to ensure liaison and thereby facilitate the smooth functioning of these arrangements'.[88] It is striking that the parties did not refer to their summit on 29 November 2015.[89] The declaration adopted on that date, the first EU-Turkey Statement, is important in two respects: first, the parties decided to activate the Joint Action Plan that had been agreed ad referenda on 15 October 2015; second, they agreed to reschedule the full application of the EU-Turkey Readmission Agreement to an earlier date. Per 1 June 2016, both parties accepted the return of illegally staying third-country nationals who, inter alia, stayed on or transited through their respective territories.[90] Between 20 March

85 Ibid 3–4.

86 Art 38(2)(c) Asylum Procedures Directive.

87 European Commission (n 84) 4.

88 EU-Turkey Statement (n 1) action point 1.

89 European Council & Council of the EU, 'Meeting of Heads of State or Government with Turkey – EU-Turkey Statement, 29/11/2015' (Press release 29 November 2015) <https://www.consilium.europa.eu/en/press/press-releases/2015/11/29/eu-turkey-meeting-statement/> accessed 1 March 2024.

90 Council Decision 2016/551/EU of 23 March 2016 establishing the position to be taken on behalf of the European Union within the Joint Readmission Committee on a Decision

2016 and 1 June 2016, the bilateral readmission agreement between Greece and Turkey continued to apply.

'For every Syrian being returned to Turkey from Greek islands, *another* Syrian will be resettled from Turkey to the EU taking into account the UN Vulnerability Criteria.'[91] By giving priority to migrants who have not previously entered or tried to enter the EU irregularly, the Statement seeks to reduce the incentive for irregular migration and to breakdown the business model of human smugglers. Knowing of adequate protection in Turkey and the possibility of resettlement to the EU, refugees and migrants should be less inclined to risk their lives on dangerous journeys across the Aegean Sea. Indeed, the number of arrivals on the Greek islands has dropped dramatically since the entry into force of the EU-Turkey Statement.[92] While the underlying strategy was thus successful, the 1:1 mechanism as such was dysfunctional. At least, it was applied in a flexible manner insofar as 18 participating Member States have resettled 27.000 refugees whereas the Greek authorities have returned only 2.735 persons since March 2016.[93] In total, the Member States pledged 72.000 places for resettlement, 'within the framework of existing commitments'.[94] The latter refers, in the first place, to the remaining commitments taken by Member States meeting within the Council on 20 July 2015 and, in the second place, to non-allocated places under the Relocation Decision 2015/1601. Following an amendment of that Decision, Member States were allowed to fulfil their quota by participating in either relocation from Italy or Greece or resettlement from Turkey.[95] According to the Commission, both admission policies 'are concrete expressions of solidarity with other Member States or third countries experiencing a mass influx of migrants'.[96]

---

of the Joint Readmission Committee on implementing arrangements for the application of Articles 4 and 6 of the Agreement between the European Union and the Republic of Turkey on the readmission of persons residing without authorisation from 1 June 2016 [2016] OJ L95/9.

91 EU-Turkey Statement (n 1) action point 2 (emphasis added).

92 See supra n 65.

93 European Commission, 'EU-Turkey Statement: Four Years On' (March 2020) <https://home-affairs.ec.europa.eu/system/files/2020-03/20200318_managing-migration-eu-turkey-statement-4-years-on_en.pdf> accessed 1 March 2024.

94 EU-Turkey Statement (n 1) action point 2.

95 Council Decision 2016/1754/EU of 29 September 2016 amending Decision 2015/1601/EU establishing provisional measures in the area of international protection for the benefit of Italy and Greece [2016] OJ L268/82 (no longer in force).

96 European Commission (n 84) 5.

3.2 *Reception at the CJEU and in Legal Scholarship*

The legality of the Statement was challenged in actions for annulment brought by two Pakistanis and one Afghan national.[97] The applicants submitted that the Statement was attributable to the European Council concluding, in violation of Article 218 TFEU, an international agreement between the EU and Turkey. They also complained about a lack of individualised assessments, contrary to the prohibition of collective expulsion, and about the human rights situation in Turkey, where applicants of international protection were not safe. The General Court did not address the substantive plea, for it dismissed the actions for lack of jurisdiction. Contrary to what the applicants maintained, the EU-Turkey Statement was attributable to the Member States acting jointly under international law. Irrespective of the legal nature of the Statement, the international activities of the Member States fell outside the jurisdiction of the EU Courts under Article 263 TFEU. The CJEU upheld the Orders of the General Court on appeal.[98]

The General Court arrived at its conclusion following a textual and contextual analysis of the EU-Turkey Statement. The circumstances in which it was adopted turned out to be decisive because the wording of the Statement was 'regrettably ambiguous'.[99] Having regard to press material and internal documents, the General Court established that the Heads of State or Government met qua European Council on 17 March 2016 whereas, on the day after, they came together in their individual capacity to adopt the EU-Turkey Statement.[100] It left open whether the parties concluded an international agreement on that occasion.

The Orders fuelled the academic debate that had been ongoing as a result of the EU-Turkey Statement. Most authors criticise the General Court for sanctioning the practice of intergovernmental decision-making outside the EU institutional framework, which the political leaders accomplished by 'changing hats' between 17 and 18 March 2016.[101] They utter this critique so fiercely

97 Case T-192/16 *NF* v *European Council* EU:T:2017:128, Case T-193/16 *NG* v *European Council* EU:T:2017:129, Case T-257/16 *NM* v *European Council* EU:T:2017:130.

98 Joined Cases C-208/17 P to C-210/17 P *NF and Others* v *European Council* EU:C:2018:705.

99 *NF* v *European Council* (n 97) para 66.

100 Ibid para 62.

101 See Jürgen Bast, 'Scharade im kontrollfreien Raum: Hat die EU gar keinen Türkei-Deal geschlossen?' (2017) Verfassungsblog <https://www.printfriendly.com/p/g/tXgPVE> accessed 1 March 2024; Enzo Cannizzaro, 'Dualism as the Supreme Expression of Realism: A Quick Comment on *NF v. European Council*' (2017) 2(1) European Papers 251; Sergio Carrera et al., 'It Wasn't Me! The Luxembourg Court Orders on the EU-Turkey Refugee Deal' *CEPS Policy Insights No 2017–15* <https://cdn.ceps.eu/wp-content/uploads/2017/04/EU-Turkey%20Deal.pdf> accessed 1 March 2024.

because of the implications for the EU legal order. If the General Court had accepted the applicants' procedural plea, it could have examined the substantive complaint as to whether the EU-Turkey Statement complies with fundamental rights enshrined in the EU Treaties. Moreover, if the European Council had been identified as the author of an international agreement, the procedure of Article 218 TFEU would have been violated. The latter requires, for most international agreements, the consent of the European Parliament and the possibility of judicial review. Circumventing that procedure is contrary to democracy and the rule of law, so the argument goes.

The General Court could have avoided these constitutional implications if it found the actions to be admissible on grounds of the EU-Turkey Statement being either an international agreement or any measure intended to produce legal effects vis-à-vis third parties. Legal scholarship is divided on these issues.[102] The following discusses the legal nature or effects of the EU-Turkey Statement for the purposes of the ERTA doctrine, which applies only if an 'international agreement' concluded by the Member States may affect common rules or alter their scope. This criterion is difficult to apply to the EU-Turkey Statement. In addition, there are normative arguments why, even assuming the ERTA doctrine was applicable, it should not be used to assess the legality of an instrument such as the EU-Turkey Statement.

3.3 *Applying the ERTA Doctrine to the EU-Turkey Statement*

3.3.1 Whether the Statement Is an 'International Agreement'

The Court interpreted the meaning of 'international agreement' to encompass 'any undertaking entered into by entities subject to international law which

102 Pro: Maarten Den Heijer & Thomas Spijkerboer, 'Is the EU-Turkey Migration and Refugee Deal a Treaty?' (2016) EU Law Analysis <http://eulawanalysis.blogspot.com/2016/04/is-eu-turkey-refugee-and-migration-deal.html> accessed 1 March 2024; Lynn Hillary, 'Down the Drain with General Principles of EU Law? The EU-Turkey Deal and "Pseudo-Authorship"' (2021) 23(2) European Journal of Migration and Law 127, 142. Contra: Steve Peers, 'The Draft EU/Turkey Deal on Migration and Refugees: Is it Legal?' (2016) EU Law Analysis <http://eulawanalysis.blogspot.com/2016/03/the-draft-euturkey-deal-on-migration.html> accessed 1 March 2024; Gloria Fernández Arribas, 'The EU-Turkey Statement, the Treaty-Making Process and Competent Organs. Is the Statement an International Agreement?' (2017) 2(1) European Papers 303. Balanced: Mauro Gatti & Andrea Ott, 'The EU-Turkey Statement: Legal Nature and Compatibility with EU Institutional Law' in Sergio Carrera et al., *Constitutionalising the External Dimensions of EU Migration Policies in Times of Crisis* (Elgar 2019).

has binding force, whatever its formal designation'.[103] Whether an undertaking has binding force depends on the intention of the parties to be bound under international law, having regard to the content and the circumstances in which it was made. As the formal designation is not decisive, the parties may express their intention to legally commit themselves in any form such as a press release.

Applying these criteria to the EU-Turkey Statement will lead to ambiguous outcomes.[104] On the one hand, an argument in favour of the binding nature is the strong, peremptory language in the paragraph introducing the separate elements of the cooperation. Having 'decided to end the irregular migration from Turkey to the EU', the parties 'agreed on [certain] additional action points'. Likewise, the context in which it was adopted might be interpreted to resemble the process of international treaty-making, starting with informal commitments such as the Joint Action Plan and culminating into a legally binding agreement like the Statement of March 2016. On the other hand, the Statement also includes rather permissive language, stating that all irregular migrants 'will be returned' from a certain date. In similar vein, if the parties actually intended to be bound, they would have taken at least some steps typical of international treaty-making such as involving the parliaments at EU or national level.

Some authors try to circumvent this analytical problem by emphasising the legal effects rather than the legal nature.[105] They argue that the Statement is a measure capable of producing legal effects because the EU, Greece and Turkey have amended their legislation for implementation purposes. However, legal effects do not affect the legal nature of a certain measure.[106] There is a broad array of international norms that give rise to legal or practical effects without being law properly so called.[107] In support of the argument that such instruments nevertheless fall within the scope of Article 3(2) TFEU, some scholars refer to the *IOM* case in which Greece was found to have interfered with the exclusive competence of the Union by submitting a non-binding proposal to

103 *Opinion 1/75* EU:C:1975:145 p 1359. Strictly speaking, the Court interpreted the term for the purposes of what is now art 218 TFEU. Consistency requires the same interpretation of arts 3(2), 216 and 218 TFEU.

104 Based on the detailed analysis in Gatti & Ott (n 102) 187–192, 195–197.

105 See Den Heijer & Spijkerboer (n 102); Narin Idriz, 'The EU-Turkey Statement or the "Refugee Deal": the Extra-Legal Deal of Extraordinary Times?' *Research Paper Series of the Asser Institute* 2017, 13 <https://papers.ssrn.com/sol3/papers.cfm?abstract_id=3080881> accessed 1 March 2024.

106 Arribas (n 102) 309–309; Joost Pauwelyn, 'Is It International Law or Not and Does it Even Matter?' in Joost Pauwelyn et al. (eds), *Informal International Lawmaking* (OUP 2012).

107 See the empirical case studies in Pauwelyn et al. (n 106).

the IOM concerning the implementation of certain conventions on maritime safety.[108] This view seems to find support in the Court's statement of principle according to which Article 3(2) TFEU applies also where an international agreement is being negotiated or implemented.[109] However, that means that legally non-binding measures fall within the scope of Article 3(2) TFEU only insofar as they are adopted in the context of an international agreement.[110] This begs the question whether the EU-Turkey Statement either prepares a new international agreement or implements an existing one. The first scenario is unlikely because, as outlined above, the Statement is rather the culmination of a political dialogue starting in 2013. The second scenario implies that the Statement is a secondary measure implementing existing obligations. Arguably, the Statement is rather a new framework for structuring and implementing the existing legal and political relations between the parties.

3.3.2 Analytical Difficulties and Normative Concerns

The previous sub-section has questioned whether the EU-Turkey Statement is an 'international agreement' for the purposes of Article 3(2) TFEU. The third limb of that provision, codifying the ERTA doctrine, might therefore not even apply. Even if it did apply, there are other analytical difficulties and normative concerns casting doubts on whether the doctrine is appropriate to new forms of governance such as the EU-Turkey Statement. The following presents three arguments to support that proposition.

First, the ERTA doctrine may be an obstacle to realising the comprehensive approach as mandated by the Treaties, covering humanitarian and control policies and bringing together the leverage of the EU and the Member States. Problems arise where legal scholars are content with observing that the Statement falls within a field already covered to a large extent by common rules.[111] This finding, as such, should not be the basis for finding exclusivity because the Treaties empower the Union and the Member States to act jointly under a common policy, not limited to legislative harmonisation for the purposes of a common European asylum system. At least, any critical examination should take the effort to elaborate if and how the Statement undermines the effectiveness of particular rules of EU law, as will be explained below. This is

108 Case C-45/07 *Commission* v *Greece (IOM)* EU:C:2009:81, referred to in Idriz (n 105).

109 *Antarctica* (n 18) para 112.

110 See also *Opinion 1/13* EU:C:2014:2303 para. 42.

111 See Carrera et al. (n 101) 8; Hillary (n 102) 147–148. See also Idriz (n 105) 12–13, who seems to adhere to the scope criterion as well. However, she demonstrates effects on the common rules in concreto.

then the basis for allocating responsibilities between the EU and the Member States, without thereby suggesting that a legal division of competences was a panacea. It gives rise to follow-up questions about cooperation and coherence, as illustrated by the EU-Turkey Statement whose separate elements had to be implemented 'in parallel'.[112] Hence, a neat allocation of competences can only give a misleading image of what it means to act under a comprehensive approach.

Second, and related to that, the EU-Turkey Statement is in many respects a framework arrangement containing open-ended norms whose meaning will only become clear when they are being implemented. For example, it provides for the establishment of a resettlement mechanism from Turkey to the participating Member States. Thus, following the adoption of the Statement, the Commission and the Turkish authorities finalised so-called Standard Operating Procedures governing the selection, assessment and transfer of refugees.[113] Constant monitoring of the implementation process is crucial since the Standard Operating Procedures confer no individual rights on the persons concerned.[114] But recalling that the ERTA doctrine already applies during the norm-making process, it is questionable to prevent the Member States from entering into an arrangement whose normative content is evolving and thus subject to change.

Finally, some authors criticise the General Court for departing from the Court's approach in ERTA where it ruled on the division of competences first and only thereafter on the admissibility of the action.[115] If it had been established that the EU was competent to conclude an international agreement (assuming that the Statement qualifies as such), Member States would have been obliged to act qua EU and to obtain the consent of the European Parliament, in accordance with Article 218 TFEU. Hence, the existence and nature of competence determines who is entitled to represent (which aspects) of the common interests externally. However, under the ERTA doctrine, either the EU institutions shall act on behalf of the Union, or the Member States are free to exercise their competences on their own behalf. The EU-Turkey Statement arguably deals with a third scenario: Member States acting voluntarily on behalf of the Union.

---

112 EU-Turkey Statement (n 1) 2.

113 Council of the EU, 'Standard Operating Procedures Implementing the Mechanism for Resettlement from Turkey to the EU as set out in the EU-Turkey Statement of 18 March 2016 – Endorsement' LIMITE 8366/16.

114 See Jorrit Rijpma, 'External Migration and Asylum Management: Accountability for Executive Action Outside EU- Territory' (2017) 2(2) European Papers 571, 582–584.

115 See Bast (n 101); Cannizzaro (n 101) 253–254.

A first indication is how the legal design of the Statement differs from traditional international agreements of the Member States. The latter often contain so-called non-affection clauses stating that the agreement concerned will not affect the application of EU law.[116] Those clauses reserve a scope of application for international and EU law respectively, trying to avoid any kind of mutual interference.[117] In comparison, the EU-Turkey Statement constitutes a framework joining together existing commitments for the purpose of a comprehensive approach. For example, the success of the resettlement scheme hinges on Greece correctly implementing and applying the Asylum Procedures Directive. EU law is thus an integral part of the overall framework.

Overall, the foregoing has demonstrated that the ERTA doctrine cannot capture the EU-Turkey Statement for analytical purposes. It is over-inclusive by precluding a framework for international migration management that will be developing over time. It is under-inclusive by failing to address the exercise of power in the implementation of the Statement. On normative grounds, the doctrine is unsatisfactory because it fails to account for voluntary action on behalf of the Union. It is submitted that the theory of the European spheres can address these concerns. As announced before, the next section will set out a re-constructed ERTA doctrine. The ambition is to allow for action in the intermediate sphere, while respecting the inner sphere of the Treaties. Hence, there is a limit to autonomous national action: self-recognition of the EU legal order.

4 Moving Inside-Out in EU External Relations

4.1 *Towards a Formal ERTA Test: The Useful Effect of EU Law*

Having regard to our theoretical lens, the ERTA doctrine is meant to demarcate the boundaries of the European spheres. In the present context of EU external relations, the ERTA doctrine is to determine whether Member States comply with the inner sphere of the Treaties. If so, they may move into the intermediate sphere to assume responsibility for the common interests (outside the EU institutional framework). This is the logical corollary of the question of competence, which the ERTA doctrine is supposed to address. Member States

116 See Marise Cremona, 'Disconnection Clauses in EU Law and Practice' in Christophe Hillion & Panos Koutrakos (eds), *Mixed Agreements Revisited: The EU and its Member States in the World* (Hart 2010).

117 For example, see Case C-467/98 *Commission* v *Denmark* (*Open Skies*) EU:C:2002:635, para 105. The relevant clause essentially guaranteed the parallel application of the international agreement in question and EU law insofar as there was no conflict.

may exercise their competences for the common purpose only if the EU is not exclusively competent. However, certain interpretations of the ERTA doctrine rule out autonomous action to the extent of calling into question the very existence of the intermediate sphere. In particular, problems arise where background assumptions about the identity of the Union as a global actor inform the legal analysis of the existence and nature of EU external competence. It is therefore suggested separating the formal rationale for the ERTA effect, that is, to safeguard the integrity of the EU legal order, from substantive considerations as to who is best placed to represent the common interests externally.

In the formal sense, the ERTA doctrine is essentially concerned with the autonomy of the EU legal order. As mentioned, the latter is independent from the national legal systems in the sense of deriving its validity from the Treaties (and thus from itself) rather than from the 27. This independence is necessary to defend the common purpose of mutual non-interference. National measures on the international scene might challenge the independent political existence of the EU in several ways. On the one hand, international commitments of the Member States might undermine the outcome of the internal political process if those commitments affect common rules or alter their scope. However, it is submitted that any such interference must reach a certain level of severity in order to affect the independent existence of the EU legal order. This will be the case when the Member States, by entering into international commitments, contradict or circumvent the common rules. In addition, they must not undermine the existence of the EU as a global actor, capable of behaving independently of the Member States vis-à-vis the outside world. To clarify, this aspect is not concerned with the Union's identity in terms of capabilities, credibility or reputation. The following will explain these requirements in more detail, using the principle of effectiveness as analytical tool.

Chapter 2 explained that the need to ensure the uniform and effective application of EU law constituted the original justification of the principle of autonomy. Today, effectiveness is still constitutive of the autonomous EU legal order insofar as the common values have been either implemented in EU legislation or specified in the jurisprudence of the Court. Though not explicitly mentioned in the Treaties, effectiveness is a meta-principle ensuring the functioning of the EU legal order, especially in conjunction with the principle of loyalty.[118] As

118 See Matej Acetto & Stefan Zleptnig, 'The Principle of Effectiveness: Rethinking its Role in Community Law' (2005) 11(3) European Public Law 375 ('governing principle'); Armin von Bogdandy, 'Founding Principles' in Armin von Bogdandy & Jürgen Bast (ed), *Principles of European Constitutional Law* (2nd edition, Hart 2009) 29–32; Klamert (n 23) ch 6; Matteo Ortino, 'A Reading of the EU Constitutional Legal System through the Meta-Principle of

the following sub-section will show, it is also a general principle informing the day-to-day interpretation and application of EU law.[119] In this regard, the proposed reappraisal distinguishes between useful and full effect.[120] The former means that EU law must not lose its capacity to produce legal effects, which would happen if Member States were allowed to circumvent the scope of the common rules. Full effect means that in case a rule of EU law may be interpreted in more than one way, one should opt for the interpretation that is most conducive to the objective of the rule in question. Unlike the former notion, full effect thus has the potential to optimise the practical effect of EU law.

It is submitted that the Member States may move into the intermediate sphere if they uphold the useful effect of EU law in the twofold sense mentioned above: the capacity of the common rules to produce practical effect in the national legal systems, and the capacity of the EU to be a global actor in its own right independent of the Member States.[121] Who is best placed to pursue the common interests is to be subject to the metaconstitutional discourse in the intermediate sphere.[122] As a consequence, the threshold for finding a violation of the EU legal order will increase, so Member States have more leeway for autonomous national action. It is not just the intention of the present proposal to make the theory of the European spheres work for EU external relations. There are additional arguments in favour of the suggested interpretation. As the next sub-section will show, it is entirely compatible with the external relations case law of the Court, including the underlying rationales for exclusivity. Even those who accord preference to EU-level action have no reason to complain because a unilateral claim to represent the Union may be rejected – even though the present proposal at least provides for the legal option to express such a claim in the first place. Finally, the legal obligations on the internal dimension will not necessarily be affected. The Member States are bound to give effect to EU law also where the Court has interpreted a certain rule so as to realise its full effect. To concede, entering into international commitments

---

Effectiveness' (2016) 52(1) Cahiers de droit européen 91; regarding EU external relations, see Anne Thies, 'The Search for Effectiveness and the Need for Loyalty in EU External Action' in Cremona (n 64) 263–290.

119 See Sibylle Seyr, *Der Effet Utile in der Rechtsprechung des EuGH* (Duncker & Humblot 2008); Anna von Oettingen, *Effet Utile und Individuelle Rechte im Recht der Europäischen Union* (Nomos 2010); Klamert (n 23) ch 13.

120 Based on von Oettingen (n 119), who distinguishes between *Wirksamkeitsgebot* (useful effect) and *Nützlichkeitsgebot* (full effect).

121 See also Thies (n 118), who makes the same distinction but without connecting it to the ERTA doctrine.

122 See Chapters 1 and 2.

might render it more difficult to actually realise the full effectiveness of EU law. However, this possibility as such is insufficient to justify a duty of abstention on the part of the Member States. It would be otherwise if national authorities had to choose which rule to apply because the two sets of legal obligations were impossible to reconcile (useful effect). In such a case, the measure in question had reached a level of severity that would jeopardise the autonomy of the EU legal order. In any event, the Member States cannot simply refer to their international commitments. They must explain that they have done their utmost best to achieve the full effect of EU law.

4.2 *The Useful Effect in the Case Law on EU External Competences*

The purpose of this sub-section is to demonstrate that the principle of useful effect could serve to scrutinise the international activities of the Member States. The intensity of judicial review is low but not ineffective. To develop the argument, this sub-section will analyse certain leading judgments in the field through the proposed lens of useful effect. National measures on the international scene may have both internal and external effects – in turn to be examined in the following paragraphs.

The already mentioned *IOM* case illustrates how unilateral behaviour of a Member State may undermine the useful effect of internal rules.[123] To recall, the Commission complained of Greece having submitted a non-binding proposal to the IOM concerning the implementation of certain conventions in the field of maritime safety. As the EU was exclusively competent on these matters while not being itself a member of the IOM, Member States must not submit national positions to that international organisation unless expressly authorised to do so by the Union. The Court ruled in favour of the Commission, explaining that the proposal could lead to the adoption by the IOM of new rules.[124] As Regulation 725/2004/EC incorporated the substance of the conventions into EU law,[125] any such rules would affect the Regulation within the meaning of the ERTA doctrine.[126] Greece thus violated the duty of abstention as derived from Article 4(3) TEU.

The Court could have found an actual as opposed to a possible interference with the common rules. Article 10(4) of the Regulation reads as follows: 'For the purposes of this Regulation and with a view to reducing the risks of conflict

123 *IOM* (n 108).

124 Ibid para 21.

125 Regulation No 725/2004/EC of 31 May 2004 on enhancing ship and port facility security [2004] OJ L129/6.

126 *IOM* (n 108) para 22.

between [EU] maritime legislation and international instruments, Member States and the Commission shall cooperate, through coordination meetings and/or any other appropriate means, in order to define, as appropriate, a common position or approach in the competent international fora.'[127] Greece argued that it tried to achieve a common position, yet the Commission refused to discuss the contested proposal in the relevant Comitology committee and thereby violated the cooperation duties under Article 4(3) TEU. The Court did not accept that argument because a Member State may not unilaterally rectify any breach of EU law by an institution.[128] It is submitted that the behaviour of Greece rendered the meaning of Article 10(4) of the Regulation devoid of any useful effect because the required coordination did not take place at all. In view of the wording of the provision, mere efforts to cooperate are not sufficient. Moreover, the rule should be interpreted strictly because of the exclusive competence of the Union.

Opinion 3/15 is a more recent example that can be read through the lens of useful effect.[129] The Court was asked for an opinion as to whether the EU had exclusive competence to conclude an international agreement in the field of intellectual property rights (the Marrakesh Treaty).[130] Directive 2001/29/EC on the harmonisation of certain aspects of copyright and related rights in the information society contains the relevant internal rules.[131] Article 5(3)(b) is an optional clause allowing Member States, for the benefit of disabled people, to provide for exceptions or to limit the exercise of intellectual property rights in any other way. By contrast, Article 4 of the Marrakesh Treaty provides for mandatory exceptions or limitations to facilitate the access of literary or artistic works for blind or visually impaired persons. After having established that the scope of the mentioned rules overlaps,[132] the Court reasoned that the EU legislature 'highly circumscribed'[133] the national discretion to provide for exceptions or limitations. For example, Article 5(3)(b) enumerates a number of cumulative conditions for the exercise of that discretion, which is also subject to the obligation not to compromise the objectives of the Directive as a whole.

---

127 Art 10(4) Regulation No 725/2004/EC.

128 *IOM* (n 108) para 26.

129 *Opinion 3/15 (Marrakesh Treaty)* EU:C:2017:114.

130 Council Decision 2018/254/EU of 15 February 2018 on the conclusion on behalf of the European Union of the Marrakesh Treaty to Facilitate Access to Published Works for Persons who are Blind, Visually Impaired, or otherwise Print Disabled [2018] OJ L48/1.

131 Directive 2001/29/EC of 22 May 2001 on the harmonisation of certain aspects of copyright and related rights in the information society [2001] OJ L167/10.

132 *Opinion 3/15* (n 129) para 112.

133 Ibid para 126.

The Court noted that following the conclusion of the international agreement, every Member State will be obliged to observe those constraints and requirements imposed by EU law.[134] It thus concluded that 'the body of obligations laid down by the Marrakesh Treaty falls within an area that is already covered to a large extent by common EU rules and the conclusion of that treaty may thus affect those rules or alter their scope'.[135]

The overlap in scope is thus liable to pose a risk to the integrity of the common rules. In line with settled case law, it was not necessary to find a contradiction between the international commitments and the rules of the EU legal order. The Court therefore rejected the argument of the intervening Member States submitting that they could implement the Marrakesh Treaty in a manner compatible with the Directive.[136] It is submitted that the conclusion of the Marrakesh Treaty by the Member States would undermine the useful effect of Article 5(3)(b) of the Directive, even though the international commitments would not require the disapplication of that rule. By de facto substituting the mandatory for the discretionary nature of that provision, the Marrakesh Treaty affects the balance of rights and obligations under the Directive. Any limitations or exceptions to the rights of holders of intellectual property rights must be interpreted narrowly, which follows from the above-mentioned rules intended to limit the discretion under Article 5(3)(b). The regulatory function of the latter, in conjunction with the other rules to which it relates, would be affected by Article 4 of the Marrakesh Treaty. The suggested interpretation is thus concerned with the nature and function of the common rules; whether the legislative objectives are more likely to be achieved following a certain interpretation is irrelevant in this context.

The latter consideration arguably informed the Court's reasoning in the above-mentioned case of *Green Network*.[137] Similar to IOM and *Opinion 3/15*, the Court found a possible interference with certain internal rules. By recognising energy imported from a third country for the purposes of Directive 2001/77/EC, Italy was less likely to increase the national production of green electricity, contrary to the aim of the Directive as interpreted by the Court.[138] However, the contested measure was but one element of the national energy policy, which is too complex to predict the effects of that measure with any reliable degree of certainty. In accordance with the proposed legal standard,

134 Ibid para 128.
135 Ibid para 129.
136 Ibid para 113.
137 *Green Network* (n 28).
138 Ibid para 59.

Italy did not infringe EU external competences. First, since Article 5 of the Directive does not regulate imports from third countries, Member States have policy discretion in that respect, without prejudice to their EU legal obligations. There is no indication that Italy violated EU law. On the contrary, it relied on the Directive as a source of empowerment, subjecting the recognition of green electricity from a third country to the same requirements as those laid down in the Directive. Second, unlike *Opinion 3/15*, any international commitments would not affect the system of the Directive since the other Member States are not required to recognise guarantees of origin from a third country. Hence, Italy would not create negative externalities, other than perhaps the far too uncertain effect on the production of green electricity in the internal market.

The sub-section now goes on to examine cases that deal with the legal capacity of the EU to act independently of the Member States on the external dimension. The first instructive example is *Commission* v *Sweden* (*PFOS*),[139] which the literature often discusses in relation to the *IOM* case.[140] However, the latter is not analysed here because the Union, not itself a member of the IOM, acted 'through the Member States'[141] to exercise an exclusive competence. *PFOS* concerned the powers of the Member States in a body established by the Stockholm Convention on persistent organic pollutants, a mixed agreement falling within the shared competence of environmental policy.[142] Sweden submitted a proposal to that body for the inclusion of PFOS into the list of prohibited substances; it did so at a time when, according to the Court, the Council had adopted a 'common strategy'[143] not to propose such an amendment of the Stockholm Convention. The Council position was 'the point of departure for concerted [Union] action'[144] giving rise to 'special duties of action and

139 Case C-246/07 *Commission* v *Sweden* (*PFOS*) EU:C:2010:203.

140 For example, see Geert de Baere, 'O, Where is Faith? O, Where is Loyalty? Some Thoughts on the Duty of Loyal Co-operation and the Union's External Environmental Competence in the light of the PFOS Case' (2011) 36(3) European Law Review 405, 413; Pieter van Elsuwege, 'The Duty of Sincere Cooperation and Its Implications for Autonomous Member State Action in the Field of External Relations' in Marton Varju (ed), *Between Compliance and Particularism – Member State Interests and European Union Law* (Springer eBook 2019) 288ff.

141 *IOM* (n 108) para 31.

142 Council Decision 2006/507/EC of 14 October 2004 concerning the conclusion, on behalf of the European Community, of the Stockholm Convention on Persistent Organic Pollutants [2006] OJ L209/1.

143 *PFOS* (n 139) para 89.

144 Ibid para 103.

abstention',[145] which flow from the requirement of unity in the international representation of the EU.[146] By making the unilateral proposal, Sweden 'dissociated itself from a concerted common strategy within the Council'.[147] Having regard to the decision-making procedures under the Convention, Sweden would also be liable to bind the Union if the proposal was accepted.[148] Even if the EU exercised the right under the Convention not to accept a certain amendment, such a declaration would cause legal uncertainty for the Member States, the Secretariat of the Stockholm Convention and third countries which are parties to that Convention.[149] For all these reasons, the Court concluded that Sweden violated the requirement of unity in the international representation of the Union and the Member States, and thus Article 4(3) TEU.

Based on the Court's reasoning, which was significantly informed by the particular circumstances of the case, it will be hard to establish to the requisite legal standard that a certain Member State has dissociated itself from a common strategy and whether that was such as to justify a duty of abstention.[150] This is of particular concern where competences are shared because an undefined duty of abstention is liable to dilute the nature of the competence division.[151] Whether the nature of a competence is exclusive or shared would, in other words, not matter. In addition, it is not clear what the legal nature and effects are of the requirement of unity in the international representation. On the one hand, it has been regarded as a specific expression of the principle of sincere cooperation in the context of mixed agreements.[152] It is thus rather intended to foster cooperation between the EU and the Member States than constituting the source of a duty of abstention eclipsing the Member States from the international scene. On the other hand, it has been argued that the requirement of unity is derived from the objective of EU external self-determination,[153] and in

145 Ibid.

146 Ibid para 73.

147 Ibid para 91.

148 Ibid paras 92ff.

149 Ibid para 99.

150 See De Baere (n 140) 416–417.

151 See Andrés Delgado Casteleiro & Joris Larik, 'The Duty to Remain Silent: Limitless Loyalty in EU External Relations?' (2011) 36(4) European Law Review 524, 538–539; but see De Baere (n 140) 417–418 and Van Elsuwege (n 140) 292–293.

152 See Christophe Hillion, 'Mixity and Coherence in EU External Relations: the Significance of the Duty of Cooperation' *CLEER Working Papers 2009/2*, 5–7 <https://www.asser.nl/upload/documents/9212009_14629clee09-2full.pdf> accessed 1 March 2024; Klamert (n 23) 191.

153 Eleftheria Neframi, 'The Duty of Loyalty: Rethinking its Scope through its Application in the Field of EU External Relations' (2010) 47(2) CML Rev 323, 353–355.

combination with the principle of loyalty, it will lead to a hierarchical ordering of foreign policies, with priority for the objectives of the Union.[154] However, this view is difficult to reconcile with the intermediate sphere, for it takes a hierarchical EU-centred perspective on the substance of European integration. The intermediate sphere, on the contrary, assumes that the constitutional relationships are plural, so the 27 co-determine the point of their joint action.

It is submitted that Advocate General Maduro proposed a more suitable legal standard in his Opinion in *PFOS*.[155] Member States violated their duties of cooperation if their exercise of a shared competence 'is liable seriously to compromise the exercise of a [Union] competence'.[156] Hence, the Advocate General was concerned about the capacity of the EU to exercise its competences in the first place, irrespective of what the international identity of the EU is or ought to be.[157] On this basis, the Advocate General concluded that the Swedish proposal did not deprive the EU from exercising its rights under the Stockholm Convention.[158] Any difficulties arising from parallel activities 'need to be balanced against the legitimate rights of Member States and the preservation of their competences'.[159] Although entitled to act, Sweden did so in a manner contrary to the internal decision-making within the Union. As discussions in the Council were ongoing, Sweden should have waited for a reasonable period before contemplating a unilateral measure.[160] One could add that Sweden, unlike Greece in the *IOM* case, did not violate a rule of EU (secondary) law requiring that a common position is to be defined. That is a reason to support the legal opinion of the Advocate General and to conclude that Sweden undermined the useful effect of the internal decision-making procedure.

While *PFOS* concerned the implementation of a mixed agreement, it is necessary to also consider a situation where the EU wants to enter into new international commitments in accordance with the procedural legal basis of Article 218 TFEU. In *Air Transport Agreement*,[161] the Commission brought an action for annulment against Decision 2011/708/EU adopted jointly by the Council and the Representatives of the Governments of the Member States meeting

---

154 Eckes (n 42) 75.
155 Opinion of AG Maduro in *Commission* v *Sweden* (*PFOS*) EU:C:2009:589.
156 Ibid para 38.
157 Compare Thies (n 118) 287–288, who argues that the ruling in *PFOS* was to protect the exercise of EU external competence 'in a particular and united way'.
158 Opinion of AG Maduro (n 155) para 39.
159 Ibid para 43.
160 Ibid paras 54, 56.
161 Case C-28/12 *Commission* v *Council* (*Air Transport Agreement*) EU:C:2015:282.

within the Council (a so-called hybrid decision).[162] The Decision authorised the signing and provisional application of certain agreements governing the accession of Norway and Iceland to the Air Transport Agreement with the USA (a mixed agreement). The Commission argued that by adopting the hybrid decision, the Council violated the decision-making procedure of Article 218 TFEU. The Court ruled in favour of the Commission, and the reasoning corresponds to the notion of useful effect. As the EU legal order is autonomous, the decision-making rules of the Treaties were not at the disposal of the Member States.[163] They were thus bound by Article 218 TFEU stipulating that a decision authorising the signing and provisional application of an international agreement is adopted by the Council. The Member States, acting qua sovereign nation states, had no role in that respect. Nonetheless, the Decision merged, under a single procedure, the act of signing the agreements concerned on behalf of the EU and their provisional application by it, and the act relating to the provisional application of those agreements by the Member States. The Council stated that it adopted the former by Qualified Majority Voting in line with Article 218(8) TFEU, while the latter met the unanimous approval of the 27 not meeting in their capacity as EU members. The Court found these voting procedures to be incompatible with one another.[164] While no explicit reason is given in the judgment, it is likely that effectiveness considerations informed the Court's reasoning since the said merging deprived Article 218(8) TFEU of its purpose to unblock decision-making precisely where there is no consensus.

At first sight, the outcome of the case appears to be detrimental to the intermediate sphere. The latter found expression in the hybrid decision adopted jointly by an EU institution and the Member States acting in their individual capacity. Indeed, the Council argued that the adoption of a joint decision reflected the mutual duties of cooperation with regard to mixed agreements,

162 Decision of the Council and of the Representatives of the Governments of the Member States of the European Union, meeting within the Council of 16 June 2011 on the signing, on behalf of the Union, and provisional application of the Air Transport Agreement between the United States of America, of the first part, the European Union and its Member States, of the second part, Iceland, of the third part, and the Kingdom of Norway, of the fourth part; and on the signing, on behalf of the Union, and provisional application of the Ancillary Agreement between the European Union and its Member States, of the first part, Iceland, of the second part, and the Kingdom of Norway, of the third part, on the application of the Air Transport Agreement between the United States of America, of the first part, the European Union and its Member States, of the second part, Iceland, of the third part, and the Kingdom of Norway, of the fourth part [2011] OJ L283/1.

163 *Air Transport Agreement* (n 161) para 42.

164 Ibid para 52.

ensuring the unified representation of the EU in international relations. While the Court insisted on compliance with Article 218 TFEU and thus on the integrity of the inner sphere, it did not rule out coordination between the EU and the Member States.[165] In terms of legal design, Advocate General Mengozzi did not even exclude coordination by means of a single act if the latter clarified which elements were an exercise of EU competence and which elements corresponded to the political will of the 27.[166] The EU had to be able to act as a 'full player on the world stage'[167] which amounted to an obligation not to conceal the 'independent and autonomous international personality'[168] of the EU. The Advocate General thus tried to strike a balance between the legal rules on the one hand, and the practice of external relations on the other.[169] That is welcome since it is then incumbent upon the 27 to assume legal and political responsibility not only for their foreign policies but also for the integrity of the EU legal order.

The foregoing suggested that the principle of useful effect is a proportionate tool to evaluate movements 'inside-out'. In any case, it requires Member States to justify their international activities by reference to specific rules of EU law. Ignoring or contradicting those rules amounts to a manifest infringement of their obligations under the EU legal order. At the same time, the proposed legal standard is mindful of national external self-determination. There is thus ample room to move into the intermediate or the outer sphere. Against this background, the EU-Turkey Statement will be regarded as action in the intermediate sphere. The question to be answered is whether the Statement is compatible with the inner sphere of the Treaties. The section hereafter follows the above regarding internal and external self-determination. More specifically, a significant part of the examination will address the useful effect of the safe third country rule on the one hand, and of Article 218 TFEU on the other.

---

165 Ibid paras 54–55.

166 Opinion of AG Mengozzi in *Commission* v *Council* (*Air Transport Agreement*) EU:C:2015:43, para 90.

167 Ibid para 86.

168 Ibid.

169 Ibid paras 3, 41.

5 Whether the EU-Turkey Statement Is Compatible with the Useful Effect of the Common Rules

5.1 *The Useful Effect of the Safe Third Country Rule*

At the outset, the Turkish law applicable in March 2016 may be summarised as follows. The Law on Foreigners and International Protection regulates the eligibility for and contents of various protection statuses.[170] Having ratified the 1951 Geneva Convention and the 1967 Protocol, Turkey maintains a geographical limitation to the scope of application. Refugee status is reserved to persons facing a risk of persecution as a result of events occurring in Europe.[171] Refugees from outside Europe are eligible for a temporary right of residence until they are resettled to a third country (conditional refugee status).[172] Furthermore, temporary protection status is conferred on groups of displaced persons arriving en masse,[173] for the conduct of individual asylum procedures would be impractical in such situations. Since 2011, Syrians displaced by the civil war have benefitted from temporary protection, the procedures and principles of which are laid down in the Temporary Protection Regulation.[174] In a nutshell, beneficiaries have a right to stay in Turkey for the duration of the temporary protection regime,[175] which may be terminated or suspended at any time,[176] or until they decide on an individual basis to no longer exercise the right.[177] In any case, they are protected from refoulement,[178] unless they fall within certain exclusion grounds according to an emergency decree adopted following the failed coup d'état in 2016.[179] Except for some basic rights, the entitlement to material reception conditions depends on the discretion of the Turkish authorities.[180] The subsequent analysis as to whether the Member States were entitled to consider Turkey a safe third country will examine these issues in more detail. Indeed, the temporary protection regime will be the focal

170 Law No 6458 of 4 April 2013 on Foreigners and International Protection ('LFIP').

171 Ibid art 61.

172 Ibid art 62.

173 Ibid art 91(1).

174 Temporary Protection Regulation 2014/6883 of 22 October 2014 ('Temporary Protection Regulation').

175 Art 25 Temporary Protection Regulation.

176 Ibid art 11(1).

177 Ibid art 12(1).

178 Ibid art 6.

179 See AIDA – Asylum Information Database, 'Country Report: Turkey (2019 Update)' (2019) 134 <http://asylumineurope.org/wp-content/uploads/2020/04/report-download_aida_tr_2019update.pdf> accessed 1 March 2024.

180 Part 6 Temporary Protection Regulation.

point because, at the time when the EU-Turkey Statement was being negotiated and adopted, Syrians were the largest group of those who arrived on the Greek islands.

According to Article 38(1) of the Asylum Procedures Directive, Member States may apply the safe third country concept only where they are satisfied that a person seeking international protection will be treated, in law and in practice, in accordance with certain principles in the third country concerned.[181] Those principles include 'the possibility (...) to request refugee status and, if found to be a refugee, to receive protection in accordance with the Geneva Convention'.[182] The first limb deals with access to a status determination procedure, and the second limb with the level of protection. In the absence of clarification by the Court, both limbs leave a lot of leeway to the Member States. Regarding the first limb, it is not clear whether status determination must meet the standards in the EU Directive, which are higher than the requirements in international law. The latter requires status determination to be fair and efficient, either in individual or generalised form such as temporary protection.[183] Regarding the second limb, it is uncertain whether it requires unconditional commitment to the 1951 Convention and the 1967 Protocol, or whether third states may formally deviate from certain obligations in accordance with international law, as long as they guarantee an equivalent level of protection in practice. At the very least, it follows from the wording of Article 38(1)(e) that the scope and level of protection must be compatible with the Geneva Convention. It is important to note that the latter confers rights relative to the degree of connection with the host state.[184] This connection hinges, in turn, on the extent to which the state has regularised the refugee's status. The more advanced the status determination procedure, the more rights the refugee has. A refugee officially recognised as such thus falls within the personal scope of all the rights enshrined in the Geneva Convention. Unlike a refugee who has just crossed the border of the host state, the former is inter alia entitled to access to the labour market and to housing. The personal and

181 Asylum Procedures Directive (n 83).

182 Ibid art 38(1)(e).

183 See Daniel Thym, 'Minimum Requirements under EU Primary Law and International Refugee Law for Rules in Secondary Legislation on the Rejection of Applicants for Asylum as Inadmissible with a view to Protection and Housing Options in Third Countries (Transit or Other Countries) or in Parts of any Such Countries' (Expert Opinion for the (German) Federal Ministry of the Interior 2017) 34 <https://papers.ssrn.com/sol3/papers.cfm?abstract_id=3163014> accessed 1 March 2024.

184 See James C Hathaway, *The Rights of Refugees under International Law* (2nd edition, CUP 2021) ch 3.

material scope as such does not determine the level of protection. The latter hinges on a comparison with the nationals or different groups of foreigners residing in the host state.

Against that legal background, it is possible to evaluate the legal situation in Turkey. As regards the first limb, Article 16(1) of the Temporary Protection Regulation reads as follows: 'Individual international protection applications filed by foreigners under this regulation shall not be processed in order to ensure the effective implementation of temporary protection measures during the period of the implementation of temporary protection.'[185] Considering the situation of Syrian nationals, they have the possibility to apply for conditional refugee status, yet their application will not be processed as long as they are protected under the temporary protection regime. When terminating the regime, the Turkish Presidency has several discretionary powers: (1) to fully suspend temporary protection and to return the beneficiaries to their countries of origin; (2) to grant conditional refugee status for the entire group or to assess the previous applications for international protection, which were not examined according to the mentioned Article 16(1); (3) to confer a right to stay in accordance with the Law on Foreigners and International Protection.[186] Depending on the Turkish practice, it could therefore be that after the termination of temporary protection, the beneficiaries will be returned to their countries of origin without getting the opportunity to apply for individual protection or to request processing of their previously submitted application. But even this worst-case scenario is not contrary to the useful effect of Article 38(1)(e) of the Procedures Directive, for temporary protection as such fulfils the minimum requirements of international law and a significant degree of executive discretion is not at odds with the requirement to provide a 'possibility' to request refugee status.

Regarding the second limb, several authors question whether Turkey is a safe third country because only refugees recognised by virtue of events occurring in Europe benefit from the full protection of the Geneva Convention.[187]

---

185 Art 16(1) Temporary Protection Regulation.

186 Ibid arts 10(1) and 11. However, the reference in that provision to the 'Council of Ministers' is no longer up-to-date since that institution was abolished in the course of the constitutional reform in 2018, see AIDA – Asylum Information Database (n 177) 120.

187 For example, see Idriz (n 105) 12; Violetta Moreno-Lax, 'Solidarity's Reach: Meaning, Dimension and Implications for EU (External) Asylum Policy' (2017) 24(5) Maastricht Journal of European and Comparative Law 740, 759–761; Sergio Carrera et al., 'The EU-Turkey Deal: Reversing 'Lisbonisation' in EU Migration and Asylum Policies' in Carrera et al. (n 102) 163ff; Tineke Strik, 'Migration Deals and Responsibility Sharing: Can the Two Go Together?' in Carrera et al. (n 102) 66–69.

Questions arise as to whether an equivalent level of protection may compensate for maintaining the geographical limitation for the purposes of EU law and, if so, whether the Turkish concept of conditional refugee status amounts to such a level of protection. The first question should be answered in the affirmative following a systematic interpretation of Article 38(1)(e) of the Directive.[188] To apply the concept of *European* safe third country, ratification of the Geneva Convention is explicitly required.[189] Had the EU legislature intended the same condition for the concept of safe third country, it would not have opted for the term 'in accordance with'. Next, an assessment in light of Article 34 of the Geneva Convention, requiring states to facilitate as far as possible the assimilation and naturalisation of refugees, does not reveal anything calling into question the legality of 'conditional refugee status'. The latter reflects the choice of the Turkish law-maker to prioritise resettlement over local integration. In the same vein, the duration of temporary protection shall not be taken into account when assessing whether the beneficiary is entitled to a residence permit or Turkish citizenship.[190] It is submitted that the Turkish rules are compatible with the useful effect of Article 38(1)(e) of the Asylum Procedures Directive and, by implication, with Article 34 of the Geneva Convention to which the former rule implicitly refers. In the first place, the latter should be qualified as an obligation of best efforts, requiring the State Parties to help refugees to live a life in dignity and self-sufficiency to the greatest extent possible. Arguably, Turkey fulfils that duty by granting socio-economic rights to every person falling within one of the mentioned protection statuses.[191] In the second place, the said obligation applies not only to the host state but to the international community as a whole, in accordance with the wording of Article 34 ('Contracting States') and the preamble of the Convention that calls for international cooperation to achieve responsibility-sharing.[192] Turkey acts accordingly by resettling refugees under the EU-Turkey Statement, for example. In the third place, it does not thereby undermine the useful effect of Article 34 of the Convention because both local integration and

---

188 See also Greek Council of State, Joint decisions 2347/2017 and 2348/2017 (unofficial English summary) <https://www.refworld.org/jurisprudence/caselaw/grccs/2017/en/120841> accessed 1 March 2024.

189 Art 39 Asylum Procedures Directive.

190 Art 25 Temporary Protection Regulation.

191 See pt 6 Temporary Protection Regulation, and section 3 LFIP. It should be noted that Turkey generally expects protection seekers to secure their own accommodation. However, it does provide emergency reception in camps, so-called temporary accommodation centres. See art 95(1) and (2) LFIP and pt 8 Temporary Protection Regulation.

192 See generally Thym (n 183) 53–56.

resettlement are durable solutions according to UNHCR.[193] Indeed, the benefits of exercising socio-economic rights are intrinsic to the individual person; they are not necessarily dependent on the place of residence. If, for example, a refugee exercises the right to education or to work in Turkey, the chances of being selected for resettlement will increase.

Article 38(1)(e) of the Asylum Procedures Directive concerns the status determination procedure and, in particular, the rights of refugees after the completion of that procedure. Letters (a) to (d) of that provision are essentially various expressions of the prohibition of refoulement, applicable irrespective of the stage of the status determination procedure.[194] Refugees have a right not to experience serious harm *in* the designated safe third country as defined in the Qualifications Directive, and not to be removed *from* that country in violation of the principle of non-refoulement.[195] Member States thus violate their obligations if returnees face a real risk of serious harm in the safe third country or following the removal from that country.

Inhuman or degrading treatment or punishment is a form of serious harm and it is prohibited by the EU Charter of Fundamental Rights and the European Convention on Human Rights (ECHR).[196] The prohibition contained in the ECHR constitutes the minimum level of protection in Europe, the Member States are bound to observe by virtue of the Charter and/or the ECHR.[197] It is therefore necessary to consider the jurisprudence of the European Court of Human Rights (ECtHR) in that respect. According to settled case law, Article 3 of the ECHR precludes a removal where substantial grounds have been shown for believing that the person concerned faces a real risk of being subjected to torture, inhuman or degrading treatment or punishment in the receiving country.[198] However, any form of ill-treatment must reach a minimum level of severity to fall within the scope of Article 3 of the ECHR, which is relative and depends on all the circumstances of the case.[199] Shortcomings concerned, on the one hand, the accessibility and reliability of the asylum system and, on the other hand, the living conditions as regards, for example, reception facilities,

193 See UNHCR Executive Committee, 'Durable Solutions and Refugee Protection No. 56 (XL) – 1989' (13 October 1989) point b) iii) <https://www.refworld.org/policy/exconc/excom/1989/en/41965> accessed 1 March 2024.

194 See Thym (n 183) 15–18.

195 Ibid.

196 Art 4 Charter; art 3 ECHR.

197 Art 52(1) and (3) Charter.

198 Recently, *Ilias and Ahmed* v *Hungary* App no 47287/15 (ECtHR, 21 November 2019), paras 124ff.

199 Ibid para 127.

detention conditions or health care services.[200] In general, the threshold for finding a violation of Article 3 of the ECHR is rather high; though it is useful to distinguish the core obligation of non-refoulement from the well-being of the person concerned in a less existential sense. Hence, a lower standard of living conditions will preclude a return only in exceptional circumstances.[201] Other than that, it is difficult to infer general principles from the casuistic approach of the Strasbourg Court.

However, there are certain objective factors that facilitate the assessment. First, the quality of reception conditions depends, to a certain extent, on the capacity of the third country concerned. The fact that many refugee-receiving countries are less developed than European states justifies a level of protection relative to the circumstances pertaining in those countries. In particular, the degree to which mass migration poses a challenge to reception capacities is relevant in this context.[202] However, it is a factor to be taken into account in the overall assessment, rather than a justification for breaching Article 3 of the ECHR.[203] In addition, it is a relevant factor in the specific context of living conditions. The ECtHR has recently clarified that it is not willing to draw a distinction between developed and developing countries as far as the principle of non-refoulement is concerned.[204] Thus, States bound by the ECHR shall ensure that safe third countries respect the prohibition of refoulement under all circumstances. Second, even poor living conditions do not necessarily preclude a removal if the sending state has taken mitigating measures. The Strasbourg Court has so far required Member States to obtain diplomatic assurances in individual cases where there is a real risk of treatment contrary to Article 3 of the ECHR.[205] However, this obligation does not prevent Member States from complementing individual guarantees with structural solutions as part of a balanced, comprehensive approach to migration. In the recent case of *Ilias and Ahmed*, Hungary could have avoided a violation of Article 3 of the ECHR if, according to the Strasbourg Court, it had obtained individual guarantees from the Serbian authorities ruling out the possibility of summary removals without an examination of their asylum applications.[206] However, the problem was of a structural nature insofar as the Serbian legislation required the authorities

200 See, in particular, *M.S.S.* v *Belgium and Greece* App no 30696/09 (ECtHR, 21 January 2011).
201 See Thym (n 183) 23–27.
202 *Khlaifia and Others* v *Italy* App no 16483/12 (ECtHR, 15 December 2016), para 185.
203 Ibid para 184.
204 *Ilias and Ahmed* (n 198) para 134.
205 *Tarakhel* v *Switzerland* App no 29217/12 (ECtHR, 4 November 2014), para 120.
206 *Ilias and Ahmed* (n 198) para 161.

to prosecute returned asylum seekers for illegal entry,[207] contrary to Article 31 of the Geneva Convention. It would therefore have been desirable if the Strasbourg Court had taken into account whether Hungary embedded the unilateral policy of designating safe third countries into a context of international cooperation aimed at actually improving the safety of those countries. As the general situation impacts on the realisation of individual rights, the ECtHR would thereby not act contrary to the tasks of a human rights court.

Before examining the legal and practical situation in Turkey, it should be reiterated that the present analysis addresses the issue as to whether the Member States respected the useful effect of Article 38(1) of the Asylum Procedures Directive when adopting the EU-Turkey Statement. That assessment will be rather lenient given that the designation of Turkey as a safe third country gives rise to a right to rebut that presumption in individual cases.[208] Having said that, Syrians do not have, in principle, a right to material reception conditions in Turkey. The Temporary Protection Regulation makes a distinction between persons staying in so-called temporary accommodation centres ('camps') and those who do not.[209] Only the former have a right to food, accommodation, health care and similar services. In any case, the provision of such services hinges on the available resources.[210] It is important to note that the Turkish authorities decide on access with regard to the reception capacity of each camp.[211] Hence, if beneficiaries of temporary protection want to live in a camp to avail themselves of the available services, they might not get access in the first place. In fact, when the EU-Turkey Statement was adopted, over 85% of the beneficiaries resided outside the camps having secured, for example, private accommodation in the cities.[212] Given the difficulties of Syrians living outside the camps to access adequate living conditions, which were reported at that time,[213] the Member States ought to have been aware of the

207 Ibid para 69.

208 Art 38(2) Asylum Procedures Directive. In practice, many asylum seekers in Greece do not exercise that right because the procedure takes too long. They rather abscond in the meantime, see European Stability Initiative, 'The EU-Turkey Statement Three Years On' (15 April 2019) 11 <https://www.esiweb.org/publications/core-facts-eu-turkey-statement-three-years> accessed 1 March 2024.

209 Art 38(1)-(2) Temporary Protection Regulation.

210 Ibid.

211 Ibid art 23.

212 See See AIDA – Asylum Information Database, 'Country Report: Turkey (2015 Update)' (2015) 73 <https://asylumineurope.org/wp-content/uploads/2015/12/report-download_aida_tr_update.i.pdf> accessed 1 March 2024.

213 Ibid 73–74.

consequences of qualifying Turkey as a safe third country. Indeed, this decision was liable to shift the responsibility to Turkey at a time when the living conditions of displaced persons had raised, at least, serious concerns under Article 3 of the ECHR. However, there were several mitigating factors. First, the high number of refugees justified the policy of dispersal, that is, of distributing the persons concerned across the country in and outside of state-funded camps. At the end of 2015, Turkey hosted the largest number of refugees worldwide (2.75 million).[214] Second, the designation of Turkey as a safe third country was part of a comprehensive cooperation. The EU and the Member States financially supported Turkey in offering humanitarian assistance and, in addition, most Member States agreed to resettle Syrian refugees. Both measures were capable of improving the living conditions on the ground (irrespective of the actual results, which will be mentioned below). It is therefore submitted that the Member States did not undermine the useful effect of Article 38(1) of the Asylum Procedures Directive on account of the living conditions in Turkey in March 2016.

Finally, at that point in time, Syrian nationals did not face a real risk of being returned to their country of origin. The Temporary Protection Regulation protected them from refoulement, only subject to 'administrative actions'[215] if a person is to be removed in accordance with another piece of legislation. However, following the failed coup d'état in July 2016, the Law on Foreigners and International Protection was amended through an emergency degree.[216] Article 54 of the Law lists the grounds for issuing a removal decision against a foreigner, including the 'association'[217] with terrorist organisations. Even though Article 54 is without prejudice to the principle of non-refoulement, several Syrian refugees were returned to their country of origin on that basis.[218] Moreover, in the summer of 2019, Turkey conducted a military operation in the Northwest of Syria to establish so-called 'safe zones' for the resettlement of Syrian refugees. It has been reported that Syrians were forced to sign 'voluntary return' forms.[219] As a result, their protection status was terminated and, in case of re-entry, it is only re-activated if the Turkish authorities issue a positive

214 UNHCR, '2015 Year-End Report (Turkey)' (25 November 2016) <https://reporting.unhcr.org/sites/default/files/pdfsummaries/GR2015-Turkey-eng.pdf> accessed 1 March 2024.

215 Art 6(2) Temporary Protection Regulation.

216 See AIDA (n 179) 134.

217 Art 54(1)(k) LFIP, as amended.

218 See AIDA (n 179) 26.

219 Ibid 124.

decision to that effect.[220] These examples demonstrate the importance of ongoing monitoring after the adoption of the EU-Turkey Statement.

By way of conclusion as far as the safe third country rule is concerned, the Member States did not undermine its integrity at the time when the Statement was adopted. However, it will lose its useful effect in the absence of adequate accountability mechanisms that are flexible enough to detect rights violations in a changing political climate. Such mechanisms would usefully complement the re-constructed ERTA doctrine. The demand for accountability is certainly not a reason to reject the present proposal, for even if the EU had formally concluded an international agreement with Turkey, the issue of how to ensure respect for human rights in the partner country would have arisen as well.

5.2 *The Union's Independent Legal Capacity to Act Internally and Externally*

Carrera et al. voice the typical criticism under this head in strong words. In their opinion, the EU-Turkey Statement is 'a form of "reverse Lisbonisation" and a step backwards to intergovernmentalism'.[221] In particular, they are concerned about the role of the European Parliament in the negotiation and conclusion of international agreements under Article 218 TFEU. In most cases, the European Parliament has the power to veto international agreements; but it was not involved in the adoption of the EU-Turkey Statement. One could add that Article 218 TFEU embodies a commitment to rule-based multilateralism in the sense that it lays down procedures for the participation of the Commission, the Council and the European Parliament, each representing different interests. In comparison, the EU-Turkey Statement is rather an example of informal multilateralism given that the 28 collectively adopted the Statement in the form of a press release.

Irrespective of the implications for democracy or the rule of law, the inner sphere is essentially concerned with the useful effect of Article 218 TFEU and other institutional rules. The Member States are obliged to act in their capacity as members of the Union, and thus in accordance with Article 218 TFEU, when they intend to enter into legally binding international agreements. Hence, they would have deprived that procedural legal basis of any useful effect if they had circumvented it despite their intention to commit themselves under international law vis-à-vis Turkey. However, as explained above, it is notoriously difficult to deduce from the wording of the Statement and the context in which

220 Art 13 Temporary Protection Regulation.

221 Carrera et al. (n 187) 161. See also Hillary (n 102) 151: 'even the general principles of EU law and the fundamental values of the EU legal order itself are being flushed down the drain'.

it was adopted, any such intention with a high degree of certainty. To determine, on that basis, whether the Member States undermined the useful effect of Article 218 TFEU will be an unsatisfactory exercise. It is therefore suggested to carry out the analysis at a higher level of abstraction, asking whether the Member States undermined the autonomy or independent existence of the EU.

For that purpose, the EU-Turkey Statement is treated as an exercise of liquid authority as defined in Chapter 2. Instead of seeking formal recognition through legally binding rules and procedures, the 28 aspire social recognition for their problem-solving capacity. But this claim could restrict, legally or practically, the exercise of competences in the inner sphere of the Treaties. It is thus possible to separate the legal nature from the actual and legal effects of the EU-Turkey Statement, and to capture it for analytical purposes despite the uncertainty as to its legal or political nature. In addition, it will be assumed that any legal and actual effects flow directly from the separate commitments, and only indirectly from the Statement as such. And these commitments concern both the internal and the external dimension of EU policies. Hence, the following will examine in how far the separate elements of the EU-Turkey Statement have a legal or practical effect on the internal or external exercise of Union competences.

5.2.1 The EU Asylum Acquis and, in Particular, the Asylum Procedures Directive

As explained above, the Member States and the Commission rely on a certain interpretation of the Asylum Procedures Directive in order to legitimise returns from Greece to Turkey. In particular, the wording of the Directive is ambiguous as to whether a third country must have fully ratified the Geneva Convention in order to qualify as 'safe'. A legal or political commitment to the EU-Turkey Statement could obstruct the capacity of the EU legislature to clarify the criteria in the future. In other words, even if the EU-Turkey Statement is not legally binding, the Commission could be reluctant to propose amendments to the Asylum Procedures Directive and, assuming it did, the Council is likely to block the legislative procedure irrespective of the attitude of the European Parliament. While not legally precluded from acting, the EU legislature might thus face practical obstacles in exercising an internal competence.

This is legally relevant insofar as the Court has consistently held that Member States, when exercising their external competences, must consider the foreseeable future development of EU law. Member States have, if not a duty of abstention, at least a duty of close cooperation vis-à-vis the EU institutions when the latter have taken sufficiently concrete steps to act themselves on the international scene. Even if this obligation is applied, mutatis mutandis, to the internal dimension, the Commission proposed to amend EU asylum laws only after the EU-Turkey Statement had been adopted. We are thus concerned with the useful effect of a competence-conferring norm as such, namely Article 78(2) TFEU. In this regard, the Court found that certain Member States failed to fulfil their obligations under Article 351 TFEU by not having taken appropriate steps to eliminate incompatibilities between their pre-accession bilateral investment treaties (BITS) and EU law.[222] The international obligation of the Member States concerned to guarantee the free flow of capital in relation to certain third countries could undermine the power of the Council to take restrictive measures against the same countries, in accordance with Articles 64, 66, 75 and 215 TFEU.[223] In a nutshell, the useful effect of the said legal basis provisions was likely to be undermined. Any Member State has, according to the Court, the possibility of taking mitigating measures by renegotiating the international agreement so as to allow and safeguard the fulfilment of their obligations 'as member of the [Union]'.[224] In these rulings, the Court set a high threshold, so the said possibility seems to be rather theoretical than real.

It is doubtful whether this case law is of broader relevance. At least it could be if obligations incumbent on Member States are derived from Article 4(3) TEU, rather than Article 351 TFEU. This is relevant insofar as the scope of the national right to exercise external powers will increase if the proposed legal standard is accepted. It is therefore imperative to reconcile the double role of the Member States qua subjects of international law and qua members of the Union. Likewise, close cooperation with the EU institutions is inevitable. The institutional mechanisms brought forward in the BITS cases just illustrate what could be envisaged, including suspension, renegotiation or, as a matter of last resort, denunciation of the relevant international agreement. Moreover, non-affection clauses could clarify the primacy of EU law.[225] It has been explained that the EU-Turkey Statement is special for integrating EU asylum law into a comprehensive framework for migration management. The common rules are thus key to achieve the aims of the common policy. The former will be amended in case they do no longer fulfil their intended purpose. Consequently, instead of obstructing the exercise of EU competences, the Statement is even premised on that possibility in light of changing circumstances. It cannot be excluded that the EU legislature will even adopt higher standards following the experience with implementing the EU-Turkey Statement. In any case, that

---

222 Case C-205/06 *Commission* v *Austria* (*Bilateral Investment Treaties*) EU:C:2009:118.

223 Ibid paras 24ff.

224 Ibid para 37.

225 See supra n 116 and accompanying text.

is for the institutions to decide, who are entitled to pursue their interests in the law-making procedure, subject to certain minimum requirements flowing from international law and the ECHR, some of which were identified in the preceding sub-section. Finally, the EU-Turkey Statement is a temporary and extraordinary measure. In such circumstances, it would be disproportionate to require the Member States to refrain from exercising their powers on account of practical difficulties in EU law-making.

5.2.2 The Resettlement Scheme

Whether the resettlement scheme as part of the EU-Turkey Statement interferes with the competence of the Union requires a different legal analysis than the remainder of this section. As the EU has not yet adopted common rules in this field, the third limb of Article 3(2) TFEU cannot serve as a basis for establishing exclusivity. In any event, the initial question is whether EU external competence exists. In the absence of an express legal basis, the EU might have an implied external competence where, in accordance with Article 216(1) TFEU, the conclusion of an international agreement 'is necessary in order to achieve, within the framework of the Union's policies, one of the objectives referred to in the Treaties'. The second limb of Article 3(2) TFEU states that an implied external competence is exclusive where the conclusion of an international agreement 'is necessary to enable the Union to exercise its internal competence'. The academic literature criticised these provisions for blurring the existence and nature of EU competence.[226]

The confusion goes back to the Court, whose jurisprudence the said provisions aim to codify. The leading case on this matter is *Opinion 1/76* in which the Court found that an implied external competence may flow not only from the adoption of internal legislation but also from norms establishing an internal competence, provided that the participation of the Union in the international agreement is necessary for attaining one of the objectives of the Treaties.[227] Under the specific circumstances of that case, the participation of the Union was necessary in the sense of indispensable because the objectives of the common policy could not be achieved through the adoption of internal legislation alone. The nature of the competence remained unclear though. Later, the Court clarified that in circumstances giving rise to *Opinion 1/76* competences

226 For example, see Marise Cremona, 'EU External Relations: Unity and Conferral of Powers' in Loïc Azoulai (ed), *The Question of Competence in the European Union* (OUP 2014) 72–74 (with further references).

227 *Opinion 1/76* (*Laying-up Fund*) EU:C:1977:63, paras 3–4.

will be exclusive.[228] Conversely, according to Dashwood and Heliskoski, competences will be shared where the conclusion of an international agreement merely facilitates the realisation of common objectives.[229]

The first step is thus to determine whether the EU has an *internal* competence to conduct a common resettlement policy. The text of the Regulation establishing a Union Resettlement and Humanitarian Admission Framework, adopted by the European Parliament in April 2024, mentions Article 78(2)(d) and (g) as a legal basis.[230] Concretely, the Framework aims at establishing common procedures for selecting persons in need of international protection from certain third countries. Member States, however, retain the power to indicate, on a voluntary basis, the maximum number of persons to be resettled annually. Moreover, they are in charge of granting international protection after having selected the individuals based on common eligibility criteria. Nevertheless, it was a political choice of the EU legislature, not mandated by the Treaties, to reserve national discretion in this sensitive area. The Treaties empower the Union to introduce a uniform status of international protection, valid in every Member State, and common procedures for granting and withdrawing that status.[231] Instead of waiting for protection seekers to arrive on EU territory, the EU or the Member States may carry out those procedures in third countries in order to 'manage' migration in an orderly way.[232] Hence, while not expressly mentioned in Article 78(2) TFEU, resettlement can be considered an integral part of the Union's comprehensive approach, as foreseen by the Treaties.

Next, as regards the existence and nature of EU external competence, the above-mentioned 'necessity' criterion has to be applied. On the one hand, the Union Resettlement Framework demonstrates that internal legislation could be adopted without, at the same time, concluding an international agreement with third countries from which resettlement was to occur. According to the preamble of the new law, the admission procedure should build on the existing resettlement and humanitarian admission experience and standards of the Member States and, if applicable, of the UNHCR.[233] This includes, as per the Commission proposal, the so-called Standard Operating Procedures under

228 *Opinion 1/03* (n 17) para 115.

229 Dashwood & Heliskoski (n 12) 16.

230 European Parliament, Text of the Union Resettlement and Humanitarian Admission Framework, adopted at 1st Reading, T9-0184/0184.

231 Art 78(2)(a)-(d) TFEU.

232 See the interpretation of art 78(2)(g) TFEU in Chapter 3.3.

233 See European Parliament (n 230) recital (14).

the EU-Turkey Statement.[234] Hence, the inevitable international cooperation may be established informally without the need to conclude an international agreement. On the other hand, it is submitted that such an agreement would 'facilitate' the mentioned comprehensive approach. The latter not only concerns administrative but also political cooperation, combining the leverage of the EU and the Member States to promote international migration governance. Indeed, according to the Commission proposal, the choice of third countries from which resettlement was to occur depended on, inter alia, the effective cooperation with the Union in the area of migration and asylum, covering more specific factors such as reducing irregular migration to the EU from the relevant third country or increasing the reception capacity there for persons in need of international protection.[235] An international agreement would certainly help to establish such a mutual give-and-take of which resettlement is one element. It can therefore be concluded that the EU has an implied shared competence to enter into resettlement commitments with third countries.

Finally, given that competences were shared, one might wonder whether it was legal for the Member States to collectively act outside the EU institutional framework. According to García Andrade, it was not because in so doing they prevented the Union from exercising its competences.[236] In her opinion, '[t]he common external rules agreed on in the Statement show that the requirements for the exercise of those Union competences – the subsidiarity principle and, eventually, the Opinion 1/76 doctrine criterion – would have been fulfilled'.[237] Put differently, the mere fact of autonomous collective action demonstrated that the Member States *could have acted* in accordance with the rules and procedures of the EU legal order. Their choice was to circumvent the EU institutional framework. If it is correct that the EU was competent in line with the *Opinion 1/76* doctrine, it then remains to be determined whether the resettlement scheme is contrary to the subsidiarity principle. According to the EU Treaties, the said principle requires that a certain proposed measure falling within a non-exclusive EU competence should be taken at Union level only if and insofar as its scale or effects go beyond the ability of the individual

234 European Commission, 'Proposal for a Regulation establishing a Union Resettlement Framework and amending Regulation No 516/2014/EU establishing the Asylum, Migration and Integration Fund' COM(2016) 468 final, 7.

235 Ibid 10. The text adopted by the European Parliament is more protection-oriented, although it does not exclude other considerations, see European Parliament (n 230) art 4.

236 Paula García Andrade, 'EU External Competences in the Field of Migration: How To Act Externally When Thinking Internally' (2018) 55(1) CML Rev 157.

237 Ibid 195–196.

Member States.[238] At the outset, the application of the proposed legal standard is rendered more difficult in this context because subsidiarity is a principle rather than rule, and a political rather than a legal principle since it has so far been of limited relevance for the reasoning of the Court.[239] To argue that the 27 have 'violated' the principle of subsidiarity might therefore not be very illuminating. This is not to suggest the irrelevance of the question who is best placed to pursue the common objectives. However, that is a matter to be determined in the intermediate sphere, with more regard to political will and the actual capacities of the Member States. However, the present EU principle of subsidiarity is but a test of comparative efficiency, without regard to the political underpinnings.[240] The latter is all the more important in the field of resettlement since durable integration into the host society will have more far-reaching implications than temporary protection. That is why the EU-Turkey Statement provides for voluntary and unequal participation, which the EU principle of subsidiarity cannot capture.

Finally, resettlement under the EU-Turkey Statement is best seen as a coordination mechanism. Apart from reaffirming the existing commitments of the Member States acting in their individual capacity, the Statement calls on the EU institutions to amend Relocation Decision 2015/1601/EU so as to allow Member States to off-set resettlements from Turkey against non-allocated places under the former Decision. It thereby establishes coherence between both levels, stimulating Member States to protect refugees from Turkey by lowering the burden imposed by EU law in return. Such coordination is permissible if EU institutional law, in particular the procedure of Article 218 TFEU, has been complied with.[241] The foregoing analysis did not lead to a definitive conclusion in that regard. But as it is possible to defend the resettlement scheme with valid legal arguments, Member States have the benefit of the doubt. Their moving 'inside-out' was legitimate.

5.2.3 The Facility for Refugees in Turkey

The Facility for Refuges is essentially a body for coordinating and managing the funds made available by the EU and the Member States for supporting Turkey in coping with the presence of Syrians under temporary protection. The

238 Art 5(3) TEU.

239 See Paul Craig, 'Subsidiarity: A Political and Legal Analysis' (2012) 50(1) Journal of Common Market Studies 72.

240 See Maria Cahill, 'Theorizing Subsidiarity: Towards an Ontology-Sensitive Approach' (2017) 15(1) I·CON 201.

241 See supra n 166 and accompanying text.

Facility was established by a Commission Decision following the EU-Turkey Joint Action Plan in which the EU pledged substantial new funds for immediate humanitarian assistance, the socio-economic integration of Syrians during their stay in Turkey and for addressing the needs of the local population affected by the population growth.[242] When the EU-Turkey Statement was adopted in March 2016, the Facility had already begun disbursing 3 billion euros based on previous commitments. The Statement called for speeding up the process and it added that the EU will mobilise an additional 3 billion euros for the Facility until the end of 2018 once the first tranche is about to the used in full and if Turkey complies with its commitments as laid down in the Statement. It follows that the EU-Turkey Statement, and the related declarations such as the Joint Action Plan, had legal effects insofar as they were the basis for disbursing funds under a newly established Facility governed by conditionality. The impact of the Facility, and the conditionality regime thereby established, on the Union's international legal personality will be considered next.

In February 2016, following an informal agreement with the 27,[243] the Commission amended the mentioned Decision.[244] The former, though not legally binding, has produced legal effects in the sense of providing the impetus for amendments, two of which are of particular interest. First, the funds will be paid out only if Turkey implements its commitments under the Joint Action Plan relating to the support for Syrians and the prevention of irregular migration.[245] The Statement of March 2016 extended the conditionality to areas not covered by the Joint Action Plan (returns and visa liberalisation). Second, the amended Decision affected the role of the Commission under the Facility. The task to coordinate the Union's and the Member States' actions no longer falls on the Commission but on the Facility and, in particular, a so-called steering committee composed of two representatives of the Commission and one of each Member State.[246] It provides strategic guidance in the sense of setting, inter alia, overall priorities and types of actions to be supported.

---

242 Commission Decision of 24 November 2015 on the coordination of actions of the Union and of the Member States through a coordination mechanism – the Refugee Facility for Turkey [2015] C407/8, recital (4).

243 Common Understanding establishing a Governance and Conditionality Framework for the Refugee Facility for Turkey between EU Member States and the European Commission [2016] <https://www.statewatch.org/media/documents/news/2016/feb/eu-com-common-understaning-for-refugee-facility-for-turkey.pdf> accessed 1 March 2024.

244 Commission Decision of 10 February 2016 on the Facility for Refugees in Turkey amending Commission Decision C(2015) 9500 of 24 November 2015 [2016] C60/3.

245 Ibid art 5(1).

246 Ibid art 3(1).

Moreover, it has monitoring functions, for example as regards the conditionality requirements. Although the Commission chairs the meetings, it arguably has been in a weaker position since the amendments. Article 5(2) of the amended Decision stipulates that the Commission shall have a 'leading role'[247] in coordinating the work of the steering committee. It replaces the following text: 'The Commission shall retain the responsibility for the final decision on the setting of priorities, on the identification of actions and on the allocation of funds.'[248] Now, the Commission has a limited right to veto strategic guidance; otherwise, it is responsible for implementation.[249] To sum up, the EU is not unconstrained in exercising its competence in the field of humanitarian and development policy. First, it is subject to migration-control implemented by Turkey; second, the Member States rather than the Commission seem to dominate the competent decision-making body.

Arguably, the integrity of the EU legal order is in no way undermined. Competence in development cooperation and humanitarian aid is shared and not subject to pre-emption.[250] Hence, the exercise of competence by the Union shall not result in Member States being prevented from exercising theirs. They are thus entitled to enter into commitments with third states, 'either collectively or individually, or even jointly with the [Union]'.[251] Likewise, where Member States exercise a competence in their individual capacity, they may allocate tasks to EU institutions provided they do not alter the essential character of the powers conferred on those institutions by the Treaties.[252] In that regard, the amended Decision did not deprive the Commission of the power to coordinate the development and humanitarian policies of the Union and of the Member States.[253] Having a less prominent role is not sufficient to affect the essential character of the Commission's task. Likewise, the power to veto strategic guidance on legal grounds is in line with Article 17(1) TEU, empowering the Commission to oversee the application of EU law. One might deplore the fact that the Commission mainly has an executive rather than a steering function, similar to traditional international organisations. Also, the nexus between development aid and migration management may be a matter of concern. However, these aspects are irrelevant as far as the inner sphere is

247 Art 5(2) Commission Decision, as amended (n 244).
248 Art 5(2) Commission Decision of 24 November 2015 (n 242).
249 Recital (3) and art 5(2) Commission Decision, as amended (n 244).
250 Art 4(4) TFEU.
251 Case C-316/91 *European Parliament* v *Council* (*Lomé Convention*) EU:C:1994:76, para 26.
252 Case C-370/12 *Pringle* EU:C:2012:756, para 158.
253 Art 210(2) and 214(6) TFEU.

concerned. What matters is the conclusion that the Facility for Refugees does not call into question the international legal personality of the Union.

5.2.4 Visa Liberalisation, the Customs Union and Accession

Finally, the EU-Turkey Statement intends to advance the political process concerning visa liberalisation, the Customs Union and Turkish accession. Most of the relevant provisions reflect the decision-making procedures of the Treaties including the role of the different institutions. For example, as regards visa liberalisation, the Commission will make a proposal after having assessed whether Turkey meets the conditions as set out in a Roadmap from 2013, and the European Parliament and the Council will take a final decision on that basis. Hence, the EU-Turkey Statement is without prejudice to the ordinary legislative procedure in accordance with Article 77(2) TFEU in conjunction with Article 294 TFEU. It fully respects the institutional balance and thus the independent legal capacity of the Union. Insofar as visa liberalisation is conditional on Turkey adhering to the Statement, one could argue that the latter has legal effects on the exercise of EU competences. However, those effects rather originate from an earlier stage in the international relations between the EU and Turkey. The visa liberalisation dialogue started in 2013 after the parties had negotiated the EU-Turkey Readmission Agreement. The first EU-Turkey Statement of November 2015 merely reaffirms that connection, stating that 'the EU-Turkey readmission agreement will become fully applicable from June 2016 (…) with a view to completing the visa liberalisation process'.[254] Instead of giving rise to legal or actual effects in itself, the EU-Turkey Statement is rather a catalyst for existing commitments that are to be realised through EU decision-making procedures.

6 Conclusion

This chapter complemented the previous one dealing with the implementation of the CEAS and selected instruments of EU migration law. It examined how Member States move 'inside-out' on the external dimension of EU migration management. More specifically, it did not deal with the implementation of EU international agreements but with the adoption by the 27 of informal arrangements, which fall under international migration governance. Hence, the chapter sought to clarify what it means to represent the Union when EU law does

254 European Council & Council of the EU (n 89) point 5.

not require the implementation of the common rules (formal representation). The challenge was rather to demonstrate that the 27 do not *undermine* those rules when claiming to represent the Union in a political or social sense.

Article 3(2) TFEU, as interpreted in a long line of case law since the leading *ERTA* judgment, precludes the Member States from concluding international agreements liable to affect common rules or to alter their scope. This means, according to legal doctrine, that envisaged international agreements must not fall within the scope of the common rules, irrespective of whether the former interfere, in fact, with the practical operation of the latter. The implications for the representation of the Union are enormous: the EU legal order cannot be a source of empowerment as far as autonomous action is concerned. It is only empowering in the sense of enabling the Member States to complete the European polity with external policies – adopted within the EU institutional framework. There, the 27 have less room to represent the national collective self, so it is doubtful whether the perspective of EU-based multilateralism sufficiently motivates joint action. However, according to legal doctrine, that is why the 27 should refrain from acting: the defence of the common purpose in a particular and united way, which is or ought to be the international identity of the EU.

It has been argued that this normative assumption is difficult to square with international migration governance as epitomised by the EU-Turkey Statement. More specifically, the latter is an extraordinary, temporary measure; its content is evolving in light of the situation on the ground; and it addresses the multiple identities of the Member States who are not only members of the Union but also sovereign nation states. Rather than the source of new international obligations, the Statement composes existing legal and political obligations into a comprehensive framework of international cooperation. To concede, there are serious shortcomings that have not been addressed in this chapter because they concern the intermediate sphere as such. In particular, Greece has not received sufficient assistance in processing applications for international protection. Moreover, voluntary relocation from Greece has been far too limited despite the deteriorating reception conditions in that country. These are certainly some of the lessons to be learned for EU-Turkey cooperation in the future.[255] The Statement examined in this chapter was de facto terminated in early 2020 when Turkey tolerated or even stimulated the departure of refugees in the direction of Greece. But as the cooperation with, inter alia, Tunisia

255 See also European Stability Initiative, 'Possible Draft Outline of EU-TUR Statement 2.0' (12 September 2023) <https://www.esiweb.org/possible-draft-outline-eu-tur-statement-20> accessed 1 March 2024.

demonstrates, informal international migration governance will continue. For inspiration purposes, the EU-Turkey Statement should be treated as a specific, imperfect manifestation the comprehensive approach to which the 28 contributed on their own behalf *and* on behalf of the Union.

To realise the external elements of the comprehensive approach, the chapter proposed to re-construct the ERTA doctrine. International agreements of the Member States would be contrary to EU law if they are liable to deprive the common rules of their useful effect. This will be the case when the Member States will be subject to conflicting rules emanating from various sources, or when international agreements are a tool to circumvent the rules of EU law. On this basis and despite some remaining uncertainty, it can be concluded that the EU-Turkey Statement is not contrary to the inner sphere of the Treaties. The suggested re-conceptualisation of the ERTA effect is of broader relevance since it is a means to reconcile the frames of legal ordering. The EU legal order continues to be autonomous in order to defend the common purpose of mutual non-interference both on the internal and the external dimension. At the same time, it will be empowering in a wider sense than currently foreseen by legal doctrine. Instead of precluding autonomous action, a certain norm of EU law like the safe third country rule will enable movements 'inside-out'. Although the Court has not yet clarified the meaning of that rule, it is possible to define the minimum requirements in accordance with international and regional (ECHR) human rights law. Compliance with those requirements safeguards the integrity of the EU legal order, and it is then easier to conduct international relations according to the national political imagination. The concrete policies to which that leads are less relevant, for a claim to represent the Union can be rejected in the intermediate sphere. The purpose of this chapter was to open up a legal opportunity to get there.

Conclusions

Since more than one million refugees and migrants arrived in the EU in 2015/2016, the Member States have claimed to act in the common interest of migration management. Or the EU institutions have called on them to behave as responsible members of the Union. In this book, several claims to represent the Union have come along. One of the most recent expressions of 'Team Europe' is the Memorandum of Understanding with Tunisia, concluded by the European Commission with support from the Italian and the Dutch Prime Minister.[1] It illustrates what has become known as the 'externalisation' and 'informalisation' of EU migration management, shifting migration control to third countries or – to be more precise – dispersing responsibilities across several legal and political orders, often in an ad hoc manner and with little institutional safeguards. The EU-Turkey Statement continues to be the most (in)famous example in this respect, expressing the identities of the (then) 28 as members of the Union and as sovereign nation states.[2] Something similar has happened on the internal dimension. We have seen that administrative cooperation between the German and the Greek authorities sought to reduce unauthorised movements of asylum seekers within the Schengen Area, with a view to upholding the area of internal free movement (for EU citizens).[3] Moreover, German policies have demonstrated that even unilateralism may be framed as representing the common European purpose. At the heat of the 'crisis' in 2015, Germany decided to suspend, in respect of Syrian refugees, the normal procedures for the intra-European allocation of applications for international protection, representing what the then Chancellor in a similar context considered to be the European responsibility for refugees.[4] More technical but no less

1 European Commission, 'Memorandum of Understanding on a Strategic and Global Partnership between the European Union and Tunisia' (Press release 16 July 2023) <https://ec.europa.eu/commission/presscorner/detail/en/ip_23_3887> accessed 1 March 2024. See also the Introduction.

2 See European Council, 'EU-Turkey Statement' (Press release 18 March 2016) <https://www.consilium.europa.eu/en/press/press-releases/2016/03/18/eu-turkey-statement/> accessed 1 March 2024; see also Chapter 5.

3 See the Administrative Arrangement between the Ministry of Migration Policy of the Hellenic Republic and the Federal Ministry of the Interior, Building and Community of the Federal Republic of Germany on cooperation when refusing entry to persons seeking protection in the context of temporary checks at the internal German-Austrian border <https://www.frnrw.de/fileadmin/frnrw/media/EU_Asylpolitik/Germany_Greece_Deal_eng.pdf> accessed 1 March 2024; see also Chapter 4.4.2.

4 See Chapters 2.2.3. and 5.3.1.

 | DOI:10.1163/9789004695733_008

controversial, Germany unilaterally enforced Schengen-wide entry bans at its internal border.[5] What these measures have in common are the controversies about their legality under European and international law. Furthermore, since the 'crisis', the question of what is legal has been informed, perhaps more than ever, by what political parties, interest groups, journalists and scholars deem legitimate. Various actors participate in a heated debate that tilts in the direction of one or the other extreme position, opposing 'open' and 'closed' borders or 'European' and 'national' solutions.

Apart from discussing the implications of migration control for individual rights, we the Europeans are debating the terms of our joint action. Hence, we got more interested in what makes us act together in the EU, adopting immigration policies as a Union. We realised that the persons arriving at our borders force us to (re-)define who we are. That is a plausible explanation for the uncompromising stance in public discourse. There are different understandings of the good life that cannot be harmonised like a product standard on the internal market. A common European policy will fail if different value conceptions are pitted against each another, or if one is taken as superior over the other. Although no one should be obliged to internalise the values of another as if those were his or her own, we should at least listen and take each other seriously. But this cannot succeed unless it is accepted that our identities are still for a significant part determined by the political, social and cultural contexts in the nation state. And each European nation state continues to identify itself as such, notwithstanding accession to the European Union and the (additional) self-recognition qua Member State. That was the empirical and normative starting point to answer the following research questions:

> How do the Member States claim to represent the Union in the management of migration, and when is such a claim legal and legitimate? In particular, what is the role of EU law in constraining and constituting (or framing) the exercise of national power on behalf of the Union?

1 Summary

To answer these questions, this book developed the notion of European spheres. The Member States are navigating between the inner sphere of the EU legal order and the outer sphere of international relations, where the frame

5 See Chapter 4.4.3.

of being and acting as a sovereign nation state continues to be predominant. They act in the intermediate sphere when using their sovereign powers to defend the integrity of the EU legal order while promoting the political goals of European integration, which often correspond to their national interests. In that sense, the approach was external to the EU legal order and multi-layered since the common rules were analysed against the background of their political underpinnings.

Chapter 1 explained that the legal and political order are interdependent. It adopted the internal angle of a we that should attribute the exercise of power under the legal order to itself, as an act of self-determination. The legal order has to represent the common purpose of the polis in order to be deemed legitimate, and the polis needs to be represented in order to recognise itself as such. Designing and implementing policies on matters like immigration is thus a way to present anew the identity of the polis or its common purpose, which will adapt to changing circumstances up to a point at which self-recognition is no longer possible and legitimacy is fading away. The common purpose of the liberal constitutional state is to safeguard its continuous existence, not only in terms of public security but also stability in a wider sense (social, economic or cultural). The precise meaning will differ because of history, political system, social customs and beliefs. The common purpose of the EU is to ensure mutual non-interference or, in less abstract terms, peaceful inter-state relationships after a violent past. That is broader than public security in the sense of defending the polity against military or terrorist threats. Pollution, uncontrolled immigration or a virus are cross-border challenges that may originate, intensify or worsen in one Member State and inflict damage in another. Integration through law has been the main decision-making paradigm. That is, an autonomous EU legal order has given rise to a dense web of principles, rules and procedures ensuring that Union law in principle applies uniformly and effectively in every Member State.

In line with our multi-layered approach, Chapter 1 added that the Member States need certain instruments to defend the common purpose. In other words, those instruments contain claims to represent or re-frame the identity of the polity. The Member States may represent the Union and the nation when implementing EU law, and it may be necessary to make a claim for formal or social recognition (or both). On the one hand, they are prima facie representing the Union in a formal sense when transposing, applying or enforcing EU law. A wide margin of (policy) discretion enables the Member States to represent national or local policy preferences while respecting the common rules, including EU fundamental rights.[6] In comparison, a narrow margin of (assessment) discretion renders the nature of representation rather bureaucratic than political, so it is more difficult to reach the intermediate sphere. On the other hand, the Member States might rather claim social recognition from the Union when acting within the scope of EU law in a wider sense. According to the Court, a Member State exercising a national competence in a field covered by Union law must not violate its EU legal obligations.[7] Here, a formal claim not to interfere with EU law will not be sufficient to represent the Union, unless the Member State concerned makes an additional claim to promote a common EU policy. Since it might not be certain that a measure falls within the scope of EU law,[8] the burden to justify it is higher than if it was somehow mediated through the EU legal order.

Chapter 2 dealt with legal and constitutional conflict, the likelihood of which increases when a Member State claims to act on behalf of the Union. But instead of analysing conflicts between the inner and the outer sphere, this chapter aimed at mitigation in the intermediate sphere. In a first step, it has been argued that existing theories are insufficient as they underestimate the national political imagination. The main reason for the continuous appeal of the constitutional state is its capacity to offer an ideational space that is greater than every individual existence. There is no other form of association that makes people give their money or even their life, and that has the power to weigh various public interests (and not just functional ends in a cost-benefit calculus). It has been submitted that reconciliation is possible rather at the deep than at the surface layer of interacting legal orders. The latter is prone to a stalemate of legal opinions about the scope of EU competences in particular, whereas the former underlines that all Member States and the EU itself are committed to democracy, the rule of law and human rights, which reflect the higher common purpose of mutual non-interference.

In a second step, attention shifted to dispute settlement since there may be disagreement about the meaning of the common purpose in a particular case. It has been argued that the degree by which the EU institutions, in particular the legislature, has specified the common purpose determines the degree of responsibility a Member State may assume on behalf of the Union. This is due to the principle of autonomy, which essentially amounts to a juridical sovereignty claim by the EU legal order. On a traditional understanding, the EU

6 See Case C-336/19 *Centraal Israëlitisch Consistorie van België and Others* v *Vlaamse Regering* EU:C:2020:1031; see also Chapter 1.4.2.

7 For example, see Case C-135/08 *Rottman* EU:C:2010:104, paras 39–41.

8 See Case C-258/14 *Florescu* EU:C:2017:448; see also Chapter 1.4.3.

legal order is autonomous because of its inherent unity, and legal doctrines like direct effect and primacy uphold this unity against recalcitrant Member States. More recently, the common values listed in Article 2 TEU became part of the autonomous EU legal order, so it is theoretically possible to 'enforce' them just like any other legally binding norm of Union law. However, that is premised on deducing rather specific rules from them, for only then can the EU legal order defend the common purpose of mutual non-interference. In other words, specification is necessary to realise legal equality on paper and in practice, because unlike a value or principle, a specific rule is capable of uniform application. But due to the value-foundation of the common rules, the EU rule of law has both formal and material elements. For example, the Court deduced from the principle of solidarity the national obligation to participate in any emergency measure adopted in accordance with Article 78(3) TFEU, when one or more Member States is confronted with a sudden inflow of third-country nationals.[9] That is a both a universal demand of justice and a particular functional demand of the EU legal order because measures taken under Article 78(3) TFEU contribute to the functioning of the Common European Asylum System (CEAS). The latter in turn meets the common purpose of mutual non-interference, which promotes lasting peace in Europe.

Chapter 2 also clarified why a Member State would bother to claim social recognition. A certain rule deduced from a higher norm does not exhaust the meaning of that norm. The Member State concerned is motivated to interpret it according to the national political imagination, in defence of the national and the EU common purpose. Indeed, the continuous viability of the EU has become an integral part of the national self after (in most cases) decades of European integration. This sense of responsibility has been conceptualised as a political obligation derived from Union membership as such. The 27 are empowered to assume responsibility for the Union insofar as the common purpose has *not* yet been specified. A common norm like Article 2 TEU is empowering as it gives expression to the political existence qua Member State, and as the Court may at any time interfere to defend the common purpose. It is thus important to note that the intermediate sphere is not a place for unconstrained political power. To cherish national diversity is not contrary to defending the fundamentals of the EU legal order by means of hierarchical judicial enforcement. However, in the judicial practice of EU migration management, the Court has so far been reluctant to engage with broader political questions,[10]

9 See Joined Cases C-643/15 and C-647/15 *Slovakia and Hungary* v *Council* EU:C:2017:631.

10 Ibid.

and with legally non-binding instruments or generally modes of governance that defy neat location into a particular legal order.[11] As mentioned, due to the juridical sovereignty claim of the EU legal order, measures at the fringes of that order entail a rather high justificatory burden.

But instead of condemning such measures a priori as deviating from a utopian ideal of European integration, it has been suggested that we should see them as a claim to represent the Union in a social sense. Chapter 2 called for political hybridity, which essentially continues the multi-layered approach consisting of a systemic dimension (deep layer) and an instrumental dimension (surface layer). Hence, international migration governance is prima facie a way to express belonging to the Union. It must therefore refer to the common purpose as laid down in any norm of EU law, complemented by a thorough explanation as to why the Member State concerned is well placed to represent the Union. It is another angle, shifting attention from agency under the EU legal order to political responsibility in a wider sense. But again, a claim so understood may be rejected as incompatible with the inner sphere of the Treaties or, assuming it to be legal, it might be rejected on political grounds because the other Member States cannot identify with it, or the claim-maker is considered incapable of defending the common purpose. Compliance with the inner sphere hinges on the relationship between EU law and governance in the specific case. Apart from capturing representations of unity, hybridity is a methodology to critically analyse EU law from an external, context-sensitive angle, and governance in light of the rule of law associated with the EU legal order. In particular, the analysis should address the impact of governance on the common rules and procedures in EU legislation as those specify the common purpose of mutual non-interference. Governance is more likely to be legitimate if it complements those rules and procedures, in comparison with more general norms that are insufficient to uphold the common purpose (like a value).

Using the theoretical framework of the three European spheres, the second part of this book went on to reappraise EU migration management since 2015/2016. The aim of Chapter 3 was to interpret the Treaties in their historical context, from the angle of the 27 in their primary law-making capacity. In their view, the common purpose of EU migration management is to ensure internal free movement within the Schengen area without prejudice to the right to seek asylum and the principle of non-refoulement. The historical interpretation of EU primary law demonstrated the actual practice of political reflexivity.

11 See Case T-192/16 *NF* v *European Council* EU:T:2017:128.

Having regard to migration flows and security challenges, various nation states were representing their political existence qua Member States over the course of European integration. It cannot be maintained that they intended to build a fortress Europe, nor did they aim at a particularly high level of international protection. Instead, they aimed at combining migration control and humanitarian policies in a coherent manner, acting on every dimension of migration management under a comprehensive approach. In particular, the Member States must correctly implement the rules of the CEAS in order not to cause secondary movements contrary to the common purpose of mutual non-interference. But in addition, the Member States intended to contribute to the common policy through resettlement and other voluntary contributions.

Chapter 4 examined to what extent EU asylum and migration law is empowering. In general, it has been shown that norms of EU secondary law are capable of facilitating the transition from the common system of rules to the wider common policy. As mentioned, discretion is a legal technique enabling the Member States to represent both the Union and the nation, especially if EU legislation recognises national power in policy-making. That is generally the case once it has been ensured that an asylum seeker enjoys temporary protection in line with the value of human dignity, which requires every Member State to satisfy the basic needs of everyone falling within its jurisdiction and to offer protection against refoulement. Hence, as far as temporary protection is concerned, the Member States only have a narrow margin of assessment discretion. That is in line with the common purpose because ill-treatment would undermine the joint commitment to international refugee and human rights law, apart from increasing the risk of secondary movements and the reintroduction of internal border controls. Violating the minimum requirements of equal human dignity leads to a shift in responsibility because the non-complying Member State is no longer legitimately representing the Union. Instead of re-allocating responsibility in that case, EU law in principle recognises national policy discretion, so any other Member State may decide to offer protection.[12]

Likewise, EU law can help reconcile the European spheres regarding migration control and the common return policy in particular. EU law has a coordinating role in finding a bilateral solution when one Member State contemplates

12 See art 17 Regulation No 604/2013/EU of 26 June 2013 establishing the criteria and mechanisms for determining the Member State responsible for examining an application for international protection lodged in one of the Member States by a third-country national or a stateless person ('Dublin Regulation') [2013] OJ L180/31; Joined Cases C-411/10 and C-493/10 *N.S. and Others* v *Secretary of State for the Home Department and Others* EU:C:2011:865; see also Chapter 4.2.2.

enforcing a return decision from another jurisdiction, or issuing an entry ban applicable in the entire Schengen area. In contrast to a national residence permit or a similar right, a return decision creates *positive* external legal effects in the sense that the Member State where the person concerned is apprehended must cooperate with the issuing Member State in order to best implement the common return policy.[13] A national residence permit creates *negative* external legal effects in the sense that a Schengen-wide entry ban must be withdrawn.[14] Hence, the Member States may formally represent the common purpose of internal free movement through the EU legal order, with additional options under national law in the intermediate or outer sphere. They could claim social recognition from the Union by granting humanitarian visas, or they could issue residence permits to satisfy the needs of the domestic labour market.

Some measures are difficult to locate in any of the European spheres. In particular, it is disputed what the responsibilities are of a Member State who has reintroduced internal border controls.[15] It is tempting to assume that the Member State concerned is acting in the outer sphere to defend its sovereignty, without prejudice to its obligations under European and international law. However, that Member State might rather act in the intermediate sphere if it is understood that it is responsible for the common purpose as if it was protecting the external border, were it not for one crucial difference: migration control at the internal border is liable to impact negatively on other Member States. That is reason enough to carefully monitor national action without precluding it a priori. It has been argued that the Dublin Regulation permits a fast-track procedure for returning asylum seekers to the Member State who registered their applications for international protection.[16] But Greece and Germany in that case failed to clarify responsibility upon return.[17] In particular, Greece did not express a claim vis-à-vis the Union, explaining how it intends to uphold the rights of the asylum seekers. Likewise, it has been argued that a Member State (Germany) may enforce a Schengen-wide entry ban at its internal border insofar as it apprehends the person concerned to remove him or her from the territory of the Union with due respect to the principle of non-refoulement.

---

13 See art 7(2) Regulation 2018/1860/EU of 28 November 2018 on the use of the Schengen Information System for the return of illegally staying third-country nationals [2018] OJ L312/1; see also Chapter 4.3.1.

14 See Case C-240/17 *E* EU:C:2018:8; see also Chapter 4.3.2.

15 In accordance with art 25 Regulation 2016/399/EU of 9 March 2016 on a Union Code on the rules governing the movement of persons across borders [2016] OJ L77/1.

16 See art 36 Dublin Regulation; see also Chapter 4.4.2.

17 See supra n 3.

However, the action might not always be recognised as a representation of the Union because the grounds for imposing entry bans differ widely between the national legal systems, and legal-cultural differences constitute a natural impediment to far-reaching harmonisation. Hence, depending on the circumstances, the burden to justify an entry ban on behalf of all might be rather high. The same applies, mutatis mutandis, concerning the enforcement of a return decision issued elsewhere in the Union.

Chapter 5 assessed whether the 27 could be seen as representing the Union on the external dimension of EU migration management. That was a legal doctrinal challenge since the only recognised situation so far is when international fora exclude or limit the participation of the EU even though the latter is competent in accordance with the Treaties.[18] But as the impact of international fora is still limited in the field of migration management, this peculiar situation was of no concern to our inquiry. In comparison, the ERTA doctrine as codified in Article 3(2) TFEU was more interesting since it essentially prohibits the Member States from acting externally in a largely harmonised field like asylum and international protection. More specifically, it precludes an international agreement of the Member States if it is liable to affect common rules or alter their scope. According to legal doctrine, the Member States must not conclude such an agreement outside the EU legal order if it falls within the scope of existing (or future) common rules, no matter whether it, in fact, undermines the practical operation of the latter. If that is correct, there cannot be an intermediate sphere since common rules are not empowering but a reason to preclude autonomous action in the first place. The ERTA doctrine is informed by an ideal of EU actorness, assuming that the Member States can address global challenges only if they act qua EU. That is in tension with EU migration management since national action outside the single institutional framework is part of the comprehensive approach, mandated by the EU Treaties in accordance with the findings in Chapter 3. In addition, based on the EU-Turkey Statement, it has been demonstrated that the ERTA doctrine is not fit for purpose when the stages of norm-making and norm-application become increasingly blurred. Then, it is all the more important to control the exercise of power *after* the purported international agreement has been concluded. These are the main reasons for re-constructing the ERTA doctrine.

Chapter 5 proposed a formal test to ensure respect for the useful effect of EU law and the EU legal order. On the one hand, EU law must be capable of producing practical effects in the national legal systems, so an international

18 See *Opinion 2/91* (*ILO*) EU:C:1993:106, para 37; see also the Introduction.

agreement must neither contradict the common rules nor circumvent their scope of application. On the other hand, the EU institutions must be capable of upholding the common purpose both internally and externally, which refers to the useful effect of EU institutional rules such as Article 218 TFEU. If these conditions are met, any Member State can reconcile its double bind qua member of the Union and qua independent nation state. The proposal is not necessarily a statement for a more state-based European Union. It simply means that the 27 could assume responsibility for the Union outside the common institutional framework, according to their national political imagination and, in this context, their actual capacity to enter into international relations. But any claim to that effect may be rejected if indeed the EU is deemed to be in a better position to defend the common purpose.

On that basis, it was possible to capture the EU-Turkey Statement as a claim for (formal and social) recognition in the intermediate sphere, and to assess its compatibility with the inner sphere of the Treaties. Indeed, unlike the majority of legal scholarship, this study has treated the Statement not as a single instrument originating from the EU *or* the Member States. It is rather the institutionalisation of the comprehensive approach to migration, or of political hybridity in general, insofar as it integrates existing obligations under EU and international law on the one hand, and national political will of the (then) 28 on the other. It has been demonstrated that the Statement does not undermine the useful effect of the safe third country rule, laid down in the Procedures Directive,[19] because asylum seekers get temporary protection in Turkey. In addition, it does not call into question the legal capacity of the EU institutions to amend the common rules and procedures based on the lessons learned with the EU-Turkey Statement. Major deficiencies should be addressed in the future, which is a reason for a final reflection.

2 The Future of Political Reflexivity

Countless publications described and analysed the maturing of state-based sectorial cooperation into an autonomous, quasi-constitutional legal order, with the EU institutions on top and the Member States acting as their agents. A non-complying Member State is said to retreat from European legal integration and to move into the sphere of power politics and selfish national

19 Art 38 Directive 2013/32/EU of 26 June 2013 on common procedures for granting and withdrawing international protection [2013] OJ L180/60.

interests. It is accused of disintegrating and of eroding the common project from within: the EU legal order would implode and the anarchy of international law and politics would return with a vengeance. This book promoted the intermediate sphere, situated in-between the inner and the outer sphere. There, the role of the Member States and of EU law is changing: the latter empowers the former to assume responsibility for the Union while permitting a simultaneous representation of national identities. EU law is empowering when it facilitates self-recognition qua member of the Union and qua nation state, and insofar as it succeeds in building mutual trust in the common institutions. After all, a claim to act on behalf of the Union will be rejected unless mechanisms for independent dispute resolution function properly. The line is a fine one as more leeway increases the difficulty of judicial or political control. Much of this book aimed at balancing respect for EU law on the one hand, with the political responsibility of the 27 on the other.

The intermediate sphere is a theoretical lens appreciating that EU law and policy has to operate in various national contexts. It cannot be denied that European integration carries a strong presumption of legitimacy since it is capable of addressing cross-border challenges in accordance with a set of values that are translated into uniform legal rules and procedures. However, supranational rule-making is rather detached from national political discourses, and if the EU institutions do try to reflect public sentiments, it is rather unlikely that all national publics will feel represented. Consequently, implementing common values may not be enough and responding to presumed societal feelings might be undesirable.[20] The intermediate sphere can address the conundrum by entrusting it to national institutions to represent the identit(ies) of their constituencies. While it is common sense that the institutions of, for example, the German state are in a perfect position to represent the German people, it seems to be an unreasonable demand to tolerate or recognise the same institutions as actors on behalf of the Union as a whole. However, neither assumption is entirely justified.

In the first place, it cannot be excluded that a national audience rejects a claim on behalf of the Union from its 'own' national institutions. Considering the dismantling of national institutions in certain Member States, that situation is far from implausible. For the time being, the EU rule of law has been specified so as to encompass the requirement of judicial independence. As representation implies the constant re-interpretation of the common purpose,

20 See Editorial Comments, 'EU Law between Common Values and Collective Feelings' (2018) 55(5) CML Rev 1329, 1340.

it is to be expected that the rule of law and other fundamental values will be further specified in the inner sphere of the Treaties.[21] In the meantime, political discourse in the intermediate sphere is taking place without it being possible to determine a priori and conclusively whether a certain representation of unity is compatible with the inner sphere. In the second place, it is thus not as uncomfortable as it might seem to accept being represented by a Member State other than one's state of nationality or habitual residence. For a claim can be rejected on legal – or if that is not (yet) possible – on political grounds, and the latter can in turn inform the development of the law. There are manifold feedback loops not all of which can be integrated into doctrinal legal interpretation.[22] It is often a matter of stimulating legal change from the outside – and of waiting for change to happen in a promising political, economic or social climate.

At the end of this book, it is suggested using the European spheres as a theoretical lens to scrutinise recent and future developments in EU law and politics. The following will briefly consider (1) the future of EU migration management and (2) attempts at increasing the Union's 'strategic autonomy'.

2.1 *New Pact on Migration and Asylum*

In December 2023, the European Parliament and the Council reached political agreement on a New Pact on Migration and Asylum, a comprehensive reform of EU legislation adopted according to Articles 78 and 79 TFEU.[23] At the time of writing in April 2024, the European Parliament has just enacted the new laws.[24] Neither a detailed description nor an assessment is appropriate here, considering the scope of this book and the fact that, pending the Council's formal approval, the laws have not even entered into force. Some remarks will therefore suffice. In general, the reform will direct EU migration management towards the external borders. After irregular migrants have been registered and screened, those with low chances of being recognised as refugees will be subject

---

21 Regarding the value of democracy, see Yasmine Bouzoraa, 'The Value of Democracy in EU Law and Its Enforcement: A Legal Analysis' (2023) 8(2) European Papers 809.

22 See Daniel Thym, 'Deciphering the Role of (Migration) Law in the Social Construction of "Otherness"' in Moritz Jesse (ed), *European Societies, Migration, and the Law: The "Others" amongst "Us"* (CUP 2020).

23 In general, see European Commission, 'Communication on a New Pact on Migration and Asylum' COM(2020) 609 final.

24 For an overview, see European Parliament, 'MEPs Approve the New Migration and Asylum Pact' (Press release 10 April 2024) <https://www.europarl.europa.eu/news/en/press-room/20240408IPR20290/meps-approve-the-new-migration-and-asylum-pact> accessed 16 April 2024.

to an expedited border procedure. Pending the outcome, their free movement will be restricted to prevent onwards travel within the Schengen Area. To counterbalance the burden on the peripheral Member States, the reform requires the other members of the Union to assist the former in situations of high pressure or when boat migrants arrived after search and rescue operations. In case of general pressure on a national system, Member States may choose between different contributions: relocating asylum seekers from the Member State concerned; taking charge of returning persons with no right to remain in the EU ('return sponsorship'); taking other operational measures to mitigate the pressure. Voluntariness is however subject to a sufficient number of pledges, so that a Member State must not refuse to help if others have not pledged enough to cover actual needs. Finally, the reform continues to aim at 'comprehensive partnerships' with third countries, who are to be incentivised to cooperate on various dimensions of EU migration management, including the prevention of irregular migration and the return and readmission of those who did travel to the EU but with no right to remain. 'Team Europe' initiatives like the recent agreement with Tunisia will be continued, according to the Commission.[25]

Taken together, the shift to external border management, limited relocation based on national preferences and the continuation and possible intensification of international cooperation have led commentators to warn against 'non-Europe'.[26] This is to be understood in the twofold sense of more national power,[27] and less commitment to the common European value of human rights.[28] Such criticism reveals a certain narrow-minded focus on the inner sphere of the Treaties. Under the frame of the *Rechtsgemeinschaft*, common action within the EU legal order is considered a value in its own right, and a guarantee for the promotion of human rights as part of the EU's mission. But, in fact, this is just a liberal constitutional imagination, which should not be taken for granted in view of its deficiencies. If, instead, thinking in terms of the common good is revitalised, as this book has argued for, then a shift to the intermediate sphere of the Member States is inevitable. For it is naïf to assume

---

25 See European Commission, 'Striking a Balance on Migration: An Approach That is Both Fair and Firm' COM(2024) 126 final, p 13.

26 See Alberto-Horst Neidhardt, 'Navigating the New Pact on Migration and Asylum in the Shadow of Non-Europe' *European Policy Centre* (Discussion Paper 26 January 2024)<https://www.epc.eu/content/PDF/2024/Non-Europe_migration_policy_DP_v2.pdf> accessed 3 April 2024.

27 Ibid 6–8.

28 See PICUM, 'Over 50 NGOs Pen Eleventh-Hour Open Letter to EU on Human Rights Risks in Migration Pact' (Blog 18 December 2023) <https://picum.org/blog/open-letter-eu-human-rights-risks-migration-pact/> accessed 3 April 2024.

that appeals to the *Rechtsgemeinschaft* and abstract human rights were sufficient to engage Member States in European cooperation in this field. EU law and politics should tap into the political imagination of the Member States, who are both members of the Union and sovereign nation states. Hence, the liberal idea under the *Rechtsgemeinschaft* of not harming other Member States in the exercise of one's powers is but one consideration. The other is a rich communitarian imagination of who we are as a polity, and what we can do to govern migration in Europe from within our ideas of the good life. In that sense, the New Pact is welcome as it is, on the one hand, unambiguous in framing migration management as a common European challenge, in particular as far as humanitarian and external border protection are concerned, while conferring a significant degree of discretion on Member States to determine how to contribute. From the angle of the European spheres, it is crucial that it is EU law itself that will regulate the exercise of national powers on behalf of Europe. In that sense, Member States will thus be moving from the inner to the intermediate sphere 'inside-out', as advocated in this book.

That requires legal and political control. The common purpose of granting humanitarian protection should not be compromised in the sense that certain essential legal norms must not be violated, of which the principle of non-refoulement is the most important in the context of refugee protection. However, our theoretical framework is opposed to a maximalist interpretation of human rights, which is common in the mainstream liberal discourse that seeks to inform the inner sphere of the Treaties. Proponents of a maximalist interpretation understand human rights as trumps against the common good, not as integral part thereof. The latter view is preferable as it sees human rights not as external constraints but as part of who we are, as a moral and legal command for which we are responsible. However, in a plural legal order, the sources of human rights are manifold, just as the conflicting interests that require careful balancing. Appropriate institutional mechanisms must therefore ensure that the essential human rights guarantees will be upheld. That is a tremendous challenge when actors from several legal orders cooperate, as recent cases brought against Frontex demonstrate.[29] Moreover, informal cooperation with third countries raises similar concerns. It is therefore to be hoped that this book inspires future research on how accountable governance could be ensured across the three European spheres.

---

29 See Case T-600/21 *WS and Others* v *European Border and Coast Guard Agency* ECLI:EU:T:2023:492; see also Joyce De Coninck, 'Shielding Frontex: On the EU General Court's "WS and Others v Frontex"' (2023) Verfassungsblog <https://verfassungsblog.de/shielding-frontex/> accessed 3 April 2024.

2.2 *Towards EU Strategic Autonomy*

This book has dealt with what has become known as the 'refugee' or 'migration crisis'. In fact, the crisis was not attributable to refugees or migrants, but to a mal-functioning legal regime and the absence of political will. Since then, the Union has been confronted with new major crises: the Covid-19 pandemic and the war against Ukraine. Although imbued with a certain degree of European responsibility, these crises were above all external shocks that have unsettled European politics, economies and societies. From a legal viewpoint, both were similar insofar as the EU is competent to coordinate the actions of the Member States in the areas of public health[30] and defence.[31] The EU institutions are thus precluded from harmonising national laws and from taking certain executive decisions, in particular those affecting the direct legal relationship between the Member States and their citizens (e.g. as to the distribution of vaccines or the deployment of soldiers). As a matter of routine, the Commission[32] and academia[33] allied to call for new EU regulation and, for that purpose, a further transfer of competences or at least a generous interpretation of existing legal bases. This is not the place to evaluate such proposals, nor to call into question their appropriateness as a matter of principle. Neither does the theoretical framework of the European spheres provide sufficient ground to reject more centralisation within the EU legal order, for the latter as such does not rule out movements 'inside-out', as this book has argued in respect of EU migration management. However, our theoretical framework does warn against a one-sided belief in the rhetorical potential of EU institutions claiming, for instance, that Ukraine is defending 'our values', to legitimise far-reaching EU institutional reforms.

Both crises rather suggest that the EU institutions, in particular the Commission, have been successful in upholding the frame of the *Rechtsgemeinschaft* and the liberal paradigm of mutual non-interference, as far

30 Art 6(a) TFEU.

31 Art 2(4) TFEU in conjunction with arts 42–46 TEU.

32 Regarding public health, see eg European Commission, 'Building a European Health Union: Reinforcing the EU's Resilience for Cross-Border Health Threats' COM(2020) 724 final; regarding defence, see eg European Commission, 'Commission Contribution to European Defence' COM(2022) 60 final.

33 Regarding public health, see eg Kai P Purnhagen et al., 'More Competences than You Knew? The Web of Health Competence for European Union Action in Response to the COVID-19 Outbreak' (2020) 11(2) European Journal of Risk Regulation 297; regarding defence, see eg Federico Fabbrini, 'European Defence Union ASAP: The Act in Support of Ammunition Production and the Development of EU Defence Capabilities in Response to the War in Ukraine' (2024) 29(1) European Foreign Affairs Review 67.

as possible according to the current division of competences. During the pandemic, this could be witnessed when, for example, the Commission persuaded all Member States to purchase vaccines on a joint basis. Negotiating with producers of vaccines on behalf of the Union, the Commission managed to avoid competition for vaccines among Member States, ensuring instead equal distribution across the EU.[34] It was then for each Member State to decide about the roll-out of vaccination campaigns, depending on ethical and epidemiological criteria. Likewise, after Russia's invasion of Ukraine, the EU has adopted several packages of sanctions to harm Russia's economic base. Imposing a uniform sanctions regime under the EU legal order has been vital for preventing Russian products such as oil and gas from entering the EU internal market via non-participating Member States. Interdependence has thus been the leitmotif. Exceptions and derogations secured the consent for an oil embargo from those Member States who, due to their geographical location, could not obtain oil from sources other than Russian pipelines, while the legal regime prohibited its re-sale or onwards transfer.[35] EU law-making thus struggled to reconcile the frame of the *Rechtsgemeinschaft* with the material constitution of the Member States, including indeed geographical considerations like access to resources that are essential for the survival of the nation.

Hence, apart from the inner sphere, we have also seen the outer sphere at work during both the pandemic and the war. Regarding the former, reintroducing border controls and restricting the export of medical equipment were the clearest expression of a nation state's raison d'être: the protection of its citizens. This implies that citizens from other Member States are not of equal concern. But that is inevitable both from a philosophical viewpoint, as one cannot include without excluding;[36] and through the theoretical lens of the nation state, which entails a constitutional obligation on state authorities to protect the common good, that is, the flourishing of the national polity,[37] which is impossible without basic medical products in time of a pandemic. However, the Covid-19 pandemic has also shown that once the basic needs of the own citizens were met, Member States revealed political will to help each other. Export bans were in fact soon lifted. In similar vein, it is impossible to explain

34 See Susanna Villani, 'Perspectives of Solidarity Within the EU Legal Order in Time of the Covid-19 Pandemic' (2023) 4(1) Yearbook of International Disaster Law 70, 86.

35 See recitals (16)-(19) Council Regulation (EU) 2022/879 of 3 June 2022 amending Regulation (EU) No 833/2014 concerning restrictive measures in view of Russia's actions destabilising the situation in Ukraine [2022] OJ L153/53.

36 See Chapter 1.

37 See ibid and the Introduction.

the unprecedented support to Ukraine without regard to the frame of the sovereign nation state or its constitutional imagination. It might be insightful to consider, for illustration purposes, the special position of the German state vis-à-vis the EU on the one hand, and Russia and Ukraine on the other. With its violent past and culture of remembrance, Germany represents par excellence the Union's commitment to lasting peace in Europe, to be secured through the EU legal order. And just as the national past informed integration policies into Western alliances such as the (then) European Communities, so has the same historical consciousness underlain the recent support to Ukraine. In particular where support takes the form of weapons and ammunition, German action – as well as inaction and hesitation – can be explained and legitimised only against the historical background of German war crimes against both Russia and Ukraine.[38] In theoretical terms, the inner sphere can coordinate support and stimulate common action to a limited degree,[39] but it is first and foremost the outer sphere that motivates action on matters of war and peace.

Finally, existential crises like a pandemic and a war do not preclude convergence in the intermediate sphere. After all, it is '[t]he *Union's* aim (...) to promote peace, its values and the well-being of its peoples'.[40] But it seems that the pandemic and the Russian aggression were the impetus to translate this aim from the language of the Treaties into practical politics. According to the notion of 'strategic autonomy', the Union aspires to become more autonomous from third countries; to increase its capabilities in, for instance, the areas of public health and defence; and to reconsider its purpose(s).[41] The 27, acting outside the EU legal order, imagined and represented the EU as a political union aiming at 'protecting our citizens, values, democracies and the European model'.[42] Like a state, the Union seeks to protect its citizens and, for that purpose, it will develop its own material constitution, with independent

---

38 See German Federal Government, 'Televised Speech by Olaf Scholz, Chancellor of the Federal Republic of Germany and Member of the German Bundestag, on the Anniversary of the End of the Second World War in Europe' (Speech 8 May 2022) <https://www.bundesregierung.de/resource/blob/998352/2037652/6e6c89881efafb3a60c426dfa5f151f4/2022-05-08-bk-ansprache-8-mai-en-pdf-data.pdf?download=1> accessed 3 April 2024.

39 See e.g. Council Decision (CFSP) of 28 February 2022 on an assistance measure under the European Peace Facility for the supply to the Ukrainian Armed Forces of military equipment, and platforms, designed to deliver lethal force [2022] OJ L60/1.

40 Art 3(1) TEU.

41 See e.g. Mario Damen, 'EU Strategic Autonomy 2013–2023: From Concept to Capacity' (Briefing European Parliament July 2022) 5–6 <https://www.europarl.europa.eu/RegData/etudes/BRIE/2022/733589/EPRS_BRI(2022)733589_EN.pdf> accessed 3 April 2024.

42 'Versailles Declaration' (11 March 2022) point 6 <https://www.consilium.europa.eu/media/54773/20220311-versailles-declaration-en.pdf> accessed 3 April 2024.

defence capabilities, a future-proof economic base, et cetera. Hence, the legal concept of the autonomous legal order, whose 'thin' common purpose is to regulate joint action, will be supplemented with or turn into a 'richer' concept embracing ideas about what common action should aim at in terms of substance. However, this should not be mistaken for centralisation within the inner sphere of the Treaties. It rather seems that pondering over the common European purpose(s) inspires (national) public debates about what Member States could do on behalf of the Union. As far as common defence policies are concerned, the Commission has followed the lead of the European Council, outlining how to strengthen the European defence technological and industrial base.[43] One of the goals is to overcome fragmented national markets and duplicated investments, moving instead towards investing 'better, together, and European'.[44] Hence, national investments should be consistent and coherent with a view to 'European Defence Projects of Common Interest',[45] which need to be identified in the first place. In this regard, the nature and possible impact of external threats should be but one consideration; another should be the characteristics and existing strengths of European defence industries. For this entails the chance to tap into the political imagination of, for instance, the Netherlands as a 'seafaring nation', encouraging the state to invest in its maritime sector on behalf of the European common good. Nonetheless, as this example shows, proceeding from the European rather than national common good might also entail that public contracts are granted to foreign (read: European) companies.[46] That in turn raises legitimate concerns about losing labour, know-how and tradition.

It will be wise not to reject such sentiments as old-fashioned nationalism,[47] nor to criticise the quest for a more autonomous or sovereign EU as a sign of 'European nationalism'[48] that requires legal containment. As this book has

43 See European Commission & High Representative of the Union for Foreign Affairs and Security Policy, 'A New European Defence Industrial Strategy: Achieving EU Readiness Through a Responsive and Resilient European Defence Industry' JOIN(2024) 10 final.

44 Ibid 8.

45 Ibid 9.

46 See Dutch Ministry of Defence, 'Contract for new submarines provisionally awarded to Naval' (News item 15 March 2024) <https://english.defensie.nl/latest/news/2024/03/15/contract-for-new-submarines-provisionally-awarded-to-naval> accessed 3 April 2024.

47 See Editorial Comments, 'Nationale kramp rond order onderzeeboten is kortzichtig' *NRC* (18 March 2024) <https://www.nrc.nl/nieuws/2024/03/18/nationale-kramp-rond-order-onderzeeboten-is-kortzichtig-a4193330?t=1712053331> accessed 3 April 2024.

48 Editorial Comments, 'Keeping Europeanism at Bay? Strategic Autonomy as a Constitutional Problem' (2022) 59(2) CML Rev 313, 313.

demonstrated, nationalism is not per se bad. In a Union that has just started to develop its own sense of the common good, which is richer than individual liberties, it is inevitable to generate and legitimise public powers on the basis of established national identities. Even if these at first lead to unilateral action or traditional international cooperation, the form does not exclude that European nation states in fact weigh in concerns reaching across their own borders, acting thus qua EU Member States. At least, membership of the Union obliges them to do just that, as this book has argued. But this obligation does not pre-empt fundamental political choices as to the Union the Member States want to form. It is in the intermediate sphere where the Member States, through joint action rather than abstract norms, determine the European common good. It is there where we the European citizens are responsible for insisting that such action takes place on our behalf. That is challenging due to the loose institutionalisation of the intermediate sphere, and our additional, main obligation to scrutinise how we are represented as nationals of European nation states. Just as Member States face a double bind, so do we. Vigilance is thus required in Brussels and Luxemburg, but also somewhere in the Union.

Bibliography

Primary Sources

European Union

Treaties Currently in Force

Charter of Fundamental Rights of the European Union [2016] OJ C202/389.

Treaty on European Union (consolidated version) [2016] OJ C202/13.

Treaty on the Functioning of the European Union (consolidated version) [2016] OJ C202/47.

Other Treaties

Agreement between the Governments of the States of the Benelux Economic Union, the Federal Republic of Germany and the French Republic on the gradual abolition of checks at their common borders [2000] OJ L239/13.

Convention determining the State responsible for examining applications for asylum lodged in one of the Member States of the European Communities [1997] OJ C254/1.

Convention implementing the Schengen Agreement of 14 June 1985 between the Governments of the States of the Benelux Economic Union, the Federal Republic of Germany and the French Republic on the gradual abolition of checks at their common borders [2000] OJ L239/19.

Treaty establishing the European Community, as amended by the Treaty of Amsterdam (consolidated version) [1997] OJ C340/173.

Treaty establishing the European Community, as amended by the Treaty of Maastricht (consolidated version) [1992] C224/6.

Treaty establishing the European Economic Community, as amended by the Single European Act, [1987] OJ L169/1.

Treaty on European Union [1992] OJ C191/1.

Legislation

Commission Decision 85/381/EEC setting up a prior communication and consultation procedure on migration policies in relation to non-member countries [1985] OJ L217/25 (no longer in force).

Council Decision (CFSP) of 28 February 2022 on an assistance measure under the European Peace Facility for the supply to the Ukrainian Armed Forces of military equipment, and platforms, designed to deliver lethal force [2022] OJ L60/1.

Council Decision (EU) 2015/1523 of 14 September 2015 establishing provisional measures in the area of international protection for the benefit of Italy and of Greece [2015] OJ L239/146.

Council Decision (EU) 2015/1601 of 22 September 2015 establishing provisional measures in the area of international protection for the benefit of Italy and Greece [2015] OJ L248/80.

Council Decision 2006/507/EC of 14 October 2004 concerning the conclusion, on behalf of the European Community, of the Stockholm Convention on Persistent Organic Pollutants [2006] OJ L209/1.

Council Decision 2016/551/EU of 23 March 2016 establishing the position to be taken on behalf of the European Union within the Joint Readmission Committee on a Decision of the Joint Readmission Committee on implementing arrangements for the application of Articles 4 and 6 of the Agreement between the European Union and the Republic of Turkey on the readmission of persons residing without authorisation from 1 June 2016 [2016] OJ L95/9.

Council Decision 2016/1754/EU of 29 September 2016 amending Decision 2015/1601/EU establishing provisional measures in the area of international protection for the benefit of Italy and Greece [2016] OJ L268/82 (no longer in force).

Council Decision 2018/254/EU of 15 February 2018 on the conclusion on behalf of the European Union of the Marrakesh Treaty to Facilitate Access to Published Works for Persons who are Blind, Visually Impaired, or otherwise Print Disabled [2018] OJ L48/1.

Council Directive 2001/40/EC of 28 May 2001 on the mutual recognition of decisions on the expulsion of third country nationals [2001] OJ L149/34.

Council Framework Decision 2002/584/JHA of 13 June 2002 on the European arrest warrant and the surrender procedures between Member States [2002] OJ L190/1.

Council Regulation (EU) 2018/1877 of 26 November 2018 on the financial regulation applicable to the 11th European Development Fund [2018] OJ L307/1.

Council Regulation (EU) 2022/879 of 3 June 2022 amending Regulation (EU) No 833/2014 concerning restrictive measures in view of Russia's actions destabilising the situation in Ukraine [2022] OJ L153/53.

Decision of the Council and of the Representatives of the Governments of the Member States of the European Union, meeting within the Council of 16 June 2011 on the signing, on behalf of the Union, and provisional application of the Air Transport Agreement between the United States of America, of the first part, the European Union and its Member States, of the second part, Iceland, of the third part, and the Kingdom of Norway, of the fourth part; and on the signing, on behalf of the Union, and provisional application of the Ancillary Agreement between the European Union and its Member States, of the first part, Iceland, of the second part, and the Kingdom of Norway, of the third part, on the application of the Air Transport

Agreement between the United States of America, of the first part, the European Union and its Member States, of the second part, Iceland, of the third part, and the Kingdom of Norway, of the fourth part [2011] OJ L283/1.

Directive 2001/77/EC of 27 September 2001 on the promotion of electricity produced from renewable energy sources in the internal electricity market [2001] OJ L283/33 (no longer in force).

Directive 2008/115/EC of 16 December 2008 on common standards and procedures in Member States for returning illegally staying third-country nationals [2008] OJ L348/98.

Directive 2011/95/EU of 13 December 2011 on standards for the qualification of third-country nationals or stateless persons as beneficiaries of international protection, for a uniform status for refugees or for persons eligible for subsidiary protection, and for the content of the protection granted [2011] OJ L337/9.

Directive 2013/33/EU of 26 June 2013 laying down standards for the reception of applicants for international protection [2013] OJ L180/96.

Joint Position 96/196/JHA defined by the Council on the basis of Article K.3 of the Treaty on European Union on the harmonized application of the definition of the term "refugee" in Article 1 of the Geneva Convention relating to the status of refugees [1996] OJ L63/2.

Regulation (EU, Euratom) 2018/1046 of the European Parliament and of the Council of 18 July 2018 on the financial rules applicable to the general budget of the Union [2018] OJ L193/1.

Regulation 2016/399/EU of 9 March 2016 on a Union Code on the rules governing the movement of persons across borders ('Schengen Borders Code') [2016] OJ L77/1.

Regulation 2018/1860/EU of 28 November 2018 on the use of the Schengen Information System for the return of illegally staying third-country nationals [2018] OJ L312/1.

Regulation No 543/69/EEC of 25 March 1969 on the harmonisation of certain social legislation relating to road transport [1969] OJ L77/49 (no longer in force).

Regulation No 604/2013/EU of 26 June 2013 establishing the criteria and mechanisms for determining the Member State responsible for examining an application for international protection lodged in one of the Member States by a third-country national or a stateless person [2013] OJ L180/31.

Regulation No 725/2004/EC of 31 May 2004 on enhancing ship and port facility security [2004] OJ L129/6.

Regulation No 810/2009/EC of the European Parliament and of the Council of 13 July 2009 establishing a Community Code on Visas [2009] OJ L243/1.

Regulation No 1099/2009/EC on the protection of animals at the time of killing [2009] OJ L303/1.

Regulation of 25 October 2012 on the financial rules applicable to the general budget of the Union [2012] OJ L298/1.

Case Law

Case 22/70 *Commission* v *Council* (*ERTA*) EU:C:1971:32.
Case 26/62 *Van Gend & Loos* EU:C:1963:1.
Case 294/83 *Les Verts* EU:C:1986:166.
Case 6/64 *Costa* v *ENEL* EU:C:1964:66.
Case C-156/21 *Hungary* v *European Parliament and Council* EU:C:2022:97.
Case C-157/21 *Poland* v *European Parliament and Council* EU:C:2022:97.
Case C-163/17 *Jawo* v *Germany* EU:C:2019:218.
Case C-202/11 *Anton Las* EU:C:2013:239.
Case C-205/06 *Commission* v *Austria* (*Bilateral Investment Treaties*) EU:C:2009:118.
Case C-208/09 *Sayn-Wittgenstein* EU:C:2010:806.
Case C-213/17 *X* v *Staatssecretaris van Veiligheid en Justitie* EU:C:2018:538.
Case C-216/18 PPU *LM* EU:C:2018:586.
Case C-240/17 *E* EU:C:2018:8.
Case C-246/07 *Commission* v *Sweden* (*PFOS*) EU:C:2010:203.
Case C-258/14 *Florescu* EU:C:2017:448.
Case C-28/12 *Commission* v *Council* (*Air Transport Agreement*) EU:C:2015:282.
Case C-284/16 *Achmea* EU:C:2018:158.
Case C-290/14 *Celaj* EU:C:2015:640.
Case C-316/91 *European Parliament* v *Council* (*Lomé Convention*) EU:C:1994:76.
Case C-336/19 *Centraal Israëlitisch Consistorie van België and Others* v *Vlaamse Regering* EU:C:2020:1031.
Case C-36/02 *Omega* EU:C:2004:614.
Case C-370/12 *Pringle* EU:C:2012:756.
Case C-391/09 *Runevič-Vardyn* EU:C:2011:291.
Case C-392/95 *European Parliament* v *Council* EU:C:1997:289.
Case C-444/17 *Préfet des Pyrénées-Orientales* v *Abdelaziz Arib and Others* EU:C:2019:220.
Case C-45/07 *Commission* v *Greece* (*IOM*) EU:C:2009:81.
Case C-467/98 *Commission* v *Denmark* (*Open Skies*) EU:C:2002:635.
Case C-47/15 *Sélina Affum* v *Préfet du Pas-de-Calais and Procureur général de la Cour d'appel de Douai* EU:C:2016:408.
Case C-528/11 *Halaf* EU:C:2013:342.
Case C-573/17 *Popławski* EU:C:2019:530.
Case C-578/16 PPU *C.K. and Others* v *Slovenia* EU:C:2017:127.
Case C-606/10 *ANAFE* v *Ministre de l'Intérieur* EU:C:2012:348.
Case C-617/10 *Åkerberg Fransson* EU:C:2013:105.
Case C-619/18 *Commission* v *Poland* (Independence of the Supreme Court) EU:C:2019:531.
Case C-621/18 *Wightman* EU:C:2018:999.
Case C-638/16 PPU *X and X* v *Belgium* EU:C:2017:173.

Case C-64/16 *Associação Sindical dos Juízes Portugueses* EU:C:2018:117.

Case C-646/16 *Jafari* EU:C:2017:586.

Case C-66/13 *Green Network* EU:C:2014:2399.

Case C-695/15 PPU *Mirza* EU:C:2016:188.

Case C-808/18 *Commission v Hungary* EU:C:2020:1029.

Case T-192/16 *NF* v *European Council* EU:T:2017:128.

Case T-193/16 *NG* v *European Council* EU:T:2017:129.

Case T-257/16 *NM* v *European Council* EU:T:2017:130.

Case T-600/21 *WS and Others* v *European Border and Coast Guard Agency* ECLI:EU:T:2023:492.

Joined Cases 281, 283 to 285 and 287/85 *Germany, France, the Netherlands, Denmark, United Kingdom* v *Commission* EU:C:1987:351.

Joined Cases C-105/15 P to C-109/15 P *Mallis* EU:C:2016:702.

Joined Cases C-208/17 P to C-210/17 P *NF and Others* v *European Council* EU:C:2018:705.

Joined Cases C-297/17, C-318/17, C-319/17, C-438/17 *Ibrahim and Others* v *Germany* EU:C:2019:219.

Joined Cases C-357/19, C-379/19, C-547/19, C-811/19 and C-840/19 *Criminal proceedings against PM and Others* EU:C:2021:1034.

Joined Cases C-411/10 and C-493/10 *N.S. and Others* v *Secretary of State for the Home Department and Others* EU:C:2011:865.

Joined Cases C-582/17 and C-583/17 *Staatssecretaris van Veiligheid en Justitie* v *H. and R.* EU:C:2019:280.

Joined Cases C-609/17 and C-610/17 *TSN and AKT* EU:C: 2019:981.

Joined Cases C-626/15 and C-659/16 *Commission* v *Council (Antarctica)* EU:C:2018:925.

Joined Cases C-643/15 and C-647/15 *Slovakia and Hungary* v *Council* EU:C:2017:631.

Joined Cases C-715/17, C-718/17 and C-719/17 *Commission v Poland, Hungary, Czech Republic* EU:C:2020:257.

Joined Cases C-8/15 P to 10/15 P *Ledra Advertising* EU:C:2016:701.

Joined Cases C-924/19 PPU and C-925/19 PPU *FMS and Others* EU:C:2020:367.

Opinion 1/03 (Lugano Convention) EU:C:2006:81.

Opinion 1/75 EU:C:1975:145.

Opinion 1/76 (Laying-up Fund) EU:C:1977:63.

Opinion 2/13 (Accession to the ECHR) EU:C:2014:2454.

Opinion 2/91 (ILO), EU:C:1993:106.

Opinions of Advocates General of the Court of Justice of the EU

Opinion of AG Bot in Case C-213/17 *X* v *Staatssecretaris van Veiligheid en Justitie* EU:C:2018:434.

Opinion of AG Bot in in *Slovakia and Hungary* v *Council* EU:C:2017:618.

Opinion of AG Kokott in Case C-240/17 *E* EU:C:2017:963.

Opinion of AG Maduro in *Commission* v *Sweden* (*PFOS*) EU:C:2009:589.
Opinion of AG Mancini in *Germany and Others* v *Commission* EU:C:1987:169.
Opinion of AG Mengozzi in Case C-638/16 PPU *X and X* v *Belgium* EU:C:2017:93.
Opinion of AG Mengozzi in *Commission* v *Council* (*Air Transport Agreement*) EU:C:2015:43.
Opinion of AG Saugmandsgaard Øe in *ASJP* EU:C:2017:395.
Opinion of AG Sharpston in *Commission* v *Poland, Hungary and Czech Republic* EU:C:2019:917.
Opinion of AG Szpunar in Case C-444/17 *Préfet des Pyrénées-Orientales* v *Abdelaziz Arib and Others* EU:C:2018:836.
Opinion of AG Wathelet in Case C-163/17 *Jawo* v *Germany* EU:C:2018:613.

European Ombudsman

Decision of the European Ombudsman in the joint inquiry into complaints 506-509-674-784-927-1381/2016/MHZ against the European Commission concerning a human rights impact assessment in the context of the EU–Turkey Agreement, 18 January 2017.

Policy Documents

Common Understanding establishing a Governance and Conditionality Framework for the Refugee Facility for Turkey between EU Member States and the European Commission [2016] <https://www.statewatch.org/media/documents/news/2016/feb/eu-com-common-understaning-for-refugee-facility-for-turkey.pdf> accessed 1 March 2024.
Commission Decision of 10 February 2016 on the Facility for Refugees in Turkey amending Commission Decision C(2015) 9500 of 24 November 2015 [2016] C60/3.
Commission Decision of 24 November 2015 on the coordination of actions of the Union and of the Member States through a coordination mechanism – the Refugee Facility for Turkey [2015] C407/8.
Commission Recommendation of 7 March 2017 on making returns more effective when implementing the Directive 2008/115/EC C(2017) 1600 final.
Coordinators' Group on the Free Movement of Persons, '"The Palma Document" Free Movement of Persons. A Report to the European Council by the Coordinators' Group' (Key texts on justice and home affairs 1976–1993) <https://www.statewatch.org/media/documents/semdoc/assets/files/keytexts/ktch1.pdf>accessed1March 2024.
Council of the EU, 'Action Plan of the Council and the Commission on How Best to Implement the Provisions of the Treaty of Amsterdam on an Area of Freedom, Security and Justice' [1999] OJ C19/1.

Council of the EU, 'Conference "Managing Migration Together"' (Vienna, 24 February 2016) <https://data.consilium.europa.eu/doc/document/ST-6481-2016-INIT/en/pdf> accessed 1 March 2024.

Council of the EU, 'European Pact on Immigration and Asylum' 13440/08.

Council of the EU, 'Resolution on Burden-Sharing with Regard to the Admission and Residence of Displaced Persons on a Temporary Basis' [1995] OJ C262/1.

Council of the EU, 'Standard Operating Procedures Implementing the Mechanism for Resettlement from Turkey to the EU as set out in the EU-Turkey Statement of 18 March 2016 – Endorsement' LIMITE 8366/16.

Council of the EU, 'Statement of the EU Heads of State or Government, 07/03/2016' (Press release 8 March 2016) <https://www.consilium.europa.eu/en/press/press-releases/2016/03/08/eu-turkey-meeting-statement/pdf> accessed 1 March 2024.

Court of Justice of the EU, 'Press Release Following the Judgment of the German Constitutional Court of 5 May 2020' (Press Release No 58/20, 8 May 2020) <https://curia.europa.eu/jcms/upload/docs/application/pdf/2020-05/cp200058en.pdf> accessed 1 March 2024.

European Commission & High Representative of the Union for Foreign Affairs and Security Policy, 'A New European Defence Industrial Strategy: Achieving EU Readiness Through a Responsive and Resilient European Defence Industry' JOIN(2024) 10 final.

European Commission, 'Action Fiche of the EU Trust Fund to be Used for the Decisions of the Operational Committee: Support to Integrated Border and Migration Management in Libya' (2017), T05-EUTF-NOA-LY-04 for the first phase and T05-EUTF-NOA-LY-07 for the second phase.

European Commission, 'Building a European Health Union: Reinforcing the EU's Resilience for Cross-Border Health Threats' COM(2020) 724 final.

European Commission, 'Commission Contribution to European Defence' COM(2022) 60 final.

European Commission, 'Communication on a New Pact on Migration and Asylum' COM(2020) 609 final.

European Commission, 'Communication on Immigration and Asylum Policies' COM(94) 23 final.

European Commission, 'Communication on the Common Asylum Policy and the Agenda for Protection COM(2003) 152 final.

European Commission, 'Communication on the Possible Application of Article K.9 of the Treaty on European Union COM(95) 566 final.

European Commission, 'EU-Turkey Joint Action Plan' (15 October 2015) <https://ec.europa.eu/commission/presscorner/detail/de/MEMO_15_5860> accessed 1 March 2024.

European Commission, 'EU-Turkey Statement: Four Years On' (March 2020) <https://home-affairs.ec.europa.eu/system/files/2020-03/20200318_managing-migration-eu-turkey-statement-4-years-on_en.pdf> accessed 1 March 2024.

European Commission, 'Joint Declaration of Intent on a Controlled Emergency Procedure – Voluntary Commitments by Member States for a Predictable Temporary Solidarity Mechanism' (23 September 2019) <http://www.statewatch.org/media/documents/news/2019/sep/eu-temporary-voluntary-relocation-mechanism-declaration.pdf> accessed 1 March 2024.

European Commission, 'Memorandum of Understanding on a Strategic and Global Partnership between the European Union and Tunisia' (Press release 16 July 2023) <https://ec.europa.eu/commission/presscorner/detail/en/ip_23_3887> accessed 1 March 2024.

European Commission, 'Next Operational Steps in EU-Turkey Cooperation in the Field of Migration' COM(2016) 166 final.

European Commission, 'President Jean-Claude Juncker's State of the Union Address 2017' (Speech 13 September 2017) <https://ec.europa.eu/commission/presscorner/detail/en/SPEECH_17_3165> accessed 1 March 2024.

European Commission, 'Proposal for a Directive on Common Standards and Procedures in Member States for Returning Illegally Staying Third-Country Nationals (Recast) – A Contribution from the European Commission to the Leaders' Meeting in Salzburg on 19-20 September 2018', COM(2018) 634 final.

European Commission, 'Proposal for a Regulation establishing a Union Resettlement Framework and amending Regulation No 516/2014/EU establishing the Asylum, Migration and Integration Fund' COM(2016) 468 final.

European Commission, 'Recommendation Addressed to the Member States on the Resumption of Transfers to Greece under Regulation (EU) No. 604/2013' C(2016) 8525 final.

European Commission, 'Remarks by President von der Leyen at the Joint Press Conference with Kyriakos Mitsotakis, Prime Minister of Greece, Andrej Plenković, Prime Minister of Croatia, President Sassoli and President Michel' (Statement 3 March 2020) <https://ec.europa.eu/commission/presscorner/detail/en/statement_20_380> accessed 1 March 2024.

European Commission, 'Report to the Council on the Possibility of Applying Article K.9 of the Treaty on European Union to Asylum Policy' SEC(93) 1687 final/3.

European Commission, 'State of the Union Address 2016: Towards a Better Europe – a Europe That Protects, Empowers and Defends' (Speech 14 September 2016) <https://ec.europa.eu/commission/presscorner/detail/en/SPEECH_16_3043> accessed 1 March 2024.

European Commission, 'Striking a Balance on Migration: An Approach That is Both Fair and Firm' COM(2024) 126 final.

European Commission, 'The European Union and Tunisia: Political Agreement on a Comprehensive Partnership Package' (News article 16 July 2023) <https://neighbourhood-enlargement.ec.europa.eu/news/european-union-and-tunisia-political-agreement-comprehensive-partnership-package-2023-07-16_en> accessed 1 March 2024.

European Commission, 'Towards More Accessible, Equitable and Managed Asylum Systems' COM(2003) 315 final.

European Commission, 'Versailles Declaration' (11 March 2022) <https://www.consilium.europa.eu/media/54773/20220311-versailles-declaration-en.pdf> accessed 3 April 2024.

European Commission, Untitled letter from European Commission President Ursula von der Leyen to the members of the European Council (25 June 2023) <https://www.statewatch.org/media/3945/eu-com-von-der-leyen-letter-euco-25-6-23.pdf> accessed 1 March 2024.

European Council and Council of the EU, 'Meeting of Heads of State or Government with Turkey – EU-Turkey Statement, 29/11/2015' (Press release 29 November 2015) <https://www.consilium.europa.eu/en/press/press-releases/2015/11/29/eu-turkey-meeting-statement/> accessed 1 March 2024.

European Council, 'Conclusions' (Meeting of 10 and 11 December 2009) EUCO 6/09.

European Council, 'Conclusions' (Meeting of 11 and 12 December 1992) SN 456/1/92 Rev 1.

European Council, 'Conclusions' (Meeting of 14 and 15 December 2023) EUCO 20/23.

European Council, 'Conclusions' (Meeting of 15 and 16 October 1999).

European Council, 'Conclusions' (Meeting of 19 and 20 June 2003) 11638/03.

European Council, 'Conclusions' (Meeting of 25 and 26 June 2015) EUCO 22/15.

European Council, 'Conclusions' (Meeting of 26 and 27 June 1989) SN 254/2/89.

European Council, 'Conclusions' (Meeting of 4 and 5 November 2004) 14292/04.

European Council, 'EU-Turkey Statement' (Press release 18 March 2016) <https://www.consilium.europa.eu/en/press/press-releases/2016/03/18/eu-turkey-statement/> accessed 1 March 2024.

European Council, 'Malta Declaration by the Members of the European Council on the External Aspects of Migration: Addressing the Central Mediterranean Route' (Press Release 43/17, 3 February 2017) <https://www.consilium.europa.eu/en/press/press-releases/2017/02/03/malta-declaration/> accessed 1 March 2024.

European Council, 'Migration: Way Forward on the External and Internal Dimension' (Leaders' Agenda December 2017) <https://www.consilium.europa.eu/media/32143/en_leaders-agenda-note-on-migration_.pdf> accessed 1 March 2024.

European Migration Network, 'The Effectiveness of Return in EU Member States: Challenges and Good Practices Linked to EU Rules and Standards – Synthesis Report' (European Migration Network 2018).

European Migration Network, 'The Effectiveness of Return in EU Member States: Challenges and Good Practices Linked to EU Rules and Standards – Response from the Netherlands' (European Migration Network 2017).

European Parliament, 'MEPs Approve the New Migration and Asylum Pact' (Press release 10 April 2024) <https://www.europarl.europa.eu/news/en/press-room/20240408IPR20290/meps-approve-the-new-migration-and-asylum-pact> accessed 16 April 2024.

European Parliament, 'Mutual Recognition of Return Decisions' (Answer to question E-002722/2017, 27 June 2017) https://www.europarl.europa.eu/doceo/document/E-8-2017-002722-ASW_EN.html> accessed 1 March 2024.

European Parliament, 'Mutual Recognition of Return Decisions' (Question for written answer E-002722-17 to the Commission, 12 April 2017) <https://www.europarl.europa.eu/doceo/document/E-8-2017-002722_EN.html> accessed 1 March 2024.

European Parliament, Text of the Asylum Procedure Regulation, adopted at 1st Reading, T9-0177/2024.

European Parliament, Text of the Union Resettlement and Humanitarian Admission Framework, adopted at 1st Reading, T9-0184/0184.

Report from the Ministers Responsible for Immigration to the European Council Meeting in Maastricht on Immigration and Asylum Policy, SN 4038/91 (WGI 930), 3 December 1991.

Secrétariat Général du Conseil de l'Union Européenne, *Conférence Intergouvernementale en vue de la Révision des Traités – Semestre de la Présidence Néerlandaise* (*Recueil de Textes*) (Secrétariat Général du Conseil de l'Union Européenne 1997).

Secrétariat Général du Conseil de l'Union Européenne; *Conférence Intergouvernementale en vue de la Révision des Traités – Semestre de la Présidence Irlandaise* (*Recueil de Textes*) (Secrétariat Général du Conseil de l'Union Européenne 1997).

Council of Europe

European Court of Human Rights

Ilias and Ahmed v *Hungary* App no 47287/15 (ECtHR, 21 November 2019).

Khlaifia and Others v *Italy* App no 16483/12 (ECtHR, 15 December 2016).

Lautsi and Others v *Italy* App no 30814/06 (ECtHR, 18 March 2011).

Tarakhel v *Switzerland* App no 29217/12 (ECtHR, 4 November 2014).

M.S.S. v *Belgium and Greece* App no 30696/09 (ECtHR, 21 January 2011).

S.S. and Others v *Italy* App no 21660/18 (communicated on 26 June 2019).

United Nations

Treaties

Convention Relating to the Status of Refugees, signed at Geneva on 28 July 1951, UNTS, vol 189, p 137.

Protocol Relating to the Status of Refugees, done at New York on 31 January 1967, UNTS, vol 606, p 267.

UN General Assembly Resolutions

UN General Assembly, Global Compact for Safe, Orderly and Regular Migration (2018) A/RES/73/195.

UN General Assembly, Global Compact on Refugees (2018) A/73/12.

UN Secretary General

UN Secretary General, 'Draft Declaration and Comprehensive Plan of Action Approved by the Preparatory Meeting for the International Conference of Indo-Chinese Refugees on 8 March 1989' A/CONF 148/2, 26 April 1989.

UNHCR

UNHCR, 'Germany: Fact Sheet' (February 2023) <https://www.unhcr.org/sites/default/files/legacy-pdf/640747697.pdf> accessed 1 March 2024.

UNHCR, '2015 Year-End Report (Turkey)' (25 November 2016) <https://reporting.unhcr.org/sites/default/files/pdfsummaries/GR2015-Turkey-eng.pdf> accessed 1 March 2024.

UNHCR Executive Committee, 'Durable Solutions and Refugee Protection No. 56 (XL) – 1989' (13 October 1989) point b) iii) <https://www.refworld.org/policy/exconc/excom/1989/en/41965> accessed 1 March 2024.

Germany

Constitution

Basic Law for the Federal Republic of Germany in the revised version published in the Federal Law Gazette Part III, classification number 100–1, as last amended by the Act of 19 December 2022 (Federal Law Gazette I p. 2478).

Legislation

Act on the Residence, Economic Activity and Integration of Foreigners in the Federal Territory in the version promulgated on 25 February 2008 (Federal Law Gazette I p. 162), most recently amended by Article 4b of the Act of 17 February 2020 (Federal Law Gazette I p. 166).

Case Law

BVerfG, Judgment of the Second Senate of 5 May 2020, 2 BvR 859/15.

BVerfG, Judgment of the Second Senate of 18 March 2014, 2 BvR 1390/12.

BVerfG, Judgment of the Second Senate of 30 June 2009, 2 BvE 2/08.

VG München, M 18 E 19.32238, Order of 8 August 2019.

Policy Documents

Christian Democratic Union (CDU), 'Beschlüsse des Koalitionsausschusses vom 5. Juli 2018' (Press release 6 July 2018) <https://archiv.cdu.de/artikel/beschluesse-des-koalitionsausschusses-vom-5-juli-2018> accessed 1 March 2024.

Federal Government, 'Rede von Bundeskanzlerin Dr. Angela Merkel' (Speech 25 November2015)<https://www.bundesregierung.de/breg-de/service/newsletter-und-abos/bulletin/rede-von-bundeskanzlerin-dr-angela-merkel-452842> accessed 1 March 2024.

Federal Office for Migration and Refugees, 'Resettlement and the NesT Programme' (14 February 2023) <https://www.bamf.de/EN/Themen/AsylFluechtlingsschutz/ResettlementRelocation/Resettlement/resettlement-node.html> accessed 1 March 2024.

German Federal Government, 'Televised Speech by Olaf Scholz, Chancellor of the Federal Republic of Germany and Member of the German Bundestag, on the Anniversary of the End of the Second World War in Europe' (Speech 8 May 2022) <https://www.bundesregierung.de/resource/blob/998352/2037652/6e6c89881efafb3a60c426dfa5f151f4/2022-05-08-bk-ansprache-8-mai-en-pdf-data.pdf?download=1> accessed 3 April 2024.

Greece

Greek Council of State, Joint decisions 2347/2017 and 2348/2017 (unofficial English summary) <https://www.refworld.org/jurisprudence/caselaw/grccs/2017/en/120841> accessed 1 March 2024.

Netherlands

Dutch Ministry of Defence, 'Contract for new submarines provisionally awarded to Naval' (News item 15 March 2024) <https://english.defensie.nl/latest/news/2024/03/15/contract-for-new-submarines-provisionally-awarded-to-naval> accessed 3 April 2024.

Turkey

Temporary Protection Regulation 2014/6883 of 22 October 2014.

Law No 6458 of 4 April 2013 on Foreigners and International Protection.

Other International Documents

Administrative Arrangement between the Ministry of Migration Policy of the Hellenic Republic and the Federal Ministry of the Interior, Building and Community of the Federal Republic of Germany on cooperation when refusing entry to persons seeking protection in the context of temporary checks at the internal German-Austrian border <https://www.frnrw.de/fileadmin/frnrw/media/EU_Asylpolitik/Germany_Greece_Deal_eng.pdf> accessed 1 March 2024.

Memorandum of Understanding on Cooperation in the Fields of Development, the Fight Against Illegal Immigration, Human Trafficking and Fuel Smuggling and on Reinforcing the Security of Borders Between the State of Libya and the Italian Republic ('Memorandum of Understanding') (2 February 2017) <https://eumigrationlawblog.eu/wp-content/uploads/2017/10/MEMORANDUM_translation_finalversion.doc.pdf> accessed 1 March 2024.

Visegrad Group, 'V4 Letter to the Prime Minister of Italy' (Letter 19 July 2017) <https://www.visegradgroup.eu/documents/official-statements/v4-letter-to-the-prime> accessed 1 March 2024.

Secondary Sources

Academic Literature

Acetto M, Zleptnig S, 'The Principle of Effectiveness: Rethinking its Role in Community Law' (2005) 11(3) European Public Law 375.

Anderson B, *Imagined Communities: Reflections on the Origin and Spread of Nationalism* (revised edition, Verso 2016).

Ankersmit FR, *Political Representation* (Stanford University Press 2002).

Augenstein D (ed), *"Integration through Law" Revisited: The Making of the European Polity* (Ashgate 2012).

Avbelj M, 'Can European Integration Be Constitutional and Pluralist – Both at the Same Time?' in Avbelj M and Komárek J (eds), *Constitutional Pluralism in the European Union and Beyond* (OUP 2012).

Avbelj M, 'Human Dignity and EU Legal Pluralism' in Gareth Davies and Matej Avbelj, *Research Handbook on Legal Pluralism and EU Law* (Elgar 2018).

Avbelj M, 'Revitalisation of EU Constitutionalism' (2021) 46(1) European Law Review 3.

Avbelj M, 'Supremacy or Primacy of EU Law? – (Why) Does It Matter?' (2011) 17(6) European Law Journal 744.

Avbelj M, 'Values, Constitutionalism and the Viability of European Integration' in Matej Avbelj (ed), *The Future of EU Constitutionalism* (Hart 2023).

Avbelj M, *The European Union under Transnational Law: A Pluralist Appraisal* (Hart 2018).

Azoulai L, '"Integration through Law" and Us' (2016) 14(2) I·CON 449.

Azoulai L, 'The Many Visions of Europe: Insights from the Reasoning of the European Court of Justice in External Relations Law' in Marise Cremona and Anne Thies (eds), *The European Court of Justice and External Relations Law: Constitutional Challenges* (Hart 2014).

Baere G de, 'O, Where is Faith? O, Where is Loyalty? Some Thoughts on the Duty of Loyal Co-operation and the Union's External Environmental Competence in the light of the PFOS Case' (2011) 36(3) European Law Review 405.

Barents R, *The Autonomy of Community Law* (Kluwer 2004).

Bast J, 'Deeping Supranational Integration: Interstate Solidarity in EU Migration Law' (2016) 22(2) European Public Law 289.

Bast J, 'Scharade im kontrollfreien Raum: Hat die EU gar keinen Türkei-Deal geschlossen?' (2017) Verfassungsblog <https://www.printfriendly.com/p/g/tXgPVE> accessed 1 March 2024.

Bekker S, 'The European Semester: Understanding an Innovative Governance Model' in Paul James Cardwell & Marie-Pierre Granger (eds), *Research Handbook on the Politics of EU Law* (Elgar 2020).

Bello Hutt D, 'Political Representation as Interpretation: A Contribution to Deliberative Constitutionalism' (2020) 33(4) Ratio Juris 351.

Betts, 'Public Goods Theory and the Provision of Refugee Protection: The Role of the Joint Product Model' (2003) 16(3) Journal of Refugee Studies 274.

Betts, and Durieux J, 'Convention Plus as a Norm-Setting Exercise' (2007) 20(3) Journal of Refugee Studies 509.

Bickerton CJ, *European Integration: From Nation States to Member States* (OUP 2012).

Bogdandy A von, 'Founding Principles' in Armin von Bogdandy and Jürgen Bast (ed), *Principles of European Constitutional Law* (2nd edition, Hart 2009).

Bogdandy A von, 'Jenseits der Rechtsgemeinschaft: Begriffsarbeit in der europäischen Sinn- und Rechtsstaatlichkeitskrise' (2017) Europarecht 487.

Bogdandy A von, and Spieker LD, 'Countering the Judicial Silencing of Critics: Article 2 TEU Values, Reverse Solange, and the Responsibilities of National Judges' (2019) 15(3) EuConst 391.

Bonelli M and Claes M, 'Judicial Serendipity: How Portuguese Judges Came to the Rescue of the Polish Judiciary' (2018) 14(3) EuConst 622.

Borger V, *The Currency of Solidarity: Constitutional Transformation During the Euro Crisis* (CUP 2020).

Bornemann J, 'Competing Visions and Constitutional Limits of Schengen Reform: Securitization, Gradual Supranationalization and the Undoing of Schengen as an Identity-Creating Project' (2024) German Law Journal 1.

Bouzoraa Y, 'The Value of Democracy in EU Law and Its Enforcement: A Legal Analysis' (2023) 8(2) European Papers 809.

Brink T van den, 'National Discretion in EU Legislation' in Sacha Garben and Inge Govaere, *The Division of Competences Between the EU and the Member States: Reflections on the Past, the Present and the Future* (Hart 2017).

Búrca, G de, Scott J, 'Introduction: New Governance, Law and Constitutionalism' in Graínne de Búrca and Joanne Scott (eds), *Law and New Governance in the EU and the US* (Hart 2006).

Burke E, 'Speech to the Electors of Bristol' in Philip B Kurland & Ralph Lerner (eds), *The Founders' Constitution* (volume 1, web edition, University of Chicago Press) <https://press-pubs.uchicago.edu/founders/documents/v1ch13s7.html> accessed 1 March 2024.

Cahill M, 'Theorizing Subsidiarity: Towards an Ontology-Sensitive Approach' (2017) 15(1) I·CON 201.

Calliess C, 'Art. 2 [Die Werte der Union]' in Christian Calliess and Matthias Ruffert (eds), *EUV/AEUV: Das Verfassungsrecht der Europäischen Union mit Europäischer Grundrechtecharta [Kommentar]* (5th edition, C H Beck 2016).

Calliess C, 'Constitutional Identity in Germany – One for Three or Three in One?' in Christian Calliess and Gerhard van der Schyff (eds), *Constitutional Identity in a Europe of Multilevel Constitutionalism* (CUP 2019).

Cannizzaro E, 'Dualism as the Supreme Expression of Realism: A Quick Comment on *NF v. European Council*' (2017) 2(1) European Papers 251.

Cappelletti M, Seccombe M, Weiler JHH, 'Integration through Law: Europe and the American Federal Experience – A General Introduction' in Mauro Cappelletti et al., *Integration through Law: Europe and the American Federal Experience* (De Gruyter 1986).

Cappelletti M, Seccombe M, Weiler JHH, *Integration through Law: Europe and the American Federal Experience* (De Gruyter 1986).

Cardwell PJ, 'Tackling Europe's Migration "Crisis" Through Law and "New Governance" (2018) 9(1) Global Policy 67.

Carrera S, Hertog L den, Stefan M, 'It Wasn't Me! The Luxembourg Court Orders on the EU-Turkey Refugee Deal' *CEPS Policy Insights No 2017–15* <https://cdn.ceps.eu/wp-content/uploads/2017/04/EU-Turkey%20Deal.pdf> accessed 1 March 2024.

Cassarino JP, 'Informalizing EU Readmission Policy' in Ariadna Ripoll Servent and Florian Trauner (eds), *The Routledge Handbook of Justice and Home Affairs Research* (Routledge 2018).

Cassarino JP, and Luisa Martin, 'The Pact on Migration and Asylum: Turning the European Territory into a Non-Territory?' (2022) 24(1) European Journal of Migration and Law 1.

Chamon M, 'Implied Exclusive Powers in the ECJ's Post-Lisbon Jurisprudence: The Continued Development of the ERTA Doctrine' (2018) 55(4) CML Rev 1101.

Chetail V, *International Migration Law* (OUP 2019).

Claes M and Bonelli M, 'The Rule of Law and the Constitutionalisation of the European Union' in Werner Schroeder (ed), *Strengthening the Rule of Law in Europe: From a Common Concept to Mechanisms of Implementation* (OUP 2016).

Classen CD, 'Die Gleichheit der Mitgliedstaaten und ihre Ausformungen im Unionsrecht' (2020) Europarecht 255.

Cliteur P, 'Strengthening the Rule of Law Within the Union: Some Advice to Break the Deadlock' in Afshin Ellian and Raisa Blommestijn (eds), *Reflections on Democracy in the European Union* (Eleven 2020).

Cloots E, 'National Identity, Constitutional Identity, and Sovereignty in the EU' (2016) 45(2) Netherlands Journal of Legal Philosophy 82.

Coninck J de, 'Shielding Frontex: On the EU General Court's "ws and Others v Frontex"' (2023) Verfassungsblog <https://verfassungsblog.de/shielding-frontex/> accessed 3 April 2024.

Contartese C, Andenas M, 'EU Autonomy and Investor-State Dispute Settlement under *Inter Se* Agreements Between EU Member States: *Achmea*' (2019) 56(1) CML Rev 157.

Craig P, 'Subsidiarity: A Political and Legal Analysis' (2012) 50(1) Journal of Common Market Studies 72.

Cremona M, 'Disconnection Clauses in EU Law and Practice' in Christophe Hillion and Panos Koutrakos (eds), *Mixed Agreements Revisited: The EU and its Member States in the World* (Hart 2010).

Cremona M, 'EU External Relations: Unity and Conferral of Powers' in Loïc Azoulai (ed), *The Question of Competence in the European Union* (OUP 2014).

Cremona M, 'Member States as Trustees of the Union Interest: Participating in International Agreements on Behalf of the European Union' in Anthony Arnull et al. (eds), *A Constitutional Order of States? Essays in EU Law in Honour of Alan Dashwood* (Hart 2011).

Cremona M, 'Structural Principles and their Role in EU External Relations Law' in Marise Cremona (ed), *Structural Principles in EU External Relations Law* (Hart 2018).

Cruz A, 'Visa Policy under the First Pillar: A Meaningless Compromise', in Monica den Boer (ed), *Schengen, Judicial Cooperation and Policy Coordination* (European Institute of Public Administration 1997).

Cuyvers A, 'The Legal Space for Structural Differentiation in the EU: Reciprocity, Interconnectedness and Effectiveness as Sources of Constitutional Rigidity' (2022) 7(3) European Papers 1165.

Dagilytė E, 'Solidarity: A General Principle of EU Law? Two Variations on the Solidarity Theme' in Andrea Biondi et al. (eds), *Solidarity in EU Law – Legal Principle in the Making* (Elgar 2018).

Dashwood A, Heliskoski J, 'The Classic Authorities Revisited' in Alan Dashwood & Christophe Hillion (eds), *The General Law of E.C. External Relations* (Sweet & Maxwell 2000).

Dawson M, 'Integration through Soft Law? New Governance and the Meaning of Legality in the European Union' in Daniel Augenstein (ed), *"Integration through Law" Revisited: The Making of the European Polity* (Ashgate 2012).

Dawson M, 'New Modes of Governance' in Dennis Patterson and Anna Södersten (eds); *A Companion to European Union Law and International Law* (Wiley 2016).

Dawson M, and Witte F de, 'From Balance to Conflict: A New Constitution for the EU' (2016) 22(2) European Law Journal 204.

Dawson M, *The Governance of EU Fundamental Rights* (CUP 2017).

Delgado Casteleiro A, 'Loyalty in EU External Relations Law: The Fabric of Competence, Autonomy and Institutional Balance' in Eleftheria Neframi and Mauro Gatti (eds), *Constitutional Issues of EU External Relations Law* (Nomos 2018).

Delgado Casteleiro A, and Joris Larik, 'The Duty to Remain Silent: Limitless Loyalty in EU External Relations?' (2011) 36(4) European Law Review 524.

Denza E, *The Intergovernmental Pillars of the European Union* (OUP 2002).

Dietze J, Kellerbauer M, Klamert M, Malferrari L, Scharf T, Schnichels D, Basedow J, Loacker LD, 'Europa – Quo Vadis? Ein kritischer Kommentar zum EZB-Urteil des BVerfG' (2020) Europäische Zeitschrift für Wirtschaftsrecht 525.

Dougan M, 'Judicial Review of Member State Action under the General Principles and the Charter: Defining the "Scope of Union Law"' (2015) 52(5) CML Rev 1201.

Dougan M, 'The Vicissitudes of Life at the Coalface: Remedies and Procedures for Enforcing Union Law before the National Courts' in Paul Craig and Gráinne de Búrca, *The Evolution of EU Law* (OUP 2011).

Eckes C, 'Disciplining Member States: EU Loyalty in External Relations' (2020) 22 CYELS 85.

Eckes C, 'The Reflexive Relationship between Internal and External Sovereignty' (2015) 18(1) Irish Journal of European Law 33.

Eckes C, *EU Powers under External Pressure: How the EU's External Actions Alter its Internal Structures* (OUP 2019).

Editorial Comments, 'EU Law between Common Values and Collective Feelings' (2018) 55(5) CML Rev 1329.

Editorial Comments, 'Keeping Europeanism at Bay? Strategic Autonomy as a Constitutional Problem' (2022) 59(2) CML Rev 313.

Eeckhout, 'Bold Constitutionalism and Beyond' in Miguel Poiares Maduro & Loïc Azoulai, *The Past and Future of EU Law: the Classics of EU Law Revisited on the 50th Anniversary of the Rome Treaty* (Hart 2010).

Eeckhout, *EU External Relations Law* (2nd edition, OUP 2011).

Eijsbouts T, 'Wir sind das Volk – Notes about the Notion of "The People" as Occasioned by the *Lissabon-Urteil*' (2010) 6(2) EuConst 199.

Elsuwege P van, 'The Duty of Sincere Cooperation and Its Implications for Autonomous Member State Action in the Field of External Relations' in Marton Varju (ed), *Between Compliance and Particularism – Member State Interests and European Union Law* (Springer eBook 2019).

Endres de Oliveira P, Schmalz D, 'Anordnung des (Europa-)Rechtsbruchs' (2018) Verfassungsblog <https://verfassungsblog.de/anordnung-des-europa-rechtsbruchs/> accessed 1 March 2024.

Erlbacher F, 'Recent Case Law on External Competences of the European Union: How Member States Can Embrace Their Own Treaty' *CLEER Papers 2017/2*, 35 <https://www.asser.nl/media/3485/cleer17-2_web.pdf> accessed 1 March 2024.

Fabbrini F, 'After the OMT Case: The Supremacy of EU Law as the Guarantee of the Equality of the Member States' (2016) 16(4) German Law Journal 1003.

Fabbrini F, 'European Defence Union ASAP: The Act in Support of Ammunition Production and the Development of EU Defence Capabilities in Response to the War in Ukraine' (2024) 29(1) European Foreign Affairs Review 67.

Farahat A, Markard N, 'Forced Migration Governance: In Search of Sovereignty' (2016) 17(6) German Law Journal 923.

Farahat A, Markard N, and Leijten I, 'Human Rights Overreach?' (2022) 40(2) Netherlands Quarterly of Human Rights 83.

Fernández Arribas G, 'The EU-Turkey Statement, the Treaty-Making Process and Competent Organs. Is the Statement an International Agreement?' (2017) 2(1) European Papers 303.

Garben S, 'Collective Identity as a Legal Limit to European Integration in Areas of Core State Powers' (2020) 58(1) JCMS 41.

García Andrade, 'EU External Competences in the Field of Migration: How To Act Externally When Thinking Internally' (2018) 55(1) CML Rev 157.

García Andrade, and Frasca E, 'The Memorandum of Understanding between the EU and Tunisia: Issues of Procedure and Substance on the Informalisation of Migration Cooperation' (2023) EU Immigration and Asylum Law and Policy <https://eumigrationlawblog.eu/the-memorandum-of-understanding-between-the-eu-and-tunisia-issues-of-procedure-and-substance-on-the-informalisation-of-migration-cooperation/> accessed 1 March 2024.

Gärditz KF, 'Die demokratische Gestaltungsverantwortung durch Recht in einer Einwanderungs-gesellschaft' (2017) 44(17–20) Europäische Grundrechte-Zeitschrift 516.

Gatti M, Ott A, 'The EU-Turkey Statement: Legal Nature and Compatibility with EU Institutional Law' in Sergio Carrera et al., *Constitutionalising the External Dimensions of EU Migration Policies in Times of Crisis* (Elgar 2019).

Gibbs A, 'Common Values, Europe's Indeterminate Nature and Enduring Sovereignty' in Matej Avbelj (ed), *The Future of EU Constitutionalism* (Hart 2023).

Goldner Lang I, 'No Solidarity Without Loyalty: Why Do Member States Violate EU Asylum and Migration Law and What Can Be Done?' (2020) 22(1) European Journal of Migration and Law 39.

Goldoni M, 'Constitutional Pluralism and the Question of the European Common Good' (2012) 18(3) European Law Journal 385.

Goldoni M, and Wilkinson MA, 'The Material Constitution' (2018) 81(4) The Modern Law Review 567.

Graßhof M, 'Artikel 78 AEUV' in Jürgen Schwarze (ed), *EU-Kommentar* (3rd edition, Nomos 2012).

Grimm D, 'Three Meanings of Constitutional Identity and Their Prospects in the European Union' in Jurgen de Poorter, Gerhard van der Schyff, Maarten Stremler, Maartje de Visser, Ingrid Leijten, Charlotte van Oirsouw (eds), A Constitutional Identity for the EU?' (2022) 4 European Yearbook of Constitutional Law 13.

Grimm D, *Sovereignty: The Origin and Future of a Political and Legal Concept* (Columbia University Press 2015).

Guild E, *Immigration Law in the European Community* (Kluwer 2001).

Guiraudon V, 'European Integration and Migration Policy: Vertical Policy-Making as Venue-Shopping' (2000) 38(2) Journal of Common Market Studies 251.

Halberstamm D and Christoph Möllers, 'The German Constitutional Court Says "*Ja zu Deutschland*!"' German Law Journal (2009) 10(8) 1241.

Halberstamm D, '"It's the Autonomy Stupid!" A Modest Defense of Opinion 2/13 on EU Accession to the ECHR, and the Way Forward' (2015) 16(1) German Law Journal 105.

Haltern U, 'Ultra-vires-Kontrolle im Dienst europäischer Demokratie' (2020) Neue Zeitschrift für Verwaltungsrecht 817.

Haltern U, *Europarecht und das Politische* (Mohr Siebeck 2005).

Hansen R, 'Making Cooperation Work: Interests, Incentives, and Action' in Randall Hansen et al. (eds), *Migration, Nation States and International Cooperation* (Routledge 2011).

Hathaway JC, Neve RA, 'Making International Refugee Law Relevant Again: A Proposal for Collectivized an Solution-Oriented Protection' (1997) 10 Harvard Human Rights Journal 115.

Hathaway JC, *The Rights of Refugees under International Law* (2nd edition, CUP 2021).

Heijer M den, Spijkerboer T, 'Is the EU-Turkey Migration and Refugee Deal a Treaty?' (2016) EU Law Analysis <http://eulawanalysis.blogspot.com/2016/04/is-eu-turkey-refugee-and-migration-deal.html> accessed 1 March 2024.

Hillary L, 'Down the Drain with General Principles of EU Law? The EU-Turkey Deal and "Pseudo-Authorship"' (2021) 23(2) European Journal of Migration and Law 127.

Hillebrand Pohl J, 'Intra-EU Investment Arbitration After the *Achmea* Case: Legal Autonomy Bounded by Mutual Trust?' (2018) 14(4) EuConst 767.

Hillion C, 'Mixity and Coherence in EU External Relations: the Significance of the Duty of Cooperation' *CLEER Working Papers 2009/2*, 5–7 <https://www.asser.nl/upload/documents/9212009_14629clee09-2full.pdf> accessed 1 March 2024.

Hilpold P, 'Understanding Solidarity Within EU Law: An Analysis of the "Islands of Solidarity" with Particular Regard to Monetary Union' (2015) 34(1) YEL 257.

Hruschka C, Maiani F, 'Binnengrenze ≠ Außengrenze: Klärendes vom EuGH zur Wiedereinführung von Grenzkontrollen' (2019) Verfassungsblog <https://verfassungsblog.de/binnengrenze-≠-aussengrenze-klaerendes-vom-eugh-zur-wiedereinfuehrung-von-grenzkontrollen/#:~:text=Der%20deutsche%20Vortrag%2C%20die%20Grenzkontrollen,carrier%20sanctions> accessed 1 March 2024.

Hruschka C, Maiani F, 'Dublin III Regulation' in Kay Hailbronner and Daniel Thym (eds), *EU Immigration and Asylum Law: A Commentary* (2nd edition, Beck 2016).

Hurwitz AG, *The Collective Responsibility of States to Protect Refugees* (OUP 2009).

Hwang S, 'Humanitäre Visa für Flüchtlinge: Einfallstor für ein unbeschränktes Asylrecht?' (2018) 53(3) Europarecht 269.

Idriz N, 'The EU-Turkey Statement or the "Refugee Deal": the Extra-Legal Deal of Extraordinary Times?' *Research Paper Series of the Asser Institute* 2017, 13 <https://papers.ssrn.com/sol3/papers.cfm?abstract_id=3080881> accessed 1 March 2024.

Isensee J, *Gemeinwohl und öffentliches Amt: Vordemokratische Fundamente des Verfassungsstaates* (Springer 2013).

Jacobsohn GJ, 'How to Think About the Reach of Constitutional Identity' (2023) 1(1) Comparative Constitutional Studies 6.

Karageorgiou E, Noll G, 'What is Wrong with Solidarity in EU Asylum and Migration Law?' (2022) 4 Jus Cogens 131.

Kaunert C, Léonard S, 'The European Union Asylum Policy after the Treaty of Lisbon and the Stockholm Programme: Towards Supranational Governance in a Common Area of Protection?' (2012) 31(4) Refugee Survey Quarterly 1.

Kelemen D, Eeckhout P, Fabbrini F, Pech L and Uitz R, 'National Courts Cannot Override CJEU Judgments: A Joint Statement in Defense of the EU Legal Order' (2020) Verfassungsblog <https://verfassungsblog.de/national-courts-cannot-override-cjeu-judgments/> accessed 1 March 2024.

Kilpatrick C, 'Are the Bailouts Immune to EU Social Challenge Because They Are Not EU Law?' (2014) 10(3) EuConst 393.

Kilpatrick C, 'The EU and its Sovereign Debt Programmes: The Challenges of Liminal Legality' (2017) 70(1) Current Legal Problems 337.

Kinneging A, *De Onzichtbare Maat: Archeologie van Goed en Kwaad* (Prometheus 2020).

Kinneging A, *Hercules op de Tweesprong* (Prometheus 2023).

Klamert M, 'The Autonomy of the EU (and of EU Law): Through the Kaleidoscope' (2017) 42(6) European Law Review 815.

Klamert M, *The Principle of Loyalty in EU Law* (OUP 2014).

Kochenov D, 'EU Law Without the Rule of Law: Is the Veneration of Autonomy Worth It?' (2015) 34(1) YEL 74.

Komárek J, 'European Constitutional Imaginaries: Utopias, Ideologies, and the Other' in Jan Komárek (ed), *European Constitutional Imaginaries: Between Ideology and Utopia* (OUP 2023).

Komárek J, 'Why Read *The Transformation of Europe* Today? On the Limits of a Liberal Constitutional Imaginary' in Jan Komárek (ed), *European Constitutional Imaginaries: Between Ideology and Utopia* (OUP 2023).

Koschorke A, 'Auf der Suche nach dem verlorenen Europa-Narrativ' in Claudius Franzius et al. (eds), *Die Neuerfindung Europas: Bedeutung und Gehalte von Narrativen für die europäische Integration* (Nomos 2019).

Krisch N, 'Authority, Solid and Liquid, in Postnational Governance', in Roger Cotterrell and Maksymilian Del Mar (eds), *Authority in Transnational Legal Theory: Theorising Across Disciplines* (Elgar 2016).

Krisch N, 'Law and Polity: Contingency, Fiction, Loss' (2018) 16(4) I·CON 1223.

Krisch N, *Beyond Constitutionalism: The Pluralist Structure of Postnational Law* (OUP 2010).

Küçük E, 'Solidarity in EU Law – An Elusive Political Statement or a Legal Principle with Substance?' (2016) 23(6) Maastricht Journal of European and Comparative Law 965.

Küçük E, 'The Principle of Solidarity and Fairness in Sharing Responsibility: More Than Window Dressing?' (2016) 22(4) European Law Journal 448.

Kumm M, 'Constituent Power, Boundaries and Identity: On the Justificatory Depth of Constitutionalism – A Rejoinder to Neil Walker' (2016) 14(4) I·CON 914.

Kumm M, 'Constituent Power, Cosmopolitan Constitutionalism, and Post-Positivist Law' (2016) I·CON 14(3) 697.

Kumm M, 'Sovereignty and the Right to Be Left Alone: Subsidiarity, Justice-Sensitive Externalities, and the Proper Domain of the Consent Requirement in International Law' (2016) 79(2) Law and Contemporary Problems 239.

Kumm M, 'The Moral Point of Constitutional Pluralism: Defining the Domain of Legitimate Institutional Civil Disobedience and Conscientious Objection' in Julie Dickson and Pavlos Eleftheriadis (eds), *Philosophical Foundations of European Union Law* (OUP 2012).

Larik J, 'From Speciality to a Constitutional Sense of Purpose: On the Changing Role of the Objectives of the European Union' (2014) 63 ICLQ 935.

Larsen SR, 'Varieties of Constitutionalism in the European Union' (2021) 84(3) Modern Law Review 477.

Lavenex S, 'Failing Forward' Towards Which Europe? Organized Hypocrisy in the Common European Asylum System' (2018) 56(5) Journal of Common Market Studies 1195.

Leeuw M de, Wichelen S van, 'Un-signing Geneva: Legal Pragmatics in the Management of Asylum' (2019) 15 International Journal of Law in Context 20.

Lev A, 'The Imaginary and the Unconscious: Situating Constitutional Pluralism' in Jan Komárek (ed), *European Constitutional Imaginaries: Between Ideology and Utopia* (OUP 2023).
Lindahl H, 'The Paradox of Constituent Power: The Ambiguous Self-Constitution of the European Union' (2007) 20(4) Ratio Juris 485.
Lindahl H, *Authority and the Globalisation of Inclusion and Exclusion* (CUP 2018).
Lindeboom J, 'Is the Primacy of EU Law Based on the Equality of the Member States? A Comment on the CJEU's Press Release Following the *PSPP* Judgment' (2020) 21(5) German Law Journal 1032.
Loughlin M, 'Constitutional Pluralism: An Oxymoron?' (2014) 3(1) Global Constitutionalism 9.
Loughlin M, 'On Constituent Power' in Michael W Dowdle and Michael A Wilkinson (eds), *Constitutionalism Beyond Liberalism* (CUP 2017).
Loughlin M, 'The Constitutional Imagination' (2015) 78(1) The Modern Law Review 1.
Loughlin M, *Against Constitutionalism* (Harvard University Press 2022).
Loughlin M, *Foundations of Public Law* (OUP 2010).
Loughlin M, *Political Jurisprudence* (OUP 2017).
Macaj G, Nicolaidis K, 'Beyond One Voice? Global Europe's Engagement with its Own Diversity' (2014) 21(7) Journal of European Public Policy 1067.
MacCormick N, 'Beyond the Sovereign State' (1993) 56(1) The Modern Law Review 1.
MacCormick N, 'The Maastricht-Urteil: Sovereignty Now' (1995) 1(3) European Law Journal 259.
MacCormick N, *Questioning Sovereignty: Law, State and Nation in the European Commonwealth* (OUP 1999).
Majone G, 'Two Logics of Delegation: Agency and Fiduciary Relations in EU Governance' (2001) 2(1) European Union Politics 103.
Markakis M and Dermine P, 'Bailouts, the Legal Status of Memoranda of Understanding, and the Scope of Application of the Charter: *Florescu*' (2018) 55(2) CML Rev 643.
Mayer FC, 'Die Europäische Union als Rechtsgemeinschaft – ein überholtes Narrativ?' in Claudius Franzius et al. (eds), *Die Neuerfindung Europas: Bedeutung und Gehalte von Narrativen für die europäische Integration* (Nomos 2019).
McCrudden C, 'Alasdair MacIntyre's Critique of Human Dignity: A Response' (2022) 189 Law & Justice: The Christian Law Review 110.
Melin P, 'The Global Compact for Migration: Lessons for the Unity of EU Representation' (2019) 21(2) European Journal of Migration and Law 194.
Middelaar L van, *The Passage to Europe – How a Continent Became a Union* (Yale University Press 2013).
Miller D, *On Nationality* (OUP 1995).
Möllers C, 'Durchführung des Gemeinschaftsrechts: Vertragliche Dogmatik und theoretische Implikationen' (2002) Europarecht 483.

Moreno-Lax V, 'Solidarity's Reach: Meaning, Dimension and Implications for EU (External) Asylum Policy' (2017) 24(5) Maastricht Journal of European and Comparative Law 740.

Moreno-Lax V, 'The Architecture of Functional Jurisdiction: Unpacking Contactless Control – On Public Powers, *S.S. and Others v. Italy*, and the "Operational Model"' (2020) 21(3) German Law Journal 385.

Neframi E, 'The Duty of Loyalty: Rethinking its Scope through its Application in the Field of EU External Relations' (2010) 47(2) CML Rev 323.

Neidhardt A, 'Navigating the New Pact on Migration and Asylum in the Shadow of Non-Europe' *European Policy Centre* (Discussion Paper 26 January 2024) <https://www.epc.eu/content/PDF/2024/Non-Europe_migration_policy_DP_v2.pdf> accessed 3 April 2024.

Nettesheim M, 'Migration im Spannungsfeld von Freizügigkeit und Demokratie' (2019) 144(3) Archiv des öffentlichen Rechts 358.

Neylon A, 'Producing Precariousness: 'Safety Elsewhere' and the Removal of International Protection Status under EU Law' (2019) 21(1) European Journal of Migration and Law 1.

Odermatt J, 'The Principle of Autonomy: An Adolescent Disease of EU External Relations Law?' in Marise Cremona (ed), *Structural Principles in EU External Relations Law* (Hart 2018).

Oettingen A von, *Effet Utile und Individuelle Rechte im Recht der Europäischen Union* (Nomos 2010).

Orgad L, *The Cultural Defense of Nations – A Liberal Theory of Majority Rights* (OUP 2015).

Ortino M, 'A Reading of the EU Constitutional Legal System through the Meta-Principle of Effectiveness' (2016) 52(1) Cahiers de droit européen 91.

Ott A, 'EU External Competence' in Ramses Wessel and Joris Larik (eds), *EU External Relations Law: Text, Cases and Materials* (2nd edition, Hart 2020).

Pauwelyn J, 'Is It International Law or Not and Does it Even Matter?' in Joost Pauwelyn, Ramses Wessel and Jan Wouters (eds), *Informal International Lawmaking* (OUP 2012).

Peers S, 'The Draft EU/Turkey Deal on Migration and Refugees: Is it Legal?' (2016) EU Law Analysis <http://eulawanalysis.blogspot.com/2016/03/the-draft-euturkey-deal-on-migration.html> accessed 1 March 2024.

Pérez CS, 'Mutual Trust as a Driver of Integration: Which Way Forward?' in Katja S Ziegler, Päivi J Neuvonen, Violeta Moreno-Lax (eds), *Research Handbook on General Principles in EU Law: Constructing Legal Orders in Europe* (Elgar 2022).

Pijnenburg A, 'Team Europe's Deal: What's Wrong with the EU-Tunisia Migration Agreement?' (2023) Verfassungsblog <http://www.printfriendly.com/print/?source=site&url=https://verfassungsblog.de/team-europes-deal/> accessed 1 March 2024.

Pitkin HF, *The Concept of Representation* (University of California Press 1967).

Podolski T, 'Ein Symbol der Humanität' (2019) Legal Tribune Online <https://www.lto.de/recht/hintergruende/h/grundgesetz-70-jahre-art-16a-interview-seegmueller/#:~:text=70%20Jahre%20Grundgesetz%20%2D%20das%20Asylrecht,GG%20%22Ein%20Symbol%20der%20Humanität%22&text=Das%20Grundrecht%20auf%20Asyl%20ist,erklärt%20Robert%20Seegmüller%20im%20Interview> accessed 1 March 2024.

Polzin M, 'Constitutional Identity as a Constructed Reality and a Restless Soul' (2015) 18(7) German Law Journal 1595.

Poorter J de, Van der Schyff G, Stremler M, Visser M de, Leijten I, Oirsouw C van (eds), A Constitutional Identity for the EU?' (2022) 4 European Yearbook of Constitutional Law.

Post R, 'Constructing the European Polity: ERTA and the Open Skies Judgments' in Miguel Poiares Maduro & Loïc Azoulai, *The Past and Future of EU Law: the Classics of EU Law Revisited on the 50th Anniversary of the Rome Treaty* (Hart 2010).

Poulou A, 'Financial Assistance Conditionality and Human Rights Protection: What is the Role of the EU Charter of Fundamental Rights?' (2017) 54(4) CML Rev 991.

Purnhagen KP, Ruijter A de, Flear ML, Hervey TK, Herwig A, 'More Competences than You Knew? The Web of Health Competence for European Union Action in Response to the COVID-19 Outbreak' (2020) 11(2) European Journal of Risk Regulation 297.

Rehfeld A, 'On Representing' (2018) 26(2) The Journal of Political Philosophy 216.

Repasi R, 'Judicial Protection Against Austerity Measures in the Euro Area: *Ledra* and *Mallis*' (2017) 54(4) CML Rev 1123.

Rhinard M, Sjöstedt G, 'The EU as a Global Actor: A New Conceptualisation Four Decades after Actorness' *Swedish Institute of International Affairs 6/2019* <https://www.ui.se/globalassets/ui.se-eng/publications/ui-publications/2019/ui-paper-no.-6-2019.pdf> accessed 1 March 2024.

Rijpma J, 'External Migration and Asylum Management: Accountability for Executive Action Outside EU-Territory' (2017) 2(2) European Papers 571.

Rizcallah C, *The Principle of Mutual Trust in European Union Law* (Bruylant 2022).

Roermund B van, *Law in the First Person Plural: Roots, Concepts, Topics* (Elgar 2020).

Ruffert M, 'Art. 3 (ex-Art. 2 EUV) [Ziele der Union]', in Christian Calliess and Matthias Ruffert (eds), *EUV/AEUV: Das Verfassungsrecht der Europäischen Union mit Europäischer Grundrechtecharta [Kommentar]* (5th edition, C H Beck 2016).

Sabel CF, Zeitlin J, 'Learning from Difference: The New Architecture of Experimentalist Governance in the EU' (2008) 14(3) European Law Journal 271.

Salomon S and Rijpma J, 'A Europe Without Internal Frontiers: Challenging the Reintroduction of Border Controls in the Schengen Area in the Light of Union Citizenship' (2023) 24(2) German Law Journal 281.

Santos Vara J and García Andrade P, Molnár T (eds), 'The Externalisation of EU Migration Policies in Light of EU Constitutional Principles and Values' (2023) 8(2) European Papers 901.

Santos Vara J, 'Soft International Agreements on Migration Cooperation with Third Countries: A Challenge to Democratic and Judicial Controls in the EU' in Sergio Carrera et al., *Constitutionalising the External Dimensions of EU Migration Policies in Times of Crisis* (Elgar 2019).

Scheffer P, *De Vorm van Vrijheid* (De Bezige Bij 2018).

Schnettger A, 'Article 4(2) TEU as a Vehicle for National Constitutional Identity in the Shared European Legal System' in Christian Calliess and Gerhard van der Schyff (eds), *Constitutional Identity in a Europe of Multilevel Constitutionalism* (CUP 2019).

Scholtes J, 'Abusing Constitutional Identity' (2021) 22(4) German Law Journal 534.

Scott J, Trubek DM, 'Mind the Gap: Law and New Approaches to Governance in the European Union' (2002) 8(1) European Law Journal 1.

Seel G, 'What is the Common Good and Why Should We Pursue it? A Philosophical Foreword to a Current European Debate' in Sonja Puntscher Riekmann et al. (eds), *Is There a European Common Good?* (Nomos 2012).

Seyr S, *Der Effet Utile in der Rechtsprechung des EuGH* (Duncker & Humblot 2008).

Spijkerboer T, 'Bifurcation of People, Bifurcation of Law: Externalisation of Migration Policy before the Court of Justice' (2017) 31(2) Journal of Refugee Studies 216.

Temple Lang J, The ERTA Judgment and the Court's Case Law on Competence and Conflict' (1986) 6(1) YEL 183.

Thielemann and Armstrong C, 'Understanding European Asylum Cooperation under the Schengen/Dublin System: A Public Goods Framework' (2013) 22(2) European Security 148.

Thielemann, 'Between Interests and Norms: Explaining Burden-Sharing in the European Union' (2003) 16(3) Journal of Refugee Studies 253.

Thies A, 'The Search for Effectiveness and the Need for Loyalty in EU External Action' in Marise Cremona & Anne Thies (eds), *The European Court of Justice and External Relations Law: Constitutional Challenges* (Hart 2014).

Thym D, 'Deciphering the Role of (Migration) Law in the Social Construction of "Otherness"' in Moritz Jesse (ed), *European Societies, Migration, and the Law: The "Others" amongst "Us"* (CUP 2020).

Thym D, 'Für ein „Helsinki" im deutschen Migrationsrechtsdiskurs' (2018) Verfassungsblog <https://verfassungsblog.de/fuer-ein-helsinki-im-deutschen-migrationsrechtsdiskurs/> accessed 1 March 2024.

Thym D, 'In the Name of Sovereign Statehood: A Critical Introduction to the Lisbon Judgment of the German Constitutional Court' (2009) 46(6) CML Rev 1795.

Thym D, 'Judicial Maintenance of the Sputtering Dublin System on Asylum Jurisdiction: *Jafari*, *A.S.*, *Mengesteab* and *Shiri*' (2018) 55(2) CML Rev 549.

Thym D, 'Minimum Requirements under EU Primary Law and International Refugee Law for Rules in Secondary Legislation on the Rejection of Applicants for Asylum as Inadmissible with a view to Protection and Housing Options in Third Countries (Transit or Other Countries) or in Parts of any Such Countries' (Expert Opinion for the (German) Federal Ministry of the Interior 2017) <https://papers.ssrn.com/sol3/papers.cfm?abstract_id=3163014> accessed 1 March 2024.

Thym D, 'Rücküberstellung von anerkannten Schutzberechtigten innerhalb der EU' (2018) 37(9) Neue Zeitschrift für Verwaltungsrecht 609.

Thym D, 'Steuerung der Migration im öffentlichen Interesse', in Georg Jochum et al.; *Grenzüberschreitendes Recht – Crossing Frontiers: Festschrift für Kay Hailbronner* (C F Müller 2013).

Thym D, 'Verfassungspatriotismus in der Einwanderungsgesellschaft – Über die gesellschaftliche Breitenwirkung des Verfassungsrechts und kulturelle Parteinahme unter dem Grundgesetz' (2020) 145(1) Archiv des öffentlichen Rechts 40.

Thym D, and Tsourdi E, 'Searching for Solidarity in the EU Asylum and Border Policies: Constitutional and Operational Dimensions' (2017) 24(5) Maastricht Journal of European and Comparative Law 605.

Thym D, *European Migration Law* (OUP 2023).

Triggs GD, Wall PCJ, '"The Makings of a Success": The Global Compact on Refugees and the Inaugural Global Refugee Forum' (2020) 32(2) International Journal of Refugee Law 283.

Tsarapatsanis D, 'Representative Legislatures, Grammars of Political Representation, and the Generality of Statutes' (2018) 31(4) Ratio Juris 444.

Tsiliou A, 'When Greek Judges Decide Whether Turkey is a Safe Third Country Without Caring Too Much for EU Law' (2018) EU Immigration and Asylum Law and Policy <https://eumigrationlawblog.eu/when-greek-judges-decide-whether-turkey-is-a-safe-third-country-without-caring-too-much-for-eu-law/> accessed 1 March 2024.

Tsourdi E, Ott A, Vankova Z (eds), 'The EU's Shifting Borders Reconsidered: Externalisation, Constitutionalisation, and Administrative Integration' (2022) 7(1) European Papers 87.

Tushnet M, Bugaric B, *Power to the People: Constitutionalism in the Age of Populism* (OUP 2022).

UNHCR, 'The Concept of Protection Elsewhere' (1995) 7(1) International Journal of Refugee Law 123.

Venzke I, Mendes J, 'The Idea of Relative Authority in European and International Law' (2018) 16(1) I·CON 75.

Verellen T, 'European Sovereignty Now? A Reflection of What is Means to Speak of "European Sovereignty" (2020) 5(1) European Papers 307.

Vermeule A, *Common Good Constitutionalism* (Polity Press 2022).

Villani S, 'Perspectives of Solidarity Within the EU Legal Order in Time of the Covid-19 Pandemic' (2023) 4(1) Yearbook of International Disaster Law 70.

Voermans W, *Het Verhaal van de Grondwet: Zoeken naar Wij* (Prometheus 2019).

Waldron J, *Political Political Theory: Essays on Institutions* (Harvard University Press 2016).

Walker N, 'Constitutional Pluralism Revisited' (2016) 22(3) European Law Journal 333.

Walker N, 'EU Constitutionalism and New Governance' in Gráinne de Búrca and Joanne Scott (eds), *Law and New Governance in the EU and the US* (Hart 2006).

Walker N, 'Flexibility Within a Metaconstitutional Frame' in Gráinne de Búrca and Joanne Scott, *Constitutional Change in the EU: From Uniformity to Flexibility?* (OUP 2000).

Walker N, 'Foundations of Public Law and Postnational Constitutionalism' in Michael A Wilkinson and Michael W Dowdle (eds), *Questioning the Foundations of Public Law* (Hart 2018).

Walker N, 'Sovereignty Surplus' (2020) 18(2) I·CON 370.

Walker N, 'The Burden of the European Constitution' in Matej Avbelj (ed), *The Future of EU Constitutionalism* (Hart 2023).

Walker N, 'The European Public Good and European Public Goods' in Jan Komárek (ed), *European Constitutional Imaginaries: Between Ideology and Utopia* (OUP 2023).

Walker N, 'The Idea of Constitutional Pluralism' (2002) 65(3) The Modern Law Review 317.

Walker N, and Búrca G de, 'Reconceiving Law and New Governance', (2007) 13 Columbia Journal of European Law 519.

Walker N, The Return of Constituent Power: A Reply to Mattias Kumm' (2016) 14(4) I·CON 906.

Ward A, 'Article 51' in Steve Peers, Tamara Hervey, Jeff Kenner, Angela Ward (eds), *The EU Charter of Fundamental Rights: A Commentary* (Hart 2021).

Weber, 'The Identity of Union Law in Primacy: Piercing Through *Euro Box Promotion and Others* (2022) 7(2) European Papers 749.

Weber, 'The Pluralism of Values in an Identity-Framed Verbund: Federal Belonging in the European Union after the Rule of Law Conditionality Judgments' (2022) 47(4) European Law Review 514.

Weiler JHH, 'In Defence of the Status Quo: Europe's Constitutional *Sonderweg'* in Joseph H. H. Weiler & Marlene Wind (eds), *European Constitutionalism beyond the State* (CUP 2003).

Weiler JHH, 'Prologue: Global and Pluralist Constitutionalism – Some Doubts', in Gráinne de Búrca & Joseph H H Weiler, *The Worlds of European Constitutionalism* (CUP 2012).

Weiler JHH, 'The Transformation of Europe' in Miguel Poiares Maduro and Marlene Wind, *The Transformation of Europe: Twenty-Five Years On* (CUP 2017).

Wendel M, 'Die Pflicht zur Berücksichtigung von anerkannt Schutzbedürftigen im EU-Ausland' (2019) 74(20) Juristenzeitung 983.

Wendel M, 'Mutual Trust, Essence and Federalism – Between Consolidating and Fragmenting the Area of Freedom, Security and Justice after *LM*' (2019) 15(1) EuConst 17.

Wendel M, 'The Refugee Crisis and the Executive: On the Limits of Administrative Discretion in the Common European Asylum System' (2016) 17(6) German Law Journal 1005.

Wischmeyer T, 'Nationale Identität und Verfassungsidentität. Schutzgehalte, Instrumente und Perspektiven' (2015) 140(3) Archiv des öffentlichen *Rechts* 415.

Witte B de and Imamovic S, 'Opinion 2/13 on Accession to the ECHR: Defending the EU Legal Order against a Foreign Human Rights Court' (2015) 40(5) European Law Review 683.

Witte B de, 'Exclusive Member State Competences – Is There Such a Thing?' in Sacha Garben and Inge Govaere, *The Division of Competences Between the EU and the Member States: Reflections on the Past, the Present and the Future* (Hart 2017).

Witte B de, Imamovic S and Martinelli T, 'Treaties between EU Member States as Quasi-Instruments of EU Law' in Marise Cremona and Claire Kilpatrick (eds), *EU Legal Acts: Challenges and Transformations* (OUP 2018).

Witte B de, Imamovic S, Martinelli T and Tsourdi E, 'Confrontation on Relocation – The Court of Justice Endorses the Emergency Scheme for Compulsory Relocation of Asylum Seekers Within the European Union: *Slovak Republic and Hungary v. Council*' (2018) 55(5) CML Rev 1457.

Wouters J, 'Revisiting Art. 2 TEU: A True Union of Values?' (2020) 5(1) European Papers 255.

Yang T, 'Eine starke oder eine schwache Konzeption der Rechtsstaatlichkeit? – Auch zur Problematik der Universalität der Rechtsstaatlichkeit' (2015) 54 Der Staat 375.

Zoeteweij M, Progin-Theuerkauf S, 'CJEU Case C-638/16 PPU, X and X – Dashed Hopes for a Legal Pathway to Europe' (2017) European Law Blog <https://europeanlawblog.eu/2017/03/10/cjeu-case-c-63816-ppu-x-and-x-dashed-hopes-for-a-legal-pathway-to-europe/#:~:text=on%20EU%20law-,CJEU%20Case%20C%2D638%2F16%20PPU%2C%20X%20and%20X,a%20legal%20pathway%20to%20Europe&text=On%207%20March%202017%2C%20the,EU%20Charter%20of%20Fundamental%20Rights> accessed 1 March 2024.

Media Reports

Alexander R, *Die Getriebenen – Merkel und die Flüchtlingspolitik: Report aus dem Innern der Macht* (Siedler 2017).

Bubrowski H, Haneke A, 'Wie Seehofer auf die Rückkehr des Clanchefs reagiert' *FAZ* (6 November 2019) <https://www.faz.net/aktuell/politik/inland/wie-horst-seehofer-auf-die-rueckkehr-des-miri-clanchefs-reagiert-16472169.html> accessed 1 March 2024.

Editorial Comments, 'Nationale kramp rond order onderzeeboten is kortzichtig' NRC (18 March 2024) <https://www.nrc.nl/nieuws/2024/03/18/nationale-kramp-rond-order-onderzeeboten-is-kortzichtig-a4193330?t=1712053331> accessed 3 April 2024.

Haneke A, 'Hat Herr Miri sich verrechnet?' *FAZ* (31 October 2019) <https://www.faz.net/aktuell/politik/inland/clan-chef-zurueck-in-bremen-hat-herr-miri-sich-verrechnet-16461341.html> accessed 1 March 2024.

Lorenzo G di, 'Meine kleine Handgranate reicht dafür nicht' *DIE ZEIT* (25 November 2020).

Matthies M, 'Asylstreit: Bundespolizei soll mit Zurückweisungen an Grenzen beginnen' *SVZ* (19 June 2018) <https://www.noz.de/deutschland-welt/politik/artikel/bundespolizei-soll-mit-zurueckweisungen-an-grenzen-beginnen-23005039> accessed 1 March 2024.

Nielsen N, Tani C, 'Slovak PM: Human Rights are not a Travel Pass to EU' *EUobserver* (14 December 2017) <https://euobserver.com/migration/140291> accessed 1 March 2024.

Pascale F, 'Italy Works to Secure Tunisia IMF Funding for Stable Cooperation' *Euractiv* (7 June 2023) <https://www.euractiv.com/section/politics/news/italy-works-to-secure-tunisia-imf-funding-for-stable-cooperation/> accessed 1 March 2024.

Phoenix, 'Sommer-Pressekonferenz der Kanzlerin zu aktuellen Themen (Teil 1) am 31.08.2015' (Press conference 31 August 2015) <https://www.youtube.com/watch?v=TQgaXHMMkwM> accessed 1 March 2024.

Zermin H, 'Nach dem G7 Gipfel Bundeskanzlerin Angela Merkel zu Gast bei ANNE WILL am 10. Juni 2018' (Interview 11 June 2018) <https://www.youtube.com/watch?v=S5dzCR06XX4> accessed 1 March 2024.

Reports from Non-governmental Organisations

AIDA – Asylum Information Database, 'Country Report: Turkey (2015 Update)' (2015) 73 <https://asylumineurope.org/wp-content/uploads/2015/12/report-download_aida_tr_update.i.pdf> accessed 1 March 2024.

AIDA – Asylum Information Database, 'Country Report: Turkey (2019 Update)' (2019) 134 <http://asylumineurope.org/wp-content/uploads/2020/04/report-download_aida_tr_2019update.pdf> accessed 1 March 2024.

European Stability Initiative, 'Possible Draft Outline of EU-TUR Statement 2.0' (12 September 2023) <https://www.esiweb.org/possible-draft-outline-eu-tur-statement-20> accessed 1 March 2024.

European Stability Initiative, 'Refugees and Asylum in the Aegean – The Impact of the EU-Turkey Statement' (26 January 2018) <https://www.esiweb.org/publications/refugees-and-asylum-aegean-impact-eu-turkey-statement> accessed 1 March 2024.

Global Legal Action Network (GLAN), Association for Juridical Studies on Immigration (ASGI), and Italian Recreational and Cultural Association (ARCI), 'Complaint to the European Court of Auditors Concerning the Mismanagement of EU Funds by the EU Trust Fund for Africa's "Support to Integrated Border and Migration Management in Libya" (IBM) Programme' <http://aa76854664da4e33.filesusr.com/ugd/14ee1a_ae6a20e6b5ea4b00b0aa0e77ece91241.pdf> accessed 1 March 2024.

Human Rights Watch, 'Libya: Events of 2023' (World Report 2024) <https://www.hrw.org/world-report/2024/country-chapters/libya#1d4050> accessed 1 March 2024.

PICUM, 'Over 50 NGOs Pen Eleventh-Hour Open Letter to EU on Human Rights Risks in Migration Pact' (Blog 18 December 2023) <https://picum.org/blog/open-letter-eu-human-rights-risks-migration-pact/> accessed 3 April 2024.

Index

www.ingramcontent.com/pod-product-compliance
Lightning Source LLC
LaVergne TN
LVHW012051011026
849162LV00017B/143

* 9 7 8 9 0 0 4 6 9 5 7 2 6 *